Ethnic Minorities in the Soviet Union

ETHNIC MINORITIES
IN THE
SOVIET UNION

EDITED BY

ERICH GOLDHAGEN

Published for the Institute of East European Jewish Studies of the Philip W. Lown School of Near Eastern and Judaic Studies, Brandeis University, by

FREDERICK A. PRAEGER, *Publishers*
New York • Washington • London

FREDERICK A. PRAEGER, PUBLISHERS
111 Fourth Avenue, New York, N.Y. 10003, U.S.A.
77–79 Charlotte Street, London W.1, England

Published in the United States of America in 1968
by Frederick A. Praeger, Inc., Publishers

Library of Congress Catalog Card Number: 67–20478

Printed in the United States of America

Contents

Introduction

ERICH GOLDHAGEN

Few aspects of Soviet society have been the object of such divergent opinions and impassioned disputes as the condition of the numerous ethnic minorities inhabiting the Soviet Union. On the one hand, some Western writers have denounced the Soviet Union as a colonial oppressor that has subjugated the non-Russian peoples, subjected them to severe treatment, and endeavored to divest them of their native cultures by imposing upon them Russification. And in the case of some minorities, so the indictment runs, the treatment was so severe that it may be said to border on genocide. On the other hand, in sharp contrast to this dark picture, the Soviet Union has presented to the world a radiant image. In it, the numerous nationalities form a fraternal and harmonious union of which the Russian people are an unprivileged member; their separate cultures are protected and fostered in equal measure; enmity and even discord among them have evaporated under the enlightenment of Communism; and no Soviet citizen suffers discrimination because of his ethnic origin. In short, in Soviet parlance, the national problem has been solved in the Soviet Union. This solution, though an unprecedented historical achievement, will however be supplanted by a still more perfect consummation whose beginnings are already discernible. In the future, all nationalities will gradually and voluntarily shed their distinctive identities, abandon their respective languages for Russian, the lingua franca of the Soviet Union, and merge into a common body from which all ethnic differences will disappear—a Russian-speaking cosmopolis.

Confronted by these sharply contrasting pictures one might be tempted to dismiss them as figments of partisan imaginations. Indeed, the truth is neither as black as some Western writers paint it nor the pastoral idyll drawn by Soviet propagandists. The condition of the ethnic minorities in the Soviet Union is complex and many-hued, a unique and novel phenomenon defying the labels of political polemics. It is the purpose of this volume to unfold before the reader the complex and unique fate of the major non-Russian peoples under Soviet rule.

The Bolsheviks began their rule with a noble promise to the nationalities. They proclaimed the right to self-determination, which meant the right of each nation to secede from the Russian empire and constitute itself as an independent state. Not that Lenin regarded self-determination as a desirable goal. On the contrary, he viewed it as detrimental to socialism, for it would produce a multitude of states hindering the creation of large-scale socialist economies essential to the flourishing of a socialist society. He believed, however, that the striving for national independence could best be checked by announcing that no obstacles stood in its way. If, out of concern for the future of socialism, one denied the right to self-determination, one would stir resentment among the nationalities and increase the desire for independence. But by leaving the door to secession wide open one would blunt the desire for it, since the nationalities, recognizing the benefits to be derived from a large socialistic commonwealth, would choose to remain within the union rather than to withdraw into the constricting framework of small statehood and a precarious, and in many cases penurious, existence. In Lenin's view the right to self-determination was to be promulgated in order to nip the desire for it in the bud.

But when, amid the turmoil of revolution and civil war, independence movements sprang up among the nationalities, rending asunder the empire, the Bolsheviks threw the promise of self-determination unhesitatingly and remorselessly to the wind and set out to subdue the national minorities that refused to submit to their authority; within a few years after the Revolution, aided by small Communist minorities within each of the nationalities, they succeeded in recapturing all of the Asian provinces and a great part of the European domain of the Czarist empire, welding them into a Communist state.

Although honored in the breach, the right to self-determination has ever since remained an article of the official creed, as though it had never been violated; and it was solemnly enshrined in the Soviet constitution—a stillborn, decorative right of which one is free to boast in the Soviet Union but which it would be dangerous to claim.

Unlike the Czarist regime—which, though desiring to Russify the whole of the empire, did not reach deeply into the internal life of any of the non-Russian peoples under its rule, except in those cases in which it felt threatened by native recalcitrance—the Soviet regime set out to transform the lives of the nationalities in accordance with the precepts of its ideology and the requirements of industrialization and modernization which it sought to effect. It viewed the nationalities not only as inhabitants of territories rich in resources, or of strategic value, but also as backward and "feudal" peoples to be radically reshaped in the socialist image. Moreover, the Bolshevik leaders of the early days were imbued with a strong sense of internationalism. They were for the most part free from ethnic prejudice; and although the Bolshevik party, composed predominantly of Russians, may have appeared to the nationalities as the heir of the Czars, the Bolsheviks thought of themselves as builders of a new society whose hallmark would be the equality of all. In the 1920's, in order to placate national sentiments and to give a native flavor to its rule, the Communist dictatorship granted to the major nationalities formal autonomy in the shape of constituent republics of a federal Soviet Union. This autonomy has ever since been spurious, for all power has remained in the hands of the central authority in Moscow, where all major decisions affecting the destinies of the minorities are taken.

Yet one should not underestimate the symbolic satisfaction that the trappings of autonomous "statehood," however insubstantial, have given to the ethnic pride of the minorities. Beyond this, the Communist regime during the 1920's encouraged the use of the native languages in local administrations and in the schools. It greatly expanded the educational systems of the minorities and launched a campaign to abolish illiteracy, widespread among most of them. It devised alphabets for unlettered peoples whose languages had never been written down. In short, it began to equip each of the non-Russian peoples with a cultural apparatus intended to transmit to them scientific knowledge and technical skills, as well as to serve as a means by which the new ideology could be implanted in the minds and hearts of its people. The statistics on the growth of schools, the increase of literacy, the numbers of educated persons and of trained engineers, scientists, and holders of academic degrees offer an impressive picture of cultural ascent of the minorities under Communist rule. The Soviet dictatorship surrounded the nationalities with an iron hedge, ruthlessly suppressing all endeavor for independence, but within these confines the national identity was given considerable freedom of scope. The dictatorship arrogated to itself, however, the right to be the arbiter of what was permissible and impermissible, which part of the national culture could be fostered and which was to be subdued or discarded. Yet whatever the intentions of the regime may have been, the cultural institutions it created among the non-Russian peoples, together with the symbols of autonomy it conferred upon them, had the unintended effect of strengthening their national consciousness, especially among the nationalities in whom it had been but feebly developed.

After the great change of the early 1930's, under Stalin's iron rule, the minorities were subjected to far sterner dispensation. The new period was characterized by the elevation of the Russian people and things Russian to a position of preeminence, and by the endeavor to draw the minorities into the orbit of Russian culture with an ultimate view to Russification and, as a corollary, the constriction of the scope and content of native cultures. It was a period in which the Russian language was exalted, the heroes of Russian history (even those who had hitherto been treated as reactionaries) celebrated, and the symbols of Russian nationhood revered. Conversely, many of the heroes of the national minorities were dethroned, many of the ethnic symbols tabooed or subdued, and every institution or person that strove or appeared to strive to protect native identity against the encroachment of Russian culture denounced as a promoter of "bourgeois nationalism," one of the chief heresies in the Soviet canon. There is scarcely a nationality that escaped the heresy hunt, and innumerable non-Russians, Party members, writers, and common people paid with their freedom or with their lives for the real or imagined sin of bourgeois nationalism.

Six ethnic groups were treated so severely that their very existence as coherent, viable entities was endangered: the Ingush, the Chechens, the Crimea Tatars, the Kalmyks, the Karachai, and the Balkars. Each of these groups had incurred the wrath of Stalin, who held all of its members accountable for the collaboration of some in their midst with the German invaders during World War II. The sins of the few were visited upon the whole community. Each group in its entirety was banished from its native land to a remote place under conditions of extreme privation, causing widespread suffering and death; and its name was expunged from the public records of the Soviet Union as though it had ceased to exist. After Stalin's death, the Soviet Government pronounced the deportation of these nationalities a "gross error" and rehabilitated them. According to Khrushchev, Stalin was tempted to mete out similar punishment to the Ukrainians, but their numbers made banishment impracticable. The experience of these groups shows that the fate of ethnic minorities, like that of other social groups, was determined not only by ideological and political considerations but also by the capricious, vengeful temper of the dictator and the irrational vagaries that marked his rule.

In exalting things Russian and in glorifying Russian nationalism, Stalin and successive Soviet leaders were moved not by chauvinistic impulses but by considerations of totalitarian *raison d'état*. They appealed to Russian national feelings because the Russians were the most numerous and the most important of all the nations of the Soviet Union and their support was necessary if Communism was to succeed. Moreover, it is easier to rule an ethnically homogeneous state than a multinational realm, which is a perpetual breeding ground of recalcitrant national feelings and aspirations. Also, insofar as the Soviet leaders were still needful of Marxian rationalizations, they could justify to themselves their policy to make the minorities surrender to Russian culture—the process they euphemistically call the "fusion of nations," or "internationalization"—as a progressive endeavor: the undoing of *Kleinvölkerei* as a step toward the creation of a universal socialist society.

Whatever the motives of the Soviet leaders, it is clear that for them the preservation of the separate identities of the ethnic minorities is not a desirable goal, and that their aim is to bring about the "fusion of nations." Every pronouncement by the Soviet leaders dealing with the future of ethnic minorities professes that aim. One such utterance by a Soviet leader, chosen almost at random, may be given here as an example. In a speech before the Twenty-second Party Congress, Khrushchev said:

> One cannot fail to note the growing striving of the non-Russian peoples to acquire the Russian language which has become in effect the second native language for the peoples of the U.S.S.R. . . . The process actually now taking place of voluntary study of the Russian language is of positive significance for the development of cooperation between nations. A process of bringing nations closer together is taking place in our country; their social homogeneity is being strengthened.

Every sign of Russification is acclaimed and every resistance to it denounced as an ignorant balking of historical progress or, worse, as a conscious or unconscious service to the enemies of the Soviet Union. Thus *Izvestiia* reported the exultation of a Caucasian poet at having been penetrated by Russian culture: "A son of the mountains I am in spirit, and in mind a Russian man. Without the Russian language, without the Russian environment, nothing in life is close to me."*

How successful has the policy of "fusion" been? If the degree of displacement of the native languages by Russian is taken as an indicator, then the inroads of Russian culture into the ethnic fabric of the minorities have not been very deep. The census of 1959 revealed that most minorities cling to their languages, and even in the case of the Jews, who have undergone a high degree of linguistic Russification, the sense of ethnic consciousness and apartness has remained alive. Fifty years after the Bolshevik Revolution, the goal of Russification must seem more remote to the Soviet leaders than it did during the 1920's or the 1930's, when the Bolshevik mind was less tempered by the complexity of reality, when it seemed that the social world was but clay in the hands of the Bolshevik potters.

If in the political and cultural spheres the Soviet Union has grossly departed from its original promise of self-determination, in the economic and social treatment of the minorities it has remained more faithful to its professed creed. The services provided by the Soviet state, such as pensions, medical treatment, holidays, etc., are more or less equitably dispensed to all Soviet citizens irrespective of their ethnic origins. Although Vsevolod Holubnychy, in his contribution to this volume, casts doubt on the belief that economic resources are equitably distributed among the various republics, one cannot call the Soviet economic policies in regard to minorities "colonialist," unless one assigns to that word a meaning quite different from its usual sense.

In any discussion of ethnic minorities in the Soviet Union, the movement of polycentrism sweeping over the Communist world, fragmenting the former monolithic unity of which it had boasted and which had for so long seemed unshakable, comes to mind. Underlying that movement is the doctrine that the will of the Soviet Union can never again be, as it was in the days of Stalin, a command for other Communist parties and states. The primacy of the Soviet Union must be replaced by the recognition of the sovereign right of all members of the Communist camp to follow their own course both in their internal affairs and in the world at large. This doctrine has been militantly asserted in many parts of the Communist world and reluctantly accepted by the Soviet Union. It might hold a perilous attraction for the leaders of some nationalities of Soviet Russia.

* *Izvestiia,* December 5, 1961.

Surely, they might argue, why should, say, Georgia and the Ukraine be entitled, if not to the full measure of sovereignty granted Poland and Rumania, at least to a greater measure of genuine autonomy within the framework of the Soviet Union? There are signs that the Soviet leaders are conscious of the danger that the spirit of polycentrism may penetrate into their own domain to inflame national feelings and stir national aspirations that could lay claim to doctrinal legitimacy. They have recently displayed a heightened alertness to the manifestations of nationalism, and a note of profound disquiet is audible in the official pronouncements on the theme. "In nationalism," *Pravda* observed on February 7, 1968, "lies the greatest danger to the fighting capability and ideological power of the Communist movement. . . . It must not be reconciled with the ideology of Marxism-Leninism." This disquiet is mingled with perplexity at a phenomenon for which Marxist theory cannot account. According to the Marxian prophecy, nationalism would wane with the advance of Communism. Yet the opposite has occurred—it has been growing. Unable to admit in public, or even to themselves, that the ideology upon which their claim to power rests has proved to be so profoundly mistaken, they have sought to persuade themselves and others that the spread of nationalism in the Communist camp is an unnatural and transient aberration. Yet as they watch the powerful currents of nationalism coursing through their camp they are overcome by worry. Never before in the history of the Soviet Union has the danger of nationalism so intensely and so anxiously preoccupied its leaders as it does today.

The verdict of the objective student on the historical performance of the Soviet Government in the treatment of ethnic minorities under its rule cannot be rendered in clear-cut and unicolored terms. The Soviet Government appears here in a manifold role. To the Asian peoples under its sway, it was the great Westernizer of their societies, imparting to them the skills and attitudes of modernity and raising them to a level of economic development which compares favorably with that of the adjacent Asian countries. In the cultural realm, however, it has been the high-handed tamperer with their cultural legacy, suppressing or curtailing many parts of their tradition. To the six nationalities that were deported, the Soviet Government appeared as the brutal assailant upon their very lives, and, to the Jews, as the enemy of the whole of their cultural legacy, excepting an emasculated and shrunken Yiddish literary estate. To the Baltic peoples, to the Ukrainians and Georgians, the Soviet Government is the undoer of their independent statehood, however short lived and imperfect it may have been, and the arbitrary manipulator of their art, literature, historiography, and the sanctities of their nation. Among most minorities material achievements, impressive as they are in many cases, have been attended by intellectual and cultural constrictions and the tailoring of their identities, and all have been exposed to the pressures of Russification. Yet all we know about the Soviet minorities suggests that their ethnic personalities are alive and that their muteness is a tribute to the efficiency of the totalitarian Leviathan rather than a sign of the absence of collective aspirations. If the incipient, feeble, and struggling trend toward pluralism in Soviet society increases, then these aspirations may assert themselves and profoundly affect the shape of Soviet society. But in any case it is doubtful whether the national minorities will conform to the blueprint of the "fusion of nations" nourished by the Soviet leadership. History may yet assign to the national minorities a role in the future of Soviet Russia quite different from that reserved for them by Lenin and Stalin in their visions of the future.

All the essays in the present volume were read at a symposium held in the fall of 1965 at the Institute of East European Jewish Studies of the Philip W. Lown School of Near Eastern and Judaic Studies of Brandeis University. Three papers read at the symposium, those of George Nakashidse, Michael Rywkin, and Severyn Bialer were not included here for purely technical reasons. In preparing this volume I was aided by many people to all of whom I owe a debt of thanks. But my special thanks are due to Marcia Case of Frederick A. Praeger, who bore with admirable patience the exasperating working habits of the editor.

This volume is the first of a series to be published by the Institute of East European Jewish Studies.

Waltham, Mass.
March, 1968

Ethnic Minorities in the Soviet Union

1

The Ethnic Scene in the Soviet Union: The View of the Dictatorship

JOHN A. ARMSTRONG

It has been customary to regard Soviet nationality policy, and, indeed, the entire ethnic problem in the U.S.S.R., as a single, homogeneous phenomenon. A major reason for this approach is the influence of the early writings of Lenin (and his protégé Stalin), which treated the nationality problem in the Czarist empire as a single facet of the revolutionary program. This tradition has been perpetuated by the Soviet Communist Party Program.[1] Although this prolix manifesto devotes 3,500 words to the nationality question, it manages to avoid mention of a single specific ethnic group other than the Russian. In his Twenty-second Congress commentary on the Program, Khrushchev devoted nearly a thousand words to the nationalities question, but apart from a passing reference to Ukrainians and Kazakhs, he mentioned no nationality other than the Russian.[2] Because of the complexity of the Soviet nationality picture, with its more than one hundred diverse ethnic groups, many non-Soviet commentators, accepting the facile generalization that it is impossible to deal with specific nationalities, embrace the basic Soviet framework by confining themselves to abstract, one might almost say philosophical, criticism of the avowed Soviet nationality position.

A failure to examine the general features of Soviet policy would be almost as wrong, however, as accepting these general features as the entire policy. Fortunately, the evolution of these general features since Stalin's death can be summarized in a brief examination of the Party Program and the speeches and publications associated with it.[3] The basic element is the stress on the development in the U.S.S.R. of a Communist culture common to all its member nations. Eventually, sometime in the indefinite future, this process, the Program states, will bring about an effacement of national distinctions. Khrushchev described this process in a dialectic framework: After an initial period in which the culture of each nation develops rapidly, the "socialist" nations in the U.S.S.R. will begin to merge. But, the Program emphasizes, a distinctive language is a persistent national characteristic. The dialectic of national merging will not lead to a composite language within a single multinational "socialist" state like the U.S.S.R., but to the adoption of the most appropriate existing national language as the "inter-national" (*mezhnatsional'nyi*) language of the socialist state. Much later, when such multinational socialist states predominate throughout the world, a world language will develop, but it is too early to predict what form it will take.[4] In one respect this argument is more moderate than the extreme views dominant in Stalin's later years, when Russian was regarded as the future world language. Still, the Program and its commentators stress the dominant position of Russian within the U.S.S.R. Individuals (or, in the case of minors, their parents) are free to choose their languages, but the "voluntary" study of Russian is warmly praised by the Program. A commentator called the increase (between the 1926 and 1959 censuses) in the proportion of non-Russians using Russian as their native language a progressive step, and noted with approval that non-Russian parents in the autonomous republics are demanding that Russian replace the local languages as the medium of secondary-school instruction.[5]

The reasons given for the increased use of Russian between the 1926 and 1959 censuses were, of course, derived from historical materialism. The rapid economic development of the U.S.S.R. necessitates, it was stated, a common medium of communication. Since Russian was the most advanced language, the language of science and technology, as well as the language of the country's majority, it would seem essential for all Soviet citizens to learn Russian, at least as a second language. The predominance of Russian publications in scientific and technical fields is advanced as evidence.[6]

Another major point of the Party Program is that Communist construction requires the continuous exchange of trained personnel. Any attitude of "national exclusiveness" is, therefore, abhorrent. Khrushchev expressed satisfaction that the population of the republics was becoming more mixed.[7] Evidently—though neither the Program nor its commentators draw the conclusion—individual members of smaller nations increasingly will find themselves in situations where they cannot effectively use their own languages or train their children in them.

In proceeding from the generalities of the Program to a consideration of the operational features of Soviet nationality policy, an analytic framework is essential. A comparative approach to the complex problem is suggested by a functional theory. Usually, sociological discussions of functional relationships treat the society as an "equilibrium system"—i.e., one in which subsystems perform latent or overt functions in maintaining the system as a whole. Such an approach to Soviet nationalities would introduce two difficulties: (1) the equilibrium model is essentially static, while it is precisely the rapidly changing nature of the Soviet nationality situation which interests the analyst; (2) while functional theory generally assumes that elements of a social system tend automatically to maintain the system or to further its unconscious goals, the direction of change in the Soviet system is clearly due, at least in part, to conscious manipulation. Consequently, the functional framework employed here will depart from the usual model. It will be assumed that the fundamental objectives of the ruling Soviet elite are to maintain control of the decision-making process in the present Soviet Union and to expand the power of the U.S.S.R. as widely as possible. It is further assumed that the elite believes (and is factually correct in its belief) that maximum centralized control and expansion of Soviet power require a unified national culture; that given the numerical and historical predominance of Russians, this culture must be Russian; but that, except in special cases, the elite is not primarily motivated by Russian ethnocentrism as such. Given these assumptions, the function of each element of the present Soviet system can be viewed not as the maintenance of the society in an equilibrium state, but as a contribution toward maximum centralization of control in the system and its maximum external expansion. Obviously such an approach neglects many aspects of the nationalities and their cultures, which are inherently interesting and (by any usual scale of values) important. But the functional approach appears the best available to bring out the relation of the nationalities and nationality policy to the dynamics of the Soviet system. There is some evidence that the regime understands the function of a nationality, but it is of course possible that in some cases the functional basis of nationality policies rests on tacit understandings.

Most available evidence on the nationality situation in the U.S.S.R. is qualitative, consisting of literary and historical interpretations, ideological exegesis, and observations (frequently intuitive in nature) by qualified observers. Although the amount available has grown immensely in the past decade, quantitative information is limited and unsatisfactory in many respects. Nevertheless it seems useful to employ certain available quantitative data as *indicators* of basic trends and policies. Since the relationship of each nationality to the Russians is the prime consideration, the Russians (or Russian culture) will generally be taken as the standard of reference. Indicators will be divided into three classes:

1. *Indicators of the extent of social mobilization (change from traditional to modernized ways of life) of the ethnic groups.* As will be shown, social mobilization is a category directly related to the function of the group. It is also indirectly related to the group's function through the impact on secondary phenomena, such as the extent of Russification. Important indicators of social mobilization are the degree of urbanization; the level of education, particularly higher education of a technical or scientific nature, and the relative education level of women; geographical mobility; and access to media of communication.[8]

2. *Indicators of the specific objectives and tactics of Soviet policy.* These indicators include the proportion of schools providing instruction in non-Russian languages and of students enrolled in them; Communist Party enrollment; publication in national languages;[9] employment of members of the national group in official posts.

3. *Indicators of the degree of Russification achieved.* The principal indicator available is the extent to which individuals of another nationality claim Russian as the language that they customarily speak. Since the available census data frequently make it possible to distinguish age groups, urban and rural inhabitants, and inhabitants of territorial divisions, this indicator is especially flexible. Where available, intermarriage rates constitute a highly significant indicator.

It should be evident that the above classification of indicators, while analytically useful, is not definitive. Particular aspects of social mobilization (e.g., level of higher education) have undoubtedly been manipulated by the regime in many instances to attain its objectives, and therefore might be considered in Class 2. For many groups use of Russian is, as the official program claims, actually a significant vehicle of social mobilization, and therefore should be considered as a Class 1 indicator. These overlapping considerations, of course, merely serve to re-emphasize the importance of considering quantitative indicators within the broader framework of qualitative evidence. In order to do this, one must turn to more concrete examination of the nationality situation.

The Internal Proletariat

Among the major functional types of ethnic groups, one stands out because of its frequency in modern industrial societies and the problems arising in connection with it. This type consists of groups that have low indexes of education, political participation, and income, but are socially mobilized in respect to geographical mobility and, to a considerable extent, exposure to mass media. An essential characteristic of such ethnic groups is that their members are easily uprooted by job (and presumably living standard) attractions in distant places, usually urban, though sometimes agricultural. Members of these groups perform the "dirty work" of society. In nearly all cases their work is unskilled and undesirable. Their material rewards are low and many show little concern for occupational advancement. Their housing is inferior, they are usually segregated by income even if they do not encounter ethnic prejudice, and their children's chances for education and occupational advancement are inferior. Obvious examples are Negroes, Puerto Ricans, and Mexican-Americans in the United States; East and West Indians in Great Britain; and Algerians and Portuguese in France. Borrowing a term (though applied somewhat differently) from Arnold Toynbee, I have designated these ethnic groups the "internal proletariat."

It is one of the great accomplishments of the Soviet system that an internal proletariat in this sense scarcely exists in the U.S.S.R. It is, of course, true that very low-skilled ethnic groups do exist there, but on the whole they remain in their own national areas, rather than following the crop cycle or doing the dirty work in the territories of the dominant ethnic group. In a few areas, it is true, there has been a slight tendency to develop internal proletariats. The rapid expansion of industry in the Urals and the Kuzbass during the early Five Year Plans and World War II brought considerable numbers of unskilled workers from the nearby Moslem tribal societies and from as far off as Central Asia into basically Russian cities (see Table XI* on the considerable *relative* as well as the enormous *absolute* increase of Tatars in Urals industrial cities). During the war, Central Asians alone constituted 18 per cent of the workers in Cheliabinsk *oblast*. They generally replaced Russians mobilized by the army.[10] But, as any visitor to the great cities of European Russia knows, the street

* Tables appear on pp. 33–44.

sweepers, ditch diggers, and washroom attendants are Russians, members of that very disadvantaged group in Soviet society—the female sex. Possibly reliance on an unskilled work force drawn from the dominant ethnic group is a feature of a modernized society in its early stages. At a similar stage, England and the northern United States used their own poor for dirty work or drew on the Irish or other closely related groups rather than on racially distinct minorities.

Mobilized Diasporas

While internal proletariats appear to be a feature of late stages of modern industrialized societies, "mobilized diasporas" clearly accompany early stages of modernization. By definition, a diaspora is a geographic dispersion of a small minority of the total population. But few diasporas exhibit a degree of social mobilization sufficient to enable them to occupy a special functional position in a modernizing society. Those that do qualify as mobilized diasporas are highly urban, have high relative educational levels, have access to mass media, and are geographically mobile. While mobilized diasporas are distinct in culture (frequently because of religious distinctiveness), their attachment to their own language is usually not too deep. They readily employ the dominant language in their homes as well as at their work. Partly as a consequence of this linguistic ability, members of this group are especially skilled in trade, communication, human relations, and other white-collar occupations. Members of mobilized diasporas have a very high achievement orientation, and women as well as men are mobilized. Therefore mobilized diasporas may be extraordinarily useful in a modernizing society where these characteristics are rare. On the whole, members of mobilized diasporas fill attractive jobs. As the society becomes more fully modernized, members of other ethnic groups seek to obtain these positions, frequently before their skills make them competitively equal to mobilized diaspora members. The result is resentment and, frequently, discrimination against the mobilized diasporas. The classic example of the mobilized diaspora in Western civilization is the Jews, but the Parsees in India, the Chinese in Southeast Asia, and the Lebanese in West Africa also fit the model.

Considering the complexity of the ethnic structure in the territories historically dominated by Russians, it is not surprising that more than one mobilized diaspora has existed there. The overlapping and succession of mobilized diasporas have been increased by the long transitional period that has characterized Russia's modernization. In many respects the Czarist empire was modernized fairly early in the nineteenth century. But the U.S.S.R. has not yet achieved a high degree of modernization in consumer goods, personal services, and rural transportation. Consequently, the functional need for mobilized diasporas has existed for more than a century. Given the occupational and educational mobility of various ethnic groups and the absence of a strong ethic of minority protection, it is not surprising that no single mobilized diaspora has been able to fill this functional need continuously.

1. In many respects the most important mobilized diaspora in the nineteenth century consisted of Germans. While most Russian Germans were sedentary farmers, a smaller but significant portion were tradesmen, engineers, physicians, teachers, and agricultural specialists scattered throughout the empire. The Baltic nobility in particular (and some bourgeois) played an almost indispensable role in the imperial bureaucracy. They readily learned Russian and many converted to the Orthodox faith. The Russian nationalist views sponsored by Alexander III encouraged exclusivist attitudes jeopardizing the Balts' position. World War I eliminated them as a significant mobilized diaspora even before the Revolution and collapse of Russian rule on the Baltic. There are still over 1.6 million Germans in the U.S.S.R., who, since the deportations of World War II, constitute a diaspora, but not a mobilized diaspora. Less than 40 per cent of the Soviet Germans are urban. It is unlikely that the regime trusts Germans enough to allow them to resume the function of a mobilized diaspora. The recent formal admission that the wholesale wartime deportations were not justified, together with minor concessions on schooling and other cultural activity, seem designed for propaganda in East Germany rather than as a major policy shift.

2. In some respects the Jews acted as a mobilized diaspora even in the nineteenth century, but the sharply restrictive policies of the Czars prevented them from fully occupying this functional role. When the Revolution temporarily reversed these policies, Jewish qualities of education, skill in human relations, achievement orientation, and personal mobility made them very useful in Soviet society. Jews rapidly acquired important positions not only in trade, the professions, and management, but in political affairs as well. By the late 1930's, however, the position of the Jews was again in jeopardy.

Today the Jews have all the social characteristics of a mobilized diaspora. In terms of the indicators of social mobilization, they rank far higher than any other Soviet ethnic group. Ninety-five per cent are urban. Their geographical dispersion is very wide, and it is very probable that individual change of residence is frequent. Women are as socially mobilized as men; proportions educated beyond the elementary level (in the R.S.F.S.R.) are virtually identical (695 and 686 per 1,000). Largely as a result of the Nazi massacres, the number of Jews, according to the official census of 1959, has declined to some 2.3 million, or 1.1 per cent of the total Soviet population. Yet as recently as about 1950, they constituted one-tenth of the nonmanual workers, one-tenth of the students in higher education, one-tenth of the writers, one-ninth of the scientific workers, and one-sixth of the physicians.[11]

Unfortunately (Soviet sources are extraordinarily reticent concerning the Jews), data to construct other indicators are sparse, but all evidence suggests that even today the Jews perform the function of a mobilized diaspora to such an extent that the Soviet system could dispense with their services only with great difficulty. In view of the general shortage of skills in the U.S.S.R., the country could ill afford the loss of roughly one-tenth of its skilled professionals. The presence of the Jewish group has another functional aspect. It serves to demonstrate the alleged ethnic equality and well-being of all nations in the U.S.S.R. On the other hand, two sets of factors prevent the Jews from fully playing their functional role. Under Stalin, irrational factors probably predominated. Stalin's anti-Semitic prejudices resulted in a secret purge of Jewish leaders in all aspects of Soviet life and, but for his timely death, might well have led to violent mass persecution. Other Soviet leaders shared these prejudices. According to Ilya Ehrenburg, Aleksander Shcherbakov was one of these, and other sources indicate that T. A. Strokach, a prominent MVD chieftain, even criticized Khrushchev for being too lenient toward Jews.[12] Very probably, irrational prejudice *among the elite* is still responsible for anti-Semitic policies. Mass anti-Semitism, on the other hand, induces official calculation that it is functionally useful to minimize the role of Jews. Khrushchev has argued that, as the level of education among non-Russian and non-Jewish ethnic groups rises, non-Russians inevitably demand a larger share of desirable posts held by Jews.[13] It is probably true that this pressure really exists. However, a regime that on the one hand does not wish to deprive the dominant ethnic group of desirable positions, but that on the other hand has no scruples about treating minority group members as just that rather than as individuals, will tend to discriminate against members of a mobilized diaspora. Moreover (according to a totalitarian ethic), Jews, particularly in consumer-goods distribution, provide convenient scapegoats for the notorious failures and inefficiencies of the regime. The liberal ethos and international associations of the Jews seem to present a threat to centralized control of totalitarian regimes.

The combination of a continued functional role for the Jews, dysfunctional aspects (from the regime's standpoint), and irrational prejudice among the leadership has led to the following basic policies in the post-Stalin period: (1) Refusal to permit Jews to emigrate; (2) avoidance of overt persecution, but large-scale intimidation; (3) severe restrictions on elements contributing to Jewish identity, including (a) prohibition of Zionism or other foreign organizational contacts, (b) unusually severe restrictions on religious practices, (c) almost complete prohibition of Yiddish cultural activities, combined with strong pressures to Russify Jews linguistically. The proportion of Yiddish-speaking Jews is now the lowest of any major ethnic group in the U.S.S.R.—about 20 per cent. Away from the former "Pale of Settlement" cities, the proportion is much lower (see Table I) The lack of Yiddish-language schools (justified by the "impracticability" of providing schools for dispersed groups) is a major factor in limiting any transmission of concepts of national identity; (4) discrimination against individuals identified as Jews. There is strong evidence to suggest that during the war quotas (of about 10 per cent) were set for Jews in higher education or certain professions,[14] regardless of whether the individuals wished to identify with the Jewish ethnic group or not. Apparently steps have been taken to reduce the proportion of Jews still further, as Table II suggests; (5) continued, though reduced, utilization of Jews, especially in areas where other trained and reliable personnel is scarce. Though there are very few prominent Jewish officials, minor Jewish officials in Belorussia immediately after the war constituted 6.1 per cent of the total (as compared to 1.9 per cent of the population). Even in 1962, Jews constituted 6.4 per cent of the Party membership there, and probably a similar proportion of the Party in the Ukraine.[15]

3. Although the regime has to a considerable degree prevented the Jews from functioning as a mobilized diaspora, the role of the Armenians suggests that such a function is still important in Soviet society. On a world-wide basis, Armenians have constituted a diaspora since the Turkish massacres of 1915. Within the U.S.S.R., the Armenian situation as a diaspora is not wholly clear from census data alone. Fifty-five per cent live in the small Armenian S.S.R. No other

nationality assigned a Union Republic has such a small proportion of its members living in it, yet, compared to the Jews, the Armenians are highly concentrated. As Table III indicates, the 45 per cent of Armenians living outside the republic is largely limited to the Transcaucasus, North Caucasus, and Transcaspian areas, and shows no signs of expanding greatly numerically relative to the total Armenian population. However, the proportion of highly trained Armenians leaving the republic is extraordinarily high (19 per cent of the scientific workers and 13 per cent of the students go to the R.S.F.S.R.—see Table XII). Fifty-seven per cent of all Armenians are urban. This is a high proportion compared to most Soviet nationalities, but it is almost exactly the same as the Russian proportion. If one looks at the Armenian S.S.R. and the dispersed Armenians separately, however, the picture is different: only 52 per cent in the republic is urban, while 62 per cent in the diaspora is urban. The urban percentage of the diaspora would be even higher were it not for concentrations of rural Armenian populations just outside the borders of the Armenian S.S.R.

The extent of social mobilization is also different for the two groups of Armenians, but unfortunately there are few data on this difference. Certainly the Armenian population as a whole has a relatively high degree of social mobilization in terms of education and occupation. Out of every 10,000 Armenians, 94 are full-time students in higher education (as compared to 90 Russians); 430 per 100,000 are scientific workers (compared to 327 Russians); 30 per 1,000 are specialists with higher educations (compared to 21 Russians).[16] In the cities, indexes of basic education are almost as high for women as for men (391 and 394, respectively, for the entire group, 398 and 387 within the republic). Yet the birth rate remains relatively high.

Armenians are, then, in a position to act as a mobilized diaspora at least in limited areas of the U.S.S.R. Armenians seem to occupy a wide range of posts (although in relatively small numbers) throughout the U.S.S.R. concerned with consumer-goods distribution, finance, and (to a lesser extent) industrial management.

Armenians also play a functional role in Soviet foreign policy. Apparently they constitute as high a proportion of senior diplomatic officers as any non-Russian nationality, including the far more numerous Ukrainians.[17] More important, the nation's remaining homeland and headquarters of the distinctive Armenian Christian church are located in the U.S.S.R. As a result, from the regime's standpoint, Armenians constitute a far more useful diaspora than Germans or Jews, whose areas of compact national settlement lie beyond Soviet control. Whereas Jews and Germans have been regarded as subject to outside attraction, the Soviet regime to some extent can manipulate developments in the Armenian homeland so as to make it attractive to diaspora Armenians. For a time this even held true for Armenians in the United States, and it is still a factor of some importance in Soviet Middle Eastern politics. There some elements in the numerous, wealthy, and socially mobilized Armenian communities have provided bases for local Communist parties; even non-Communist Armenians have at times shown a certain sympathy for Soviet policies. Recently the U.S.S.R. appears to have been exploiting Armenian ability to get along in the Middle East by sending technical assistance to Iraq from the Armenian S.S.R.[18]

The linguistic capabilities of the Armenians make them functionally useful in Soviet society as well as abroad. Their attachment to their language is fairly high. Even in cities outside Armenia, among a heavily Russian population, the proportion speaking Russian as the native language rarely rises over two-fifths, though it has greatly increased (see Table III) under Soviet rule. On the other hand, Armenians readily learn Russian and Asian languages. From the regime's standpoint, however, the position of the Armenians is not without its dysfunctions. In the first place, there is a strong current of anti-Soviet feeling among Armenians, fostered by the nationalist Dashnak organization. Secondly, like all mobilized diasporas, the Armenians arouse resentment. Among the Russians this resentment seems to be mild, mainly expressed in jokes like calling rumors "Armenian broadcasts" or saying that the British Ambassador, Sir Humphrey Trevelyan, "is one of the two most important Armenians in Moscow." But the Azerbaidzhanis and some other Turkic groups have a tradition of bitter animosity to Armenians. It is probably significant that in spite of the large-scale experimentation in multinational schools in the Azerbaidzhan republic, none is reported as encompassing only Armenians and Azerbaidzhani children.[19]

Soviet policies appear to take these functions and dysfunctions into account:

1. Apparently no limit is placed on Armenians in higher education or highly skilled occupations. While Armenians still constitute a far smaller proportion of highly skilled professionals than do Jews, the Armenian proportion has remained virtually constant (see Table IV).

2. Publicized Armenian cultural activities are largely confined to the Armenian S.S.R. Publicized symbols of Armenian activity in the Azerbaidzhan and Georgian S.S.R.'s are few, probably fewer than the actual extent of Armenian cultural activity there. For example, of 973 books published in Armenian in 1963, 939 were published in the Armenian S.S.R.; none were explicitly identified as published in Georgia or Azerbaidzhan. There were four Armenian-language newspapers with an annual printing of 12 million in Azerbaidzhan, but these constituted only 6 per cent of the newspaper circulation, though Armenians constituted 12 per cent of the Azerbaidzhan S.S.R.'s population (corresponding figures for Georgia: two newspapers, 1.5 per cent of total circulation, 11 per cent Armenians in population).[20] At the more symbolic level, in spite of the large number of Armenian writers (thirty-six, or 5 per cent of the total) at the Second Writers' Congress in 1954, only two identifiable Armenians were included in the large Georgian and Azerbaidzhani delegations.[21] Armenian representation in Party and state bodies in those republics is also very low.

3. A relatively wide range of tolerance is accorded to Armenian national organizations within the Armenian S.S.R., particularly to the Church.[22]

4. At the all-Union level, prominent Armenians are given great recognition, and, in fact, occupy a considerable number of major posts—the ubiquitous Mikoyan was long the most obvious example. Party membership (67 per 1,000 population) is slightly higher than for Russians (64).[23]

5. Armenian-language schools exist outside the Armenian S.S.R., even in urban areas.

6. Since 1953, published references to the Transcaucasus occasionally appear to favor Armenians over Georgians. Several reports have identified Georgians as black marketeers in a context suggesting they may be the scapegoats for other Caucasians.

Younger Brothers

The presence of mobile diasporas in the U.S.S.R. indicates incomplete modernization of the society. Similarly, the presence of large ethnic groups, which I shall designate the "younger brothers," is characteristic of a transitional society. Younger brothers are nationalities low in social mobilization, yet close to the dominant ethnic group in major cultural aspects. In terms of relative social mobilization, the younger brothers are rural, low in education and access to skilled occupations and mass media, and low in geographical mobility except when transplanted by the dominant nationality. Women are somewhat less mobilized than men. The cities in the younger-brother areas are relatively small, but contain large majorities of members of the dominant group, mobilized diaspora members linguistically assimilated to it, and younger brothers themselves, who gradually, over a long period of time, have been linguistically assimilated by the dominant nationality. The cities are, therefore, fortresses from which dominant ethnic forces sally forth to control the countryside economically and politically, and (through control of rural socialization and communication processes) to effect a measure of assimilation even there. As the initial stages of modernization are succeeded by rapid industrialization, however, the picture changes rapidly. Large numbers of the younger-brother peasants pour into the cities, mainly as unskilled labor, but with a growing educated stratum as opinion leaders. At this point, as Karl Deutsch has pointed out, two divergent developments are possible.[24] If the erstwhile dominant ethnic group in cities in the younger-brother territory is cut off from areas where large numbers of the dominant group predominate in the rural as well as the urban population, the dominant group may be swamped by the influx of younger brothers, and the assimilative process may gradually reverse itself. If, on the other hand, the dominant ethnic group in the younger-brother cities can draw massive reinforcements from its own compact ethnic areas, it may successfully assimilate the enlarged influx of younger brothers. Then, as urbanization proceeds, assimilation of increasing proportions of the younger-brother group will eventually reduce it to insignificance as a distinct nationality.

One need not subscribe completely to Deutsch's analysis, which may well overemphasize the purely demographic side of the interaction. (Deutsch does not restrict the model to culturally close nationalities.) The power and skill of the central government, its policies, and the extent of organized expression of national identity among the younger brothers is also highly important. Nevertheless, in broad outline the type of interaction described here is easily recognizable. In some such fashion the French have largely assimilated the Provençals and the Alsatians; the Germans the Plattdeutsch and the Bavarians; and the English the Lowland Scots. The importance of factors other than social mobilization and cultural affinity is shown by the Irish and Luxembourgers' resistance to assimilation. A relatively small proportion of the Soviet younger brothers—4 million—consists of the Finnic or semi-Finnic ethnic groups of the upper Volga region.[25]

These groups are linguistically quite distinct from the Russians. But their low degree of social mobilization, the primitiveness of their original culture, and centuries of acculturization by Russian Orthodox missionaries have evidently made the Finnic groups, once they are drawn to the cities, highly susceptible to assimilation. As Table V indicates, the rate of linguistic Russification among the urban portions of these groups is high, especially among adolescents, even in their own autonomous republics, and very high in the adjacent Russian *oblasts.*

Far more important numerically are the Ukrainians and the Belorussians; the latter number 8 million, the former more than 37 million, making them by far the largest minority in the U.S.S.R. Both groups are similar to the Russians in their predominantly Orthodox culture and in their East Slav languages. Soviet theorists rely heavily upon this linguistic affinity to strengthen Russian influence.[26]

As Table VI indicates, Ukrainians and Belorussians are far behind the Russians in higher education, with indexes running from less than one-half to three-quarters of the Russians'. The urbanization indicator is similar: 40 per cent for the Ukrainians and 33 per cent for the Belorussians, as compared to 57 per cent for the Russians. Given the vast extent of the R.S.F.S.R., there is no easy way to compute indicators of East Slav relative geographical mobility, but they would appear to be much closer together. To a large extent, movement of Ukrainians and Belorussian peasants outside their republics is the result of deliberate (often forced) transplantation by the regime. On the other hand, the extraordinarily large number of Ukrainian and Belorussian students (one-eighth in each case) who attend R.S.F.S.R. institutions of higher education, and scientific workers who settle there (nearly one-fifth in each case), probably indicate voluntary personal mobility (see Table XII).

Furthermore, while the *degree* of urbanization is much lower for the smaller East Slav groups, their *rate* of urbanization has recently exceeded the Russian: 2.7 times as many Russians were urban in 1959 as in 1926; the corresponding rate for Ukrainians is 3.8, and for Belorussians, 3.2. In view of this rapid urbanization, the educational situation (see Table VI) is puzzling. When urbanized, Ukrainians and Belorussians apparently acquire *basic* education more readily than Russians (however, even when the urban factor is constant, Ukrainian and Belorussian women, in contrast to Russian women, lag behind men). Educational attainment above the elementary level for Russian urban males is 363 per 1,000, for females, 375; the Ukrainian rates are 426 and 385, respectively; and the Belorussian are 411 and 399, respectively. But, considered over almost any interval and under any classification of highly skilled training, the proportion of Ukrainians or Belorussians has dropped, or at the most remained approximately constant compared to the Russian. The failure of these ratios to increase during the postwar as they did in the prewar years is largely due to the incorporation in the U.S.S.R. of a large population of educationally depressed Ukrainians and Belorussians from Poland; but it is hard to understand why the smaller East Slav groups have not shown a higher educational gain since 1950 corresponding to their urbanization.

As Table VII indicates, the proportion as well as the absolute number of Ukrainians in the cities of the Ukrainian S.S.R. has increased enormously since 1939. The stage has therefore been set for the theoretical interaction described by Deutsch. As Table VII shows, large majorities in all Ukrainian S.S.R. cities except those in the Black Sea, Donbas, and Kharkov areas now speak Ukrainian, whereas these same cities were Russian-language fortresses until the Five Year Plans.[27] Not only have the Russian-speaking majorities given way to Ukrainian-speaking majorities, but the proportion of Ukrainians giving their language as Russian (Table VIII) has also greatly diminished. From this point of view, it would appear that the Ukrainian language has won out in the assimilation interaction. In fact, however, a large *absolute* number of Ukrainians coming to the cities adopts Russian as their language, as Table IX indicates. The net loss to the Ukrainian-speaking group from urbanization is, therefore, well over a million persons. The loss as a result of emigration from the republic is even greater. Consequently (as one Soviet source notes complacently), in spite of the enormous annexations of Ukrainians during the war period, the proportion speaking Ukrainian increased scarcely at all between 1939 and 1959—from 87.6 to only 88.8 per cent.[28] Moreover, there is no general diminution in the use of the native language among younger age groups. While urban adolescents are somewhat less apt to use Ukrainian than other age groups, the tendency is very slight compared to Armenian and Asian adolescents. The Belorussians, though of course more Russified on the whole, exhibit an even smaller tendency toward progressive Russification. On the other hand, the rate of intermarriage between Ukrainians and non-Ukrainians (obviously mostly Russians) in the Ukrainian S.S.R. is now 18.5 per cent, an enormous increase over the 3.4 per cent (for males only) reported for 1927.[29]

The question of the ultimate assimilation of the younger brothers therefore hangs in the balance. If all could be completely assimilated, the Russian ethnic group would constitute 76 per cent of the total Soviet population. The proportion of the core ethnic group would not be much below that of such nationally stable societies as the United Kingdom or the United States. Members of the group would be assignable throughout the territory and range of positions of the U.S.S.R., thus making for greater flexibility, efficiency, and centralized control. Ukrainians and others could be used to support Russian control in Central Asia, an objective already accomplished to a considerable extent: Ukrainians in Kazakhstan constitute 8 per cent of the population, nearly one-fifth as many as Russians there; Ukrainians constitute 7 per cent of the Kirgizstan population (more than one-fifth as many as the Russians); and 1 per cent of the Uzbekistan population (one-twelfth as many as the Russians). Ukrainians have constituted an even larger proportion of the Party membership and apparatus in the Asian areas.[30] Because many early Ukrainian immigrants in these areas have become assimilated to the Russians, the contribution of the Ukrainian ethnic group to Soviet power in Asia is undoubtedly much higher. The Soviet commentator on nationality theory repeatedly cited estimates that about half of the European settlers in Siberia between 1896 and 1914 were from Ukrainian and Belorussian territories. He remarks that "in the eyes of the Kazakh, the Tatar, the Kirgiz, the Turkmen, or the Uzbek, the Ukrainian or the Belorussian are to an equal degree 'Russian,' " and that before the Revolution, Uzbeks used to say, "among the Russians there are many *khokhols* [the somewhat derogatory term for Ukrainian peasants]."[31]

Though the functional importance of the younger brothers in general, and the Ukrainians in particular, is overwhelming for the Soviet system, the presence of these ethnic groups is dysfunctional in some respects. Alignment of East Slavs inevitably arouses resentment among the other ethnic groups. It also tends to undermine the consistent Soviet claim to be a true union of disparate nations on the road to a world Communist society. The younger brothers also have certain social weaknesses that limit their usefulness. Their relatively low rate of social mobilization and their seeming inability to increase their share of highly trained manpower have already been noted. One might expect a less socially mobilized group to have a high birth rate. In fact, however, the Ukrainian and the Belorussian birth rates are about the same as the Russian (i.e., about 21 per 1,000). There are proportionately fewer Ukrainians and Belorussians under twenty (33.5 per cent and 35.8 per cent, respectively) than Russians (37 per cent).[32]

Certain irrational prejudices on the part of the Russians also limit the usefulness of Ukrainians. Rank-and-file Russians often regard a Ukrainian somewhat contemptuously as a "country cousin" (*khokhols*) or kulak (*kurkul*), terms which sometimes even find their way into print.[33] Khrushchev, when he headed the Party and state, was careful to stress that he was not a Ukrainian: "I can tell you that I know Ukrainian rather well, but when people speak it rapidly I also must ask them to speak slowly. Naturally it is easier to speak in one's native language."[34]

A far greater dysfunction, however, arises from the attitudes of the Ukrainians toward the Russians. A considerable portion of this antagonism has its source in pride in Ukrainian historical and cultural accomplishments made in opposition to, rather than in collaboration with, the Russian "elder brothers." Probably more significant, however, are events associated with the totalitarian policies of the Soviet regime. Collectivization is an especially traumatic memory for the Ukrainians. Rightly or wrongly, Ukrainians felt that this repression, carried out by Russian-speaking officials and coinciding with attacks on Ukrainian literature and a purge of Ukrainian Party officials, was a discriminatory national as well as a "class warfare" measure. As a result, Ukrainians, largely still peasants, are extraordinarily suspicious of Soviet measures affecting the agricultural population. The need to take this factor into account puts a severe burden upon the regime's economic policy-making as well as its nationality policy.

In view of the factors just discussed, it is understandable that Soviet policy toward the Ukraine has been unusually devious:

1. The injustices heaped on the Ukrainians during Stalin's rule are admitted. Many prominent Ukrainians have been publicly rehabilitated.

2. Symbolic recognition of Ukrainian importance has been accorded through the transfer of the Crimea to the Ukrainian S.S.R. and the appointment (for the first time in Soviet history) of clearly identifiable Ukrainians such as A. A. Kirichenko and N. V. Podgornyi to high posts.

3. There has been a great increase in Party membership of Ukrainians and Belorussians. In 1952, Ukrainian Party membership, in proportion to population, was probably no more than 40 per cent of the Russian, and Belorussian scarcely more than 35 per cent. By 1961,

each of the two East Slav groups had about 70 per cent as many members proportionately as the Russians, and, by 1965, 77 per cent (ratios per 1,000 population in that year were Russian, 64; Ukrainian, 49; Belorussian, 49). Whatever the increase in Party membership may mean in terms of political control, near equality of Ukrainians and Belorussians was an important symbol of the regime's desire to demonstrate that the opportunities of members of the three groups were equal.

4. In fact, Ukrainians (and to a lesser extent Belorussians) have been employed in key control and managerial positions throughout the U.S.S.R., and abroad. This is concrete evidence that members of these groups are not discriminated against if they acquire the proper education and submit to Russification.

5. Considerable latitude of literary and historical expression has been granted to Ukrainians in the Ukrainian S.S.R. High praise may at times be heaped on Ukrainian cultural accomplishments, and even the purity of the Ukrainian language has been stressed, so long as hostility or overt aloofness toward things Russian is avoided.

While the above moves are designed to assuage Ukrainian feeling, they have been accompanied by these firm measures to promote assimilation:

1. Reiteration of the theme that the Russians are the elder brothers and teachers, and that the accomplishments of Ukrainian history have been achieved with Russian help. The anniversary of the 1654 "union" with Russia at Pereiaslav was elaborately celebrated as the beginning of Ukrainian liberty.

2. Continued emphasis on Russian in Ukrainian-language schools, and strong influence of Russian-language schools in urban areas in the Ukrainian S.S.R. Apparently, schools are set up in rough proportion to existing ratios of Ukrainian and Russian *speakers* rather than of members of the Ukrainian and Russian groups.[35] Consequently, if the schools do not serve on the balance as a Russifying agency, they can do little to draw Ukrainian children back to their native tongue. This is apparently in accord with the policy of encouraging parents "voluntarily" to choose Russian-language instruction.

3. Fierce repression of any organized manifestation of Ukrainian national distinctiveness, especially in the Catholic West Ukraine.

4. The transfer of hundreds of thousands of Ukrainians and Belorussians outside their republics, both to strengthen Russian influence in Asia and to promote assimilation of the dispersed Ukrainians and

Belorussians. In striking contrast to the treatment of nationalities like the Armenians and Tatars, who are not scheduled for immediate, complete Russification, virtually no Ukrainian and Belorussian publications are issued outside the home republics. No Ukrainian newspaper or periodical is published outside the Ukraine, and of the 3,321 books published in the Ukrainian language in 1963, only 4 were printed beyond the borders of the Ukrainian republic. Similarly, only 3 of 359 Belorussian books and no periodicals or newspapers appeared outside Belorussia.[36] Even if, according to the official assertion, only "compact" areas of minority settlement are to be served by a local native-language press, settlers outside the two republics were obviously being discriminated against, for in considerable rural areas their settlements constituted majorities. The picture is probably no better in education. While there may be some rural Ukrainian-language schools, there are almost none in the cities of Russia or Kazakhstan in which Ukrainians are numerous. Soviet ethnographical studies generally try to minimize the importance of older Ukrainian settlements in areas like the Kuban and Kursk *oblast*. Census returns have called the huge areas of Belorussian language (as a recent Soviet map indicates)[37] east of the present Belorussian S.S.R. boundary purely Russian.

5. In addition to all the above measures, the regime has sponsored a very large influx of Russians into the Ukraine, especially into the newly acquired western territories. No doubt this influx is designed partly to increase assimilation through greater exposure of the Ukrainians to Russian influence, but it is probably also designed to provide a cadre of thoroughly reliable personnel in case the assimilation efforts are not successful.

State Nations

As compared to the mobilized diasporas and the younger brothers, the "state nations" are groups typical of the ethnic interaction patterns that have prevailed in modern Europe. This category consists of nationalities with strong traditions of national identity, including distinctive languages, well-developed cultures, and distinctive historical traditions. From the standpoint of their functional relationship to the aims of the dominant ethnic group's elite, however, both the degree of social mobilization and the ease of assimilation of the state nations are of secondary importance. The prime importance of the state nations lies in the strategic territory they occupy. The dominant elite (if it is pursuing an expansive policy in competition with other powers) must at least control this territory.

The ethnic groups in the U.S.S.R. that most closely fit this model are the Baltic nations. While all were associated with the Russians for several centuries, they maintained distinctive languages and cultures which developed rapidly in the nineteenth century. During the two decades between the world wars, each possessed an apparently viable national state. The degree of social mobilization (as indicated in Table X) varies considerably among the three nationalities, but in no case is it very different from the Russian. Consequently, it is not surprising that an overwhelming majority of all groups, urban and rural, regardless of age level, use their native tongues. Moreover, children born after World War II tend to turn back to their native language at adolescence, probably in a spirit of national pride and defiance.

The Baltic nations occupy a position of extreme strategic importance for the Soviet regime, hence the regime is firmly determined to hold the territories. The Russians remain to guarantee strategic control (20 per cent of the population in Estonia, 27 per cent in Latvia, and 9 per cent in Lithuania, plus very large numbers of military personnel). On the other hand, there has been considerable improvement in the treatment of the native intellectuals, including permission for many to return from exile. Some relaxation of control of national cultural life has occurred, though any manifestation of "bourgeois nationalism" is rigidly repressed. Apparently the regime relies on the sheer weight of numbers and the pervasiveness of Russian culture to achieve a measure of assimilation, but is not overly sanguine on the matter.

The regime's view on the continuing unreliability of these groups (as well, possibly, as their aversion to the regime's agencies) is indicated by the low ratios of Party membership: 34 per 1,000 for Estonians; 32 for Latvians, and 26 for Lithuanians, as compared to 64 for Russians. Given the unreliability of the Baltic groups, the regime apparently does not try to use them for skilled manpower, except to a limited degree within the Baltic republics. On the other hand, there has been increasing public recognition of the superior ability of the Latvians and Estonians in orderly, efficient management of community affairs and goods distribution.[38]

In contrast to the Baltic nations, the Finns, Poles, and Moldavians are irredentas—fragments torn from historic state nations. The Soviet regime obviously considers the strategic territory occupied by these irredentas well worth the resentment aroused in the parent nations, which are in no position to react forcibly. As there are only 260,000 Finns and Karelians, the significance of this minority is minimal. The position of the Poles is only a little more significant than that of the Finns. The most compact and nationally conscious Polish minorities were transferred to Poland shortly after World War II. In the Ukraine, most of the remaining Poles (363,000) have never lived in a Polish state. Widely dispersed among the Ukrainian population, both urban and rural groups have for the most part adopted Ukrainian or Russian as their native language and apparently possess only vestigial national feeling. Both absolutely (539,000) and proportionately (6.7 per cent of the total population), the Poles are more important in Belorussia and in Lithuania (230,000, 8.5 per cent of the total). Until 1939, they had been the dominant ethnic group in most of these areas. The almost unrivaled low rate of Party membership among Poles in Belorussia (5 per 1,000) indicates their alienation from the regime. The Poles therefore are typical irredentists, but in view of their low degree of social mobilization (see Table X), the weakness vis-à-vis the U.S.S.R. of their parent state, and the fact that they are surrounded by East Slavs and Lithuanians, the Poles scarcely pose a significant problem for the regime.

The Moldavians live in a compact area on the border of the parent Romanian state, but apparently their national consciousness is lower than that of the Poles. The Moldavians' Orthodox religious background makes them closer culturally to the Russians, while their very low degree of social mobilization makes them somewhat susceptible to assimilation measures. Recently Romania has begun to refer to Moldavia as an irredenta region. It is hardly likely that this poses a real threat to Soviet control, though the extremely low Party membership (19 per 1,000) suggests political unreliability.

The Georgians have occupied a unique position among the state nations. Though the independent Georgian republic (1918–21) was considerably more stable and successful than its counterparts in the Ukraine, Belorussia, Armenia, and the Moslem areas, it scarcely compares as an experience in national identification with the Baltic republics. The extraordinarily high sense of Georgian national identification probably rests more firmly on the unusual role of the Georgians under Stalin, when they shared the role of dominant Soviet ethnic group with the Russians. Attachment to the native language is high (although a decline has been noted in the very young age groups), and Georgian is employed to a high degree in publications and scholarly activity. According to educational indicators, the Georgians are very highly mobilized socially. On the other hand, their urban proportion is quite low, and they are strikingly immobile geographically. (Only 4 per cent of scientific workers and 7 per cent of students leave for the R.S.F.S.R.—see Table XII.)

Like the other nation states, the Georgians occupy a strategic position. Also, they serve a functional purpose in the Soviet system by providing a considerable portion (2–3 per cent) of its highly skilled manpower. This manpower resource is not as valuable as it would be if it were mobile, but it can be utilized in the highly developed scientific and educational institutions within the republic. Georgians have a reputation of being personally pleasant, but the fact that some Georgians were secret-police officials under Beria made the whole nation suspect throughout the U.S.S.R. In their own Caucasian area, Georgian officials displayed "imperialist" tendencies that tended to alienate neighboring ethnic groups. Occasionally, Georgians are blamed explicitly for what are probably general Transcaucasian tendencies toward petty speculation. Prompt measures to curb Georgian linguistic dominance within the republic, and retrocession of territory north of the Caucasus acquired by the Georgian S.S.R. when Moslem groups were banished are signs that the Georgians are no longer privileged politically. While Georgian Party membership (72 per 1,000) is proportionately still very high, it has not grown rapidly in the past twelve years, probably because the regime wishes to eliminate the impression that Georgians are favored politically.

Colonials

Like the nation states, "colonials" are a common ethnic phenomenon in the contemporary world. By colonials I do not mean members of a dominant ethnic group living abroad, but a subject nationality sharply differentiated from the dominant group in cultural background, physical appearance, and degree of social mobilization. Typically, colonials are just entering the transition to modernized society. The traditional culture pattern of the colonials (frequently shaped by a religion very different from the dominant group's) is regarded by the dominant elite as a barrier to modernization. The colonial language is regarded as inadequate for modern communication. Since language, religion, and traditional cultural patterns are closely linked, the potential for conflict between colonials and dominants is great during the transitional period. The higher and more integrated the traditional culture, the greater the likelihood of friction. As social mobilization (especially urbanization and access to mass media) increases, resentment rises. Sometimes the dominant nation will try to stem resentment by symbolic incorporation of the colonial group in the dominant nation, by providing educational opportunities, and by assigning some desirable posts to colonials, but this tactic has rarely succeeded.

The relationship of the Russians to the ethnic groups of Moslem background in the Asian-European borderlands and in Central Asia closely fits the model just presented.[39] Failure to recognize this phenomenon in the U.S.S.R. is due partly to Soviet propaganda, partly to the gradual way in which physical traits change from the Baltic to the Altai, and partly to the fact that the Soviet colonies are not overseas.

While groups of Moslem background constitute less than one-eighth of the Soviet population, they are largely scattered over about a third of its vast territory. It is not surprising, therefore, that the Islamic groups vary greatly in traditional culture and language. It is impossible to discuss these factors in detail here, but some of the salient contemporary characteristics of the major groups must be noted.

1. The second largest group numerically, the Tatars, have played an extraordinarily important role in the Russian-colonial relationship. As Table XI indicates, the Tatars are very widely dispersed—more so, in fact, than any major Soviet ethnic groups except the Jews and Germans. The Tatar levels of education and urbanization are much below the Russian, and not much higher than those of the other Moslem groups, but in the years preceding and immediately following the Revolution, Tatar social mobilization was much higher than that of the Moslem groups. At the same time, the principal Tatar group, the Volga or Kazan Tatars, had developed a high degree of national consciousness. Partly out of resentment toward Orthodox missionary and Czarist Russifying activities, many Volga Tatars at first sided with the Bolsheviks. Though this honeymoon was brief, Tatar services in propagating Communism and raising educational levels among the Central Asian and steppe Moslem groups (most of whom speak related Turkic languages) were very important, as Soviet sources recognize even today. In 1926, there were, for example, 26,000 Volga Tatars in Uzbekistan; in 1939, 159,000; and today, 400,000, including a very significant portion of the urban population.[40]

In view of their wide dispersion, it is not surprising that a considerable number of Tatars have become linguistically assimilated under Soviet rule (in 1926, the proportion of Russian-speaking Tatar was still negligible), especially when they live in thoroughly Russian ethnic environments (see Table XI). Tatar adolescents tend to abandon their native tongue. On the other hand, the Soviet press has frequently criticized "nationalist deviations" in the substantial Tatar literary and historiographical output. Separate religious headquarters have been maintained in Ufa for those Tatars (and related Bashkirs) who still practice Islam.[41] Furthermore, the Tatars in dispersion enjoy the extraordinary privilege of schools using their own language. Slightly less than half the Tatar-language schools are located in the Tatar A.S.S.R. (the proportion of these schools parallels the proportion of Tatars in the total A.S.S.R. population). There are 1,450 Tatar-language schools in Bashkiria, 120 in Orenburg *oblast,* 150 in Tiumen *oblast,* but none for the large Tatar population in Uzbekistan.[42]

2. Azerbaidzhanis, though far less mobile geographically, have much higher educational and urbanization indexes than the Tatars. The Azerbaidzhani position grew out of the rapid industrialization of their petroleum-rich country before the Revolution, and the native population's exposure to a large immigration of socially mobilized Russians and Armenians. Culturally, however, the Azerbaidzhanis (traditionally Shi'a Moslems) are not as close to other Turkic-speaking groups as are the Tatars. This factor, together with their low geographic mobility, has apparently restricted their use as a vehicle of Russian influence. A relatively sedentary group, the Azerbaidzhanis have preserved use of their own language to a greater extent than the Tatars, though adolescents are somewhat prone to abandon it in favor of Russian.

3. The Turkic-speaking Bashkirs, Kazakhs, and Kirgizes were, until fairly recently, nomadic. As Table XII shows, though these groups are less urban than the more sedentary Uzbeks and Turkmens, the Kazakhs and Kirgizes already have about as many scientists and specialists with higher education in proportion to their total populations, and a significantly higher proportion of students in higher education. In many cases, however, Central Asian students and scientific workers tend to an overwhelming extent to remain in their home territories. Part of this trend is undoubtedly due to the very large proportion of East Slavs living among the erstwhile nomads (46 per cent in Bashkiria, 37 per cent in Kirgizia, and 52 per cent in

Kazakhstan). Quite possibly the regime has deliberately accelerated the educational progress of the former nomads (as it almost certainly has their entry into the Party). The fact remains that social mobilization appears now to be progressing somewhat faster and more smoothly among the ex-nomads, with their relatively primitive cultural background, than among the sedentary peoples.

4. One possible reason for the sedentary peoples' relative lag is that Moslem culture in their cases developed in a stricter, more fanatical form than among the nomads. As Table XII indicates, Tatar urban women have the same access to education as men, but in all other groups there are distinct differences. In addition, the oasis Moslems seem to have clung more closely to other forms of maintaining the inferior status of women, such as bride purchase and kidnaping. From the regime's standpoint, these practices and attitudes are undesirable not only because they have religious roots, but because they waste work time, prevent economic development, and, above all, adversely affect the recruitment of women into the skilled labor market. For example, only seven Uzbek girls graduated from the Tashkent Textile Institute between 1943 and 1953.[43] The situation is especially interesting as far as marriages are concerned. In 1959, 5.4 per cent of the families in Tashkent (the most urbanized) were Russo-Uzbek, and the rate of intermarriage in 1958 was about the same. Only one-fourth of the brides in these mixed marriages were Uzbek. The Soviet commentator notes with satisfaction that the Russian wives exerted a strong cultural influence in the mixed families.[44]

5. The small Moslem groups in the North Caucasus are divided between those who were banished en masse by Stalin at the end of World War I and those who, more loyal to the Soviet regime, were allowed to remain. In the former category, the Chechens are most numerous; while the Kabardins are not the most numerous of the more loyal groups, they can be taken as fairly typical. As Table XII shows, the degree of social mobilization among the Chechens is very low. This is due partly to the frightful losses the Chechens suffered in their years of banishment (only 19 per cent of the present population is in the thirty to fifty-nine age group). But it is also due to the Chechens' very conservative, clannish traditions, which accentuate the attitudes toward women described above. These same national traditions, of course, have been instrumental in fostering the fierce resistance to Russification demonstrated by the Chechen adherence to the native language.

Some of the functional aspects of the colonial ethnic groups are peculiar to each of these varied nationalities. Nevertheless, some important over-all functions can be identified: (1) In terms of sheer manpower, the colonials are important to the Soviet system, since they constitute about 12 per cent of the population. Because of their high relative birth rates, their value as a source of labor will increase. This value will also be increased by the growing level of education, though at present the colonials are much less useful as skilled manpower than the Europeans. On the other hand, on farms in the warmer Central Asian oases and parts of Azerbaidzhan they are able to produce some products more efficiently than is the case in other parts of the U.S.S.R. (2) Strategically, the territories inhabited by the colonials provide a vast *glacis* vis-à-vis both China and the American CENTO allies. (3) The claim of the U.S.S.R. of being a truly multinational and multiracial society rather than merely a European federation depends upon continued, and at least ostensibly happy, association of the colonials in the U.S.S.R.

There are, on the other hand, a number of important general dysfunctions the regime must take into account: (1) The effort to increase the colonials' level of social mobilization is expensive in proportion to their contribution to the Soviet gross national product.[45] (2) Almost all the groups present strong traditional barriers to the full utilization of their labor. Their treatment of women also is a standing defiance of one of the major tenets of Communist ideology —however much it may be covertly flouted in other parts of the U.S.S.R. (3) The history of colonial relations suggests that, no matter what policy the regime may pursue, there is always a chance of sudden rebellion among a rapidly modernizing colonial group. There is, therefore, an unavoidable danger that the Soviet regime might be badly weakened in its propaganda and military posture at a crucial moment of its contest with China and the West. (4) While Russians (and other Soviet Europeans) do not exhibit much prejudice toward Asians, the two groups remain aloof, especially as far as intermarriage is concerned. (5) In view of the high relative birth rate of the Central Asians, it is questionable whether the regime can promote assimilation and control there (as it has in the past) by increasing the European portion of the population. A possible course (also advantageous in view of labor shortages in Europe resulting from low birth rates) would be to transfer Asians to the metropolitan areas— but this would create an internal proletariat, with all its disadvantages.[46]

The policies adopted by the regime to deal with the complex functional position of the colonials have been equally complex. Some of these policies are designed to conciliate the colonials and to modernize them in a way that will bring them material benefits as well as make them more productive. (1) Strong efforts have been made to achieve rapid social mobilization. Very likely this has often involved giving the colonials preferential treatment, at least in funds. (2) The impression that the regime offers equal chances to colonials is fostered by strong efforts to enroll them in the Party. The Azerbaidzhani, Kazakh, and Kirgiz membership rates (48, 50, and 36 per 1,000, respectively) are not much below the Russian (64). The sedentary Central Asian groups have lower rates (Uzbek, 32; Turkmen, 32; Tadzhik, 30), but this may be due in part to resistance of these groups to association with Russians. (3) The impression of equality of opportunity is enhanced by giving high posts to symbolic figures such as M. D. Bagirov and N. A. Mukhitdinov. At present no colonial occupies a truly major post, while many important positions in colonial areas are held by Europeans. One Soviet source, however, emphasizes the importance of Asians (60.5 per cent) and Uzbeks in particular (43 per cent) in the Uzbekistan MVD.[47] (4) Stalin's injustice in expelling Moslem Caucasian groups was publicly admitted in 1957 and the survivors returned to their homelands, which were again given administrative recognition. The Crimean Tatars were not, however, returned to their more strategic homeland. (5) Policies in relation to language and culture are more ambiguous. Probably the assurance (often expressed by regime spokesmen of Moslem background) that national languages will persist and be further developed is sincere. The firm adherence of the colonial groups to their own languages has probably convinced the regime that outright Russification would be a very long and costly process. Furthermore, as Soviet writers point out, it is simply impracticable to educate children in a language other than their native one if that language is as dissimilar to Russian as the Turkic tongues are. In some areas a considerable proportion of colonial children are enrolled in Russian-language schools (27 per cent in Kazakhstan),[48] but the regime is disturbed by the virtually complete segregation of colonial and European school children (99 per cent of Uzbek children in Uzbekistan attend Uzbek-language classes in which there are practically no Europeans). Conversely, 90 per cent of the students in Uzbekistan with Russian as the language of instruction are of European background. In an effort to overcome this segregation, some Uzbek S.S.R. schools (with over half the enrollment in Tashkent *oblast* outside Tashkent city) have been converted into dual or multilanguage schools. Ordinarily the children receive their instruction in Russian or Uzbek (or occasionally in another Central Asian language) in accordance with their backgrounds, but, a Soviet commentator notes, "in the process of daily study, occupation, and play, the children get accustomed to Russian." By 1960 nearly 10 per cent of the schools in the Azerbaidzhan Republic had been reorganized on this basis.[49] The process is hardly likely to assimilate many Asians, but it may enable them to use Russian effectively. The fact that many colonials cannot now do so poses an additional barrier to their full utilization. In Asia, the regime's avowed aim of bilingualism has very concrete meaning. Since Stalin's death there has been a considerable relaxation of cultural controls. Sometimes even Russians urge colonials to exploit their rich literary lore and to write.[50] The requirement that historiography should unfailingly praise everything associated with Russia has been somewhat modified. It is now possible to point out that Czarist colonizers used deplorable methods, but the end result—attachment of colonial areas to Russia—must still be acclaimed.[51] Khrushchev himself emphasized that the "voluntary" incorporation of Kirgizia into the Russian Empire had been a "progressive" step.[52] The role of Russian as a transmitter of all the benefits of culture is constantly stressed and colonials are urged to borrow new terms from it rather than adapt old words from their own languages.[53] Conversely, the millennium-old ties of the colonials with the great Middle Eastern cultures are ignored or minimized.[54]

Some policies pursued by the regime are even more definitely aimed at breaking down elements of the colonial people's traditions which stand in the way of Soviet aims: (1) The attacks on Islam, while falling short of those directed at Judaism and the Ukrainian Catholic Church, are very sharp. As suggested earlier, they are especially directed against elements associated with Islam which have stood in the way of full social mobilization. (2) The policy of divide and conquer has been assiduously pursued by the regime ever since the Civil War. In the great oases of Central Asia, artificial divisions among republics were created on a linguistic basis, whereas historically (and sociologically), the division has been between the sedentary "Sarts" and the nomads. A similar multiplicity of divisions was created in the North Caucasus. The Bashkirs, who were (see Table XI) well on the way to Tatarization, have been "revived" as a separate nation. Now, however, the regime considers it safe, and more efficient, to promote change and consolidation. Important irrigable districts of Kazakhstan have been transferred to the Uzbek S.S.R. This move is praised as being in accord with Lenin's statement that nationality is merely one, and not the most important, principle for territorial division.[55] Experimentation with a council of national economy and a Communist Party Bureau for Central Asia (not including Kazakhstan) is obviously in accord with that concept. (3) As in other areas, Russians (and other Europeans, mainly East Slav) have been poured into the territories of the colonial nationalities to further assimilation, to promote modernization, and to serve as a bulwark of Soviet control. (4) Beyond all these policies aimed at *securing* the colonial areas and *exploiting* their resources are the policies directed at using them as a springboard for influencing the Asian and African world. Yet the Soviet regime is obviously uneasy concerning this tactic. Up to 1959, only two Asians were employed at the diplomatic first secretary level or above, both in minor countries.[56] In his speech in Kirgizia, Khrushchev boasted that he and his audience were in the "very center of Asia," but he was careful to point out that the U.S.S.R. also had a claim to be Asian because of the *Russian* settlement of Vladivostok. Obviously the quarrel with China lay behind these nuances, but long before this quarrel was avowed the Soviet regime hedged on its use of Asians to appeal to Asians. Most of the delegates to the October, 1958, "Conference of Writers of the Countries of Asia and Africa" in Tashkent, were from Asia and Africa, with a few European and white American guests. The Soviet contingent, on the other hand, included many delegates of European background (as well as Georgians and Armenians, who were only geographically "Asian"). An obscure Dagestani, very likely inspired by the regime, emphasized that this distinction between continents was insignificant:

> My people live at the foot of the Caucasian ridge that divides Europe and Asia. But this ridge cannot separate the culture of Europe and Asia, of East and West. Peoples do not oppose one another in their literature.
>
> Mankind would be a thousand times poorer spiritually if the great culture of the West and the East did not feed him with its two breasts, just as a mother feeds her children. Possibly there is a border between East and West, but there is no border between their culture and literature.[57]

While awaiting more precise studies, it is the hope of the author that the functional examination of Soviet nationalities has provided a perspective for analyzing the broad policy statements that have characterized the regime's over-all approach to the nationality question. The denial of a proximate intention to merge non-Russian groups with the Russians linguistically is meaningful as far as the colonials and the state nations go, but dubious for the mobilized diasporas and the younger brothers, who appear to be scheduled for Russification. The other nationalities probably would satisfy the regime, for the time being at least, if they could use Russian fluently and willingly in occupational and political activity, retaining their native languages for use in the home and limited cultural pursuits.[58] The opposition to national aloofness and the stress on the mingling of populations, on the other hand, fit in with the effort to provide strong Russian or Russified cadres in all strategic regions. Intermingling of populations is also an essential aspect of the process of isolating and then Russifying major elements of the younger-brother groups.

The analysis also suggests that the major thrust of Soviet nationality policy in the short run (the next decade or two) will be toward drawing the younger brothers (especially the Ukrainians) into indissoluble junior partnership with the Russians as the dominant ethnic group, but avoiding the dysfunctions that open avowal of this aim would entail. If this aim is accomplished, the relatively small state nations can be "contained" without undue effort, and the mobilized diasporas can be treated as pawns. The situation of the colonials is more critical, mainly because of their importance for the Soviet image in the outside world. Overreliance on Slavs in Asia will tarnish this image, yet all precedents, and many concrete features of the Soviet system, suggest that the relationship with colonials is explosive. Finally, as far as the younger brothers are concerned, the success of their absorption depends in considerable measure upon the regime's implementation of programs that will greatly enhance the dignity and well-being of submerged social strata, particularly the peasantry. But the totalitarian system has yet to demonstrate that it has the will to undertake this, or the capacity to accomplish it. In the final analysis, the totalitarian ethos of the Soviet elite not only provides the motivation for its handling of the nationalities problem but erects what may well be insurmountable barriers to its solution.

TABLE I
Jews in Selected Urban Areas

Area	Total Urban Population (*in thousands*)	Jews (*in per cent of total urban population*)	Jews Speaking Yiddish (*in per cent of urban Jewish population*)	Russian Speakers (*in per cent of total urban population*)
"Pale"				
Belorussia				
Brest	284	2.0	20	47
Gomel	389	11.0	26	44
Grodno	251	1.4	21	37
Minsk (city)	509	7.7	15	48
Minsk (oblast)	273	2.8	23	29
Mogilev	365	7.6	27	40
Vitebsk	410	4.4	22	41
Ukraine				
Khmelnitskii	305	5.9	27	22
Kiev (city)	1,104	13.9	13	54
Kiev (oblast)	444	3.1	33	18
Odessa	957	12.4	12	64
Vinnitsa	363	11.5	36	27
Zhitomir	417	9.5	29	26
Non-"Pale"				
Baku (Azerbaidzhan S.S.R.)	643	4.0	17	50
R.S.F.S.R.				
Dagestan A.S.S.R.	315	7.0	85[a]	49
Leningrad (city)	3,321	5.1	9	97
Moscow (city)	5,086	4.7	8	96
Rostov (oblast)	1,899	1.1	7	95
Ukraine				
Chernovitsy[b]	203	20.0	50	34
Crimea	775	3.1	9	90
Donetsk	3,656	1.2	7	59
Kharkov	1,574	5.3	8	50
Lvov[c]	821	3.6	17	28
Poltava	484	2.5	13	18
Transcarpathia[d]	265	3.5	44	13

Sources: *Itogi vsesoiuznoi perepisi naseleniia 1959 goda: RSFSR,* and the 1959 censuses of the various republics.

[a] Probably includes many "mountaineer" Jews speaking Tati.

[b] In Rumania before 1940.

[c] In Poland before 1939.

[d] In Czechoslovakia before 1945.

TABLE II
JEWISH SCIENTIFIC WORKERS

Year	Number (*in thousands*)	Percentage of Total Soviet Scientific Workers
1956	24.6	11.0
1958	28.9	10.0
1959	30.6	9.9
1960	33.5	9.5
1961	36.2	9.0
1963	48.0	8.7
1964	50.9	8.3
1965	53.0	7.9

SOURCES: *Bulletin d'études et d'information politique internationale,* No. 195 (May 16–31, 1958), p. 21 (based on a Soviet source for 1956); *N. Kh. 1959,* p. 757; *N. Kh. 1960,* p. 785; *N. Kh. 1961,* p. 704; *N. Kh. 1963; N. Kh. 1964,* p. 701; *N. Kh. 1965.* No new data on scientific workers were published in *N. Kh. 1962.*

TABLE III

ARMENIANS IN SELECTED AREAS

Area	Total Population (in thousands)	URBAN: Armenians (in per cent of urban population)	URBAN: Armenian Absolute Increase 1926–59[a] (in per cent of Armenian population)	URBAN: Armenian Relative Increase 1926–59[a] (in per cent of total population)	URBAN: Armenians Speaking Armenian (in per cent of Armenian population)	URBAN: Russian Speakers (in per cent of urban population)	URBAN: Armenians Speaking Russian (in per cent of Armenian population) 1959	URBAN: Armenians Speaking Russian (in per cent of Armenian population) 1926[a]	RURAL: Armenians (in per cent of rural population)	RURAL: Armenians Speaking Armenian (in per cent of Armenian population)
Armenian S.S.R.										
Erevan (city)	509	93	720	4	98	6	2	—		
Other	1,254	92	260	—3	99	6	1	—	84	100
Azerbaidzhan S.S.R.										
Greater Baku	971	18	110	—6	69	47	31	—		
Other	2,727	10	320	60	90	17	10	—	9	99
Georgian S.S.R.										
Abkhazia A.S.S.R.	405	8	300	—25	90	45	10	—	20	92
Tbilisi (city)	695	21	50	—38	70	26	16[b]	5		
Other	2,944	10	60	—70	82	20	7	1	9	91
Turkmen S.S.R.										
Ashkhabad (city)	170	5	...	...	67	59	33	...		
Other	1,346	1	...	...	69	35	31	...	—	—
R.S.F.S.R.										
Dagestan A.S.S.R.	1,062	2	—	—	66	49	34	5	—	—
Greater Moscow	5,086	0.4	...	...	34	96	66	...		
Krasnodar (oblast)	3,762	2.4	}	}	66	95	34	}	1.9	86
Rostov (oblast)	3,312	1.7	}—8	}—50	59	95	41	}14	—	—
Stavropol (oblast)	1,883	3	}	}	61	93	40	}	—	—

SOURCES: 1959 censuses of the various republics.

[a] Approximations only, due to changes in administrative boundaries.

[b] Nearly all of the remainder (here and in other parts of the Georgian S.S.R.) speak Georgian.

Note: In this table and elsewhere, dashes are used to indicate that the amount is negligible, ellipses indicate that information is not available.

TABLE IV

ARMENIAN PROFESSIONAL MANPOWER

SCIENTIFIC WORKERS			SPECIALISTS WITH HIGHER EDUCATION			FULL-TIME STUDENTS IN HIGHER EDUCATION		
Year	Number (*in thousands*)	Percentage of Total Soviet Supply	Year (*as of December 1*)	Number (*in thousands*)	Percentage of Total Soviet Supply	Year	Number (*in thousands*)	Percentage of Total Soviet Enrollment
1939	2.1	2.2	1957	62.2	2.2	1927–28	3.4	2.0
1950	3.9	2.4	1959	69.0	2.1	1957–58	22.0	1.7
1955	5.1	2.3	1960	74.1	2.1	1958–59	21.2	1.6
1957	5.9	2.3	1961	79.4	2.1	1959–60	20.4	1.5
1958	6.4	2.3	1962	83.2	2.1	1960–61	21.1	1.5
1959	7.3	2.3	1964[a]	91.4	2.1	1961–62	23.5	1.6
1960	8.0	2.3				1962–63	26.2	1.6
1961	9.1	2.3						
1962	. . .	. . .						
1963	12.0	2.1						
1964	12.8	2.0						

SOURCES: *N. Kh. 1958,* pp. 688, 846; *N. Kh. 1959,* pp. 617, 752, 757; *N. Kh. 1960,* pp. 663, 780, 785; *N. Kh. 1961,* pp. 586, 704; *N. Kh. 1962,* pp. 473, 573; *N. Kh. 1963,* p. 591; *N. Kh. 1964. Total* enrollment in the Armenian S.S.R. institutions of higher learning has been 1 to 5 per cent below the total Armenian higher education enrollment shown in the table. Even though Armenian S.S.R. schools of higher education must accommodate students of other nationalities (11 per cent in the republic), it appears probable that they provide places for very many students from the diaspora. A Soviet source (Loretta Kh. Ter-Mkrtichian, *Armiane v stranakh arabskogo vostoka* [Moscow, 1965], p. 57) notes that 100 Arabs and Near Eastern Armenians were studying in Armenian S.S.R. institutions of higher education in 1962–63.

[a] As of November 15.

TABLE V
Use of Russian among Volga Finnic Groups

			Rural Population in Nationality's A.S.S.R.		Urban Population in Nationality's A.S.S.R.			Urban Population in Selected Adjacent Areas	
Nationality	Nationality in A.S.S.R. Population	Children in Nationality Language Schools	Russian Speakers in Total Rural Population	Russian Speakers in Nationality	Russian Speakers in Total Urban Population	Russian Speakers in Nationality	Urban Nationality Population 10–19 Age Group Speaking Russian (*estimated*)	Russian Speakers in Total Urban Population	Russian Speakers in Nationality
	(*in per cent*)								
Chuvash	70	54	14	1	65	16	34	91[a]	23
Mari	43	27	38	1	80	16	28	92[b]	26
Mordvin	36	23	55	2	86	22	58	94[c]	47
Udmurt	36	15	45	3	79	23	36	89[d]	40

Sources: Column 2 ("Children in Nationality Language Schools") from *Kul'turnoe stroitel'stvo RSFSR* (Moscow, 1958), pp. 206–7; all other columns from *Itogi vsesoiuznoi perepisi naseleniia 1959 goda: RSFSR,* Table 54.

[a] Ulianovsk oblast.
[b] Sverdlovsk oblast.
[c] Kiubyshev oblast.
[d] Perm oblast.

TABLE VI
East Slav Professional Manpower

Scientific Workers (*per 100,000 population*)				Specialists with Higher Education (*per 1,000 population*)				Full-time Students in Higher Education (*per 10,000 population*)			
Year	Russian	Ukrainian	Belorussian	Year	Russian	Ukrainian	Belorussian	Year	Russian	Ukrainian	Belorussian
1939	59	35	32	1957	14	11	9	1927–28	12.1	8	9.6
1950	87	39	34	1962	21	16	14	1950–51	45	29	22
1955	127	59	52	1964	23	17	14	1957–58	72	49	45
1963	327	159	132					1962–63	90	60	57
1964	354	172	145								
1965	386	190	163								

Sources: *N. Kh. 1958,* pp. 688, 846; *N. Kh. 1959,* p. 752; *N. Kh. 1962,* pp. 473, 573; *N. Kh. 1963,* p. 591; *N. Kh. 1964,* pp. 517, 691, 701; *N. Kh. 1965,* pp. 701, 711; 1939 data calculated to base of 1939 census data, *Bol'shaia sovetskaia entsiklopediia: SSSR* (1st ed.; Moscow, 1948), p. 59; 1927–28 data calculated to base of 1926 census data, as cited in Frank Lorimer, *The Population of the Soviet Union* (Geneva, 1946), p. 55.

TABLE VII

URBAN GROWTH, UKRAINIAN NATIONALITY, AND THE USE OF UKRAINIAN IN URBAN AREAS OF THE UKRAINIAN S.S.R.

Oblast	Rate of Growth of Urban Population 1939–59 (*in per cent of total oblast population*)	Percentage of Ukrainians in Urban Population 1959	Percentage of Total Population Speaking Ukrainian 1959
Cherkassy	64	81	77
Chernigov	44	82	70
Chernovitsy	30	49	46
Crimea	25	19	8
Dnepropetrovsk	32	72	64
Donets	12	52	39
Ivan Franko	—	82	80
Kharkov	17	61	49
Kherson	82	72	61
Khmelnitskii	58	72	69
Kiev (city)		60	43
Kiev (oblast)	117	81	79
Kirovograd	63	80	75
Lugansk	20	53	44
Lvov	22	70	66
Nikolaev	44	68	51
Odessa	24	44	31
Poltava	50	84	80
Rovno	31	74	71
Sumy	68	82	75
Ternopol	21	83	82
Transcarpathia	. . .	61	58
Vinnitsa	42	70	66
Volhynia	63	83	82
Zaporozhe	46	62	51
Zhitomir	24	66	62

SOURCE: *Itogi vsesoiuznoi perepisi naseleniia 1959 goda: Ukrainskaia SSR.*

TABLE VIII
USE OF THE RUSSIAN LANGUAGE IN URBAN AREAS OF THE UKRAINIAN S.S.R.

Oblast	Percentage of Total Urban Population Speaking Russian	Percentage of Ukrainian Urban Population Speaking Russian	
	1959	1959	1926[a]
Cherkassy	21	4	...
Chernigov	28	14	36
Chernovitsy	34	7	...
Crimea	90	57	...
Dnepropetrovsk	35	11	34
Donets	59	25	50
Ivan Franko	16	2	...
Kharkov	50	19	26
Kherson	38	16	44
Khmelnitskii	22	5	6
Kiev (city)	54	28	35
Kiev (oblast)	18	3	2
Kirovograd	23	6	21
Lugansk	54	16	46
Lvov	28	5	...
Nikolaev	47	26	53
Odessa	64	31	63
Poltava	18	4	8
Rovno	25	4	...
Sumy	24	9	25
Ternopol	14	2	...
Transcarpathia	13	3	...
Vinnitsa	27	6	8
Volhynia	17	2	...
Zaporozhe	48	18	26
Zhitomir	26	6	8

SOURCES: Data for 1926 are taken from Tsentral'noe statisticheskoe upravlenie, *Recensement de la population de l'URSS,* First Series (Moscow, 1927–28). Data for 1959 are from *Itogi vsesoiuznoi perepisi naseleniia 1959 goda: Ukrainskaia SSR.*

[a] Since administrative boundaries have changed considerably since 1926, comparisons are very approximate. In most cases, the 1926 urban areas, in the smaller okrugs, contained a higher proportion of inhabitants in the central cities. Since these were usually older, relatively large cities, the proportion of Russian speakers is in many cases significantly greater than would have been the case if it had been feasible to calculate the total urban population of areas exactly comparable to the present oblasts.

TABLE IX
ABSOLUTE NUMBERS OF UKRAINIANS SPEAKING RUSSIAN, IN SELECTED URBAN AREAS OF THE UKRAINIAN S.S.R.
(in thousands)

Oblast	1959	1926[a]
Chernigov	40.6	14.5
Dnepropetrovsk	145.9	49.9
Donets	476.8	34.7
Kharkov	183.7	71.7
Kherson	38.3	17.5
Khmelnitskii	10.0	1.9
Kiev (city)	186.3	74.8
Kiev (oblast)	11.3	1.3
Kirovograd	16.8	15.4
Lugansk	168.0	44.1
Nikolaev	69.5	24.2
Odessa	128.6	32.5
Poltava	16.6	7.2
Sumy	35.0	19.3
Vinnitsa	14.4	4.1
Zaporozhe	92.7	4.3
Zhitomir	16.6	6.0

SOURCES: *Recensement de la population de l'URSS; Itogi vsesoiuznoi perepisi naseleniia 1959 goda: Ukrainskaia SSR.*

[a] In most cases, the vast majority of Ukrainians speaking Russian have been concentrated in the central cities; the major exception is the Donbas oblasts, where large industrial centers contain many Ukrainian Russian-speakers. Consequently, the fact that the okrugs of 1926 do not coincide with the oblasts of 1959 distorts the comparison significantly only in the case of the Donbas oblasts.

TABLE X
Social Mobilization of State Nations

Nationality	Total Number (*in thousands*)	Approximate Birth Rate (*per 1,000*)	Percentage Under Age 20	Percentage of Urban Population	Urban Population with Higher than Elementary Education (*per 1,000*)		Scientific Workers 1963 (*per 100,000 population*)	Specialists with Higher Education 1962 (*per 1,000 population*)	Full-time Students in Higher Education 1962–63 (*per 10,000 population*)	Percentage Living in Nationality's Republic
					Male	Female				
Estonian	989	. . .	25.8	47	433	437	307	22	94	90
Georgian	2,692	25	36.1	36	551	546	435	36	105	97
Latvian	1,400	17	26.2	48	494	473	274	20	81	93
Lithuanian	2,326	22	34.3	36	314	310	200	15	90	93
Moldavian	2,214	28	40.7	13	313	246	45	6	42	85
Russian	*114,114*	*21*	*37.0*	*58*	*363*	*375*	*327*	*21*	*90*	*86*

Sources: *N. Kh. 1962,* p. 573; *N. Kh. 1963,* pp. 493, 591; Karl-Eugen Waedekin, "Nationalitaetenpolitik und Lebenskraft der Voelker in der Sowjetunion heute und morgen," *Osteuropa,* XIV (November, 1964), pp. 830, 844.

TABLE XI
Tatars in Selected Areas

Area	Urban						Rural				
	Tatars (*in thousands*)	Tatars (*in per cent of urban population*)	Tatar Absolute Increase 1926–59[a] (*in per cent of Tatar population*)	Tatar Relative Increase 1926–59[a] (*in per cent of total population*)	Russian Speakers (*in per cent of urban population*)	Tatars Speaking Russian (*in per cent of Tatar population*)	Tatars (*in thousands*)	Tatars (*in per cent of rural population*)	Tatar Absolute Increase 1926–59[a] (*in per cent of Tatar population*)	Russian Speakers (*in per cent of rural population*)	Tatars Speaking Russian (*in per cent of Tatar population*)
R.S.F.S.R.											
Astrakhan (oblast)	31	8	35	–27	88	5	26	8	4	71	2
Bashkir A.S.S.R.	242[b]	19	764	58	70	4	527[c]	26	16	31	1
Cheliabinsk (oblast)	130	6	4,200	50	89	11	60	9	216	76	5
Orenburg (oblast)	42	5	110	–140	87	8	79	8	132	70	2
Perm (oblast)	98	6	1,130	50	89	12	68	6	1,300	79	5
Tatar A.S.S.R.	396	33	509	38	64	3	949	57	–14	32	0
Tiumen (oblast)	15	4	650	33	92	9	57	8	110	82	2
Ulianovsk (oblast)	21	5	450	20	91	6	76	11	114	74	1
Uzbek S.S.R.	287	10	1,200	400	40	8	157	3	2,750	4	4

Source: *Itogi vsesoiuznoi perepisi naseleniia 1959 goda: RSFSR* and *Uzbekskoi SSR*.

[a] Approximations only, due to changes in administrative boundaries.

[b] In addition, there are about 22,000 Tatar-speaking urban Bashkirs.

[c] In addition, there are about 280,000 Tatar-speaking rural Bashkirs.

TABLE XII
SOCIAL MOBILIZATION OF COLONIALS

Nationality	Total Number (*in thousands*)	Approximate Birth Rate (*per 1,000*)	Percentage Under Age 20	Percentage of Urban Residence	Urban Population with Higher than Elementary Education (*per 1,000*) Male	Female	Scientific Workers 1963 (*per 100,000 population*)	Specialists with Higher Education 1962 (*per 1,000 population*)	Full-time Students in Higher Education 1962–63 (*per 10,000 population*)	Percentage Living in Nationality's Republic	Percentage of Scientific Workers Living in R.S.F.S.R.[a]	Percentage of All Students in Higher Education Studying in R.S.F.S.R.[a]
Azerbaidzhani	2,940	42	45.9	35	374	248	244	18	75	85	1.5	2.5
Bashkir	989	...	44.0	18	222[b]	182[b]	68	7.5	...	75	...	...
Chechen	419	...	48.8[b]	22	106[b]	13[b]	13	1.5	...	58	...	...
Kabardin	204	...	44.9[b]	14	220[b]	174[b]	83	12	...	93	...	...
Kazakh	3,622	38	47.9	24	315	196	104	11	86	77	[c]	[c]
Kirgiz	969	35	47.1	11	438	293	86	12	84	86	0.5	8.5
Tadzhik	1,397	...	48.6	21	308	165	85	9	58	75	2.5	3.5
Tatar	4,968	28	41.4	42	299[d]	310[d]	126	12	...	27	...	...
Turkmen	1,002	...	45.5	25	331	202	100	12	77	92	2.0	4.0
Uzbek	6,015	38	48.7	22	316	209	99	10	68	84	2.0	2.5
Russian	*114,114*	*21*	*37.0*	*58*	*363*	*375*	*328*	*..21*	*90*	*86*		

SOURCES: *N. Kh. 1962*, p. 573; *N. Kh. 1963*, pp. 493, 591; Waedekin, *op. cit.*, pp. 830, 844.

[a] Calculations of these indicators of personal mobility (and others given in the text) made as follows: Data on the number of scientific workers for 1963 in the U.S.S.R. (*N. Kh. 1963*) and in the R.S.F.S.R. (Tsentral'noe statisticheskoe upravlenie, *Narodnoe khoziaistvo RSFSR, 1963* [Moscow, 1965], p. 381) are available, as are data on *all* students in higher education in the R.S.F.S.R. for 1956–57 (*Kul'turnoe stroitel'stvo RSFSR*). The number of all students by nationality in higher education in the U.S.S.R. for 1956–57 can be estimated fairly closely. Consequently, the proportions of students and scientific workers of each nationality can be calculated. From these are subtracted proportions equivalent to the proportion of the general population of each nationality living in the R.S.F.S.R., on the assumption that students from the R.S.F.S.R. group do not represent mobile individuals. Obviously the indicator understates the extent of personal mobility by omitting both the movement of students and scientists *to* the nationality S.S.R. and the movement of students and scientists *from* the nationality republic to republics other than the R.S.F.S.R.

[b] Population in R.S.F.S.R. only.

[c] Reverse movement.

[d] Population in the R.S.F.S.R. and Uzbek S.S.R. only.

NOTES

1. *XXII s"ezd Kommunisticheskoi Partii Sovetskogo Soiuza: Stenograficheskii otchet* (Moscow, 1962), III, 312–15 (translated in the *Current Digest of the Soviet Press* [hereafter cited as *CDSP*] XIII, No. 46, 14–15).
2. *XXII s"ezd KPSS,* I, 215–17 (translated in *CDSP,* XIII, No. 30, 19–20).
3. I have not made any attempt to present a chronological treatment of the development of Soviet policy since 1953. There is considerable reason to support Paul Urban's view ("Moskaus heutige Kulturpolitik gegenueber den nichtrussischen Voelkerschaften der Sowjetunion," *Osteuropa,* XI [March, 1961], 213–26) that an initial "thaw" (approximately 1953–57) was followed by an intensified drive for Russification after Khrushchev had consolidated his power. There are some faint signs that Khrushchev's successors may permit a second "thaw." (See the discussions translated in *CDSP,* XVII, Nos. 15 and 16, on national characteristics and folk art, mainly related to Russians; and the sharp polemic against "assimilators" in A. M. Egiazarian, *Ob osnovnykh tendentsiiakh razvitiia sotsialisticheskikh natsii SSSR* [Erevan, released to press January, 1965].) It seems safest, however, to view the official Program and its exegeses as the basic current position.
4. K. Kh. Khanazarov, *Sblizhenie natsii i natsional'nye iazyki v SSSR* (Tashkent, 1963), pp. 82, 83, 222–23. This monograph provides an unusually detailed and explicit exposition of Soviet views, as well as much interesting factual material. Many of its points apply primarily to Central Asian nationalities, but its general significance appears to be enhanced by the fact that an Asian wrote it, just as Stalin's early essay on the national question (suggested by Lenin) had greater impact because it was written by a non-Russian. Khanazarov's book is introduced by the prominent philosopher M. D. Kammari.
5. *Ibid.,* pp. 165, 203.
6. *Ibid.,* pp. 180, 189–90.
7. *XXII s"ezd KPSS,* I, 215–17 (translated in *CDSP,* XIII, No. 30, 19–20).
8. The discussion of social mobilization draws heavily upon Karl W. Deutsch, "Social Mobilization and Political Development," *American Political Science Review,* LV (September, 1961), 493–514. In addition to the four indicators I have listed, Deutsch proposes voter participation (meaningless for comparative purposes in the U.S.S.R., in view of the universal participation reported); "exposure to modernity," a concept which I find impossible to quantify, at least in Soviet conditions; the shift out of agriculture (which in the U.S.S.R. is virtually identical to urbanization); and per capita income (which, insofar as it is determinable by nationality in Soviet statistics, is also almost identical to rural-urban differences). It should be noted that Deutsch anticipates the fact that indicators of social mobilization will tend to be identical. In the four indicators that I use, divergence is more frequent, however, than his model would suggest. It is, therefore, especially important for me to employ as many indicators (especially of different kinds of education) as is feasible. Unfortunately, I have not often been able to use indicator 4, exposure to mass media. At first sight it would seem simple to utilize the easily available data on publications in the national languages as indicators of exposure to printed mass media. In fact, however, a member of a nationality may obtain most of this exposure through Russian-language publications imported from

Moscow or other centers. For example, in 1940, out of 5 million books printed in the Azerbaidzhanian S.S.R., 3.9 million were in Azerbaidzhani, whereas, in 1958, 6.5 out of 8.3 million were in that language. (Tsentral'noe statisticheskoe upravlenie, *Narodnoe khoziaistvo SSSR* [hereafter cited as *N. Kh.*] *1960* [Moscow, 1961], p. 811.) These books constituted only a very small portion of all books *sold* in the republic, however: 14.4 million in 1940 and 47.0 million in 1958. (M. K. Kurbanov, *Kul'tura Sovetskogo Azerbaidzhana* [Baku, 1959], p. 32.) Since almost no books were printed in Azerbaidzhani outside the republic, evidently—in sharp contrast to the impression created by the first statistics—the predominance of non-Azerbaidzhani books has increased from 73 per cent in 1940 to 86 per cent in 1958. Unfortunately, there are very few instances in which readily available data permit such comparative language calculations, or even an estimate of the *total* exposure of nationalities to printed media, films, radio, or television. Very intensive research in local publications might provide important additional data, but even Yaroslav Bilinsky's extremely detailed investigation has not turned up much for recent years (*The Second Soviet Republic: The Ukraine after World War II* [New Brunswick, N.J.: Rutgers University Press, 1964], p. 180).

9. In fact, because of the difficulties discussed in note 8 above, I have been cautious in using, for example, the per capita newspaper circulation as an indication of the relative exposure of ethnic groups to their own language or culture. If one group has a high index on this score, yet also (though the data do not inform us on the point) reads numerous Moscow newspapers, its relative exposure to its own language may be less than that of another group with a low per capita newspaper circulation in its own language but with a far lower circulation of Moscow and other Russian-language papers. I have not used employment of national cadres extensively because the subject is treated at length by Dr. Seweryn Bialer in a paper that will appear in a separate work now in progress. In general, I want to emphasize that my essay is by no means exhaustive; it is an effort at outlining the problem, presenting an approach to it, and applying this approach in an illustrative fashion.
10. *Formirovanie i razvitie sovetskogo rabochego klassa* (*1917–1961 gg.*): *Sbornik statei* (Moscow, 1964), pp. 264–65.
11. John A. Armstrong, *The Politics of Totalitarianism* (New York: Random House, 1961), p. 242. At least Jews were 10 per cent of the delegates to the Second Writers' Congress, which is very unlikely to have overrepresented Jewish writers. (*Vtoroi vsesoiuznoi s''ezd sovetskikh pisatelei: Stenograficheskii otchet* [Moscow, 1956], p. 79.)
12. Ilya Ehrenburg, *The War: 1941–1945* (Cleveland: World Publishing Co., 1965), p. 121. Cf. Armstrong, *The Politics of Totalitarianism,* p. 154; and John A. Armstrong (ed.), *Soviet Partisans in World War II* (Madison, Wis.: University of Wisconsin Press, 1964), p. 68.
13. From an interview quoted in "Jews in the Soviet Union," *The New Leader,* September 14, 1959.
14. Armstrong, *The Politics of Totalitarianism,* p. 154. Ehrenburg's treatment (*op. cit.*) of this period (particularly Shcherbakov's role) seems to substantiate this conclusion.
15. Armstrong, *The Politics of Totalitarianism,* p. 242; and *Kommunist Belorussii,* No. 5 (May, 1962), p. 57. The Ukrainian calculation is based on the fact that about 10 per cent of the members in the Ukraine are unac-

counted for ethnically (see V. M. Churaev, "Kommunisticheskaia Partiia Ukrainy v tsifrakh," *Partiinaia zhizn'*, No. 12 [1958], pp. 57–59), and seem likely to be predominantly Jewish.

16. *N. Kh. 1962,* p. 573; and *N. Kh. 1963,* pp. 493, 591. In all instances in this and subsequent indexes for the postwar period the population base for calculation is taken from the 1959 census, *Itogi vsesoiuznoi perepisi naseleniia 1959 goda* (16 vols. [one for the U.S.S.R. and one for each Union republic]; Moscow, 1962–63). This census is also the source of other quantitative data when the origin is not otherwise indicated. Using the 1959 base gives an upward bias to indexes for the 1960's, since the population has been growing rapidly, and an even heavier downward bias for the early 1950's and late 1940's. Since, however, there are no reliable estimates on nationalities for other years, and since the main use of the indexes is for comparison (though nationality population growth rates have differed, these differences introduce less bias than the over-all growth rate), it has seemed advisable to use the single base.
17. Judging by the biographies in *Diplomaticheskii slovar'* (3 vols.; Moscow, 1960–64). Armenians are readily identified by their names, which (in the U.S.S.R.) almost always end in "ian."
18. M. Keresselidze, "Transkaukasien im Jahr 1962," *Osteuropa,* XIII (May, 1963), 319, 322–23.
19. See below, p. 30. Of course, this lack of Armenian-Azerbaidzhani schools may be partly due to the regime's desire to mix all of them with Russian children. In view of the very high proportion of Armenians in the republic however, it is curious that there should be no cases where it is convenient to mix Armenians and Azerbaidzhanis alone.
20. *Pechat' SSSR v 1963 godu* (Moscow, 1964), pp. 24, 115, 119, 121, 125, 152.
21. *Vtoroi vsesoiuznoi s"ezd sovetskikh pisatelei,* pp. 79, 594–95.
22. M. Keresselidze, "Transkaukasien im Jahr 1963," *Osteuropa,* XIV (July–August, 1964), 540–41.
23. Armenian Party membership is about 30 per cent higher outside than inside the Armenian S.S.R., but this is largely accounted for by the higher proportion of adults in the diaspora. Except where otherwise indicated, current Party membership is based on data from *Partiinaia zhizn',* No. 10 (1965), pp. 8–17 (translated in *CDSP,* XVII, No. 29, 14–18); 1961 data is from *Partiinaia zhizn',* No. 1 (1961), pp. 44–54 (translated in *CDSP,* XIV, No. 3, 3–6).
24. Karl W. Deutsch, *Nationalism and Social Communication* (Cambridge, Mass.: The M.I.T. Press, 1953), chap. vi.
25. The Chuvash speak a basically Turkic language with a strong Finnic influence. Though predominantly Orthodox, they were also influenced by Islam. As Table V indicates, the Chuvash seem distinctly less susceptible to Russification than the other groups.
26. Khanazarov, *op. cit.,* pp. 137, 140, 203.
27. See also the table in John A. Armstrong, *Ukrainian Nationalism* (2d ed.; New York: Columbia University Press, 1963), p. 324. The reduction of the proportion of Russian speakers was due partly to Nazi massacre of the large Jewish urban populations; but the influx of Russians has largely replaced the Russian-speaking Jews in the linguistic sense.
28. I. M. Bogdanov, *Gramotnost' i obrazovanie v dorevoliutsionnoi Rossii i v SSSR* (Moscow, 1964), p. 134.

29. V. I. Naulko, in *Narodna tvorchist' ta etnohrafiia* (May–June, 1964) (translated in *Digest of the Soviet Ukrainian Press,* VIII, No. 10, 13). Professor Bilinsky has suggested to me, however, that the 1959 figure (in contrast to the 1927 one) probably refers to *urban* Ukrainians only.
30. Armstrong, *The Politics of Totalitarianism,* p. 278. The ratio of Ukrainian Party membership to Ukrainian population has been significantly higher in some parts of Asia than in the Ukraine. See *Rost i regulirovanie sostava Kommunisticheskoi Partii Kirgizii* (Frunze, 1963), p. 254.
31. Khanazarov, op. cit., pp. 145–46.
32. Karl-Eugen Waedekin, "Nationalitaetenpolitik und Lebenskraft der Voelker in der Sowjetunion heute und morgen," *Osteuropa,* XIV (November, 1964), 839, 844.
33. "Is Such Generosity Necessary?," *Izvestiia,* September 6, 1961 (translated in *CDSP,* XIII, No. 36, 26).
34. Interview with the British journalist I. McDonald, *Pravda,* February 16, 1958 (translated in *CDSP,* X, No. 7, 16).
35. This calculation is based on inferences from fragmentary data. In 1958 there were 25,464 Ukrainian-language schools and 4,355 Russian schools (*Radians'ka Ukraïna,* February 1, 1959 [translated in *Digest of the Soviet Ukrainian Press,* II, No. 5, 17]). Since the proportion of Ukrainian speakers in the urban population was 53 per cent, and that of Russian speakers was 44 per cent, one can calculate (the total number of urban schools being available in *Narodne hospodarstvo Ukraïns'koi RSR v 1960 rotsi* [Kiev, 1961], pp. 439–41) that there should have been (according to the criterion suggested above) 2,777 Ukrainian-language and 2,314 Russian-language urban schools; similarly, there should have been 22,736 Ukrainian-language and 2,021 Russian-language rural schools. The estimated total of 25,514 Ukrainian and 4,435 Russian schools is so close to the figures reported by the regime that one is led to feel that the calculation is sufficiently exact to enable one to proceed to the next step of inferring that Ukrainian and Russian-language schools in the same types of areas have on the average similar attendance figures, and that, therefore, rural Ukrainian pupils are overwhelmingly instructed in Ukrainian, but that a high proportion of urban Ukrainians are instructed in Russian.
36. *Pechat' SSSR v 1963 godu,* pp. 25, 55, 61, 90, 93, 96, 97, 100, 102.
37. F. T. Zhylko, *Narysy z dialektologiï Ukraïns'koï movy* (Kiev, 1955), facing p. 308.
38. "Street Lights in the Evening," *Pravda,* July 14, 1965 (translated in *CDSP,* XVII, No. 28, 37).
39. For the sake of brevity the present discussion will omit the groups of Buddhist background, which are relatively insignificant numerically. Similarly, the primitive, northern tribal-culture groups will be omitted. It can be argued that they should be considered a distinctive class (like the Australian, Papuan, and other primitive groups) from the functional standpoint; but their significance for the future of the Soviet system scarcely warrants extended treatment.
40. Khanazarov, *op. cit.,* p. 106.
41. "L'Islam en URSS après 1945," *La documentation française,* December 8, 1953 (translated in *Ost-Probleme,* VI [April 24, 1954], 657).
42. F. F. Sovetkin (ed.), *Natsional'nye shkoly RSFSR* (Moscow, 1958), p. 180; and Khanazarov, *op. cit.,* p. 176.

43. Kamil Faizulin, "Interrupted Wedding," *Literaturnaia gazeta,* December 10, 1953 (translated in *CDSP,* V, No. 50, 7).
44. A. G. Kharchev, *Brak i sem'ia v SSSR* (Moscow, 1964), pp. 193, 195.
45. Analysis of union republic budgets is very complicated, but might be revealing in this respect.
46. Waedekin, *op. cit.,* p. 849. A Soviet writer (Egiazarian, *op. cit.,* p. 94) sharply rejects the possibility of large-scale labor transfer.
47. Hamid Inoiatov, *Otvet fal'sifikatoram istorii Sovetskoi Srednei Azii i Kazakhstana* (Tashkent, 1962), p. 119.
48. Baymirza Hayit, "Turkestan in der Sowjetpolitik," *Osteuropa,* XII (January–February, 1962), 120.
49. Khanazarov, *op. cit.,* pp. 176–78, 196–98. See also A. M. Afanas'ev, *Narodnoe obrazovanie v Uzbekistane* (Tashkent, 1962), pp. 16–17.
50. See the speech by S. P. Borodin, in *II s"ezd intelligentsii Uzbekistana, 11–12 dekabria 1959 goda: Stenograficheskii otchet* (Tashkent, 1960), pp. 169–71.
51. Report on a conference of historians in Leningrad in *Vestnik Akademii Nauk SSSR,* No. 1 (1962), pp. 138–40 (translated in *CDSP,* XIV, No. 15, 12).
52. Speech at Central Committee and Supreme Soviet meeting in Kirgizia, *Pravda,* August 17, 1964 (translated in *CDSP,* XVI, No. 35, 3).
53. Khanazarov, *op. cit.,* pp. 64, 211.
54. See especially Inoiatov, *op. cit.;* and the critical articles by Urban, *op. cit.,* and Baymirza Hayit, "Turkestan im Lichte der KP–Kongresse," *Osteuropa,* X (July–August, 1960), 523.
55. P. V. Presniakov (ed.), *Formirovanie kommunisticheskikh obshchestvennykh otnoshenii* (Alma-Ata, 1964), p. 170.
56. Hans Koch and Leo Bilas, "Slawen und Asiaten in der UdSSR," *Osteuropa,* IX (July–August, 1959), 437–38.
57. *Tashkentskaia konferentsiia pisatelei stran Azii i Afriki* (Tashkent, 1960), p. 215.
58. Cf. Khanazarov, *op. cit.,* p. 189.

2

Some Economic Aspects of Relations Among the Soviet Republics

VSEVOLOD HOLUBNYCHY

The State of General Theory on the Subject in the Communist World

The main contribution to the Communist theory of the economic aspect of the "national" and "colonial" problem has been made by V. I. Lenin,[1] although he built his theories largely on the broad foundations of the writings of Marx and Engels.[2] Marx and Lenin were, of course, the first to correctly foresee the true gravity of the "national" and "colonial" problem as well as the oncoming disintegration of the Western colonial empires, which the world has witnessed recently. For this reason, careful attention ought to be paid to their views, even though they may be not as theoretically rigorous as modern theory requires.

The quintessence of Lenin's contribution to our subject can be summarized as follows: Capitalist society is characterized not only by class inequalities and the class struggle, but also by equally antagonistic inequalities and struggle among nationalities within the multinational states and among the colonial and imperialist, and the underdeveloped and developed countries. According to the general philosophy of historical materialism, the latter inequalities, like the former, originate in and are determined by the unevenness of the levels of economic development. Under conditions of capitalism and imperialism, according to Lenin, the unevenness in the levels of development of the metropolitan and the colonial countries leads to a break in the "weakest link" of the "chain," and results in the national-liberation movements and even in socialist revolutions in the underdeveloped countries. On the other hand, under socialism, the unevenness in the levels of development of the socialist nations makes it imperative for them to join forces among themselves and with the developed socialist nations in order to be able to survive the capitalist encirclement and to get aid from the developed socialist nations.[3]

Lenin saw the key to the solution of the national and colonial question under socialism in the economic, and therefore also social, cultural, and political equalization of all nationalities and races. He believed this solution to be possible only under socialism, because only a socialist government would be in the position to furnish the underprivileged and underdeveloped nationalities not only with legal, political, and social but—and most important of all—also with economic aid, that is with direct aid to their economic development, industrialization, technical modernization, education of native professional and leadership cadres, and the development of their culture in general.

Lenin did not favor nationalistic demands for the dissolution of multinational states such as the former Russian Empire; he did not prefer small national states. Neither did he favor the eternal preservation of the division of mankind into separate nationalities. At least prior to World War I he had stated many times that he preferred assimilation of small non-Russian nationalities by the Russians, and he never explicitly repudiated this view. However, he is also on record as saying that force must not be used in any form to achieve assimilation, because it would only produce and strengthen nationalistic reaction on the part of minorities. He vigorously condemned Great Russian chauvinism among Russian Communists, and specifically accused Stalin of fostering it.

One early pre-Stalinist interpretation of Lenin's views on the ways and means of solving the problem of nationalities, especially popular among the non-Russian Soviet Communists,[4] held that Lenin *de facto* repudiated his earlier views on the desirability and inevitability of the assimilation of the non-Russian nationalities by the Russians. Since in the last five years of his life he unequivocally supported preferential development of the non-Russian nationalities aimed at their actually becoming equal in all respects with the Russians, this interpretation maintained that he no longer believed in any advantages deriving from the merger and disappearance of nationalities, or that he at least foresaw such a merger as possible only in a very distant, implicitly unrealistic future.

A second interpretation is also possible, provided historical evolution and change of Lenin's views is not assumed. Preferential economic and cultural development of the non-Russian regions of the Soviet Union, in Lenin's view, did not of course preclude the simultaneous continuation of the development of Russia proper. The Russian population would also grow, and the Russians would always remain a majority in the U.S.S.R. Once, as a result of the Russian aid, the minorities in all respects (education, income, wealth, culture, etc.) become equal to and identical with the Russians,[5] presumably they would no longer have any reason to feel hostility toward Russians. At this point in history neither the non-Russians nor the Russians would have any reasons to oppose their mutual integration and assimilation. But since the Russians would be numerically in the majority, it would be they who would assimilate the non-Russians, rather than the other way around. When qualitative differences are no more, sheer quantity, according to the Third Law of Dialectics, transforms itself into a new quality.

Lenin's theory and prescriptions for the solution of the "problem of nationalities" were repeatedly accepted by the Russian Communist Party. The thesis that it is primarily economic underdevelopment and inequality that underlie the "national" and "colonial" problems was explicitly adopted while Lenin was still alive, in the resolutions of the Tenth (March, 1921) and Twelfth (April, 1923) Congresses of the Russian Communist Party.[6] Both congresses also resolved that the solution of the "question of nationalities" in the U.S.S.R. was to be achieved primarily by means of equalization of the levels of economic and cultural development of the republics and regions inhabited by different non-Russian nationalities. Specifically, industry was to be "implanted in a planned way" in the Turkic and Caucasian republics, according to the resolution of the Tenth Congress.[7] The Twelfth Congress spoke of the "formation of industrial centers" in the republics "of the previously oppressed nationalities" as the "foremost" task of the Party.[8] It also called on the "Russian proletariat" in Russia and in the non-Russian republics to do its best to help "actually and for a long time to come" the non-Russian nationalities to "raise themselves to a higher level of development so as to catch up with the advanced nationalities."[9] Both congresses also resolved[10] that on the basis of, and along with, the preferential economic development of the non-Russian republics, the education of their native cadres and the development of their cultures were also to be promoted.[11] The Twelfth Congress also resolved specifically that the government agencies in the non-Russian republics and regions must be staffed "for the most part" by native personnel, speaking local languages and practicing local cultures.[12] Extraterritorial nationalities, such as Jews and the immigrants from Latvia, Poland, and other countries, were also promised complete equality and freedom to develop their capabilities and cultures.[13] Both congresses also condemned Great Russian chauvinism for being both the provoker of non-Russian nationalisms and an enemy of the Soviet Union more dangerous than these nationalisms.[14]

Undoubtedly there was little refined economic analysis in this Leninist theory of the economic aspect of the problem of nationalities, especially in the solution offered. For this reason, it could, and did in fact, contradict the purely economic Russian theories of the spatial location of industries which were to come later. However, this was only an economic aspect of a noneconomic problem. Furthermore, neither Lenin nor the Party resolutions have ever said that the goal of the economic equalization of nationalities ought to be the sole, or even the main, criterion of the spatial resource allocation. In fact, in addition to the "nationalities" criterion, Lenin also advocated at one place in his voluminous writings two other criteria for the location of industries, viz., placing them closer to the sources of raw materials and holding the expenditure of social labor costs on production and transportation at a minimum.[15] *A priori* this may appear as contradictory to the "nationalities" criterion, unless of course proven by economic analysis that raw materials and least-cost combinations both happen to be located in the territory of the underdeveloped nationalities. On the other hand, however, this apparent contradiction of Lenin's can also be easily explained in the usual dialectical terms, as, for example, in Engels' locational model, which Lenin undoubtedly knew. Engels specifically assumed a very high level of development and of diversification which permitted the location of the Socialist industries with equal costs of production to be dependent on the minimum transportation costs alone. Under such a degree of diversification Engels assumed that, transportation costs permitting, the necessary raw materials could be imported into any place. As a result, industrialization would spread equiproportionately all over the country and the world, and there would be no unequally developed industrial clusters and/or backward regions.[16] If applied to the "question of nationalities," this would simply mean that in the territories of the underdeveloped nationalities those equal-cost industries must be developed which are economical from the viewpoint of transportation costs—and not only those for which raw materials are available on the spot. Within given demand-and-supply limits, the rule of the minimization of transportation costs automatically presumes a location of industries that is as close to their sources of factor supply as economically possible. (This makes a separate rule of bringing the industries closer to their supply sources redundant rather than contradictory.)

In his many writings on the "question of nationalities," Stalin failed to contribute anything substantially new to the theory of its economic aspect. He is on record, back in 1921, as repeating Lenin's theory that it is necessary to give economic aid to the underdeveloped non-Russian republics.[17] His practice was for the most part anti-Leninist, however. This conclusion comes out in part from our analysis of his policies toward the republics in the period of his reign. But in the ideological sphere also, especially since 1930, he clearly supported and fostered Russian chauvinism as a political weapon and used it against the interests of the non-Russian nationalities.[18]

Stalin's successors did not contribute anything positive to the theory either. Molotov admitted publicly that they neglected the "national" and "colonial" problem in Stalin's time to such an extent that the Soviet Union "suffered from the underestimation" of the "unprecedented rise" of the struggle of the colonial and dependent nations abroad and failed to exploit this struggle in its foreign policies.[19] Khrushchev, too, admitted publicly that Stalin had committed grave mistakes in his attempts to solve the "question of nationalities" both inside the Soviet Union and inside the whole Socialist camp.[20] However, quite like Stalin, Khrushchev repeatedly insisted that the "question of nationalities" no longer existed in the U.S.S.R.; in his opinion, it had been solved.[21] Such statements were sheer "socialist realism," of course, or wishful thinking in plain language, for at the same time Khrushchev contradicted his own statements many times (see the discussion below).

For a brief period during 1955–58, non-Russian Soviet Communists raised a desperate cry for a "return to Leninism" in the nationalities policy, and especially in respect of the development of local cadres, but the Russians behind Khrushchev quickly hushed them by pointing out that the "return to Leninism" could also mean a return to Lenin's overt statements on the desirability of the merger and assimilation of nationalities. There this attempt at a theoretical discussion of the meaning of Leninism rested, at least for the time being.

The State of the Specific Theory: Economic Colonialism in the U.S.S.R.?

Many Western writers have accused the U.S.S.R. of colonial practices in respect to its non-Russian nationalities. The accusation has come from political scientists and scholars, and from such eminent political figures as William O. Douglas, Robert F. Kennedy, Adlai Stevenson, and John G. Diefenbaker.[22] What characterizes these writings and statements, however, is that they are for the most part purely political. From the point of view of political science, the arguments advanced in these writings may be sufficient to prove the case. Of course, colonialism per se is much more than merely an economic phenomenon; however, none of these writings take proper cognizance of the economic aspect. None adequately deals with the economic colonialism present in the U.S.S.R. Therefore, we can accept these arguments only as statements of a hypothesis requiring further analysis.[23]

The only acceptably comprehensive study of the economic aspect of Soviet nationality policies that is available thus far is the well-known paper on Central Asia by a team of economists of the United Nations' Economic Commission for Europe.[24] It clearly implies the existence of discrimination against the Central Asian Soviet republics, but it stops short of accusing the Soviet Union of colonialist policies. But, the reason for this hesitancy may also have been political.

The Soviet Union has been bitterly accused of colonialist practices by many émigré writers.[25] Especially numerous and comprehensive are Ukrainian writings on this subject, and it is also the Ukrainians who, more than others, have attempted to prove the presence of economic colonialism in the Soviet Union.[26] Although many of their writings contain important and reliable data, they are frequently hampered by faulty economic analysis. Some are also tendentious: separate and scattered bits of information are used to illustrate the presumed thesis rather than to test one or another hypothesis.

The methodologically most consistent of all these studies to date is that on the capital balance of the Ukraine during the years 1928–32, by Dr. Z. L. Melnyk, Professor of Finance at the University of Cincinnati.[27] Using a national budget method of comparison of total revenues and expenditures at all levels of government in the Ukraine, he established the very important fact that almost 30 per cent of total revenue (some 5 billion rubles of capital funds) collected in the Ukraine during that period were withdrawn from the Ukraine by the central government in Moscow and spent somewhere else. Melnyk suggests that his finding indicates that the Ukraine was being exploited as a colony. The arguments supporting this conclusion are essentially threefold: (1) On balance, the Ukrainian economy suffered a considerable loss; (2) capital withdrawn from the Ukraine was not borrowed and was not to be returned later, nor was there any interest paid on it; and (3) since the Ukraine was not a politically sovereign state, the capital was taken away without the permission or consent of Ukraine taxpayers. Melnyk's method and findings coincide with several other similar studies accomplished by Soviet Ukrainian economists discussed below. Unfortunately, no similar studies are known to exist for other Soviet republics or regions.

That economic exploitation may indeed have been practiced, if not inside the U.S.S.R. then inside the Soviet bloc among the different Communist nations has been charged and debated in a considerable body of recent scholarly literature. The Soviet Union has been accused of economically exploiting such other Communist nations as Yugoslavia, Poland, East Germany, Hungary, Romania, Albania, China, and North Korea by such means as price discrimination, rigged exchange rates, enforced specialization, joint-stock companies, long-term loans, indemnities, and reparations. What is even more important is that these charges were advanced not only by Western economists and researchers, but also by the Communists of the injured nations themselves.[28]

On the other hand, under the pressure of the 1956 uprisings in Poland and Hungary, the Soviet Union publicly admitted that there had been, on its part, "violations and errors which demeaned the principle of equality in relations among the socialist states."[29] It also unequivocally implied, in a joint statement with the Polish Government, that it had failed to pay the "full value" for Silesian coal delivered to it by Poland from 1946 to 1953, and that its loans to Poland had been excessively burdensome.[30] Under the impact of recent Chinese criticism the U.S.S.R. insists, however, that it has already "corrected Stalin's errors and restored the Leninist principle of equality in its relations with fraternal parties and countries."[31] Yet, if such practices have been present within the Soviet bloc, there can be no a priori reason why they might also not be present within the Soviet Union. It is as naïve to assume that the interests of different republics and economic regions in the U.S.S.R. (or in any other country) are always coincident as it is to assume that they are always or inevitably inimical. This is why an inquiry into this subject seems both justified and interesting.

The Methods of Inquiry and the Theories to Test

The task of the economist in this case consists, first of all, in ascertaining whether or not there has been a normal interspatial transfer of resources for a stated, sufficiently long period of time. As the first step, it is necessary to compute resource balances for each given economic region. The best, though also the most difficult to compute is the regional balance of payments. Balances of the regional national incomes[32] and/or of gross social (in the Soviet sense) or national (in the Western sense) products[33] are also among the best tools of analysis, although, like the balances of payments, they are very difficult to compute today largely because of the lack of necessary statistics. Balances of trade, and the implicit terms of trade, are also useful, but they are partial balances only. In case of the federal states, and especially under specific Soviet conditions where almost 70 per cent of the national income is siphoned via the government budgets, a balance of fiscal transactions, of revenues and expenditures, on a regional basis is also highly significant.[34] Capital transfer balances consisting of direct capital investments and banking or government loans are also quite meaningful;[35] and so are the population and labor transfer balances, although of course they represent only individual, separate resources. The official Soviet methodological instructions on the choice of location of industries also call for the calculation of regional supply-and-demand balances of raw materials, of the production and consumption of specific commodities, and of their substitutes (all in kind, of course, rather than in money).[36] No doubt such balances—especially if they are interindustry input-output matrixes—are also useful for the solution of partial and specific problems, but more generalized and synthetic balances are more useful and more economically meaningful.[37]

If and when such balances show considerable and persistent deficits (or surpluses on the opposite side), this may signal the presence of a problem. No doubt such imbalances indicate a net interregional transfer of resources. We need to know, therefore: (1) What is the effect of these resource movements on the economic growth, employment, and welfare of the respective regions? (2) Do these movements of resources promote a convergence of the differentials in regional per capita incomes, meaning both material incomes as well as psychic, such as culture, education, health, etc.? (3) Are these transfers of resources economically justified; are they not arbitrary in the sense that their direction and extent could be different and more economical; in other words, do these transfers maximize the total income, employment, and welfare of all the regions combined and taken as a whole?

The purpose of study of the conterminous regional balances is, first of all, to trace the movement of resources among the regions; second, to establish whether or not such resource movements produce a trend in regional development toward an optimum equilibrium in interregional economic efficiency and welfare; or, on the other hand, whether or not the observed regional inequalities in income, employment, and welfare, as well as in their comparative rates of growth, might be attributed to such resource transfers. The latter case would imply the presence of interregional discrimination and exploitation, if the observed inequalities do not decrease with time; as a result they would probably intensify the acuteness of the "colonial" or "national" question.[38]

The basic definition of a balance-of-payments equilibrium is well known, of course; it may be depicted, for example, as follows:

	Exports of goods and services
minus	Imports of goods and services
minus	Net outflow of capital
equal	Zero
equal	Net outflow (inflow) of capital
minus	Net outflow (inflow) of gold.

All this is simple in case of relations among sovereign states, or even among regions, provided they possess gold or some hard currency to plug the deficit holes. The case ceases to be so simple when there is no gold, or when all its reserves have been exhausted. To plug the deficit, the state or the firms and the population in a region may go into debt for some time, provided credit is available. The real problem begins when deficit persists and credit is exhausted. The sovereign state must devalue its domestic currency at this point. The relative structure of the domestic/foreign price ratios changes as a result, and so do relative costs. This brings about, in due time, a structural change in the economy and its new specialization vis-à-vis foreign markets. Obviously the same trend of events must also occur in case of similar relations among the economic regions, except that "currency devaluation" appears in a different form in this case. Since currency is the same "at home" and "abroad" in case of interregional relations, it is its local purchasing power and/or total volume of local moneyed demand that undergoes a "devaluation." Local prices of goods and services imported into the region may rise, local prices of regional exports may fall, or both, and total moneyed income of the region may decline either because of falling export prices or because of rising unemployment, or again both. The structure of the region's economy as well as its specialization must undergo a change in any case.[39]

The Soviet students of Belorussia's balance of payments (although not explicitly stating that there was a deficit) have been quite right in pointing out that the mere discovery of a *"saldo"*—a deficit or a surplus—in the process of the balance-of-payments calculations does not in itself really say much; what is needed, they stress, is "to reveal the material contents" of such an imbalance, and that "not only in physical measures (which is done in case of individual commodities), but also in terms of money for the most important commodity groups."[40] The latter is, of course, most significant because it would show changes in the relative price and cost structures, and would produce an impact on the regional income, employment, and welfare.

A deficit in the balance of payments can be likened to a hole in a vessel of the national or regional economy through which it loses its contents and becomes emptier as time goes by. It loses income and wealth. Its natural resources and raw materials may become cheaper and be exploited more intensively, and be exhausted in a shorter period of time. Its population and labor force may flee the region in search of higher real income and welfare. It may lose its scientific and artistic talent for the same reasons. Even its art objects and museum treasures may be removed to plug the payments gap, which all would adversely affect its culture, education, human dignity, and self-respect. This is how economic exploitation generates nationalism and anticolonialist feelings.

In purely economic respect, however, the interregional transfer of resources that leads to their persistent loss on the part of a given region produces a clearly retarding impact upon that region's economic growth and development because it diverts the region's economy into such types of activity and lines of specialization which require less resources than before, reduces the scope and opportunities for technological progress and diversification, diminishes external and internal economies, and removes the secondary and cumulative effects that could have been produced by the investment and employment of the transferred resources. The rate of reproduction of the region's economy slows down, and may even come to a standstill, after which absolute decay might ensue.

In most cases it is probable that if one region loses resources some other region or regions gain them at its expense.[41] If and when the juxtaposed regional balances show considerable and persistent surpluses, this means that the regions in question enjoy actual gains. The gain is not only absolute in the sense of wealth and resources added, which is self-evident. It is also relative, in comparison to the region that lost. The relative gain is in the ability to use the added resources to diversify the economy and to make it more complex, to enlarge the scope and opportunities for technological innovations and for the economies of scale, and to reap subsequent cumulative and compounded gains as time goes by. The fruits of this progress are as a rule distributed to producers in the form of rising incomes (rather than to consumers in the form of lower prices) and as the region's economy becomes more and more developed its terms of trade with the underdeveloped regions become more and more tilted in its favor and against the underdeveloped regions. Gradually, the rich region becomes richer, whereas poor regions become relatively poorer (in comparison to the rich).

If and when persistent and sufficiently large imbalances (deficits and surpluses) in the interregional balances have been empirically established, the next step in the purely economic analysis is to find out why these imbalances obtain. In other words, one must establish the economic rationale behind the fact of the interregional transfer of resources. As a rule, one must first assume an open economy in this analysis in order to be able, second, to reverse this rule and thus test the hypothesis of whether or not there has been interregional discrimination and exploitation. Thus a region is assumed to be an open part of a country or a state; the latter, in its turn, may be a part of some larger spatial complex, such as a customs union, a common market, a bloc or camp, or of the world economy as a whole, provided that with each of the larger spatial complexes its economic frontiers are assumed to be opened.[42] (Frontiers among the Soviet republics and economic regions are of course open; hence, the assumption is quite realistic in this case, and the U.S.S.R. as a whole can therefore be taken as one space complex, of which the republics are regional units.)

Under this assumption it is now necessary to inquire whether or not the observed interregional transfers of resources have had purely economic justification from the point of view of all concerned; that is, from the point of view of the sum total of regions taken as one single spatial complex. This is accomplished by means of testing of whether or not the resources in question have been transferred and allocated in accordance with economically rational criteria of the maximization of the specified ends, minimization of means, and equalization of the marginal returns to the said resources. If and when such tests indicate that the transferred resources have not been allocated in accordance with the rule of equalization of their marginal productivities in all the respective regions, it would mean therefore that some noneconomic criteria or motives (such as regional nationalism, for example) have been applied in their transfer and allocation, and that interregional economic discrimination and exploitation have been practiced. This also would mean that some region has gained at the expense of another region, while the total space that they comprise has sustained a relative loss because it failed to attain maximum possible growth.

The rational economic policy in the interregional resource transfers must, as a rule, aim at the attainment of, or at least the ever closer approach to, the optimum economic effect of such transfers. An optimum in the regional allocation of resources is an allocation that maximizes total output, income, and welfare simultaneously (i.e., during identical periods of time) in all the pertinent regions combined and taken together as one whole spatial complex. Conventionally, this is a Pareto-type optimum in the sense that, under it, it is impossible to increase the output, income, and welfare of any region without decreasing them, even relatively, in other regions and in the total space as a whole.[43]

However, Pareto's optimum is static, and it also abstracts from the possibility of increasing or decreasing economies of scale. Therefore, at least in theory—if in practice such calculations are perhaps impossible—we must strive to approach a dynamic optimum by including the time-cost factor for the time period necessary to achieve it and by assuming the shape of the production functions themselves as time-dependent. The necessary and sufficient conditions for such an equilibrium are, first, that the price of each transferable resource be the same in all regions in which it is used—the price in this case explicitly including all transportation costs as well as a compound interest charge for the time it takes both to transfer resources and to reproduce or recoup them in their new locations; second, that the price (again, in the above sense) of all identical products be the same in all the regions; third, that the output or profitability of any one product per identical unit of each resource and the same length of time be the same in all regions. All these conditions combine into one necessary and sufficient condition for this type of spatial equilibrium over a given period of time, viz., that the price (in the above sense) of each resource be equal to full cost of its marginal product in all the regions. Only under such conditions will the policy of resource transfers result in the simultaneous and equal gain of all the regions concerned and in the maximum gain of the total space they comprise.

To sum up, economic efficiency rules for the interregional transfer of resources which would not hurt any region and would not create conditions for a "national" or "colonial" problem (or which would alleviate and eliminate the existing ones), and which at the same time would maximize the growth of output, income, employment, and welfare of the sum total of all regions combined, must be formulated as follows.

1. Capital, labor, and all other mobile resources should be allocated among regions so as to equate their marginal costs and/or products in all lines of production. In export and import industries resources must be allocated so as to hold their marginal costs below those prevailing in other regions, and/or marginal products above those prevailing in other regions.

2. Each region must export resources with a lower marginal productivity at home than in other regions and must import resources with higher productivity at home than in other regions. The volume of such resource transfers will be optimum when their marginal costs will differ among the regions only by the amount of transfer costs for the same periods of time.

3. In case of immobile natural and other resources, the rule must be that they should be employed to the optimum which is reached when total output cannot be increased any more by any other combination of factors and of their substitutes, and when its cost of production does not exceed marginal cost plus the cost of transportation of a similar product imported from other regions. If a region lacks some particular resource, it must be imported up to the point where its "foreign" marginal cost and transportation cost are equal to the local equilibrium price.

4. Mobile resources must be transferred on a free loan basis,

rather than on a permanent ownership or retained control basis. They must be subject to return conditions, or conditions relinquishing control. The interest charge must be determined by supply and demand in different regions, and such an alternatively determined interest rate must figure explicitly in all comparative costs.

It is perhaps worth mentioning at this point that some modern Soviet theories of interregional resource allocation have recently been evolving in the direction of the above-mentioned principles. In particular, the most advanced among them advocate now the use of the average national normatives of the marginal capital efficiency of from 10–25,[44] 17,[45] and 15 per cent,[46] corresponding to the compounded recoupment periods of about four to nine years. It is proposed that the actual capital-investment projects be then compared with these normatives. As a criterion of rational spatial resource allocation, the minimum, full, imputed costs are advocated, which would be the sum total of (a) direct production costs, (b) additional or new capital investments, multiplied by the marginal efficiency coefficient (or the "profitability normative"), and (c) the c.i.f. costs of transportation and delivery of goods to the consumers.[47] Needless to say, such methods are a great step forward, even though they are not yet generally applied. The main shortcoming of the just-mentioned proposal, advocated by the U.S.S.R. Gosstroy, is the conspicuous absence of a time-cost charge (interest) for the alternative use of resources, and of a proviso that the resources are being transferred on a loan basis and must therefore be returned in the due time. Much worse in its practical implications, however, is a methodology advocated by two agencies of the U.S.S.R. Academy of Sciences—The Scientific Council on the Problem of Economic Efficiency of Fixed Capital, Capital Investments, and New Technology (T. S. Khachaturov, Chief) and the Sector on the Effectiveness of the Location of Industries of the Institute of Economics (Y. G. Feigin, Chief). While also ignoring interest charges and the returnability of investments, this methodology suggests that the efficiency normatives be differentiated according to regions, and that the empirical efficiency indicators be allowed to deviate from the normatives, "if necessary."[48] If such a methodology is adopted in practice, it would obviously do away with any semblance of genuine economic rationality and would leave the door wide open to subjective and arbitrary decisions, influenced by possibly spurious motives.[49]

The empirical methods of testing the economic rationale of the interregional transfer of resources are well known today. The most advanced and accurate are the methods of mathematical programming—nonlinear and linear, as well as those using regional input-output models.[50] Some major problems involved in the use of these methods must be mentioned at this point to make the reader aware of their significance. In most mathematical programming models of the interregional transfer and location of resources, the dual objective functions are (a) to minimize the total transportation and delivery costs and (b) to maximize some appropriate aggregate output, such as national income. In applying these models to the analysis of the Soviet economy one must be well aware of the arbitrary peculiarity of Soviet transportation tariffs: they have been made to decrease with the distance, rather than increase or be constant.[51] The transferability of goods and people is thereby artificially increased, and tilted in favor of the Russian republic. It is comparatively cheaper to haul heavy freights to and from the small border republics hundreds and thousands of miles to and from Russia, and within Russia, than within even such medium-sized republics as the Ukraine or Uzbekistan. Historically, back in the 1930's, this tariff policy was explicitly designed to aid in the acceleration of the economic development of the eastern parts of the R.S.F.S.R.[52]

The elasticities of demand for and supply of the transportation services in the Soviet Union's consuming regions must accordingly be expected to be more effective than in the producing regions, and even more than in a free market economy.[53] This would appropriately affect the shadow prices within the mathematical programs, while the cost minimums, too, would necessarily be smaller than they would in a normal competitive economy. Furthermore, it must be kept in mind that Soviet freight rates are insufficiently and arbitrarily differentiated among commodities as well as among types of carriers. As one Soviet author has recently stated outright, they do not reflect actual transportation costs.[54]

As to the maximizing objective function of the dual program, very much, of course, depends on what goes into the aggregate output or the national income, especially if it is taken as a measure of welfare. There still exist some doubts, for example, as to whether or not to include in the national income such items as investment and collective goods, or communal consumption supplied by the government free of charge, and how to value them if they are included.[55] While for the purpose of measuring welfare there must be no question that these items must be included (at cost to the government), for our particular purpose of appraising the welfare and the "psychic income" of different nationalities it is even more true. In the Soviet Union, government financing of very wide programs of collective consumption (especially such as the free-of-charge education in the native tongues, research in local history, social sciences, and humanities, subsidization of publishing, national theaters, museums, public libraries, clubs, recreational and medical facilities, and so forth almost *ad infinitum*) directly affects the culture and welfare of different nationalities in different regions. Since all such financing is centralized and disbursed from Moscow through the state budget, and since the republics of the U.S.S.R. do not have the right of self-taxation or self-crediting, it is obvious that the distribution of the budget funds can be, technically speaking, used as a tool of fostering the culture and welfare of some nationalities, while others might be forced to remain culturally underdeveloped so as to gradually succumb to assimilation and extinction. It is therefore imperative to find out whether or not such is in fact the case.

With the analysis of the economic rationale of the observed interregional transfer of resources and of its effects on the regional economy completed, the last remaining step is to find out whether or not the levels of regional economic development display a long-run tendency to converge. This is a purely mathematical exercise, of course, but one thing must be stressed in this connection. However we measure the comparative levels of economic development (by national income, personal disposable income, real wages, industrial output, etc., per capita or per unit of productive factors), we must be aware of the fact that the equalization of such levels is possible only in the sufficiently long run. The comparative regional endowment with natural and other "fixed" resources, geographic location and distances from and to markets, the historically given levels of economic development and the given structure of industries, as well as the sociocultural and political conservatism on the part of local population and leadership may all combine to hinder, if not completely prevent, the equalization and convergence of the levels of development in the short run. Time is indeed needed to develop natural resources, to expand and specialize local industries and the regional export-import relations, and to break through conservative traditions.

Furthermore, the mathematics of the comparison of the levels of development also deserves some careful consideration. The convergence or divergence of the regional levels of development might appear evident at first sight, as soon as the absolute or relative gaps over limited periods of time are compared. However, such evidence may also be misleading as far as the actual trend of the comparative developments is concerned.[56] Even if the observed percentage rate of growth (per unit of time) of the comparatively lower level is larger than the comparative rate of growth of the higher level—and this is clearly the only possible case where the gap between the two levels would converge[57]—the gap between the two levels might not necessarily decrease at once. Rather, it might first increase, reach a maximum, and only then begin to decrease. (In case of divergence of the comparative levels, especially if it happens at a slow rate, the opposite might be true for some time.) The gap between the two levels decreases from the beginning only if the absolute increment in the comparatively higher level is absolutely smaller than the absolute increment of the comparatively lower level, and this happens at the point in time where the gap between the two levels is a maximum. What all this actually depends on are the comparative percentage rates of growth of the two levels, averaged per unit of time over the (limited) period of observation but then extrapolated into the future until the levels meet. The trend toward convergence or divergence of the two levels is necessarily an extrapolating exercise that must go beyond the limited period of time given in the comparison.

The average rate of growth of a region's economic development (a given aggregate per capita of the population) is the familiar geometric mean that can be computed in a number of ways. The following is an example of one of the possible formulas:

$$k_x = \frac{(\log X_t - \log X_o)\ 230.259}{t} \qquad (1)$$

where k_x is the rate of growth of the level X; X_o is that level at the beginning of the given period t and X_t is the level at the end of the period; t is the number of years or other time units in the given period; *log* is the common logarithm of the given number, and 230.259 is the natural logarithm of 10 multiplied by 100. Having similarly computed k_y for the level Y, we compare them, as well as X_o with Y_o. The two levels will converge if, and only if, the following is true: either $Y_o \geqq X_o$ and $k_x \geqq k_y$, or $X_o \geqq Y_o$ and $k_y \geqq k_x$. If these conditions hold, then we may calculate when (i.e., after how many units of t) in the future the gap between the X and Y will be closed—even though, as mentioned above, this gap may in the meantime absolutely increase for some time. This is calculated according to the following formula:

$$t = \frac{(\ln Y_o - \ln X_o)\ 100}{k_x - k_y} \qquad (2)$$

where all the symbols are the same as in (1), while *ln* stands for the natural logarithms.

Formula (2) tells us whether or not, and if yes, when, the two comparative development levels will become equal. From (2) we can also derive the formula of the rate of growth of the lower level required to catch up with the initially higher level within some specified period of time:

$$k_x = k_y + \frac{(\ln Y_o - \ln X_o)\ 100}{t} \qquad (3)$$

Both rates of growth are assumed to be constant in the meantime, of course. They may also be changed into variable over time in accordance with one or another function, but this would severely complicate the calculations in practice.

THE GROWING GAP BETWEEN RUSSIA AND THE NON-RUSSIAN REPUBLICS[58]

What remains to be done now is to apply the above theories and methods to the analysis of the available Soviet facts and data. This is not an easy task in view of its enormous scope and the paucity of available statistics. That what follows must be considered only a preliminary test of correlation and comparison of facts and theories, and most conclusions must be considered tentative mainly because this is essentially the first inquiry of its kind,[59] and it is as such still incomplete: not all the available data have been studied with equal thoroughness, particularly not all the available statistical handbooks of the Soviet republics and regions. The incompleteness of the inquiry is evident especially from the fact that the autonomous republics and the economic regions of the R.S.F.S.R. have not been treated separately; the present paper does not go any deeper than the level of the union republics.

To begin with, our first task is to establish whether or not considerable inequalities in the levels of economic development of different union republics still prevail in the U.S.S.R., and if so, whether or not the gap tends to decrease over time. Several indicators may be employed to measure such differences, but our choice is unavoidably limited only to those available.[60]

The most widely used measure in the world is the per capita national income or product, but Soviet statistical sources have not so far published these data in analyzable form. The calculation of the national income in the union republics began in 1957, but only indexes of growth have been revealed thus far (see Table I). This of course prevents a comparison of the levels of income among the republics. Two Soviet authors who presumably had access to the national income figures in absolute form have come up with different results. Ya. Feigin has found that "in 1960, the ratio between the maximum and the minimum amounts of national income per capita of the population of the union republics was 3:1" and that the "highest level of national income per capita was found in the Latvian and Estonian S.S.R.s, and then in the R.S.F.S.R."[61] On the other hand, Yu. F. Vorob'yov has found that, in 1961, the same ratio between the highest and the lowest per capita national income levels was only 2.4:1, with, indeed, Latvia, Estonia, and the R.S.F.S.R. heading the list in that order, and Uzbekistan and Tadjikistan being at the very bottom.[62] A jump from the level of 3 to 2.4 in one single year is not easily imaginable, although there might have been a decline in the per capita income in Latvia in 1961 (cf. Table I). In any case, a more definite picture of the actual and stable difference in the per capita national income of the Soviet republics must await publication of more evidence than is now the case.[63]

Assuming that the maximum interrepublic differences in the levels of national income per capita lie within the range of 1:2.4 and 1:3, we may conclude that this range is quite a bit larger than in the developed capitalist countries, such as France, England, and the United States.[64] Perhaps one might have expected that in a socialist planned economy this difference could have been smaller.

Whether or not these observed interrepublic national income inequalities diminish as time goes by cannot be ascertained because of the absence of data for sufficiently long periods. The only available data are those reproduced in Table I, and they only cover the seven-year period 1958–65. Even for such a short period, however, these statistics do not indicate any significant convergence in the levels of income among the republics; this is particularly evident when the income is calculated per capita and compared with 1958. Turkmenia, Kazakhstan, and Azerbaidzhan display particularly poor and divergent growth compared to Lithuania, Estonia, and Belorussia. The table also shows that in some republics in some years the national income even declined absolutely in comparison with the previous year; such is the case in the Ukraine, Moldavia, and Kazakhstan. This of course was due to bad harvests, but it also shows how dependent on agriculture the economies of these republics still are.

TABLE I
GROWTH INDEXES OF THE NATIONAL INCOME OF THE SOVIET REPUBLICS, 1958–65
(1958 = 100)

Republics[a]	1958	1960	1962	1963	1964	1965	Per Capita National Income 1965
R.S.F.S.R.	100	117	132	138	149	159	147
Ukraine	100	111	129	127	142	158	145
Belorussia	100	128	133	149	169	178	166
Uzbekistan	100	115	128	137	149	167	130
Kazakhstan	100	117	131	133	158	152	115
Georgia	100	108	123	124	131	146	130
Azerbaidzhan	100	117	127	128	136	147	117
Lithuania	100	124	130	156	172	188	171
Moldavia	100	110	139	136	154	178	152
Latvia	100	121	121	142	158	172	159
Kirghizia	100	114	126	149	155	174	136
Tadjikistan	100	117	138	157	169	181	139
Armenia	100	122	140	146	161	181	146
Turkmenia	100	111	113	127	132	139	110
Estonia	100	125	135	152	169	180	168

SOURCES: Central Statistical Administration, *Narodnoe khozyaystvo SSSR v 1962 godu: Statisticheskiy ezhegodnik* (Moscow, 1963), p. 484; *Nar. khoz. SSSR v 1963 g.* (Moscow, 1965), p. 576; *Nar. khoz. SSSR v 1965 g.* (Moscow, 1966), pp. 9, 590. The data are in "comparative" prices.

[a] The order in which the republics are listed in this and subsequent tables is that used in the original Soviet tables.

Another accepted way of comparing the levels of economic development of the Soviet republics is to analyze the structure of their populations, viz., their distribution between urban and rural communities. These statistics are more readily available, and they are reproduced in Table II. It emerges that, at the present time, Estonia, Latvia, and the R.S.F.S.R. are the most highly urbanized republics of the U.S.S.R., while Uzbekistan, Tadjikistan, and Moldavia are still very much agrarian. This finding exactly coincides with their respective levels of national income per capita, discussed above, and illustrates again the well-known fact that income and wealth grow with urbanization, while rural environment generates relative poverty and relative economic underdevelopment.

Today, most of the Soviet republics trail Russia in the level of urbanization by far, but that was not always so. The R.S.F.S.R. made

TABLE II
URBAN-RURAL POPULATION RATIO IN THE SOVIET REPUBLICS, 1914–65[a]

Republics	1914	1926	1933	1939	1959	1965
R.S.F.S.R.	17:83	17:83	25:75	33:67	52:48	59:41
Ukraine	21:79	17:83	22:78	34:66	46:54	52:48
Belorussia	17:83	15:85	16:84	21:79	31:69	39:61
Uzbekistan	15:85	22:78	25:75	23:77	33:67	35:65
Kazakhstan	10:90	...	...	28:72	44:56	48:52
Kirghizia	12:88	...	...	19:81	34:66	38:62
Turkmenia	7:93	14:86	19:81	33:67	46:54	49:51
Tadjikistan	2:98	9:91	11:89	17:83	33:67	35:65
Georgia	26:74	24:76 (Georgia, Azerbaidzhan, Armenia combined)	29:71 (Georgia, Azerbaidzhan, Armenia combined)	30:70	42:58	47:53
Azerbaidzhan	24:76			36:64	48:52	50:50
Armenia	10:90			29:71	50:50	55:45
Lithuania	13:87	...	...	23:77	39:61	45:55
Latvia	38:62	...	...	35:65	56:44	62:38
Estonia	19:81	...	...	34:66	56:44	63:37
Moldavia	13:87	...	...	13:87	22:78	28:72

SOURCES: Central Administration of National Economic Accounts, *The U.S.S.R. in Figures* (Moscow, 1934), p. 133; *Nar. khoz. SSSR v 1963 g.*, p. 11; *Nar. khoz. SSSR v 1965 g.*, p. 11.

[a] Frontiers of 1926, 1933, and 1939 are as of January 1, 1939; those of 1914, 1959, and 1965 are as of January 1, 1965.

the greatest progress in urbanization in the post–World War II period, leaving behind Azerbaidzhan, the Ukraine, and Turkmenia, whose levels of urbanization as late as 1939 surpassed or were equal to Russia.[65] In the post–World War II period, the annexation of the western, predominantly rural regions to the Ukraine and Belorussia undoubtedly lowered their levels of urbanization compared to Russia's, but not by much. For example, the proportion of urban to rural populations in the eastern provinces of the Ukraine (i.e., excluding seven western provinces) was 36:64 in 1940, 50:50 in 1959, and 55:45 in 1963, while the same proportion in Russia in 1963 was 58:42.[66]

Table III data supplement those of Table II, and reinforce its evidence and implications. The share of "workers and employees," which comprises all those individuals who are not members of collective farms or dependents is again the highest in Estonia, Latvia, and Russia, and the lowest in Moldavia and Central Asia. A comparative study of the structure of the labor force according to employment, profession, and sources of income, the data for which presumably are available in the fifteen republic volumes of the 1959 population census,[67] would probably show additional interesting interrepublic differences, but this study could not be undertaken in connection with this paper.

Differences in the levels of economic development can also be measured by the per capita industrial output. In a way it is a better indicator than even the national income per capita because it shows the level of industrialization attained by an economic region, making its level of development independent of agriculture and other non-industrial sectors of the economy. This indicator also suits very well the Leninist theory of the economic aspect of the "question of nationalities," expressed in the resolutions of the Tenth and Twelfth Party Congresses referred to above.

TABLE III

PERCENTAGE OF WORKERS AND EMPLOYEES IN THE TOTAL POPULATION OF THE SOVIET REPUBLICS, 1940, 1956, AND 1963[a]

Republics	1940	1956	1963
R.S.F.S.R.	19.2	29.1	35.4
Ukraine	15.1	21.7	27.2
Belorussia	11.9	16.2	25.8
Uzbekistan	11.0	15.1	18.9
Kazakhstan	14.7	25.9	31.9
Georgia	12.6	18.7	24.9
Azerbaidzhan	14.2	18.5	20.0
Lithuania	6.4	18.3	27.9
Moldavia	3.8	13.2	17.7
Latvia	13.9	28.8	37.7
Kirghizia	11.0	16.9	21.5
Tadjikistan	9.3	13.8	16.1
Armenia	10.9	19.4	25.6
Turkmenia	14.4	18.2	19.1
Estonia	17.9	33.4	40.1

SOURCES: Central Statistical Administration, *Narodnoe khozyaystvo SSSR: Statisticheskiy sbornik* (Moscow, 1956), p. 18; *Nar. khoz. SSSR v 1958 g.* (Moscow, 1959), p. 660; *Nar. khoz. SSSR v 1963 g.*, pp. 9, 477.

[a] Frontiers are post–World War II.

Per capita industrial production in the Soviet republics is presented in Table IV, which gives absolute output figures of all industries,[68] in constant 1926–27 rubles (linked up by a chain index formula to the subsequent constant-price years 1952 and 1955).[69] The defects of the 1926–27 prices are of course well known, but this is not relevant in our case. We do not compare growth here with that of foreign countries; since the same methods of index construction and the same prices had been used consistently in all Soviet republics, this makes the data sufficiently comparable for our purposes.[70]

Table IV provides evidence for some rather grave conclusions. First, in spite of the undoubtedly outstanding progress of industrialization in all non-Russian republics, their level of industrialization attained thus far is still very much below that of Russia. Second, the gap between the levels of industrialization of Russia and the non-Russian republics continued to grow until 1958; then, during the Seven-Year Plan, it decreased, but only very slightly. In terms of the gap, the non-Russian republics today are industrially more underdeveloped compared to Russia than they were before the Bolshevik Revolution: in 1913, they produced 44 per cent of per capita Russian production, while in 1965 they produced only 29 per cent.[71]

Some republics fared especially badly compared to the R.S.F.S.R.; they are Tadjikistan, Turkmenia, and Kirghizia, whose level of industrialization remains incredibly low. Others, such as Azerbaidzhan, Ukraine, Uzbekistan, Belorussia, and Georgia increased their gaps in relation to Russia very rapidly. Only Armenia and Moldavia have gained some ground, and Kazakhstan remained on the same relative level of development compared to Russia as in the past.

Lenin's exhortation to achieve equality between the levels of industrialization of the non-Russian republics and the R.S.F.S.R. has clearly not been realized thus far. During Stalin's reign practical policies in this respect obviously differed: the industrialization of Russia proceeded faster than that of the non-Russian regions. Only between 1958 and 1965, as mentioned before, did the gap between them decrease a little. The average annual rate of growth of per capita industrial production in this seven-year period was 7.4 per cent in Russia and 8 per cent elsewhere. (This has been computed from data in Table IV by means of Formula 1, above.) From Formula 2 we can compute now that, if the 1958–65 trend were to continue unchanged into the future, the equalization of the non-Russian republics, taken together, with the level of Russia could be attained only by the year 2170. If, however, the long-range trend prevails—that of 1913–65—the two levels would never meet, for the Russian output would grow by 7.9 per cent a year and that of the non-Russian republics by only 7 per cent.

The findings of Table IV can be compared with those of Tables V and VI, which show the per capita levels of electrification and of the consumption of energy in the Soviet republics. Table V, to be exact, shows only the production of electric power in each republic, but interrepublic exports and imports of this commodity are known to have been negligible.[72] Therefore, production can be indicative of

TABLE IV

Per Capita Production of All Industries in the Soviet Republics, 1913–65[a]

Republics	1913		1940		1958		1965	
	Rubles	Index	Rubles	Index	Rubles	Index	Rubles	Index
R.S.F.S.R.	130	100	923	100	3,376	100	5,671	100
Ukraine	120	92	576	62	1,693	50	2,884	51
Belorussia	51	39	261	28	854	25	1,801	32
Uzbekistan	67	51	332	36	572	17	1,380	24
Kazakhstan	36	28	260	28	978	29	1,560	27
Georgia	45	35	339	37	1,067	32	1,647	29
Azerbaidzhan	145	111	743	80	1,417	42	1,784	31
Lithuania	57	44	140	15	1,127	33	2,502	44
Moldavia	25	19	148	16	748	22	1,569	28
Kirghizia	35	27	188	20	700	21	968	17
Tadjikistan	12	9	71	8	186	5	350	6
Armenia	56	43	375	41	1,540	46	3,001	53
Turkmenia	39	30	201	22	520	15	587	10
Average for non-Russian republics	57	44	303	33	950	28	1,669	29

SOURCES: Central Administration of National Economic Accounts, Gosplan, *Sotsialisticheskoe stroitel'stvo Soyuza SSR (1933–1938 gg.): Statisticheskiy sbornik* (Moscow, 1939), pp. 8–9, 145; *Planovoe khozyaystvo,* No. 5 (1939), p. 174; U.S.S.R. Academy of Sciences, Institute of Economics, *Ekonomika sotsialisticheskoy promyshlennosti* (Moscow, 1940), p. 297; *Strany mira: Ezhegodniy spravochnik* (Moscow, 1946), pp. 186–251; S. E. Kamenitser and M. S. Urinson, *Rossiyskaya federatsiya v novoy pyatiletke* (Moscow, 1947), p. 28; *Bol'shaya sovetskaya entsiklopediya,* volume on the U.S.S.R. (1st ed.; Moscow, 1948), pp. 1827–1925; *Narodnoe khozyaystvo SSSR* (1956), p. 51; Statistical Administration of the R.S.F.S.R., *Narodnoe khozyaystvo RSFSR* (Moscow, 1957), pp. 3, 66; Statistical Administration of the Ukrainian S.S.R., *Narodne hospodarstvo Ukrayins'koyi RSR* (Kiev, 1957), p. 22; Central Statistical Administration of the Belorussian S.S.R., *Razvitie narodnogo khozyaystva Belorusskoy SSR za 20 let* (Minsk, 1964), p. 29; Central Statistical Administration of the Turkmenian S.S.R., *Sovetskiy Turkmenistan za 20 let* (Ashkhabad, 1964), p. 19; Central Statistical Administration, *SSSR v tsifrakh* (Moscow, 1958), pp. 16, 139–69; *Nar. khoz. SSSR v 1964 g.* (Moscow, 1965), pp. 4, 128, 802; *Nar. khoz. SSSR v 1965 g.*, pp. 9, 127.

[a] Production and population data apply to the area of each republic for the given year.

consumption in this case. Also, Table VI basically substantiates the evidence of Table V. Both tables show a slightly different picture from that arising out of Table IV; viz., electric power output and consumption of energy have been distributed between the R.S.F.S.R. and the non-Russian republics somewhat more equally than the production of all the industries combined. But the basic conclusions from Table IV still stand. One observes again vast differences in the levels of electrification and in general consumption of energy between the R.S.F.S.R. and the other Soviet republics, especially those of Central Asia. Also, in the comparison over time, the gap between the electrification of Russia and of the non-Russian republics, taken together, increased rather than decreased, especially in the post–World War II period.[73]

Of course, it may be said that the absolute gap between the highest and the lowest levels of electrification, shown in Table V, had decreased from a proportion of 4820:1 in 1913 (Azerbaidzhan com-

TABLE V
PER CAPITA ELECTRIC POWER OUTPUT IN THE SOVIET REPUBLICS, 1913, 1940, AND 1965

	1913		1940		1965	
Republics	Kwt. hrs.	Index	Kwt. hrs.	Index	Kwt. hrs.	Index
R.S.F.S.R.	14.7	100.0	284	100.0	2,639	100.0
Ukraine	15.4	104.9	306	107.7	2,088	79.1
Belorussia	0.4	2.9	57	20.1	980	37.1
Uzbekistan	0.7	5.1	75	26.4	1,104	41.8
Kazakhstan	0.2	1.6	105	37.0	1,602	60.7
Georgia	7.6	51.7	212	74.6	1,338	50.7
Azerbaidzhan	48.2	327.5	571	201.0	2,265	85.8
Lithuania	2.0	13.8	28	9.8	1,298	49.2
Moldavia	0.4	3.0	7	2.5	932	35.3
Latvia	5.9	40.2	132	46.5	660	25.0
Kirghizia	0.01	0.06	34	12.0	883	33.4
Tadjikistan	0.01	0.06	41	14.4	619	23.4
Armenia	5.1	34.7	304	107.0	1,320	50.0
Turkmenia	2.5	17.0	70	24.6	745	28.2
Estonia	6.1	41.5	190	66.9	5,548	210.2
Average for non-Russian republics	10.3	70.3	212	74.6	1,527	57.9

SOURCES: Central Statistical Administration, *Promyshlennost' SSSR: Statisticheskiy sbornik* (Moscow, 1964), pp. 234–35; *Nar. khoz. SSSR v 1965 g.*, p. 99.

pared to Tadjikistan) to a mere 9:1 (between Estonia and Tadjikistan) by 1965, but this is hardly of much consequence as far as the question of nationalities is concerned.[74] No one denies that there has been remarkable progress in the economic development of the non-Russian republics in the past fifty years. It is also readily granted that their progress was rapid compared to, let us say, Afghanistan, Saudi Arabia, or the former colonial countries of Africa, and that this difference was due to the difference in their respective economic, social, and political systems. However, what matters most as far as the solution of the nationalities question in the U.S.S.R. is concerned is how the growth of the non-Russian nationalities compares to that of Russia. Russia is the "elder brother" of them all, Russia is the largest by far of the republics, and Russia was an imperialist oppressor of the other nationalities before the October

TABLE VI

CONSUMPTION OF ENERGY IN THE SOVIET REPUBLICS, 1962

Republics	All Types of Energy	Electric Power	Mineral Fuel	Population	Per Capita Consumption Index, All Types of Energy (R.S.F.S.R. = 100)
	(in per cent of the U.S.S.R. total)				
R.S.F.S.R.	63.6	68.0	72.2	55.5	100.0
Ukraine	22.1	18.2	16.2	19.8	97.4
Belorussia	1.9	1.2	1.8	3.8	43.6
Uzbekistan	1.6	1.9	0.9	4.1	34.0
Kazakhstan	4.5	3.7	2.9	5.0	78.5
Georgia	0.9	1.2	0.8	1.9	41.4
Lithuania	0.6	0.4	0.7	1.3	40.2
Azerbaidzhan	1.7	1.9	1.4	1.9	78.1
Moldavia	0.5	0.3	0.4	1.4	31.1
Latvia	0.7	0.6	1.0	1.0	61.1
Kirghizia	0.4	0.4	0.3	1.0	34.9
Tadjikistan	0.2	0.4	0.1	1.0	17.4
Armenia	0.3	0.9	0.4	0.9	29.0
Turkmenia	0.4	0.3	0.2	0.8	43.6
Estonia	0.6	0.6	0.7	0.6	87.3
Average for non-Russian republics					51.3

SOURCES: *Nar. khoz. SSSR v 1963 g.*, p. 61; *Nar. khoz. SSSR v 1961 g.* (Moscow, 1962), p. 9.

Revolution—or at least Lenin said so. This is why the comparison must be made, first of all, with the achievements of Russia.

Also, as Table IV shows, the absolute gap between the highest and the lowest levels of *total* industrialization increased in any case from a proportion of 12:1 in 1913 (between Azerbaidzhan and Tadjikistan) to 16:1 in 1965 (between Russia and Tadjikistan). This fact alone merits further investigation.

Transfer of Resources to the R.S.F.S.R.?

The question why the gap between Russia and the non-Russian republics has increased needs to be answered at this point. Part of the answer has already been given in Table IV, which shows that the growth of industry in Russia has been consistently faster than in most of the non-Russian republics. Even when that growth was relatively slower in Russia than in some non-Russian republics, it still contributed a larger absolute increment to the total output of Russia because the volume of Russia's output is, of course, much larger than that of the smaller republics. Hence, the gap is also not a mere "telescopic mirage" of percentages multiplying from a near-zero base. Russia's 1913 industrial base was not smaller, but much larger, than that of the non-Russian republics combined.

The main reason for the growing gap can be seen more clearly from Tables VII and VIII, which show per capita capital investments. Both tables, but especially Table VIII, indicate that the R.S.F.S.R. has enjoyed clear priority in the allocation of investments per capita: It has received considerably more per capita from the U.S.S.R. treasury than other republics, and this inequality has increased over time. Of all the republics, only Azerbaidzhan has gotten somewhat more investments per capita than the R.S.F.S.R., but most of these investments have been absorbed by its depleting oil industry; as Table IV suggests, other industries have not been developed sufficiently rapidly in Azerbaidzhan.[75]

By itself the fact that there has been considerable inequality in the per capita distribution of capital in the different republics still does not imply any inequity in the distribution. We have seen that the per capita national income in Russia is higher than in most other republics. From Table XV below we also observe that the population of the R.S.F.S.R. has been paying higher income taxes per capita (because of their higher income). All this suggests that higher investments per capita in Russia could at least in part be explained on equity grounds

TABLE VII

Per Capita Capital Investments of State and Cooperative Enterprises, 1918–60

Republics	1918–32		1933–40		1941–60		1946–60		1918–60	
	Rubles	Index	Rubles	Index	Rubles	Index	Rubles	Index	Rubles	Index
R.S.F.S.R.	50	100.0	194	100.0	1,309	100.0	1,221	100.0	1,531	100.0
Ukraine	48	97.2	116	59.7	905	69.1	864	70.8	1,050	68.6
Belorussia	30	61.0	63	32.4	569	43.4	551	45.1	657	42.9
Uzbekistan	34	67.5	100	51.5	544	41.5	505	41.3	636	41.5
Kazakhstan	...	...	172	88.3	1,254	95.7	1,188	97.3	1,385	90.5
Georgia	...	...	166	85.5	817	62.4	764	62.6	991	64.7
Azerbaidzhan	...	...	247	126.9	1,176	89.8	1,122	92.0	1,416	92.5
Lithuania	...	...	...	...	...	...	557	45.6	...	...
Moldavia	...	...	...	...	...	...	395	32.3	...	...
Latvia	...	...	...	...	...	...	873	71.5	...	...
Kirghizia	...	...	99	50.9	683	52.1	645	52.8	763	49.8
Tadjikistan	56	111.6	126	64.7	640	48.8	610	49.9	765	50.0
Armenia	...	...	176	90.4	783	59.8	743	60.8	929	60.7
Turkmenia	47	93.4	160	82.6	1,124	85.8	1,060	86.8	1,274	83.2
Estonia	...	...	...	...	...	...	1,283	105.1	...	...
Average for non-Russian republics	44	89.0	122	63.0	875	66.8	817	66.9	1,011	66.0

Sources: Central Statistical Administration, *Kapital'noe stroitel'stvo v SSSR: Statisticheskiy sbornik* (Moscow, 1961), pp. 80–109; *The U.S.S.R. in Figures,* p. 133; *Nar. khoz. SSSR v 1960 g.* (Moscow, 1961), p. 10.

TABLE VIII

PER CAPITA CAPITAL INVESTMENTS IN INDUSTRY, 1918–60

	1918–40		1941–60		1946–60		1918–60	
Republics	Rubles	Index	Rubles	Index	Rubles	Index	Rubles	Index
R.S.F.S.R.	104	100.0	651	100.0	602	100.0	745	100.0
Ukraine	91	87.5	476	73.1	452	75.1	541	72.6
Belorussia	25	24.0	198	30.4	193	32.0	214	28.7
Uzbekistan	40	38.5	239	36.7	216	35.9	267	35.8
Kazakhstan	82	78.8	480	73.9	450	74.7	528	70.9
Georgia	74	71.1	373	57.3	352	58.5	434	58.2
Azerbaidzhan	181	174.0	685	105.2	655	108.8	829	111.4
Lithuania	...	...	...	...	224	37.2	...	...
Moldavia	...	...	...	...	142	23.6	...	...
Latvia	...	...	...	...	283	47.0	...	...
Kirghizia	31	29.8	319	49.0	301	50.0	339	45.5
Tadjikistan	36	34.6	274	42.2	261	43.3	300	40.3
Armenia	85	81.7	377	57.9	357	59.3	435	58.4
Turkmenia	44	42.3	507	77.9	475	78.9	540	72.5
Estonia	...	...	...	...	501	83.2	...	...
Average for non-Russian republics	79	76.0	414	63.6	378	62.8	475	63.7

SOURCES: *Kapital'noe stroitel'stvo v SSSR,* pp. 80–109; *The U.S.S.R. in Figures,* p. 133; *Nar. khoz. SSSR v 1960 g.,* p. 10.

—after all, a considerable proportion of them stems from taxes. However, the solution of the question of nationalities through the equalization of the levels of economic development presumes an inequitable distribution of resources on a loan basis; otherwise, without economic aid by the developed countries, there can be no economic solution of this problem. Hence, had the Soviet capital investments been guided at least to a substantial extent by the desire to alleviate and solve the nationalities question, a different picture of the allocation of investments from that in Tables VII and VIII should have emerged.

The actual degree of equity or inequity in the larger per capita allocations in the Russian republic cannot, unfortunately, be ascertained as yet. A thorough analysis of the equity of taxation is necessary. Since this cannot be accomplished here, it is an additional important reason that the conclusions reached in this paper must still be considered as tentative. If it were true that the whole differential in the higher capital investments in Russia could be explained on equity grounds, all our findings would amount to a conclusion that the Russians did not want to aid economically the underdeveloped republics of the U.S.S.R. and did not care to solve the Soviet problem of nationalities by economic means. Of course, this still would be an important finding.

However, there are many grounds for suspecting that the rules of equity can explain only a part of the investment differential in case of the R.S.F.S.R. As Table XV shows, taxes per capita in the R.S.F.S.R. are not even 34 per cent higher than in the non-Russian republics combined—34 per cent being the investment differential in the last column of Table VII. Hence, a considerable proportion of the investment differential in the Russian republic must have come from the transfer of investment capital to Russia from other republics of the Union. If so, this is something quite different from the equity principle.

That capital funds have in fact been transferred from one Soviet republic to another without respect to equitable taxation has been explicitly acknowledged in more than one official statement. Thus Khrushchev wrote in *Pravda,* on March 30, 1957:

> Socialist accumulations must be distributed in accordance with the all-Union interests, and primarily in accordance with national economic priorities. It must be kept in mind in this connection that, in a number of cases, capital formation may take place in some republics and the government may decide to develop the economy—in other republics. If centralized leadership is relaxed in such a case, funds may become spread too thinly and would be spent not on economic growth but on various other needs, on which we still cannot afford to spend a larger share of investments.

Khrushchev expressed this point even more clearly in *Pravda,* on May 8, 1957:

> There may develop a situation when monetary accumulations of the enterprises of industry and of other sectors, which are located in the territory of that or another republic, would happen to be insufficient to finance the economic development targets established by the national economic plan, while at the same time, in other republics, capital would be formed in the amounts exceeding the needs foreseen in the plan. In all such cases the funds must be redistributed among the republics through the Union budget. This can be explained by the following example. In the Kazakh S.S.R., where there are very rich deposits of natural resources, it is necessary to develop iron and nonferrous metallurgy, the mining of coal and of iron ore. For this, large capital investments are required. Yet, all the revenues that are collected in the terri-

tory of Kazakhstan are insufficient to secure the financing of the measures already in progress. Hence, the shortage of funds must be covered from the Union budget out of the redistribution of the general, all-Union revenues. The same situation can also develop in other republics.

Let us take good note of the fact that it did not occur to Khrushchev to suggest that Kazakhstan borrow the necessary funds from other republics, or at least from the Union treasury or the State Bank. No, on the contrary, he deliberately spurned the equity and the economy principles in this case while suggesting that the taxpayers of other republics carry the burden Kazakhstan is unable to bear. Furthermore, how could Khrushchev be so sure that it was economical to develop Kazakhstan's resources in comparison with the already-developed resources of some other republic if he did not propose to charge interest on the investments in Kazakhstan and therefore failed to take the time factor into account? We must keep all this in mind for further consideration.

Khrushchev tried to justify the transfer of capital resources from one republic to another. Some half-dozen Soviet economists who partook in the discussion of the methods of calculation of the national income of the republics simply stated, as a matter of fact, that the transfer of one republic's national income to another republic via the all-Union budget is definitely taking place.[76] A. Zverev, the former Minister of Finance of the U.S.S.R., even went so far as to apply the Marxian term "surplus product" to that part of the accumulated funds which is transferred from one republic to another.[77] Logically, this means that one republic exploits another in the Marxian sense of exploitation!

In no other republic but the Ukraine have the actual calculations of the transferred funds been accomplished and published thus far. In 1963, the Academy of Sciences of the Ukrainian S.S.R. published a monograph on the national income of the Ukraine—the collective work of twenty-six economists. The monograph establishes that, in the period 1959–61 alone, considerable funds were withdrawn from the Ukraine into the all-Union treasury and were never returned. The difference between the Union budget revenues and expenditures in the Ukraine has amounted to 3.8867 billion rubles in 1959, 4.1758 billion in 1960, and 3.6648 billion in 1961.[78] These net losses of the Ukraine constituted about 14 per cent of its national income.[79]

These newest Soviet calculations sustain similar data for preceding periods, calculated by a similar method of financial balances: calculations by Professor Melnyk, quoted above, which produced a net loss of about 5 billion rubles for the Ukraine during the First Five-Year Plan period; calculations of Soviet economists of the Ukrainian Gosplan in the 1920's, which produced a net loss for the Ukraine for the period 1923–24 to 1927–28 of some 500 million rubles.[80] Also I have found, in an as yet unpublished paper which was read at the Shevchenko Scientific Society, in New York, on January 27, 1957, that in 1940, the Ukraine's deficit in relation to the all-Union budget amounted to at least 2.1 billion rubles. Hence, there is no doubt that funds have been withdrawn from the Ukraine in considerable amounts and used by the U.S.S.R. treasury outside of the Ukraine. These funds have never been returned, and neither were they borrowed from the Ukraine to bear an interest. Hence, from the Ukrainian point of view, the charge that the Ukraine has been exploited financially by Moscow makes clear sense. These facts have undoubtedly contributed to the existence of Ukrainian nationalism.[81]

However, the charge of colonialist exploitation is not *a priori* or necessarily true if looked upon from the point of view of the U.S.S.R. as a whole, and also possibly from the viewpoint of other republics. Similar calculations of financial balances of the other Soviet republics do not exist or are not being published. Hence, there exists no evidence that all or any one of them is not exploited as much as the Ukraine. Suppose for discussion's sake that Moscow withdraws identical proportions of resources from all republics and uses these resources abroad—to supply foreign aid to the underdeveloped countries of the world, for example, to finance space explorations, oceanographic research, etc. If this aid and expense is extended in the form of loans with an appropriate interest, or when research equally benefits all republics, there is no exploitation, of course. But this objection is purely academic. There is no doubt that the U.S.S.R. does not spend 14 per cent of its national income abroad. Hence, it is quite probable that not all the republics bear the burden of 14 per cent withdrawals; some probably lose less, others maybe even more, while some probably do not lose anything but gain from the transfer of funds from others. This inequity can produce conditions accounting for the existence of the question of nationalities in the U.S.S.R.

Since there is no doubt that the unpaid-for funds are transferred within the U.S.S.R., something can be learned about their distribution from studying the shares of different republics in the total capital investments of the U.S.S.R. These data are reproduced in Table IX. The first thing that can be learned from this table is the change of

TABLE IX
Share of the Soviet Republics in Total Capital Investments, 1928–60
(in per cent)

Republics	1928–32	1933–37	1938–41	1941–45	1946–50[a]		1951–55	1956–60
R.S.F.S.R.	67.8	69.5	69.7	73.5	(61.2)	62.7	66.3	65.5
Ukraine	18.5	16.6	14.4	12.3	(20.7)	19.2	15.8	16.1
Belorussia	2.0	1.4	2.3	1.0	(2.9)	2.3	1.9	2.0
Uzbekistan	2.0	2.1	2.1	2.3	(1.6)	1.9	1.8	2.0
Kazakhstan	3.3	3.4	3.5	4.7	(3.7)	3.7	4.8	6.5
Georgia	1.8	2.0	1.9	1.5	(1.7)	2.0	1.6	1.1
Azerbaidzhan	2.1	2.5	2.6	1.5	(2.5)	2.5	2.5	1.6
Lithuania	...	...	0.1	0.2	(0.6)	0.5	0.6	0.8
Moldavia	0.1	0.1	0.1	0.2	(0.5)	0.5	0.5	0.5
Latvia	...	...	0.2	0.3	(0.9)	0.9	0.7	0.8
Kirghizia	0.3	0.4	0.6	0.6	(0.5)	0.5	0.7	0.6
Tadjikistan	0.9	0.7	0.6	0.5	(0.5)	0.5	0.6	0.6
Armenia	0.6	0.7	0.8	0.5	(0.6)	0.7	0.6	0.6
Turkmenia	0.6	0.6	0.6	0.7	(0.7)	0.8	0.8	0.7
Estonia	...	...	0.5	0.2	(1.5)	0.9	0.7	0.6
Non-Russian republics combined	32.2	30.5	30.3	26.5	(38.8)	37.3	33.7	34.5

SOURCES: *Kapital'noe stroitel'stvo v SSSR*, pp. 74–75; *Bor'ba KPSS za vosstanovlenie i razvitie narodnogo khozyaystva v poslevoenniy period (1945–1953 gody): Dokumenty i materialy* (Moscow, 1961), pp. 90–117.

[a] The figures in parentheses represent the share assigned to the republics under the Fourth Five-Year Plan. Note that the R.S.F.S.R. actually received more than was allocated to it by the Plan.

shares over time. It is evident that the R.S.F.S.R.'s share constantly increased before and during the war; then it declined, partly due to the incorporation of new republics into the Union, and then sharply increased and slightly decreased again. The share of all the non-Russian republics taken together fluctuated in an inverse proportion, of course. As far as the individual non-Russian republics are concerned, these noteworthy factors have emerged: a considerable decline in the Ukraine's and Estonia's share, irregular fluctuations in the shares of Belorussia, Uzbekistan, Kirghizia, and the three Trans-Caucasian republics, and noticeable increases in the shares of Moldavia, Lithuania, and especially Kazakhstan in recent years. What can be concluded from the analysis of this table is that the Ukraine has undoubtedly been a net loser, while earlier Russia and lately Kazakhstan have undoubtedly been net gainers. However, since even Kazakhstan's share in the total is relatively small, while the R.S.F.S.R. has had the lion's share, there is the strong suspicion that the R.S.F.S.R. must have been a gainer in the long run.

This finding coincides with the evidence presented in Tables VII and VIII, and also with that of Table X. The last, in particular, shows that the Russian republic's share in U.S.S.R. investments was larger than its share in already accumulated productive capital. This disproportion was not due to any high productivity of Russian capital; as can be seen from Table XII, marginal productivity of capital in the R.S.F.S.R. in the same period was less than 1 per cent (0.78, in fact). Hence, the larger share of capital investments did not result from the increment produced by the R.S.F.S.R.'s own capital. Rather, that larger share means that investments were being obtained by the R.S.F.S.R. from sources other than its own capital. Of course, this does not yet prove beyond any doubt that capital investments were transferred to the R.S.F.S.R. from other republics, but it makes the case for such a hypothesis very strong.

Another piece of significant circumstantial evidence that suggests that resources have probably been transferred to the R.S.F.S.R. is the well-known official priority policy of accelerated development of the so-called eastern regions of the U.S.S.R. This policy was initiated in 1930, and it has remained substantially unchanged until now.[82] The "eastern regions" were allotted "about one-half" of all capital investments in heavy industries during the Second Five-Year Plan of 1933–37,[83] and in the Seven-Year Plan of 1959–65 they were still being given "more than 40 per cent" of all capital investments in the total economy of the U.S.S.R.[84]

Generally speaking, the term "eastern regions" that figures in numerous official documents is usually understood to mean the Asian part of the U.S.S.R.—the Ural area, Siberia, the Far East, and the Maritime provinces, but also Kazakhstan and the four Central Asian republics.[85] In practice, however, as Table IX indicates, in Central Asia only Kirghizia enjoyed some slight advantage in capital alloca-

TABLE X

SHARE OF THE SOVIET REPUBLICS IN FIXED CAPITAL AND NEW INVESTMENTS IN INDUSTRY

(*in per cent*)

Republics	Fixed Capital 1955	Investments 1956–60
R.S.F.S.R.	63.8	66.6
Ukraine	20.2	17.5
Belorussia	1.6	1.5
Uzbekistan	1.7	1.9
Kazakhstan	3.4	4.9
Georgia	1.8	1.1
Azerbaidzhan	3.1	1.8
Lithuania	0.5	0.7
Moldavia	0.4	0.5
Latvia	0.8	0.6
Kirghizia	0.4	0.5
Tadjikistan	0.3	0.5
Armenia	0.7	0.6
Turkmenia	0.6	0.7
Estonia	0.7	0.5
Non-Russian republics combined	36.2	33.4

SOURCES: *Promyshlennost' SSSR: Statisticheskiy sbornik* (Moscow, 1957), p. 18; *Kapital'noe stroitel'stvo v SSSR,* p. 72.

tions in the postwar, as compared to prewar, period, and Kazakhstan was given noticeable priority only in the post-1950 period. The eastern regions of the R.S.F.S.R., on the other hand, viz., the Ural area, western and eastern Siberia, the Far East, and the Maritime provinces, have headed the priority lists continuously since about 1930. Their comparative growth between 1940 and 1964 is clearly evident from Table XI. Also such regions of the R.S.F.S.R. as Upper Volga (Povolzh'ye, sometimes also called Middle Volga), the central region (around Moscow, Ivanovo, and Tula), and the northwestern region (Leningrad), in spite of the fact that they are not classified among the

TABLE XI

Share of the Eastern Regions in the Total Output of the Soviet Union, 1940 and 1964

Area	Electric Power (*in billion kwt. hrs.*)		Coal (*in million tons*)		Crude Oil (*in million tons*)		Gas (*in billion cubic meters*)		Pig Iron (*in million tons*)		Steel (*in million tons*)		Rolled Steel (*in million tons*)		Mineral Fertilizers (*in million tons*)	
	1940	1964	1940	1964	1940	1964	1940	1964	1940	1964	1940	1964	1940	1964	1940	1964
U.S.S.R.	48.3	459.0	165.9	554.0	31.1	223.6	3.20	108.6	14.9	62.4	18.3	85.0	11.4	57.4	3.2	25.6
All eastern regions	10.7	190.0	59.5	275.3	3.6	62.3	0.03	14.6	4.3	23.5	5.9	35.3	3.7	24.0	1.0	9.4
Kazakhstan and Central Asia[a]	1.3	31.4	8.3	49.8	1.4	12.2	0.00	10.1	0.0	1.5	0.0	0.9	0.0	0.6	0.0	2.8
As per cent of U.S.S.R.	*2.6*	*7.0*	*5.0*	*9.0*	*4.4*	*5.5*	*0.00*	*9.4*	*0.0*	*2.4*	*0.0*	*1.0*	*0.0*	*1.0*	*0.0*	*11.0*
Eastern regions of the R.S.F.S.R.[b]	9.4	158.6	51.2	225.5	2.2	50.1	0.03	4.5	4.3	22.0	5.9	34.4	3.7	23.4	1.0	6.6
As per cent of U.S.S.R.	*19.5*	*34.9*	*30.9*	*40.7*	*7.1*	*22.4*	*0.90*	*4.1*	*28.8*	*35.2*	*32.2*	*40.5*	*32.4*	*40.8*	*31.2*	*25.8*

SOURCE: *Nar. khoz. SSSR v 1964 g.*, pp. 148–49, 158, 164, 166, 168, 170.

[a] Uzbekistan, Turkmenia, Kirghizia, and Tadjikistan.

[b] The Urals, Siberia, the Far East, and the Maritime provinces.

"eastern regions," have received top priority in the allocation of capital investments.[86] Their economic growth has been more rapid than that of the U.S.S.R. average almost uninterruptedly.[87] This is additional circumstantial evidence that the R.S.F.S.R. has probably grown at the expense of capital transfers from the non-Russian republics. Ultimately, however, this hypothesis can be proved or disproved only by the calculation of the Russian republic's financial or national income balances.

Methods and Criteria of Spatial Resource Allocation in Soviet Practice

A pertinent question at this stage of our discussion is the following: By which methods and on what grounds does the U.S.S.R. decide to allocate resources among the republics and economic regions? Major decisions on the allocation of resources in the Soviet Union are made in the appropriate departments of the Central Committee and in the Politburo of the Communist Party; the draft proposals for such decisions and the details on their execution are prepared by the Gosplan of the U.S.S.R., by various government ministries, and by the Central Committees, Gosplans, and governments of the Union republics.[88] All major decisions are made by the politicians, not by the economists. Economists—and, at that, only those who work for the Gosplans and the government agencies, not professors—prepare and elaborate only technical details of various projects and provide analyses of the proposed drafts and of decisions already made. Consequently, in Soviet practice, spatial resource allocation in its decision-making stage is a political process, full of arbitrary rules and compromises. Thus, Mikoyan stated on this matter: "This is not a strictly peaceful process. Each struggles for his particular plans and plant—inside the all-Union Gosplan and the Gosplans of the Union republics, until a decision is reached. Most issues can be smoothed out by argument and figures, but sometimes the Government must make the decision."[89] In these internal fights the question of nationalities seems to loom very large. Consider, for example, the following revelations made by Khrushchev in his fateful speech, in which he attacked the centralizers in the Party and Government and proposed to dichotomize the Party along agro-industrial lines:

> The planning agencies do not always start with the need to develop the economy in a complex way; they fail to show initiative in the elaboration of the most economical decisions, frequently wrongly determine

the sequence of construction of the most important national economic projects.

Were the planning agencies and the U.S.S.R. Ministry of Energy and Electrification correct in their approach to the proposals of the Central Asian republics to build there big hydrostations and powerful irrigation systems? It was not because of the central agencies' initiative, for example, that construction began on the Nurek and Toktogul hydroelectric stations, which have great importance not only for the development of the economy of Central Asia, but of the whole country.

. . . Central Asia is rich in mineral resources. With cheap electric power it is possible to develop large-scale industry there. The planning agencies must take everything into consideration while deciding where first to build big hydrostations—in Central Asia or, for instance, in Siberia.

There was a heated controversy about whether or not to build the Kiev hydroelectric station on the Dnieper River. Yet now, as you know, it is already being built. We are also building the Dnieprodzerzhinsk HES, and soon we will build the one at Kanev. However, the people at Gosplan once thought that these stations should not be built. Why? Because they took the prime cost of a kilowatt-hour of the Kiev Station, for example, and compared it with the prime cost at the Bratsk HES. Obviously such a comparison was not in favor of the stations on the Dnieper River. But can one approach such a serious problem in such a simplified manner? Would it be more profitable to build thermal stations in the Ukraine and to develop the industry based on Donbas coal? Nothing of the sort. Donbas coal is expensive; it is mined at very great depths and from poor strata. The power of the thermal stations working on Donbas coal cannot compete with Dnieper hydroelectric power. Therefore, one should not add a sparrow and a camel and count them as two equal heads of cattle.

Yet some still figure according to this "method." When we interfered and insisted on the construction of the Dnieper hydrostations, there were "planners" who reasoned like this: "Well, Khrushchev knows the Ukraine and it is difficult to argue with him, but nevertheless money is not allocated there where it should be in the first place." What can one answer to this![90]

Many interesting conclusions can be drawn from this speech, but one should also take into account its background. It deals with the perennial struggle in the upper echelons of the Soviet power pyramid over the question of which regions should have priority in resource allocations. The struggle for and against the construction of the huge hydroelectric power stations in Siberia—as before this on the Volga River—began in Stalin's time. The struggle concerns the future industrial development of Central Russia versus the Ukraine and the western parts of the U.S.S.R. The whole of the European part of the

U.S.S.R. is presently short of fuel and electric power, and this scarcity will increase in the future. Ukrainian economists, planners, and politicians have for some time been leading a fight for the construction of a number of powerful hydroelectric power stations on the Dnieper, especially in its upper parts around Kiev, from where power could be supplied to the northwestern Ukraine, Belorussia, and Lithuania—the overpopulated and industrially underdeveloped parts of the U.S.S.R.[91] In this struggle, the Ukrainians were supported by other Europeans and some Russians who want to build atomic power stations in European Russia.[92] The Russians in the U.S.S.R. Gosplan, however, pushed their own pet project of developing the eastern parts of the U.S.S.R. at all costs.[93] Central Asia was neglected by all sides, and so was the Caucasus. The Gosplanners' argument in favor of Siberia has been typically Stalinist economics: only prime costs of production were compared, social overhead costs of development were neglected, a very long-run time horizon was assumed, and no interest rate was included into the cost and recoupment calculations. The arguments of the proponents of European development have been economically more plausible, although not always consistent. For instance, none of them proposed to calculate the interest. But they pointed out that social overhead costs of developing Siberia, of building cities, roads, housing facilities, and of transferring population there were prohibitive in the short run, while transportation of electric power from Siberia to European Russia—as long as the Siberian industries remained undeveloped and it could not be consumed on the spot—was also pretty expensive. Nevertheless, the Gosplanners won the first rounds of this fight, and the construction of the Siberian complex of hydrostations began. However, at the Twenty-first CPSU Congress, the Europeans won their first battle: The Congress resolved that, at least theoretically, it was cheaper to develop the already-developed economic regions than to start from scratch—a self-evident truth unknown thus far only to the ignoramuses.[94] The Twenty-third Congress finally resolved that it was necessary to intensify the search for fuels in the European parts of the U.S.S.R., and implied that they ought to be cheaper there than elsewhere.[95]

The case of Siberian versus Ukrainian electric power stations is only one yet typical example of the essentially political processes of decision-making in spatial resource allocation in the U.S.S.R. Concomitant with the electric power question has been the question of the underdevelopment of the coal, oil, and gas industries in the Ukrainian republic; Ukrainian Party leaders and economists have vigorously fought for an increase of investment allocations in their region, and in part have won the battle.[96] There was also a remarkable attack by the Ukrainians on the U.S.S.R. Gosplan for the latter's refusal to develop chemical industries in the Ukraine at a sufficient rate, but this has had no effect thus far.[97] Another perennial, as yet unsuccessful, campaign has been the fight by the Uzbeks for the development of cotton textile manufacturing in their republic, the largest producer of raw cotton in the U.S.S.R.[98] The employment interests of Russian textile workers in the Moscow region have been clearly opposed to the Uzbeks' demands.[99] The complaints by the Azerbaidzhanis have also been very ominous. Their republic's oil deposits are approaching exhaustion, and few other industries have been developed instead to secure full employment. Recently agriculture has been growing faster than industry in this republic, but it lacks a sufficient supply of water. The First Secretary of the Azerbaidzhan Party poignantly referred to "western imperialists" who "threaten the very existence of nations" by their exploitation, while discussing the decay of Azerbaidzhan's economy.[100] The growth of industry in the Georgian Republic since 1956 has also been slower than that of agriculture, and an oblique Georgian complaint is on record that the republic's industry has been undercapitalized.[101] Similar more or less sharp and explicit criticisms of the central, Moscow authorities have been voiced in the cases of Belorussia and Moldavia, as well as even in small autonomous republics of the R.S.F.S.R. such as Tataria and the Mari A.S.S.R.[102]

What probably affects national idiosyncrasies most, however, is the arbitrariness of Moscow's decisions. There is unanimous dissatisfaction among all complainants, who, as a rule, raise objective, purely economic, arguments in defense of their interests. Usually they stress the disproportionately small investments made in their regions, their regions' comparatively higher profitability or productivity, unused productive capacity, and hidden labor unemployment in their overpopulated areas. On the other hand, Moscow never furnishes any explanations for its decisions. Khrushchev himself blatantly recalled how, in the past, Stalin personally, without consulting anyone even at the U.S.S.R. Council of Ministers, made decisions about one or another national economic plan.[103] And yet, at the same time, it was also Khrushchev himself who, in his turn, personally refused Belorussia investment funds for draining her marshlands,[104] and he published decisions bearing only his signature to construct plants in the Ukraine.[105]

Each arbitrary political decision to allocate resources over the territory of the multinational Soviet Union probably touches upon the sensitive question of nationalities, because men who made decisions are inevitably themselves members of one or another nationality and because resources are allocated to one place and not to another. It resembles the allocation of new taxes among different income groups in an ethnically homogenous but socially differentiated society; or the allocation of educational and welfare funds in a religiously differentiated society like that in the United States. The decision-maker is suspected of favoring his social class, his religion, his state, or his race and nationality. The issue becomes especially acute when evidence of favoritism or bias exists.

The economic rules for the allocation of resources discussed earlier provide objective criteria for such decision-making. If they are strictly observed, the economic bases of the question of nationalities are eliminated; if they are observed at least partially, the intensity of suspicions and animosities can be alleviated to some extent. However, at this time hardly any evidence exists that these rules have been observed in Soviet practice. One major rule, viz., that resources be transferred from one republic to another on a loan basis and with interest paid in full has not been observed at all, even in theory. As to the remaining rules, some elements appeared in Soviet theory for the first time only at about 1960–62,[106] while their nonobservance in practice seems to be clearly evident from the data in Tables X, XII, and XIII.

Table X shows that the Russian republic has obtained much more in new investment funds than her share in the already accumulated fixed funds. The Ukraine, on the other hand, has got much less than her rational proportion. Table XII demonstrates that such a decision to allocate investments was arbitrary and not justified by economic considerations. The correlation regression between investment shares in Table X and the marginal capital products in Table XII has a very low coefficient. Data in Table XII also show that both marginal productivity of investments and their profitability have been considerably lower in Russia than in the Ukraine and a number of other republics. This means that had a transfer of resources from the Ukraine to Russia taken place, it would not only not have been in the interest of the Ukraine, but also contrary to the interests of the Soviet Union, because both the Soviet Union as a whole and the Ukrainian Republic have increased their output, income, employment, and welfare by a smaller percentage and increment than they might have. In

TABLE XII

CAPITAL INVESTMENT EFFICIENCY AND PROFITABILITY IN THE SOVIET REPUBLICS

Republics	Marginal Capital Product in Industry (Per Cent Growth of Output Divided by Per Cent Growth of Investments)		Profit on Investments 1959–63 (*in per cent*)	Profitability Index
	1933–41	1954–62		
R.S.F.S.R.	2.40	0.78	14.9	100.0
Ukraine	2.47	0.92	17.6	117.8
Belorussia	2.14	0.89	20.8	139.2
Uzbekistan	0.80	0.53	14.1	94.2
Kazakhstan	1.49	0.70	2.2	15.1
Georgia	2.79	1.11	14.7	98.2
Azerbaidzhan	1.24	1.21	11.6	77.8
Lithuania	. . .	0.63	19.2	128.9
Moldavia	2.44	0.57	28.8	193.2
Latvia	. . .	0.63	31.2	208.8
Kirghizia	1.10	0.70	12.8	86.0
Tadjikistan	2.41	0.57	11.7	78.4
Armenia	1.69	0.89	14.6	97.6
Turkmenia	1.15	0.67	7.2	48.3
Estonia	. . .	0.45	16.9	113.2

SOURCES: *Promyshlennost' SSSR* (1964), pp. 49, 74–75; *Kapital'noe stroitel'stvo v SSSR,* pp. 80–109; *Nar. khoz. SSSR v 1963 g.,* pp. 458, 638.

such a case Russia would have gained, there is no doubt, while the U.S.S.R. and a number of republics would have lost a foregone opportunity to increase their economic growth to the maximum. Even less economical and efficient than the investments in the R.S.F.S.R. were the investments in Kazakhstan; they produced a bare 2.2 per cent profit (Table XII). This sort of relative misallocation of capital in space, the wasteful sinking of funds into Siberia and Kazakhstan, has undoubtedly been one of the reasons for the post-1950 slowdown in the economic growth of the U.S.S.R—as this writer had an opportunity to observe earlier.[107]

Pre–World War II data also support these conclusions. The incremental capital/output ratio in large-scale industry in Siberia during the First and Second Five-Year Plans (1928–37) was 1.87, whereas in Uzbekistan it was 1.64, in Tadjikistan, 0.88, and in the Ukraine,

0.74.[108] In other words, for each additional ruble of output it was necessary to invest 1 ruble and 87 kopeks of capital in Siberia, only 88 kopeks in Tadjikistan, and only 74 kopeks in the Ukraine. It is therefore obvious that it was not worthwhile to invest in Siberia on the scale that the Soviet Government did. It was more economical to invest in the Ukraine and Central Asia, and possibly also in the European parts of the R.S.F.S.R. It can be argued, however, that defense considerations necessitated the construction of industries behind the Ural Mountains. Perhaps this was true, although to be certain it would be necessary to calculate whether or not the increment in growth of the defense industries forgone in the European parts of the U.S.S.R. would not have been larger than that gained in the Urals.[109] What is more important, however, is the fact that this defense argument is no longer valid in the post–World War II period. Today, nuclear bombs and missiles can reach any part of the U.S.S.R. Hence, there is no justification whatsoever for pushing the development of Siberia and Kazakhstan so hard.

TABLE XIII
COMPARATIVE LABOR PRODUCTIVITY IN THE INDUSTRY OF THE SOVIET REPUBLICS, 1960

	INDUSTRIAL OUTPUT PER WORKER		CAPITAL INVESTMENT PER WORKER	
Republics	Rubles	Index	Rubles	Index
R.S.F.S.R.	7,212	100.0	687	100.0
Ukraine	9,136	126.7	695	101.2
Belorussia	7,414	102.8	542	78.9
Uzbekistan	9,341	129.5	824	119.9
Kazakhstan	7,993	110.8	1,598	232.6
Georgia	8,889	123.2	741	107.9
Azerbaidzhan	9,132	126.6	1,370	199.4
Lithuania	7,619	105.6	476	69.3
Moldavia	10,656	147.7	820	119.3
Latvia	8,088	112.1	368	53.6
Kirghizia	8,411	116.6	934	135.9
Tadjikistan	10,811	149.9	1,351	196.6
Armenia	8,451	117.2	704	102.5
Turkmenia	8,955	124.2	1,492	217.2
Estonia	8,074	111.9	621	90.4

SOURCE: U.S. Congress, Joint Economic Committee, *Dimensions of Soviet Economic Power* (87th Cong., 2d sess.; Washington, D.C., 1962), pp. 704–32.

Table XIII is reproduced here as evidence that the allocation of resources illustrated by Tables X and XII was also not guided by the traditional rules of Marxian economics. In the latter, capital should be invested where the rate of "surplus value," and therefore of profit, is comparatively higher. The rate of surplus value is higher where labor productivity and the "organic structure of capital" (that is, capital per unit of labor) are comparatively higher. Both labor productivity and capital per worker have been higher in the Ukraine than in Russia, for example, as they were in a number of other republics (Table XIII). Hence, investment in Russia on the scale undertaken by the Soviet Government was not justified from the Marxian point of view either. Again one cannot escape the conclusion that the investment bias in favor of Russia has been highly arbitrary.

Comparative Material and Cultural Living Standards

Space does not permit a sufficiently detailed discussion of the interrepublic allocation of such resources as labor, land, natural resources, etc., although there is no doubt that the questions which—or rather whose—oil fields are pumped out and depleted before others, for example, or whose lands are used for dust-bowl wheat planting instead of possibly more economical and profitable sheep, camel, and steer grazing, also bear significantly upon the question of nationalities in the U.S.S.R. As far as labor is concerned, the CPSU Program calls specifically for the "continuous exchange of trained personnel among [Soviet] nations,"[110] which in practice frequently means the inflow of Government and Party officials and various specialists from Russia to the western Soviet republics; the transfer of Russian, Ukrainian, and Belorussian university graduates and skilled workers to Central Asian and Caucasian republics, instead of training and employing local personnel.

The last question that must be dealt with in this paper is whether or not the transfer of capital resources to the R.S.F.S.R., which has been circumstantially indicated, has resulted in some real gain for that region. This is not an easy question, even in theory. In practice, however, the dearth of statistical information creates difficult problems and permits only very tentative conclusions to be drawn.

The pertinent statistical data that can be assembled thus far are presented in Tables XIV through XXV. Comparative nominal wages in Table XIV have been computed by subtracting the total wage fund of the R.S.F.S.R. from that of the Soviet Union. Wage data for individual republics have not been available. It is only known that, in 1956, the lowest average money wages were paid in Moldavia, Belorussia, and Lithuania, while the highest wages among the non-Russian republics were paid in Kazakhstan and Estonia; the difference between the highest (Kazakhstan) and the lowest (Moldavia) was 41 per cent. The data for the R.S.F.S.R. as a whole for that year have not been given in the source, but from the data for the individual economic regions of the R.S.F.S.R. it would appear that the R.S.F.S.R. average was somewhere below that of Estonia and more or less on a par with that of the Ukraine.[111] Data in Table XIV also show that the money wages in the Russian republic have been higher, on the average, than in all the non-Russian republics combined, but after the war this difference was not very large, and it has been decreasing.

An average money wage does not tell much, of course. It conceals rather than reveals the true significance of income differentiation. In this connection, data in Tables XV and XVI are obviously more interesting. From Table XV it can be seen that the per capita income tax collections in the non-Russian republics are 30.7 per cent smaller than in Russia, whereas sales tax collections are only 26.5 per cent smaller. This indicates not only a considerable difference between the levels of total income in the R.S.F.S.R. and the non-Russian republics, but also that income distribution is more differentiated in the R.S.F.S.R. than in the non-Russian republics. A larger proportion of income tax revenue comes from the upper income groups, while the incidence of the sales taxes falls predominantly on the lower income groups. The data in Table XV seem to suggest that more rich people live in the R.S.F.S.R., while the poor predominate in the non-Russian

TABLE XIV
AVERAGE MONTHLY WAGES OF WORKERS AND EMPLOYEES IN THE SOVIET REPUBLICS, 1940–65
(*in current, local rubles*)

Republics	1940	1950	1955	1960	1965
R.S.F.S.R.	35.1	65.9	73.6	82.5	98.0
Non-Russian republics combined	29.0	60.0	67.6	75.9	91.7
As per cent of R.S.F.S.R.	*82.6*	*91.0*	*91.8*	*92.0*	*93.6*

SOURCES: *Nar. khoz. SSSR v 1965 g.*, pp. 557, 567; Central Statistical Administration, *Narodnoe khozyaystvo RSFSR v 1965 godu* (Moscow, 1966), pp. 394, 397.

TABLE XV

PER CAPITA INCOME AND SALES TAXES COLLECTED FROM THE POPULATION OF THE SOVIET REPUBLICS, 1960–65 ANNUAL AVERAGE

(in current, local rubles)

	INCOME TAX		TURNOVER TAX	
Republics	Rubles	Index	Rubles	Index
R.S.F.S.R.	19	100.0	192	100.0
Ukraine	14	77.9	134	70.1
Belorussia	10	53.0	141	73.5
Uzbekistan	9	48.4	110	57.6
Kazakhstan	15	80.2	141	73.4
Georgia	12	63.4	113	59.2
Azerbaidzhan	9	48.4	113	59.2
Lithuania	13	71.0	163	85.0
Moldavia	7	39.4	122	63.8
Latvia	20	105.1	250	130.6
Kirghizia	13	71.0	118	61.7
Tadjikistan	12	63.4	113	59.2
Armenia	12	63.4	127	66.4
Turkmenia	12	63.4	124	64.7
Estonia	23	117.7	209	109.0
Average for non-Russian republics	13	69.3	141	73.5

SOURCES: U.S.S.R. Ministry of Finance, Budget Administration, *Gosudarstvenniy byudzhet SSSR i byudzhety soyuznykh respublik: Statisticheskiy sbornik* (Moscow, 1962), p. 15; *Gosudarstvenniy byudzhet SSSR i byudzhety soyuznykh respublik* (Moscow, 1966), p. 18; *Nar. khoz. SSSR v 1964 g.*, p. 9.

republics. Strikingly, this finding is also corroborated by Table XVI; bank savings per capita of the population in the Russian republic are almost twice as large as in all the non-Russian republics combined.

In Table XVII an attempt has been made to construct something resembling a measure of the personal disposable income before taxes. No doubt, it is an incomplete measure, because it consists only of the sum total of (a) consumption expenditures in the government and cooperative retail outlets and public catering (retail sales in current prices); (b) net savings in banks; (c) net government bonds purchased; and (d) direct tax collections. Expenditures in collective farm markets, payments for communal services, social security taxes, savings hidden under mattresses and in stockings, etc., could not be accounted for to arrive at the true total disposable income. However, the totals comprising the data in Table XVII are proportionately

TABLE XVI
PER CAPITA SAVINGS IN BANKS OF THE SOVIET REPUBLICS, 1940, 1958, AND 1964
(*in current, local rubles*)

Republics	1940	1958	1964
R.S.F.S.R.	4.91	49.91	82.75
Ukraine	2.32	37.38	63.84
Belorussia	1.92	24.72	48.30
Uzbekistan	2.66	20.19	27.24
Kazakhstan	2.37	27.71	44.99
Georgia	3.46	38.87	60.50
Azerbaidzhan	2.47	23.79	33.82
Lithuania	. . .	21.98	44.08
Moldavia	. . .	17.46	27.48
Latvia	. . .	36.88	69.89
Kirghizia	2.29	26.04	38.74
Tadjikistan	3.40	20.62	29.98
Armenia	2.34	30.64	60.60
Turkmenia	3.68	24.27	34.82
Estonia	. . .	40.68	87.98
Average for non-Russian republics	2.69	27.94	48.01
As per cent of R.S.F.S.R.	*54.8*	*56.0*	*58.0*

SOURCES: *Nar. khoz. SSSR v 1963 g.*, p. 9; *Nar. khoz. SSSR v 1964 g.*, p. 597.

probably not very much different from the true totals, and therefore can be taken as representative.

The inferences from Table XVII are significant and interesting. The data are the most complete available on per capita incomes in the Soviet republics. The table shows, of course, that, on the average, per capita incomes in the R.S.F.S.R. are about one-fourth larger than in the non-Russian republics combined. This gap seems to remain constant over time. However, if we exclude the three Baltic republics and Moldavia and thus compare Russia with the non-Russian republics approximately within the old, pre-1939 frontiers of the U.S.S.R., the results are striking: while in 1940, Russia's per capita income was 26.5 per cent higher than in ten old non-Russian republics combined, in 1958, it was 31.2 per cent higher, and by 1964, this gap increased to 34.1 per cent!

To make this finding more reliable, retail price changes in different republics since 1940 have been taken into consideration.[112] The thus deflated, "real" personal disposable income per capita in

TABLE XVII

PER CAPITA PERSONAL DISPOSABLE INCOME (BEFORE TAXES) IN THE SOVIET REPUBLICS, 1940, 1958, AND 1964

(*in current, local rubles*)

Republics	1940 Rubles	1940 Index	1958 Rubles	1958 Index	1964 Rubles	1964 Index
R.S.F.S.R.	121	100.0	449	100.0	589	100.0
Ukraine	90	74.4	341	75.9	468	79.4
Belorussia	71	58.7	273	60.8	397	67.4
Uzbekistan	91	75.2	291	64.8	341	57.9
Kazakhstan	77	63.6	364	81.1	466	79.1
Georgia	105	86.8	333	74.2	404	68.6
Azerbaidzhan	102	84.3	277	61.7	326	55.3
Lithuania	...	...	307	68.4	459	77.9
Moldavia	...	...	237	52.8	328	55.7
Latvia	...	...	511	113.8	682	115.8
Kirghizia	72	59.5	288	64.1	367	62.3
Tadjikistan	79	65.3	275	61.2	326	55.3
Armenia	94	77.7	305	67.9	408	69.3
Turkmenia	113	93.4	339	75.5	381	64.7
Estonia	...	...	530	118.0	734	124.6
Average for non-Russian republics	89	73.5	333	74.2	434	73.7
Average for non-Russian republics, excluding Baltic republics and Moldavia	89	73.5	309	68.8	388	65.9

SOURCES: Central Statistical Administration, *Sovetskaya torgovlya: Statisticheskiy sbornik* (Moscow, 1964), pp. 301–15; *Nar. khoz. SSSR v 1964 g.*, pp. 9, 579, 627; *Gosudarstvenniy byudzhet SSSR i byudzhety soyuznykh respublik* (1966), p. 18.

1964 (in 1940 prices) was 421 rubles in Russia and 287 rubles in the ten non-Russian republics. The gap was still 31.8 per cent in 1964, as compared to only 26.5 per cent in 1940.

Can such an interregional income gap be called significant? The answer is yes, especially because in this case different nationalities inhabit different regions. For even in the ethnically more homogenous societies such gaps happen to be smaller. In Great Britain, for example, in 1963, the proportion of the gap between the lowest regional income per capita (Northern Ireland) and the highest (London and southeast) was only 1:1.35.[113] In the United States, in 1965, the same range between the minimum (Mississippi) and the maximum

(Connecticut) was 1:2.16.[114] In the Soviet Union, however, in 1964, it was 1:2.25 (between Azerbaidzhan and Estonia), or 1:1.80 (between Azerbaidzhan and Russia). Interregional income differentials in such countries as Canada, Switzerland, Sweden, the Netherlands, and West Germany are also smaller than in the U.S.S.R.[115]

The data in Tables XVIII and XIX showing regional per capita retail sales also partially corroborate the previous findings on income inequalities between the Russian and the non-Russian republics. Since these data are in local prices, however, they are not completely comparable. About one-half of all consumer goods in the U.S.S.R. have their prices differentiated according to three territorial belts. The first belt includes the Ukraine, Moldavia, the Baltic republics, Belorussia, Kazakhstan, the republics of Central Asia, and the southern parts of the R.S.F.S.R. The second belt consists of the center and

TABLE XVIII
PER CAPITA RETAIL SALES OF STATE AND COOPERATIVE STORES IN THE SOVIET REPUBLICS, 1963[a]
(R.S.F.S.R. = 100)

	IN URBAN AREAS			IN RURAL AREAS		
Republics	All Types of Goods	Food Items	Non-food Items	All Types of Goods	Food Items	Non-food Items
R.S.F.S.R.	100.0	100.0	100.0	100.0	100.0	100.0
Ukraine	91.2	84.3	102.1	66.9	53.7	84.8
Belorussia	103.1	96.3	113.7	55.4	53.0	58.6
Uzbekistan	80.2	72.6	92.1	66.1	61.2	72.7
Kazakhstan	81.2	76.9	88.0	114.2	103.0	129.3
Georgia	90.6	78.2	109.9	48.5	39.5	60.6
Azerbaidzhan	73.7	68.3	82.1	32.6	30.6	35.3
Lithuania	115.9	103.4	135.3	45.5	44.8	46.5
Moldavia	111.2	89.4	145.2	52.4	38.8	70.7
Latvia	128.8	116.7	147.7	88.4	91.0	84.8
Kirghizia	75.8	69.1	86.3	80.7	74.6	88.9
Tadjikistan	77.9	67.8	93.8	57.9	51.5	66.7
Armenia	75.7	69.1	85.9	56.6	50.0	65.6
Turkmenia	77.6	74.5	82.6	66.9	61.9	73.7
Estonia	128.4	118.6	143.6	106.0	114.2	94.9
Average for non-Russian republics	93.7	84.7	107.7	67.0	62.0	73.8

SOURCE: *Sovetskaya torgovlya* (1964), p. 49.
[a] Data calculated on the basis of local prices.

northwestern regions of the R.S.F.S.R., the Urals, and the Trans-Caucasian republics. The rest—Siberia and the north—belong to the third price belt. In the second belt prices are 10 per cent higher than in the first, and in the third belt they are 20 per cent higher than in the first.[116] In addition, in 1963, all prices in the rural areas of the U.S.S.R. were 7 per cent higher than in the urban areas. The remaining prices of about half of all consumer goods are fixed locally—by the governments of the Union and autonomous republics, provincial and city soviets, etc. Interregional differences among these prices are somewhat larger than the differences among the three belts of the centralized prices, but which way these differences tend is not known.[117] All this implies that higher money incomes in the R.S.F.S.R. may be offset, in part, by a somewhat higher cost of living, although by how much higher and whether it is in fact so is not known.[118] One Soviet source says that the difference in the cost of living between the "south" and the "far north" amounts to 70–80 per cent, but this is probably the most extreme range.[119] That higher costs of living do not completely offset the Russian republic's income preferentials is clearly borne out by data in Table XVI.

TABLE XIX
PER CAPITA RETAIL SALES OF STATE AND COOPERATIVE STORES IN THE MAJOR CITIES OF THE SOVIET REPUBLICS, 1955
(*in current, local rubles*)

R.S.F.S.R.	Rubles	Non-Russian Republics	Rubles
Moscow	9,304	Kiev (Ukraine)	5,699
Leningrad	7,001	Minsk (Belorussia)	5,510
Gorky	4,273	Tashkent (Uzbekistan)	3,951
Kuibyshev	3,852	Alma-Ata (Kazakhstan)	5,307
Saratov	4,286	Tbilisi (Georgia)	4,587
Stalingrad	4,104	Baku (Azerbaidzhan)	6,002
Rostov-on-Don	5,110	Vilnius (Lithuania)	5,260
Molotov	4,886	Kishinev (Moldavia)	4,880
Sverdlovsk	5,171	Riga (Latvia)	6,914
Chelyabinsk	4,310	Frunze (Kirghizia)	4,435
Omsk	3,864	Stalinabad (Tadjikistan)	4,155
Novosibirsk	4,226	Erevan (Armenia)	3,527
Krasnoyarsk	4,580	Ashkhabad (Turkmenia)	6,140
		Tallin (Estonia)	7,870
Average for Russian cities	6,632	Average for non-Russian cities	4,968

SOURCES: *Sovetskaya torgovlya* (Moscow, 1956), pp. 194–200; *Narodnoe khozyaystvo SSSR* (1956), pp. 24–25.

Furthermore, Soviet authors use per capita retail sales data for the same purposes as we have done here, and even insist that they are a "decisive index that characterizes the level of people's consumption."[120] While not sharing the "decisive" aspect of this statement, we may nevertheless observe that the data in Tables XVIII and XIX probably reflect not only the unknown territorial price differentials but also actual physical per capita purchases as well as supplies. Especially noteworthy is the fact recorded in Table XVIII that the non-Russian rural areas fared very badly compared to Russia and to Kazakhstan. In part, of course, this is because the Russian countryside is short of food, and Russian peasants must purchase food. But then it also means that the Russian countryside is much more moneyed than the countryside in the non-Russian areas, which fact is also reflected in the comparative purchases of nonfood items. Table XIX, on the other hand, strikingly reflects the differentiated supply of cities with consumer goods. It is well known, of course, that different cities in the U.S.S.R. are assigned different priorities in their supply with various goods. Moscow and Leningrad have always headed the list, as did other industrial centers—most of which happen to be located in central Russia. The above-mentioned Soviet study claims, however, that the differences in the per capita retail sales among different cities have decreased lately.[121]

Table XX corroborates the data in Tables XVIII and XIX in physical terms. In it we have the distribution of the so-called marketable

TABLE XX
ALLOCATION OF SELECTED DURABLE CONSUMER GOODS AMONG THE SOVIET REPUBLICS, 1963

Consumer Goods	Percentage in R.S.F.S.R.	Percentage in Non-Russian Republics
Vacuum cleaners	65.06	34.94
Cameras	64.06	35.94
Watches	61.41	38.59
Television sets	61.08	38.92
Furniture	60.23	39.77
Bicycles	58.33	41.67
Washing machines	58.28	41.72
Radios	56.31	43.69
Refrigerators	55.65	44.35

SOURCES: *Sovetskaya torgovlya* (1964), pp. 378–83; *Nar. khoz. SSSR v 1962 g.*, p. 9.

fund (*rynochny fond*) of consumer goods that are allocated among different regions by the central planning authorities via the so-called material balances in kind. The fact that the R.S.F.S.R. gets a disproportionately larger share of these goods in comparison to its population (55.19 per cent of the U.S.S.R.'s people live in the R.S.F.S.R., and 44.81 per cent in the non-Russian republics) clearly indicates that its population possesses a disproportionately large purchasing power to buy these expensive goods.

Of considerable interest is Table XXI. It shows that in the non-Russian republics 28.5 per cent less of new urban housing per capita was built at government expense than in the R.S.F.S.R., while the non-Russians built 23.1 per cent more on credit and at private expense than did the Russians. What does this strange difference imply? Certainly not that the non-Russians were richer and could provide housing for themselves at their own expense. Does this, then, mean

TABLE XXI

PER CAPITA OCCUPANCY OF NEW URBAN HOUSING UNITS IN THE SOVIET REPUBLICS, TOTAL FOR 1951–60

	BUILT AT GOVERNMENT EXPENSE		BUILT ON CREDIT AND AT PRIVATE EXPENSE	
Republics	Square Meters	Index	Square Meters	Index
R.S.F.S.R.	351	100.0	121	100.0
Ukraine	230	65.5	141	116.5
Belorussia	241	68.7	165	136.4
Uzbekistan	174	49.6	185	152.9
Kazakhstan	417	118.8	208	171.9
Georgia	188	53.6	107	88.4
Azerbaidzhan	192	54.7	87	71.9
Lithuania	205	58.4	88	72.7
Moldavia	157	44.7	138	114.0
Latvia	259	73.8	73	60.3
Kirghizia	172	49.0	225	185.9
Tadjikistan	185	52.7	99	81.8
Armenia	200	56.9	120	99.2
Turkmenia	221	63.0	114	94.2
Estonia	228	64.9	62	51.2
Average for non-Russian republics	251	71.5	149	123.1

SOURCES: *Kapital'noe stroitel'stvo v SSSR,* pp. 196–97; *Nar. khoz. SSSR v 1960 g.,* p. 10.

that the Soviet Government favored the R.S.F.S.R. with housing at the expense of all Soviet taxpayers? If so, this would be a case of very gross discrimination, indeed.[122]

Differences in the rural living standards are partially revealed in Table XXII. The table is reproduced merely for the sake of observation; any meaningful inferences from it are rather difficult to obtain. It is not clear, for example, why the Ukraine fares so badly in livestock per household compared to all other republics but Moldavia. Differences in tax rates are explained in part by the intensity of cultivation and the profitability of crops: irrigated lands in Central Asia and citrus crops in the Caucasus. Why the Baltic republics seem to have tax privileges is not clear.

Last but not least important for our topic are the comparative cultural living standards from the economic point of view. The financing of cultural activities is highly centralized in the U.S.S.R. Since the republics do not possess the right to tax their population or

TABLE XXII

PRIVATE HOUSEHOLD ECONOMY OF THE COLLECTIVE AND STATE FARMERS IN THE SOVIET REPUBLICS, 1959–60 AVERAGE

Republics	Livestock per Household (= *cows*[a])	Land Plot per Household (*in hectares*)	Average Tax per 0.01 Hectares (*in rubles*)
R.S.F.S.R.	1.52	0.29	8.50
Ukraine	0.89	0.36	7.50
Belorussia	1.53	0.37	5.00
Uzbekistan	1.33	0.15	16.50
Kazakhstan	2.00	0.16	8.00
Georgia	1.36	0.40	13.00
Azerbaidzhan	1.42	0.15	12.00
Lithuania	1.69	0.52	3.00
Moldavia	0.43	0.29	6.00
Latvia	1.87	0.49	4.00
Kirghizia	1.37	0.22	9.00
Tadjikistan	1.27	0.10	16.50
Armenia	1.16	0.13	13.00
Turkmenia	1.59	0.17	15.50
Estonia	1.35	0.54	4.00

SOURCES: Central Statistical Administration, *Sel'skoe khozyaystvo SSSR: Statisticheskiy sbornik* (Moscow, 1960), pp. 43, 49, 52, 124, 272–93; G. L. Mar'yakhin, *Ocherki istorii nalogov s naseleniya SSSR* (Moscow, 1964), p. 220.

[a] Pigs, sheep, and goats were translated into "cow equivalents" by the standard coefficients given in *Statisticheskiy slovar'* (Moscow, 1965), p. 275.

economies, they have no funds of their own with which to finance their cultures. It is the U.S.S.R. Ministry of Finance, for instance, that allocates to the republics lump sums for education, maintenance of theaters, museums, libraries, and various other social and cultural programs.[123] The U.S.S.R. Ministry of Higher and Special Education establishes for the republics specific quotas for the enrollment of student candidates for the particular professions, while the U.S.S.R. Gosplan allocates the graduates from the republics to various job placements throughout the U.S.S.R.[124] The centralization of financing and decision-making in cultural matters inevitably produces suspicions that some national cultures are being short-changed and gradually squeezed into oblivion, while the Russian culture is being subsidized at their expense. That some such suspicions are current even on the highest levels in the Soviet Union was testified to by Khrushchev, who said this at the Twentieth CPSU Congress in 1956:

TABLE XXIII

Per Capita Expenditures from the Republic Budgets on Social and Cultural Measures, 1940, 1956, and 1960

	1940		1956		1960	
Republics	Rubles	Index	Rubles	Index	Rubles	Index
R.S.F.S.R.	15.33	100.0	46.78	100.0	87.44	100.0
Ukraine	13.33	86.9	43.13	92.2	70.95	81.1
Belorussia	14.14	92.2	39.15	83.7	66.89	76.5
Uzbekistan	15.47	100.9	39.36	84.1	63.47	72.6
Kazakhstan	14.88	97.1	42.18	90.2	71.48	81.7
Georgia	22.05	143.8	50.85	108.7	82.66	94.5
Azerbaidzhan	20.68	134.9	47.26	101.0	73.17	83.7
Lithuania	...	...	43.03	92.0	71.89	82.2
Moldavia	4.32	28.2	36.66	78.4	57.16	65.4
Latvia	...	...	61.70	131.9	102.23	116.9
Kirghizia	15.46	100.8	44.00	94.0	70.13	80.2
Tadjikistan	19.93	130.0	46.33	99.0	68.09	77.9
Armenia	24.46	159.5	57.56	123.1	86.68	99.2
Turkmenia	25.16	164.1	49.78	106.4	75.50	86.3
Estonia	...	...	68.09	145.5	114.75	131.2
Average for non-Russian republics	13.66	89.1	43.87	93.8	71.65	81.9

Sources: *Gosudarstvenniy byudzhet SSSR i byudzhety soyuznykh respublik* (1962), p. 28; *Narodnoe khozyaystvo SSSR* (1956), p. 18; *Nar. khoz. SSSR v 1960 g.*, p. 8.

Let us take distribution of the budgetary funds among Union republics. By and large, the funds are distributed properly, although we should think seriously of enhancing the role and authority of the republics in these matters. Some comrades have complained that there is as yet no proper system of determining allocations for public education, health services, housing construction, and the building of cultural and service establishments, city improvements, etc. As a result, we sometimes have a wholly inexplicable gap between the appropriations for some of the republics. Can such a state of affairs be regarded as normal? Of course not, primarily because it violates the basis of fair relations: equality for all.[125]

In Tables XXIII, XXIV, and XXV we have reproduced some of the comparative data on this topic. The conclusions to be drawn are too obvious to require comment. "Wholly inexplicable gaps" among the Soviet republics do exist, and they in all probability represent "violations of fair relations" and of "equality for all." This is why further research along these lines is both worthwhile and necessary.

TABLE XXIV
PER CAPITA EXPENDITURES FROM THE REPUBLIC BUDGETS ON EDUCATION, 1960

	TOTAL		ON HIGHER EDUCATION ALONE	
Republics	Rubles	Index	Rubles	Index
R.S.F.S.R.	38.96	100.0	5.80	100.0
Ukraine	32.40	83.2	4.22	72.7
Belorussia	36.48	93.6	3.57	61.5
Uzbekistan	33.79	86.7	4.34	74.8
Kazakhstan	36.34	93.3	3.44	59.3
Georgia	43.30	111.1	6.33	109.1
Azerbaidzhan	37.10	95.2	4.16	71.7
Lithuania	41.57	106.7	5.50	94.8
Moldavia	30.30	77.8	2.73	47.1
Latvia	48.14	123.5	6.00	103.4
Kirghizia	38.90	99.8	4.22	72.7
Tadjikistan	41.33	106.1	4.38	75.5
Armenia	48.52	124.5	6.26	107.9
Turkmenia	39.81	102.2	4.93	85.0
Estonia	55.91	143.5	7.00	120.7
Average for non-Russian republics	35.58	90.8	4.30	74.1

SOURCE: *Gosudarstvenniy byudzhet SSSR i byudzhety soyuznykh respublik* (1962), pp. 29, 48; *Nar. khoz. SSSR v 1960 g.*, p. 8.

TABLE XXV

SELECTED CULTURAL ACTIVITIES IN THE SOVIET REPUBLICS, 1964
(*per 1,000 population*)
(R.S.F.S.R. = 100)

Republics	Children in School	Students in Higher Education	Radios Owned	Visits to the Movies	Books in Public Libraries	Books Published	Copies of Newspapers Read	Children in Summer Camps
R.S.F.S.R.	100	100	100	100	100	100	100	100
Ukraine	92	81	90	85	106	32	57	62
Belorussia	100	64	73	74	101	24	69	60
Uzbekistan	111	86	66	52	43	28	40	31
Kazakhstan	107	63	71	85	64	20	48	58
Georgia	95	95	63	48	86	38	56	35
Azerbaidzhan	114	74	63	44	86	35	40	35
Lithuania	84	82	62	61	107	59	86	42
Moldavia	114	57	71	57	82	35	51	28
Latvia	70	79	108	79	124	76	88	55
Kirghizia	109	64	57	56	70	25	44	57
Tadjikistan	100	61	49	48	52	25	44	29
Armenia	122	90	70	59	85	46	53	44
Turkmenia	112	56	56	66	60	26	50	29
Estonia	100	89	126	106	191	111	128	79
Average for non-Russian republics	102	74	73	66	90	42	61	46

SOURCE: *Nar. khoz. SSSR v 1964 g.*, pp. 74–75, 80–83, 674–75, 681–83, 708–9, 719, 721.

NOTES

1. Lenin's writings that are directly relevant to this topic are: *On the "Cultural-National" Autonomy* (November, 1913); his letter to S. G. Shaumian, dated December 6, 1913, but published in 1920; *Imperialism as the Highest Stage of Capitalism* (1916); *The Draft of the Program of the RCP(b)* (1919); *Report to and the Concluding Statement at the Eighth Congress of the RCP(b) on March 19, 1919; Speech at the Second All-Russian Congress of the Communist Organizations of the Oriental Peoples* (November, 1919); *The Initial Draft of the Theses on the National and Colonial Questions* (June, 1920); *Report by the Commission on the National and Colonial Questions on July 26th* (1920); *To the Communist Comrades of Azerbaidzhan, Georgia, Armenia, Daghestan, and the Mountaineer Republic* (April, 1921); and *On the Question of Nationalities, Or Concerning "Autonomization"* (end of December, 1922).
2. Selections from Marx and Engels on the subject have been recently published in several languages in Karl Marx and Friedrich Engels, *On the Colonial System of Imperialism* (Moscow, 1959). The newest independent but scholarly reinterpretation of the original Marxian views on the "question of nationalities" is to be found in a monographic study by Roman Rosdolsky, "Friedrich Engels und das Problem der 'Geschichtslosen' Völker," *Archiv für Sozialgeschichte* (Hanover), IV (1964).
3. See V. I. Lenin, "Zakon neravnomernosti ekonomicheskogo i politicheskogo razvitiya," in G. A. Kozlov and S. P. Pervushin (eds.), *Kratkiy ekonomicheskiy slovar'* (Moscow, 1958), p. 81.
4. See G. Safarov, *Natsional'niy vopros i proletariat* (Petrograd, 1922); G. Safarov, "Natsional'niy vopros," in Tsentral'niy komitet, RKP(b), *Za 5 let* (Moscow, 1922); M. Ravich-Cherkassky (ed.), *Marksizm i natsional'niy vopros* (2 vols.; Kharkov, 1922); I. P. Traynin, *SSSR i natsional'naya problema* (Moscow, 1924); M. Skrypnyk, *Statti i promovy* (3 vols.; Kharkov, 1931); M. Skrypnyk, "Zblyzhennya i zlyttya natsiy za doby sotsializmu," *Bil'shovyk Ukrayiny* (Kharkov), No. 8 (April 30, 1931); B. S. Borev (ed.), *Natsional'ne pytannya: Khrestomatiya* (Kharkov, 1931); and A. Khavin, *Sotsialisticheskaya industrializatsiya natsional'nykh respublik i oblastey* (Moscow, 1933). See, also, early articles in journals devoted to the nationalities question, such as *Zhizn' natsional'nostey*. Also of interest is A. E. Khodorov, "Lenin i natsional'niy vopros," *Noviy Vostok* (Moscow), No. 5 (1924).
5. Perhaps, a better understanding of the semantics of the Russian language would also help in interpreting Lenin's dialectic correctly. In Russian etymology and synonymity the words *"ravniy," "sravnivat'," "uravnyat',"* and *"ravenstvo"* (i.e., "equal," "to equal," "to equalize," "equality") mean and are used interchangeably as *"odinakoviy, sovershenno skhozhiy," "delat' ravnym, to-yest' odinakovym, takim zhe samym,"* and *"polnoe skhodstvo, tozhdestvo,"* which in Western languages all mean "identical," "to identify, to make the same," and "complete identity." Identity and equality are, of course, two different things in Western languages, whereas in Russian their meanings are basically the same. Hence, when the Russians speak of the "equality of nationalities," they do not necessarily mean making nationalities equal only before the law, or socially and economically; rather, they probably also understand this to mean "making them identical, not different from us, the same as we are," which implies

merger, assimilation, the same language, culture, etc. Similarly, the Russian term *"edinstvo"* (as in *"edinstvo natsional'nostey SSSR"*) does not mean simply a "unity of nationalities of the U.S.S.R." in the face of some danger, for example; its meaning is broader, viz., "complete sameness" (*"polnoe skhodstvo"*), of opinions, views, tastes, etc. Unity in diversity, unity and equality of *different* people or things are meanings that are not easily conveyed in Russian and require interpretation. For additional discussions of the Russian language in connection with Lenin's dialectics, see Vsevolod Holubnychy, "Der dialektische Materialismus Mao Tse-tungs im Vergleich mit den Klassikern des Marxismus-Leninismus," *Der Ostblock und die Entwicklungsländer* (Hanover), No. 8–9 (1962), p. 37, *et passim;* and Vsevolod Holubnychy, "Mao Tse-tung's Materialistic Dialectics," *The China Quarterly* (London) (July–September, 1964), p. 32, *et passim.* For general theory on the subject, see Benjamin L. Whorf, *Language, Thought, and Reality* (Cambridge, Mass., 1956).

6. *Kommunisticheskaya Partiya Sovetskogo Soyuza v rezolyutsiyakh i resheniyakh s"yezdov, konferentsiy i plenumov TsK* (7th ed.; Moscow, 1953), Part I, pp. 559, 713.
7. *Ibid.,* p. 560.
8. *Ibid.,* p. 714.
9. *Ibid.*
10. The Ukraine was the subject of the first separate resolution in this series, adopted by the Eighth Conference of the RCP(b) in December, 1919. See *ibid.,* p. 459.
11. *Ibid.,* pp. 559, 715–18.
12. *Ibid.,* p. 716.
13. *Ibid.,* p. 561.
14. *Ibid.,* pp. 562–63, 713, 715, 717–18.
15. V. I. Lenin, "A Note on the Plan of the Scientific and Technical Research," in his *Sochineniya* (4th ed.; Moscow, 1950), XXVII.
16. Friedrich Engels, *Anti-Dühring,* Part III, chap. iii: "Production."
17. See J. V. Stalin, *Sochineniya* (Moscow, 1947), V, 57–58.
18. Stalin's revision of Leninist theory and practice in the "question of nationalities" can be traced in his writings. See, especially, his *Report to the XVIIth Congress of the CPSU(b) on the Work of the Central Committee* (January, 1934); his letter to the Politburo members, dated July 19, 1934, but published seven years later, "On Engels' Article 'Foreign Policy of Russian Tsarism,'" *Bol'shevik* (Moscow), No. 9 (1941); his wartime speeches, *On the Great Patriotic War of the Soviet Union* (1946); and his *Marxism and the Questions of Linguistics* (1950).
19. V. M. Molotov, *Rech' na XX s"yezde KPSS* (Moscow, 1956), pp. 16–17.
20. See *Protokoll der Verhandlungen des VI. Parteitages des Sozialistischen Einheitspartei Deutschlands* (Berlin, 1963), I, 331–32.
21. N. S. Khrushchev, *Stroitel'stvo kommunizma v SSSR i razvitie sel'skogo khozyaystva* (Moscow, 1962), II, 297.
22. See Walter Kolarz, *Russia and Her Colonies* (New York, 1952); Georg von Rauch, *Russland: Staatliche Einheit und nationale Vielfalt* (Munich, 1953); Olaf K. Caroe, *Soviet Empire: The Turks of Central Asia and Stalinism* (New York, 1953); Robert Conquest, *The Soviet Deportation of Nationalities* (New York, 1960); Geoffry Wheeler, *Racial Problems in Soviet Muslim Asia* (2d ed.; New York, 1962); Hugh Seton-Watson, *The New Imperialism* (Chester Springs, Pa., 1962); U.S. Congress, Senate

Committee on the Judiciary, *The Soviet Empire* (Washington, D.C., 1958; rev. ed., 1965); M. Holdsworth, "Soviet Central Asia, 1917–1940: A Study in Colonial Policy," *Soviet Studies* (Oxford), January, 1952; Olaf K. Caroe, "Soviet Colonialism in Central Asia," *Foreign Affairs,* October, 1953; Geoffry Wheeler, "Colonialism and the U.S.S.R.," *The Political Quarterly* (London), July–September, 1958; Richard Pipes, "Soviet Moslems Today," *The New Leader,* December 29, 1958; "L'Empire colonial de l'Union soviétique," *Est & Ouest* (Paris), July 16–31, 1960; E. Mettler, "Soviet Colonialism in Asia," *Swiss Review of World Affairs* (Geneva), August, 1963; Hugh Seton-Watson, "Moscow's Imperialism," *Problems of Communism,* January–February, 1964; William O. Douglas, "Soviet Colonialism—Product of Terror," *Look,* December 13, 1955; Robert F. Kennedy, "The Soviet Brand of Colonialism," *The New York Times Magazine,* April 8, 1956; Adlai Stevenson's statement in the U.N. debate on colonialism, November, 1961, as quoted in *The Soviet Empire* (rev. ed.), p. 169; and "Moscow Berated on Own 'Colonies,'" *The New York Times,* November 17, 1961.

23. Soviet counter-criticism of Western critiques has also been very weak thus far. See, for example, G. D. Krikheli, *Protiv fal'sifikatsii natsional'noy politiki KPSS* (Moscow, 1964).
24. "Regional Economic Policy in the Soviet Union: The Case of Central Asia," *Economic Bulletin for Europe* (Geneva), November, 1957.
25. See, for example, "Theorie und Praxis der Sowjetkolonialismus," *Sowjetstudien* (Munich), December, 1961; B. Hayit, "Turkestan as an Example of Soviet Colonialism," *Studies on the Soviet Union* (Munich), No. 2 (1961); M. Tachmurat, "Colonization in Turkestan," *Problems of the Peoples of the U.S.S.R.* (Munich), No. 9 (1961); and A. Adamovich, "Soviet Internal Colonialism," *Studies on the Soviet Union,* No. 1 (1962).
26. See Konstantyn Kononenko, *Ukraine and Russia: A History of the Economic Relations Between Ukraine and Russia (1654–1917)* (Milwaukee, 1958); D. F. Solovey, "The Colonial Victimization of the Ukraine," *Problems of the Peoples of the U.S.S.R.,* No. 9 (1961); D. F. Solovey, *Ukrayina v systemi sovets'koho koloniyalizmu* (Munich, 1959); B. Vynar, *Ekonomichny koloniyalizm v Ukrayini* (Paris, 1958); D. Andrievsky, *Rosiys'ky koloniyalizm i sovets'ka imperiya* (Paris, 1958); M. Velychkivsky, *Sil's'ke hospodarstvo Ukrayiny i koloniyal'na polityka Rosiyi* (New York, 1957); and B. Vynar, "The Establishment of Soviet Economic Colonialism in Ukraine," *The Ukrainian Quarterly* (New York), XIII (Spring, 1957). See also *The American Economic Review,* March, 1960, p. 218.
27. Z. L. Melnyk, *Soviet Capital Formation: Ukraine, 1928/29–1932* (Munich, 1965). The initial version of this monograph was defended at Michigan State University in 1961 as a Ph.D. dissertation entitled *Ukrainian Capital and the Soviet Economy*. See also *The Slavonic and East European Review* (London), July, 1967, pp. 568–71.
28. See, among others, Oleg Hoeffding, in Abram Bergson (ed.), *Soviet Economic Growth: Conditions and Perspectives* (Evanston, Ill., 1953); Alfred Zauberman, *Economic Imperialism: The Lessons of Eastern Europe* (London, 1955); Nicholas Spulber, *The Economics of Communist Eastern Europe* (Cambridge, Mass., 1957); Frederic L. Pryor, *The Communist Foreign Trade System* (Cambridge, Mass., 1963); as well as the articles by Horst Mendershausen in *The Review of Economics and Statistics,*

May, 1959, and May, 1960; and in *Osteuropa-Wirtschaft,* June, 1962; Hiroshi Kato, "Soviet East European Trade Relations," *Keio Economic Studies* (Tokyo), No. 1 (1963); and Mah Feng-hsia, "The Terms of Sino-Soviet Trade," *The China Quarterly,* January, 1964. See also, for example, *O kontrarevolucionarnoj i klevetnickoj kampanji protiv socialisticke Jugoslavije* (2 vols.; Belgrade, 1949–50); *Seven Letters Exchanged Between the Central Committees of the Communist Party of China and the Communist Party of the Soviet Union* (Peking, 1964); and "Soviet Revisionism's Neo-Colonialist 'Aid,'" *Peking Review,* No. 40 (September 29, 1967), which concerns Mongolia.

29. Statement of the Soviet Government, in *Pravda,* October 31, 1956.
30. Soviet-Polish statement, in *Pravda,* November 19, 1956.
31. *Seven Letters . . . ,* p. 70.
32. This method has been used, e.g., by the Academy of Sciences of the Ukrainian S.S.R., Institute of Economics, in its *Natsional'ny dokhod Ukrayins'koyi RSR v period rozhornutoho budivnytstva komunizmu* (Kiev, 1963); see the review of this work in *The American Economic Review,* LIV, No. 5 (September, 1964). Another example, though with much less statistical data, is A. A. Abduganiev, U. N. Mirzakhodzhaiev, and V. A. Osminin, *Obshchestvenniy produkt i natsional'niy dokhod Uzbekskoy SSR* (Tashkent, 1960).
33. On this, see the purely theoretical analysis by L. A. Tarasov, "O sostavlenii balansa obshchestvennogo produkta v soyuznoy respublike," in U.S.S.R. Gosekonomsovet, Economic Scientific Research Institute, N. M. Osnobin (ed.), *Ocherki po sovremennoy sovetskoy i zarubezhnoy ekonomike* (Moscow, 1962), III; and also a predominantly methodological study based in part on statistics of the Belorussian S.S.R. by the R.S.F.S.R. Ministry of Higher and Special Education, Moscow Economic-Statistical Institute, *Balans obshchestvennogo produkta soyuznoy respubliki* (Moscow, 1962). The latter states that the Central Statistical Administrations of the Union republics have been computing such planned balances for each republic since 1957 (p. 3), and mentions that in the 1920's such balances were calculated in several Union and autonomous republics, and even in some provinces (*oblasts*) (p. 11). The study complains, however, that statistics on the fulfillment of the planned balances today are quite insufficient (pp. 65–66).
34. This method was used by Professor Z. L. Melnyk, *op. cit.* See also, for example, George F. Break, *Intergovernmental Fiscal Relations in the United States* (Washington, D.C.: The Brookings Institution, 1967); as well as Roland Parenteau, "Les problèmes du développement régional dans un Etat fédératif—L'expérience canadienne," *Revue d'Economie Politique* (Paris), No. 2 (1963). According to a recent Soviet source, such balances are being computed by the Soviet Union republics today; see R.S.F.S.R. Ministry of Higher and Special Education, The All-Union Financial-Economic Correspondence Institute, *Planirovanie narodnogo khozyaystva SSSR* (Moscow, 1965), p. 531. Like most other data of this kind, however, the statistics have not been made public. (The following, presumably important, monograph was published after work on this paper was completed: M. A. Binder, *Gosudarstvenno-pravovye problemy vzaimopomoshchi sovetskikh narodov* [Alma-Ata, 1967]. Part III, chap. ii, discusses the interrepublic flow of budgetary funds, although its economic analysis does not seem to be on a sufficiently adequate level.)

35. On this method see, for example, J. Thomas Romans, *Capital Exports and Growth among U.S. Regions* (Middletown, Conn., 1965); and also a general discussion in P. Bauchet, "La Comptabilité économique régionale et son usage," *Economie Appliquée* (Paris), No. 1 (1961).
36. *Metodika opredeleniya ekonomicheskoy effektivnosti razmeshcheniya promyshlennosti pri planirovanii i proektirovanii novogo stroitel'stva* (Moscow, 1966), pp. 7–8. On how such balances are calculated on the all-Union and republic levels, see G. I. Grebtsov and P. P. Karpov (eds.), *Material'nye balansy v narodno-khozyaystvennom plane* (Moscow, 1960), pp. 15–25.
37. It has been reported that such matrixes are being computed for the Union republics in the current Five-Year Plan. See *Voprosy ekonomiki,* No. 2 (1967), p. 150.
38. Historically, Marx seems to have been the first to identify the imbalance in the balance-of-payments as a measure and an index of international economic exploitation. See *Capital,* Vol. III, chap. xxxv, sec. 2, "England's Balance of Trade." It is easy to imagine exploitation in terms of labor-hours calculus; it is what Marx called the "inequitable exchange." In more realistic and empirical terms, however, the calculus is much more difficult. For high-caliber modern Western theories on this subject, see, for example, Harry G. Johnson, "A Theoretical Model of Economic Nationalism in New and Developing States," *Political Science Quarterly,* LXXX (1965), 169–85; Anne O. Krueger, "The Economics of Discrimination," *The Journal of Political Economy,* LXXI (1963), 481–86; A. Breton, "The Economics of Nationalism," *The Journal of Political Economy,* LXXII (1964), 376–86; and Gary S. Becker, *The Economics of Discrimination* (Chicago, 1957).
39. For a very lucid further analysis, see S. Andrew Oźga, *The Rate of Exchange and the Terms of Trade* (Chicago, 1967), chaps. iii, iv, and vii. See also Charles P. Kindleberger, *Balance-of-Payments Deficits and the International Market Liquidity* (Princeton, N.J., 1965).
40. *Balans obshchestvennogo produkta soyuznoy respubliki,* p. 65.
41. This rule is not without exceptions, however. In some cases, losses are nobody's gains; they are simply unaccounted for. This is true, for example, in the case of a monopsonistic market situation, where the factors of production are underpaid; i.e., the sellers lose part of their income completely and absolutely, while the monopsonist's gain is at best only relative (comparative). This relates to the monopsonistically exploited agricultural regions and colonies, among others. Marx had this in mind when he noted that the "majority of agricultural nations are compelled to sell their produce *below* value." (*Teorii pribavochnoy stoimosti* [Moscow, 1957], Part II, p. 480 [italics in original].) See also, *ibid.,* p. 7, as well as H. W. Singer, "The Distribution of Gains between Investing and Borrowing Countries," *The American Economic Review,* XL (May, 1950).
42. It can be argued that, in the case of an "open" world economy, "discrimination" and/or "colonialism" would turn themselves into the constrained time-horizon functions of pure competition, in spite of the fact that at first glance this sounds like a paradox. For example, world resources are the subject of competition between the interest in the conquest of space and in the increased production of food for the overpopulated areas, etc.
43. See A. C. Pigou, *The Economics of Welfare* (4th ed.; London, 1950), pp. 647–55, for a purely theoretical discussion of which the above is an

analogue. See also A. P. Lerner, *The Economics of Control* (New York, 1946), chaps. xxvi–xxvii, for some basic ideas. It may be worth noting that this marginalist dialectic was not entirely unknown to Karl Marx either. See, for example, his statement that whenever capital resources are being transferred to an underdeveloped industry or to a region with "low organic capital structure," the result "to be true, would lower the specific surplus profit obtainable in the latter, but would also raise the over-all level of profit" in all the industries combined or in the country as a whole. (*Teorii pribavochnoy stoimosti,* Part II, p. 438 *et supra.*)

44. A. G. Aganbegyan, "Ekonomiko-matematicheskoe modelirovanie i reshenie otraslevykh zadach," in U.S.S.R. Academy of Sciences and the U.S.S.R. Gosplan, *Primenenie matematiki pri razmeshchenii proizvoditel'nykh sil* (Moscow, 1964), p. 23.
45. U.S.S.R. Gosstroy, Scientific Research Institute of the Economics of Construction, *Metodicheskie ukazaniya po opredeleniyu optimal'nykh skhem perevozok, snabzheniya i razmeshcheniya predpriyatiy s pomoshch'yu lineynogo programmirovaniya* (Moscow, 1964), p. 84 and *passim.*
46. U.S.S.R. Academy of Sciences, *Metodika opredeleniya ekonomicheskoy effektivnosti razmeshcheniya promyshlennosti pri planirovanii i proektirovanii novogo stroitel'stva* (Moscow, 1966), p. 14. A few hints about the background of the formulation of this methodology can be found in A. A. Mints, "Obsuzhdenie proekta metodiki opredeleniya ekonomicheskoy effektivnosti razmeshcheniya promyshlennosti," *Izvestiya Akademii Nauk SSSR: Seriya Geograficheskaya,* No. 5 (1965).
47. *Metodicheskie ukazaniya po opredeleniyu optimal'nykh skhem . . . ,* pp. 83 ff.
48. *Metodika opredeleniya ekonomicheskoy effektivnosti razmeshcheniya promyshlennosti . . . ,* pp. 8, 14–15.
49. Such a well-known Russian scholar in the field as V. V. Kossov (Central Economic Mathematical Institute of the U.S.S.R. Academy of Sciences) also advocates a regional differentiation of the marginal efficiency coefficients, without explaining his reasons. See his "Metody optimal'nykh raschetov na osnove territorial'nykh modeley," in A. N. Efimov (ed.), *Problemy optimal'nogo planirovaniya* (Moscow, 1966), p. 226. (This is a symposium of Soviet-bloc economists on the problems of optimization, held in East Berlin in April, 1965.)
50. The earliest classic in this field seems to be Frank L. Hitchcock, "The Distribution of a Product from Several Sources to Numerous Localities," *The Journal of Mathematics and Physics,* XX (1941), 224 ff. A useful collection of models and an extensive, pertinent bibliography can be found in S. Vajda, *Readings in Mathematical Programming* (New York, 1962). The Soviet work in the field is described in U.S.S.R. Academy of Sciences and the U.S.S.R. Gosplan, Laboratory of Mathematical Methods of the Research Council on Productive Forces, *Primenenie matematiki pri razmeshchenii proizvoditel'nykh sil* (Moscow, 1964). A significant new contribution in this field is L. Johansen, "Regionaløkonomiske problemer belyst ved lineaer programmeringsteori," *Sosialøkonomen* (Oslo), No. 2 (1965). (I am obliged to Mrs. Sigrid Sereda for helping me read Johansen's paper.) The application of linear programming models to the optimization of foreign trade has been successfully developed by an East German economist, G. Otto, "Optimierung der territorialen Struktur des Aussenhandels," *Der Aussenhandel* (Berlin), No. 3 (1965). These models can

be easily adapted to the optimization of the regional balance of payments. A current, world-wide bibliography can be found in All-Union Institute of Scientific and Technical Information, *Referativniy sbornik: Ekonomika promyshlennosti,* Series D: *Primenenie matematicheskikh metodov v ekonomicheskikh issledovaniyakh i planirovanii* (Moscow). Specialized, but nonetheless interesting, is V. S. Mikheyeva, *Matematicheskie metody v planirovanii razmeshcheniya sel'sko-khozyaystvennogo proizvodstva* (Moscow, 1966).

51. See I. V. Ivliev and V. P. Potapov (eds.), *Transportnye tarify* (Moscow, 1960); and A. V. Kreynin (ed.), *Passazhirskie tarify na transporte SSSR* (Moscow, 1966). The historical background of this policy is given in Holland Hunter, *Soviet Transportation Policy* (Cambridge, Mass., 1957). See also Sh. Ya. Turetsky, *Ocherki planovogo tsenoobrazovaniya v SSSR* (Moscow, 1959), pp. 341 ff.
52. See, for example, *Zheleznodorozhniy transport SSSR v dokumentakh Kommunisticheskoy Partii i Sovetskogo Pravitel'stva* (Moscow, 1957), pp. 319–20. See also Hunter, *op. cit.,* p. 212 and *passim;* Franklyn D. Holzman, "Soviet Ural-Kuznetsk Combine," *The Quarterly Journal of Economics,* LXXI (August, 1957), 384–85; and H. Chambre, *L'Aménagement du territoire en U.R.S.S.: Introduction à l'étude des régions économiques soviétiques* (Paris, 1959), pp. 45–50, 142–48.
53. See S. Kobe, "Elasticity of Derived Demand for Transportation Services," *Waseda Economic Papers* (Tokyo), No. 3 (1959), pp. 58–59.
54. A. M. Shul'ga, "Voprosy opredeleniya sebestoimosti zheleznodorozhnykh perevozok po napravleniyam," *Voprosy ekonomiki zheleznodorozhnogo transporta,* Issue No. 215 (1966), p. 98. (A publication of the Moscow Institute of Railroad Engineers.)
55. See Abram Bergson, *Essays in Normative Economics* (Cambridge, Mass., 1966), pp. 149–53.
56. I am greatly indebted to Dr. D. Lazdinš for her discussion of this point with me and for mathematical clarification of the conditions necessary for the relationships (2) and (3) below to hold true. See also a discussion of these problems in Vsevolod Holubnychy, "Le ralentissement des rythmes d'accroissement de l'économie soviétique," *Problèmes soviétiques* (Munich), No. 2 (1959), pp. 64–65; and Vsevolod Holubnychy, "Problemy 'osnovnoy ekonomicheskoy zadachi' SSSR (Dognat' i peregnat' Ameriku)," *Uchenye Zapiski Instituta po Izucheniyu SSSR* (Munich), I, No. 1 (1963), 71–73.
57. Obviously, if both levels grow by identical rates, they will never meet, although the absolute gap between them may narrow for some time and then widen again in a cyclical pattern. If the lower level's rate of growth is smaller than that of the higher level, the levels will start diverging immediately and the gap between them will grow absolutely. In all three cases the rates of growth are assumed to be constant. If the rates vary with time, the trends in the two levels will depend on the shape of the rates' functions.
58. The remaining part of this paper was read on March 4, 1967, at a meeting of the Economics and Law Section of the Ukrainian Academy of Arts and Sciences in New York City, Professor B. M. Martos presiding. The author has benefited from the criticism and comments of those present.
59. The impact of the location of industries in the U.S.S.R. upon the relations among its nationalities has been treated in relatively few books and

papers, and then only in relation to individual, separate republics and without interrepublic or interregional comparisons. See U.S.S.R. Academy of Sciences, *Bibliografiya po voprosam razmeshcheniya i rayonirovaniya promyshlennosti SSSR, 1901–1957* (Moscow, 1960), pp. 27, 166–315; U.S.S.R. Academy of Sciences, *Bibliografiya po voprosam razmeshcheniya i rayonirovaniya promyshlennosti SSSR, 1958–1964* (Moscow, 1966), pp. 15, 114–220; and U.S.S.R. Academy of Sciences, V. P. Volgin Fundamental Library of Social Sciences, *Kapitalovlozheniya v narodnoe khozyaystvo SSSR: Osnovnye fondy promyshlennosti i ikh ispol'zovanie—Ukazatel' sovetskoy literatury 1945–1964* (Moscow, 1966), pp. 9, 13–15, 18, 60–64, 104–9. The only significant exceptions are a book by Yu. F. Vorob'yov, *Vyravnivanie urovney ekonomicheskogo razvitiya soyuznykh respublik* (Moscow, 1965), 215 pp.; and his articles, "Vyravnivanie urovney promyshlennogo razvitiya natsional'nykh respublik Sovetskogo Soyuza v period stroitel'stva sotsializma," *Istoriya SSSR,* No. 4 (1962), and "Fakty i fal'sifikatory," *Ekonomicheskaya gazeta,* No. 51 (December, 1966). Vorob'yov's method, however, is strange, to say the least. While explicitly discussing the economic aspects of the problem of nationalities, he compares the levels of development and growth over time of the non-Russian republics either among themselves or with the U.S.S.R. average, consistently avoiding any comparison with the R.S.F.S.R., as if the latter was not a part of the Union. Why such a strange method was chosen is perhaps suggested by the findings of this paper. Somewhat more objective is a similar paper by V. A. Shpilyuk, "Vyravnivanie urovnya promyshlennogo razvitiya soyuznykh respublik posle obrazovaniya SSSR," in Supreme Party School of the Central Committee of the CPSU, *Torzhestvo leninskoy natsional'noy politiki* (Moscow, 1963), pp. 311–36. He makes a few timid and selective comparisons of the achievements of the non-Russian republics with the R.S.F.S.R., but his comparisons are conspicuously incomplete and he uses for comparison the output of large-scale industries only, which makes the picture of some non-Russian republics look better than it is in reality. A method identical to that of Vorob'yov (i.e., excluding the R.S.F.S.R. from the interrepublic comparison) but limited historically to the pre–World War II period alone is also used in the otherwise apparently respectable volume of the U.S.S.R. Academy of Sciences, Institute of Economics, *Sotsialisticheskoe narodnoe khozyaystvo SSSR v 1933–1940 gg.* (Moscow, 1963), pp. 314–51. This book tries to impress upon the reader the view that the economic aspect of the problem of nationalities had already been resolved before the war. This opinion is *not* shared by an eminent Soviet student of pre-war economic history, who compared the non-Russian republics with the R.S.F.S.R.; viz., Peter I. Lyashchenko, *Istoriya narodnogo khozyaystva SSSR* (Moscow, 1956), III, 504. See also U.S.S.R. Academy of Sciences, Institute of Economics, *Ekonomika sotsialisticheskoy promyshlennosti,* ed. E. L. Granovsky and B. L. Markus (Moscow, 1940), pp. 296–97, which also did not claim that the problem had been solved.

60. The Soviet authors admit that even the methods of interregional comparisons of the levels of development have not yet been agreed upon in the U.S.S.R., not to speak of actual indicators of such levels. See, for example, Sh. L. Rozenfel'd, "O metodologii sopostavleniya urovney razvitiya ekonomicheskikh rayonov," *Planovoe khozyaystvo,* No. 9 (1966), p. 71; also his *Opredelenie urovney razvitiya promyshlennosti v rayonakh* (Moscow, 1963). In addition, see "Diskussiya o regional'nykh osobennostyakh eko-

nomicheskogo razvitiya," *Voprosy ekonomiki,* No. 2 (1967), pp. 149–50. On the other hand, compare the high caliber of the methodological work in this field in Yugoslavia, for example, B. Ivanović, "Classification of Underdeveloped Areas According to Level of Economic Development," *Mathematical Studies in Economics and Statistics in the USSR and Eastern Europe* (New York), I, No. 3 (Spring, 1965).

61. Ya. Feigin, "Problemy razdeleniya truda v promyshlennosti mezhdu respublikami i ekonomicheskimi rayonami," *Voprosy ekonomiki,* No. 8 (1962), p. 34.
62. Vorob'yov, *Vyravnivanie urovney ekonomicheskogo razvitiya soyuznykh respublik,* p. 193.
63. However, the rough estimates of the per capita personal disposable income provided in Table XVII suggest that the actual difference is probably close, and certainly not larger than that mentioned by Feigin and Vorob'yov.
64. Cf. U.S. Department of Commerce, Bureau of the Census, *Statistical Abstract of the United States, 1964* (Washington, D.C., 1964), p. 329.
65. The reduction in the proportions of urban population of the Ukraine and Belorussia between 1914 and 1926 is due to the official change in the definition of urban centers in these two republics adopted in 1924. In Belorussia, the new title "towns and cities" was not connected with any statistical definition; rather, the number of towns was reduced by decree. In the Ukraine, only urban centers with a population of 10,000 or more were classified as urban after 1924; a large number of towns and cities so called in 1914 were deprived of these designations. In the R.S.F.S.R., on the other hand, inhabited centers with a population of only 1,000 or more were classified as urban. As a result of this reform, the R.S.F.S.R. became at once more "urbanized" than the other republics; it probably had to look statistically more "proletarian" than the others. This was also important from the point of view of priorities in the allocation of resources. Other republics, too, had different definitions of "urban" centers during the 1920's and 1930's. See O. A. Konstantinov, "Sovremennoe sostoyanie deleniya naselennykh punktov SSSR na gorodskie i sel'skie," *Izvestiya Akademii Nauk SSSR: Seriya Geograficheskaya,* No. 6 (1958), pp. 70–71.
66. Central Statistical Administration, *Itogi vsesoyuznoy perepisi naseleniya 1959 goda: Ukrainskaya SSR* (Moscow, 1963), p. 16; and Central Statistical Administration, *Narodnoe khozyaystvo SSSR v 1963 godu: Statisticheskiy ezhegodnik* (Moscow, 1965), pp. 15–16. The Ukrainian republic includes, in this case, the Crimea and excludes the Moldavian A.S.S.R.
67. See an advertisement on p. 863 of *Nar. khoz. SSSR v 1961 g.* (Moscow, 1962). If there were also data on the structure of the labor force of each republic by nationality, remarkable differences would undoubtedly become apparent. It is probable, for example, that in the republics of Central Asia, and elsewhere, workers in heavy industry are for the most part Russians and other Slavs, not members of local nationalities. The same is probably even more true of the nationality structure of the republic government and Party bureaucracy, professionals, and intellectuals. In spite of the professed Party policy of training local, endemic cadres, there is some evidence that discrimination against local nationalities, deliberate or not, has been practiced in the Soviet Union. Cf. the nationality structure of students, specialists, and scientists in *Nar. khoz. SSSR v 1961 g.,* pp. 586, 700, 704. See also U.S. Department of Labor, Bureau of Labor Statistics,

Division of Foreign Labor Conditions, *Discrimination in the Field of Employment and Occupation in the Soviet Union* (Washington, D.C., 1957).

68. These figures are given for all industries, as distinguished from large-scale industries, the data for which are more often found in Soviet sources, but which are also very frequently mixed in with the data for all industries. Examples of such confusion can be found in Vorob'yov, *Vyravnivanie urovney ekonomicheskogo razvitiya soyuznykh respublik,* p. 82; and in Shpilyuk, *op. cit.,* pp. 325–26. There is no doubt that the use of data from large-scale industries artificially embellishes the picture in some republics. In the case of Turkmenia and Uzbekistan, for example, the exclusion of the cotton-gin shops from industrial output statistics because they are small-scale enterprises leaves both republics almost bare of any industry; then, construction of one single gin-building factory and its inclusion into the industrial output index (because it is large-scale) skyrockets that index from the almost-zero base artificially and without any justification.
69. Cf. *Nar. khoz. SSSR v 1965 g.* (Moscow, 1966), p. 815.
70. An objection has been raised to this method of comparison of the levels of industrialization on the ground that different republics have different types of industries. Some industry products are high-priced, others are low-priced, and therefore production levels in price terms do not reflect actual productivity; only labor-values do. (See S. M. Yugenburg, *Indeksniy metod v sovetskoy statistike* [Moscow, 1958], pp. 179–82.) This argument is rather strange. Although it is well known that Soviet prices have at times been fixed quite arbitrarily, what is important for the measurement of the level of industrialization is not so much the prices of individual goods as the total volume of output. If production is planned rationally, its volume will be large enough to bring in a maximum volume of profit, irrespective of whether prices are high or low. It is only when the volume of output (i.e., quantity produced) is not large enough that the marginal productivity levels of individual goods become distorted. But then the total output of all industries combined would be smaller than normal, and this would mean that a given republic was arbitrarily kept underdeveloped.
71. This conclusion is also implicit in the findings of the Soviet scholar V. A. Shpilyuk, *op. cit.,* p. 326. He produces per capita output data of large-scale industries for the R.S.F.S.R. and eight non-Russian republics in the years 1913, 1940, and 1961, but stops short of drawing any conclusions as far as the comparison with the Russian republic is concerned. His data for the R.S.F.S.R. for the given years are 80.2, 578.9, and 2719.0 rubles; the average for the non-Russian republics comes out as 47.8, 224.9, and 738.3 rubles. The level of the non-Russian republics compared to the R.S.F.S.R. has therefore declined from 60 per cent to 39 per cent and 27 per cent, respectively.
72. Central Statistical Administration, *Promyshlennost' SSSR: Statisticheskiy sbornik* (Moscow, 1957), pp. 58–100.
73. Another check substantiates these same conclusions, that of the per capita haul of freight by railroads and other carriers. The figures are not reproduced here because they give the same results. Cf. Central Statistical Administration, *Transport i svyaz' SSSR; Statisticheskiy sbornik* (Moscow, 1957), p. 67.
74. This is the argument employed by Shpilyuk, *op. cit.,* to prove that the gap decreases after all. Unfortunately, such an argument only dodges the problem.

75. For a worried statement to this effect by V. Yu. Akhundov, First Secretary of the Azerbaidzhan Communist Party, at the Twenty-third CPSU Congress, see *XXIII s"yezd Kommunisticheskoy Partii Sovetskogo Soyuza: Stenograficheskiy otchet* (Moscow, 1966), I, 376.
76. M. Bor, "Planoviy balans natsional'nogo dokhoda v soyuznykh respublikakh," *Voprosy ekonomiki,* No. 3 (1960). See also similar statements and discussions in A. Zverev, "Voprosy metodologii ischisleniya narodnogo dokhoda," *Voprosy ekonomiki,* No. 11 (1960); A. Lyando, "O sostavlenii svodnykh otchetnykh balansov finansovykh resursov i zatrat soyuznykh respublik," *Vestnik statistiki,* No. 3 (1961); L. A. Tarasov, *loc. cit.;* A. Balashova, V. Vorotnikov, and L. Grinyakina, "Problemy planovogo balansa natsional'nogo dokhoda soyuznykh respublik," *Planovoe khozyaystvo,* No. 4 (1962); V. Kuts, "Rozpodil natsional'noho dokhodu cherez derzhavny byudzhet URSR," *Ekonomika Radyans'koyi Ukrayiny* (Kiev), September-October, 1962; and L. A. Tarasov, "O vliyanii ekonomicheskikh svyazey na razmery obshchestvennogo produkta i natsional'nogo dokhoda soyuznoy respubliki," *Nauchnye doklady vysshey shkoly—ekonomicheskie nauki,* No. 6 (1962).
77. A. Zverev, "Rol' gosudarstvennogo byudzheta v raspredelenii obshchestvennogo produkta i natsional'nogo dokhoda," *Voprosy ekonomiki,* No. 6 (1964), p. 51.
78. *Natsional'ny dokhod Ukrayins'koyi RSR v period rozhornutoho budivnytstva komunizmu,* p. 151.
79. The authors of these calculations admit that for a number of statistical reasons their figures underestimate, rather than overestimate, the actual losses of the Ukraine. A recent émigré attempt at a recalculation by means of a more complete statistical coverage has produced a figure of losses of 6.021 billion rubles for the year 1962. These recalculations are debatable, however. See D. Solovey, *Finansovy vyzysk Ukrayiny* (Detroit, 1965), p. 57.
80. Cf. Ukrgosplan, *Materialy dlya opredeleniya roli Ukrainy v obshchegosudarstvennom byudzhete SSSR v 1913, 1922/23, 1924/25 gg.* (Kharkov, 1925); V. Dobrogayev, "Problemy finansovogo balansa Ukrainy," *Khozyaystvo Ukrainy* (Kharkov), No. 2 (1927); V. S. Myshkis, "Balans narodnogo khozyaystva Ukrainy," *Khozyaystvo Ukrainy,* No. 1 (1928); M. Volobuyev, "Do problemy ukrayins'koyi ekonomiky," *Bil'shovyk Ukrayiny,* Nos. 2 and 3 (1928); and *Zvit Narodnyoho Komisariyatu Finansiv USRR pro vykonannya Derzhavnoho byudzhetu USRR za 1927/28 r.* (Kharkov, 1929).
81. Cf., for example, A. Richytsky, *Do problemy likvidatsiyi perezhytkiv kolonial'nosti ta natsionalizmu* (*Vidpovid' M. Volobuyevu*) (Kharkov, 1928); also the writings of B. Vynar and D. Solovey, referred to above.
82. Cf. Ya. Ioffe and G. Lebedev, "Promyshlennost' peremeshchaetsya na Vostok," *Puti industrializatsii,* No. 13 (1930); *Za industrializatsiyu Sovetskogo Vostoka,* Nos. 1–4 (1932); *Direktivy KPSS i Sovetskogo Pravitel'stva po khozyaystvennym voprosam* (Moscow, 1958), IV, 846; R. S. Livshits, *Ocherki po razmeshcheniyu promyshlennosti SSSR* (Moscow, 1954); S. P. Tokarev, *Uskorennoe razvitie promyshlennosti vostochnykh rayonov SSSR* (Moscow, 1960); A. E. Probst, *Razmeshchenie sotsialisticheskoy promyshlennosti* (Moscow, 1962); and *XXIII s"yed KPSS . . . ,* II, 18–21, *et passim.*

83. *Direktivy KPSS i Sovetskogo Pravitel'stva po khozyaystvennym voprosam* (Moscow, 1957), II, 401.
84. *KPSS v rezolyutsiyakh i resheniyakh s"yezdov, konferentsiy i plenumov TsK* (7th ed.; Moscow, 1960), Part IV, p. 459. Also, a faster rate of growth was planned for the "eastern regions" than for the rest of the U.S.S.R. See N. A. Mukhitdinov's speech at the Twenty-first Party Congress, in *Izvestiya,* January 31, 1959.
85. This whole area is sometimes called the "east and southeast" of the U.S.S.R. (See U.S.S.R. Academy of Sciences, Institute of Economics, *Ekonomika promyshlennosti SSSR: Uchebnik* [Moscow, 1956], p. 175.) This term is, of course, less misleading than the former. In a few official sources, the "eastern regions" also include the Upper Volga region, in addition to the regions mentioned above. See S. G. Strumilin (ed.), *Ekonomicheskaya zhizn' SSSR: Khronika sobytiy i faktov 1917–1959* (Moscow, 1961), p. 415, citing the Gosplan report on the fulfillment of the 1943 economic plan.
86. *Direktivy KPSS i Sovetskogo Pravitel'stva* . . ., II, 403, 575, III, 8 ff., and IV, 583–84; *KPSS v rezolyutsiyakh* . . . , Part IV, pp. 460–62; and *XXIII s"yezd KPSS* . . . , II, 18–22. See also N. K. Belyayev, *Sotsialisticheskaya industrializatsiya Zapadnoy Sibiri* (Novosibirsk, 1958); Ya. E. Chadayev, *Noviy etap ekonomicheskogo razvitiya RSFSR* (Moscow, 1959); V. Kistanov, *Budushcheye Sibiri* (Moscow, 1960); U.S.S.R. Academy of Sciences, Institute of Economics, *Razvitie proizvoditel'nykh sil vostochnoy Sibiri* (Moscow, 1961); and A. I. Zubkov, *Osobennosti razmeshcheniya promyshlennosti RSFSR* (Moscow, 1964). See also the publication by the U.S.S.R. Academy of Sciences, Siberian Branch, *Sibir' v period stroitel'stva sotsializma* (Novosibirsk); six issues, containing important economic-historical papers, had been published by 1966.
87. Rozenfel'd, *Opredelenie urovney razvitiya promyshlennosti v rayonakh,* p. 17.
88. For more details, see Alfred Oxenfeldt and Vsevolod Holubnychy, *Economic Systems in Action* (3d ed.; New York, 1965), pp. 93 ff.
89. Victor Perlo, *How the Soviet Economy Works: An Interview with A. I. Mikoyan* (New York, 1961), pp. 17–18.
90. N. S. Khrushchev, "Razvitie ekonomiki SSSR i partiynoe rukovodstvo narodnym khozyaystvom," *Pravda,* November 20, 1962, p. 5.
91. See G. B. Yakusha, *Osnovy planirovaniya energeticheskikh sistem* (Kiev, 1963); Academy of Sciences of the Ukrainian S.S.R., Institute of Economics, *Ekonomichna efektyvnist' kapital'nykh vkladen' i vprovadzhennya novoyi tekhniky u promyslovosti* (Kiev, 1962); G. B. Yakusha, *Tekhniko-ekonomicheskie osnovy razvitiya elektroenergetiki ekonomicheskikh rayonov Ukrainskoy SSR* (Kiev, 1965), especially pp. 51, 88–89, 101–2, 126–34. In defending the electrification of the Ukraine against that of Siberia, Yakusha also points out that the East European socialist countries need to import electric power from the Ukraine (ibid., pp. 11, 101). See also the comments of N. S. Khrushchev, in *Pravda,* July 30, 1962. The fight for the extension of electric power development in the Ukraine continued even at the Twenty-third CPSU Congress; see V. V. Shcherbitsky's speech, in *XXIII s"yezd KPSS* . . . , II, 71.
92. V. F. Rubanik, "K voprosu o putyakh razvitiya sovetskoy elektroenergetiki," *Trudy Kievskogo tekhnologicheskogo instituta pishchevoy promyshlennosti* (Kiev), No. 20 (1959); and V. A. Shelest, "Razvitie i razmeshchenie

elektroenergetiki," in U.S.S.R. Academy of Sciences, *Voprosy razmeshcheniya proizvodstva v SSSR: Sbornik statey* (Moscow, 1965), who tries to find a compromise solution.

93. S. P. Tokarev, *Uskorennoe razvitie promyshlennosti vostochnykh rayonov SSSR, 1959–1965* (Moscow, 1960); and L. A. Melent'yev, M. A. Styrikovich, and E. O. Shteyngauz, *Toplivno-energeticheskiy balans SSSR* (Moscow, 1962). The latter proposed closing down Donbas coal fields and slowing down the economic development of the Ukraine almost to a standstill (pp. 174–75, as quoted by Yakusha, *Tekhniko-ekonomicheskie osnovy razvitiya elektroenergetiki . . .* , p. 102).
94. *KPSS v rezolyutsiyakh . . .* , Part IV, p. 391.
95. *XXIII s"yezd KPSS . . .* , II, 336.
96. In addition to the sources quoted in footnotes 91–95, see two works of the Academy of Sciences of the Ukrainian S.S.R., Institute of Economics, *Shlyakhy pidvyshchennya ekonomichnoyi efektyvnosti kapital'nykh vkladen' u promyslovist' Ukrayins'koyi RSR* (Kiev, 1967), pp. 10, 15, 22–54; and *Razvitie neftyanoy i gazovoy promyshlennosti USSR i effektivnost' kapital'nykh vlozheniy* (Kiev, 1964).
97. V. Bayevich and V. Sklyar, "Bogatstva nedr Ukrainy dlya razvitiya khimii," *Pravda,* August 5, 1964, p. 2.
98. See, for example, S. Petrakov, "Gde vygodneye pererabatyvat' khlopok," *Ekonomicheskaya gazeta,* September 29, 1965, p. 19; and the speech by R. Kurbanov, Uzbekistan's Premier, in *XXIII s"yezd KPSS . . .* , II, 222.
99. See the speech by Z. Pukhova, in *XXIII s"yezd KPSS . . .* , I, 351.
100. See the speech by V. Yu. Akhundov, in *ibid.*, I, 375–76.
101. A. Guniya, *O tempakh i proportsiyakh sotsialisticheskogo vosproizvodstva v ekonomike Gruzii* (Tbilisi, 1966), pp. 56–58.
102. S. Malinin, "Nuzhno respublike, vygodno strane," *Ekonomicheskaya gazeta,* October 6, 1965, p. 15; A. Diorditsa, "V yedinoy bratskoy sem'ye narodov SSSR," *Sovetskaya Moldavia* (Kishinev), December 28, 1965; Z. Muratov, "Perspektivy razvitiya ekonomiki Sovetskoy Tatarii," *Pravda,* May 5, 1957, p. 3; and *XXIII s"yezd KPSS . . .* , II, 213.
103. See Khrushchev's speech, in *Plenum Tsentral'nogo Komiteta Kommunisticheskoy Partii Sovetskogo Soyuza, 18–21 iyunya, 1963 goda: Stenograficheskiy otchet* (Moscow, 1964), p. 289. Another vivid example of how decisions were made in Stalin's time within the U.S.S.R. Gosplan is described in the recollections of Jack Miller, "Soviet Planners in 1936–37," in Jane Degras (ed.), *Soviet Planning: Essays in Honor of Naum Jasny* (New York, 1964). Of special interest is his description of the Gosplan of Uzbekistan, pp. 127–32.
104. See Khrushchev's speech in *Plenum Tsentral'nogo Komiteta KPSS . . .* , p. 291.
105. See *Pravda,* July 20, 1959, p. 1.
106. See F. Kotov, "Novye metodicheskie polozheniya k sostavleniyu gosudarstvennogo plana," *Planovoye khozyaystvo,* No. 10 (1960), p. 32; and "Polozhenie o poryadke vybora rayona i punkta stroitel'stva novykh promyshlennykh predpriyatiy i ob osnovnykh pokazatelyakh tekhniko-ekonomicheskogo obosnovaniya razmeshcheniya predpriyatiy," *Planovoye khozyaystvo,* No. 5 (1962), pp. 92–93. In the international economic relations among the sovereign socialist states, almost all capital transfers have been on a loan basis, and with appropriate interest. A contribution on this subject, almost unique in socialist literature, and published by the

Czechoslovak Academy of Sciences, is Čestmir Konečný, *Socialistický mezinárodni úvěr* (Prague, 1964). Interregional transfers of investible capital on a loan basis, though interest-free, are being carried out in Yugoslavia today. A special credit fund for the industrialization of the underdeveloped republics of Macedonia and Montenegro and the Kosovo-Metohija autonomous province was established in 1965. See "Zakon o oslobodenju od plaćanja kamate na fondove u privredi," *Službeni list SFRJ* (Belgrade), No. 5 (1965).

107. Vsevolod Holubnychy, "Problemy 'osnovnoy ekonomicheskoy zadachi' SSSR," p. 78.
108. A. S. Moskovskiy, "Razvitie promyshlennosti Sibiri v gody vtoroy pyatiletki," in *Sibir' v period stroitel'stva sotsializma* (Novosibirsk), VI (1966), 139–40; Livshits, *op. cit.*, p. 225 (see p. 222 for 1933–40 figures); and Ivan S. Koropeckyj, "The Economics of Investment in Ukrainian Industry, 1928–1937" (unpublished Ph.D. dissertation, Columbia University, 1964), p. 87.
109. See Ivan S. Koropeckyj, "The Development of Soviet Location Theory before the Second World War," *Soviet Studies,* July and October, 1967.
110. *Program of the CPSU,* adopted by the Twenty-second Congress (October 31, 1961), Part II, sec. 4.
111. B. Bukhanevich and M. Sonin, "O mezhrayonnom regulirovanii zarabotnoy platy v SSSR," *Voprosy ekonomiki,* No. 1 (1957), p. 21.
112. The deflator indexes were calculated from the indexes of retail sales in current prices and physical volume of sales for each republic. Central Statistical Administration, *Sovetskaya torgovlya: Statisticheskiy sbornik* (Moscow, 1964), pp. 31, 47.
113. M. J. Pullen, "Regional Development in the United Kingdom," in W. Birmingham and A. G. Ford (eds.), *Planning and Growth in Rich and Poor Countries* (New York, 1965), p. 118.
114. U.S. Department of Commerce, Bureau of the Census, *Statistical Abstract of the United States, 1966* (Washington, D.C., 1966), p. 330.
115. See The Chase Manhattan Bank, *The European Markets* (New York, 1964), p. 33.
116. I. Ya. Matyukha, *Statistika byudzhetov naseleniya* (Moscow, 1967), p. 101.
117. A. G. Aganbegyan and V. F. Mayer, *Zarabotnaya plata v SSSR* (Moscow, 1959), p. 192.
118. Comparative interregional real-income studies were not made officially in the U.S.S.R. until 1964. Since then they have been made, but none has been published so far. Cf. V. F. Mayer, "Nekotorye voprosy metodologii planirovaniya real'nykh dokhodov naseleniya," *Planovoe khozyaystvo,* No. 9 (1964), p. 41.
119. E. Manevich, "Vseobshchnost' truda i problemy ratsional'nogo ispol'zovaniya rabochey sily v SSSR," *Voprosy ekonomiki,* No. 6 (1965), p. 26. He cites these figures to explain why people flee from Siberia; in his view the differences in wages are insufficient to balance the cost-of-living differences.
120. V. G. Lopatkin, "Vyravnivanie urovney roznichnogo tovarooborota po ekonomicheskim rayonam SSSR," in Supreme Party School of the Central Committee of the CPSU, *Uchenye zapiski: Politicheskaya ekonomiya* (Moscow, 1961), III, 125.
121. *Ibid.,* p. 131.

122. In *Vestnik statistiki,* No. 2 (1960), pp. 89–90, there are statistics on urban housing credit outstanding, which also show the same facts, namely, that the non-Russian republics are proportionately much more in debt than the R.S.F.S.R.
123. See K. Subbotina, *Narodnoe obrazovanie i byudzhet* (Moscow, 1965), pp. 96, 107.
124. See G. A. Dorokhova, *Upravlenie narodnym obrazovaniem* (Moscow, 1965), pp. 98, 115–16.
125. N. S. Khrushchev, in *XX s"yezd KPSS: Stenograficheskiy otchet* (Moscow, 1956), I, 89.

3

*Soviet Language Policy: Continuity and Change**

JACOB ORNSTEIN

General Background

The Soviets came to power committed to allow the ethnic minority groups to develop according to the Leninist slogan "national in form, socialist in content." With some 200 distinct languages within its borders, the U.S.S.R. has been the scene of the vastest and most complex official language-planning effort known in history.

The first period in the history of Soviet language policy, following the revolution and during the 1920's, was one of relative liberalism.[1] The larger ethnic groups were encouraged to develop their languages and make them "sociologically complete," which according to Heinz Kloss signifies that they can handle the communication tasks of a modern, industrialized society.[2] This was done either by borrowing from a "culture language" (for instance, Azerbaidzhani from Osmanli Turkish), or by sending out linguist teams to seek lexical items in more remote areas, where they might possibly have survived in a more pristine form. Important languages were codified and standardized, and writing systems were worked out for then unwritten languages. Dictionaries and normative grammars were written or revised. The Latin alphabet was promoted as a weapon in the struggle for an international society and adopted by the various languages. Well over sixty languages began to be used in primary schools, and some of them past that level. Book and periodicals publication in the minority tongues was enthusiastically supported.

In the early 1930's, a sharp reversal took place and a new policy was initiated, which, with modifications, has obtained to this very day. The role of Russian in the Soviet communication network steadily increased, and that of the minority tongues decreased, with their

* Appreciation is expressed to Mr. William A. Stewart, Center for Applied Linguistics, Washington, D.C., for his helpful comments on this paper.

functions quite rigidly circumscribed. Lexical coinage—the main device whereby a language is made to keep abreast of current needs—had to follow a uniform pattern. Words in the "obligatory categories" of socio-political, economic, and scientific-technical vocabulary were to be borrowed from Russian, either directly or as loan translations (*calques,* in linguistic terminology). Writers who insisted on employing "archaic" or "feudal" terms ran the risk of being branded "bourgeois nationalists."

In addition to this, the Latin alphabet was declared undesirable and, except for Georgian, Armenian, Abkhazian, and Yiddish, the Cyrillic system was adapted for all languages. All this necessitated constant changes in orthography and lexicography and engendered considerable confusion. The codification and standardization processes continued, and special attention was paid to finding "dialect bases" thought to be most representative of the languages spoken by the broad masses.[3]

Other measures included the implementation of *korenizatsiya,* i.e., the appointment of officials fluent in local languages to administrative positions in the non-Russian areas. In the public media, as well as in written and spoken official and administrative communication, attempts were made to make the widest use of important local languages.

The use of important minority languages, however, was continued as a medium of instruction in primary, and to a lesser extent in secondary schools, in "grass roots" political work, particularly at the primary Party level and other administrative and official levels, and of course, in everyday intercourse. More and more, publication in Russian rather than the minority languages was encouraged, although technical and agricultural publications aimed at the "working level" were still widely printed in the minority languages.

Certain languages enjoyed more sanctioned use than others. At the bottom of the list was Yiddish, which has hardly had more than token use since the early 1930's, followed by the languages of small groups with little cohesion that were not "mobilized" for intensive sociopolitical communication, to use Deutsch's term.[4] Georgian, Stalin's native tongue, of course, was in a privileged position, while Armenian and Ukrainian, and to some extent languages like Uzbek, each for different reasons, were allowed relatively wide usage.

Before beginning our discussion of recent developments, let us look at the main linguistic and extralinguistic features of the language situation[5] in the Soviet Union. Language planning, it goes without saying, never takes place in a linguistic vacuum, isolated from socio-political factors.[6]

The nature of the linguistic diversity of the Soviet Union has been vastly oversimplified or treated with naïveté. The fact is that within its borders the widest spectrum of language situations occur, ranging from such highly homogeneous Russian areas as Kursk to Dagestan in the Caucausus, which has more than thirty distinct languages and numerous dialects. According to the 1959 census, 54.7 per cent of the population gave Russian as their mother tongue, meaning that almost half speak minority languages.

All this signifies that there is a high incidence of contact situations, particularly interesting from a sociolinguistic viewpoint, since the nature of the Soviet system is such that it can apply a maximum of pressure to the direction of linguistic change or drift toward Russian rather than toward the minority languages. However, vocabulary and phonology are the factors most vulnerable to change; grammar and syntax are far more resistant.

The task of analyzing Soviet bilingualism or multilingualism (the terms are becoming more and more interchangeable) is indeed a Herculean one, in which both linguistic and nonlinguistic factors are closely intertwined. The ability to switch from Russian to a minority language or languages and vice versa (code-switching, in linguistic terminology) varies a great deal among Soviet citizens, depending upon age, sex, geographical location, education, political affiliation, and individual "language loyalty" toward a given language. Idiosyncratic factors also play a role, in the form of poor or high language-learning aptitude or even of a block against learning a given tongue because of some unpleasant incident associated with it.

Of great importance, in any discussion of our subject, is also an element that Joshua Fishman has termed "ethnicity"[7]—that whole complex of attitudes toward one's own group and the degree of attachment to the native language. In Soviet Georgian speech or the Armenian community, a high degree of this can be found, while by contrast some groups, partly through the force of historical circumstances, are unable to maintain very much group solidarity. Cases in point are the Kereki, a Paleo-Asiatic speech community of only a hundred persons or so, which are rapidly losing ground to Russian, or such Balto-Finnic languages as Ludic, Olonetsian, and Votic, spoken virtually only by the older generations.[8]

It goes without saying that there are many aspects of Soviet multilingualism[9] about which Western scholars have only the sparsest information and impressions. We would like to know much more about the varieties of Russian that are in the making within the borders of the Soviet Union. We know that English, today employed as a "language of wider communication" throughout the world, develops special features in every country where it is used (for example, India, Pakistan, Kenya). That a similar process is certainly occurring in the U.S.S.R. is indicated by a statement made at the Alma-Ata Conference by Academician V. V. Vinogradov, who complained of the following:

> As a result of the influence of the numerous national languages on the Russian literary language, in the republics one finds phenomena against which one should struggle, just as we fight against dialectal peculiarities in Russian, which violate its rules. For example, we can note such things as distortions of the features of vowels and consonant phonemes, misplaced stresses, incorrect syntax, violation of stylistic and pronunciation norms of Russian, and so forth. It is inadmissable that the national republics should develop their own norms for the Russian literary language.[10]

Too little is known by us, likewise, of the types of pidgins that have been developing at work sites and communal living and working enterprises involving a variety of nationalities.[11] That these are developing not only at industrial and agricultural multilingual enterprises but also in the Soviet public media is reflected by an observation of Candidate of Philological Sciences B. K. Balkarov, a Kabardin linguist. Speaking at the Alma-Ata Conference, he complained that partly because standardization of Kabardin has not been entirely completed, as well as because of faulty command of Russian, there are serious problems in the translation of sociopolitical material and in the language of newspapers and radio broadcasting.

Although our sources of information on the language situations of the Soviet Union are in many ways limited, it is possible to tap the available ones and to draw up tentative "language profiles." What can be done despite limited sources is illustrated by Yaroslav Bilinsky, a political scientist, whose recent book, *The Second Soviet Republic: The Ukraine after World War II,*[12] contains a forty-four-page chapter on "Soviet Linguistic Policy: Extent of the Ukrainian Language in the Ukrainian Socialist Republic," in which the University of Delaware scholar has utilized both Western and Soviet written sources, scholarly as well as journalistic, statistical reference works, and the testimony of refugees, including those interviewed by the Harvard Project on the Soviet Social System, as well as reports of travelers.

While there are understandable gaps in the picture drawn by Dr. Bilinsky, it remains the most complete description of the language situation in a large area of the Soviet Union by any Western researcher.

No matter what the political system, however, the problems of conducting affairs in a multilingual state tend to be compounded by each additional language that must be reckoned with. Language frictions and disorders have been noted in Canada and Belgium. If these can occur where only two languages are at issue, it is easy to comprehend that even in a rigidly controlled country, a great linguistic diversity, no matter how fascinating to the linguist, creates problems for political leaders, administrators, and educators. And yet, particularly in its attempts to woo and win the uncommitted and underdeveloped nations, or submerged ethnic groups outside its boundaries, the Soviet Union obviously counts heavily on the appeal of ethnolinguistic self-expression. When the new state of India was established, a committee of linguists was dispatched to the U.S.S.R. to study at first hand the functioning of Soviet policy toward its minority tongues.

Soviet educational periodical literature carries frequent complaints of poor knowledge of Russian on the part of students graduating from secondary school and desiring to enter the *vuz'es* or the labor force as technicians and experts. Few complaints are, however, registered about the opposite—the command of the native languages. These do crop up occasionally, nevertheless, with regard to administrators who cannot handle the local tongue. One of the most common types of complaint is the overloading of youngsters in polyglot areas. In 1959, V. Danilov, an educator in Yakutia, wrote:

> One must recognize as wrong the simultaneous study in Yakut schools of three languages, demanding 50 per cent of the students' classroom time. This leads to neglect of other disciplines and overloads the student. . . . Such a heavy load makes too great a demand on the intellect and nervous system of their not yet fully developed organism.[13]

Developments in Language Policy in the Post-Stalin Period

Observers of the Soviet scene who expected to see an abrupt volte-face in linguistic policy after Stalin's death have had to realize that few areas of Soviet affairs have been so little affected by the "thaw" and subsequent liberalization measures. Soviet leaders, by and large, continue to favor the general line established in the early 1930's. It even appears that, if anything, it might be intensified. At best, official multilingualism is difficult to administer, and the prospect of Russian as an ever more widespread lingua franca appears to loom large in the Soviet communication network.

Unlike his predecessors, Khrushchev showed scant interest in language problems. Instead, Soviet linguistic policy has been interpreted mostly by high Party officials of republic or Central Committee rank or by leading linguistic scholars. At the same time, an unbroken chorus of paeans, both by Russian and non-Russian writers, has continued to exalt Russian as the "second native language" of every Soviet citizen, as the "inter-national language of the Soviet multilingual society," and as the unfailing source of "enrichment" of the minority languages.

Let us examine the question of the language of instruction in Soviet schools. The higher one goes in Soviet education, the greater the use of Russian, and the less frequent the use of the minority languages, except possibly in the case of Armenian and Georgian, which along with Russian are apparently used in some professional and specialized training, some of it at *vuz* level. But, by and large, our generalization holds true in the non-Russian areas, and significant native tongues are used as a medium of instruction at the primary (sometimes even the secondary) levels, and at the faculties of languages, literature, and pedagogy in *vuz'es*.

After about fifty years of use of some sixty minority tongues in primary education, there are signs that the regime wishes to de-emphasize the former in favor of Russian. On November 12, 1958, the Central Committee approved "theses" outlining an impending school reform. "Thesis 19" dealt with language policy, proposing to grant parents a choice between Russian or the minority language—if existing facilities made such an option possible. Thus, it was proposed that the children of parents opting for a Russian-language school could also study the native language, and vice versa, if there were a sufficient number of children to form classes in the optional tongue, and of course, if a teacher was available. This proposal was heatedly debated in both chambers of the Supreme Soviet on December 24, 1958, and its adoption was left to the individual republics. Almost all adopted it.

Yaroslav Bilinsky has made a careful analysis of this piece of legislation in an article in *Soviet Studies*.[14] He notes that in the five central Asian republics of Kazakhstan, Uzbekistan, Tadzhikistan,

Turkmenistan, and Kirgizia, sentiment was markedly for the compulsory study of Russian, with scant support for native language teaching. A second type of reaction was expressed in Georgia, Armenia, and other parts of Transcaucasia, Moldavia, the Ukraine, Lithuania, Latvia, and Estonia, where opposition to Thesis 19 was fairly strong, and where there was a marked insistence on the teaching of the native tongue along with Russian. This may very credibly be interpreted as a desire to stand firmly on the shoulders of the lingua franca Russian, to guarantee continued teaching and use of the minority languages.

Be that as it may, Thesis 19 was not without serious consequences, quite outside the areas of education and linguistics. In both Azerbaidzhan and Latvia, for example, purges took place at the ministerial level, with considerable indication that resistance to the school reforms was a factor in these moves.[15] One of those removed was Deputy Prime Minister Berklav of the Latvian S.S.R., who argued that the education reform linking school and life necessitated the continuation of the obligatory teaching of the three traditional tongues —Latvian, Russian, and a world foreign language.

Of all this, Bilinsky remarks:

> Today the wider implications of Thesis 19 is clear to every observer of the Soviet Union; it suffices merely to place Thesis 19 in the context of Gafurov's programmatical article. The assimilationists were again to be openly supported by the regime as during the 1930's and 1940's and early 1950's.[16]

The mention of Gafurov in the previous citation provides a fitting opportunity for us to examine an important statement made by him while he was director of the Oriental Institute in the U.S.S.R. Academy of Sciences.

In a 1958 issue of *Kommunist,* B. G. Gafurov in effect reaffirmed that the policies initiated in the 1930's would be continued. He extolled Russian as the "second native language" of all the nationalities inhabiting the land of socialism,[17] and at the same time remarked that: "All encouragement is due the practice, which has proved its merit, of the study by our people of the language of the locale in which they live and work."[18]

The fact remains, however, that despite the talk of "mutual enrichment," "fusion of languages," and the like, the linguistic drift is actually overwhelmingly toward Russian. Exception is made, of course, of specialized regional terms. For example, in the Far North, many terms relating to reindeer herding have been incorporated from the Paleo-Asiatic languages. Moreover, apart from linguists and some teachers, few native Russian speakers appear to bother with the local tongues, although the native elite are expected to handle the minority languages. A correspondent of the *Central Asian Review,* published in London, in a recent article titled "Some Impressions of the Central Asian Republics," notes the following:

> I never met a Russian or Ukrainian throughout my travels who admitted speaking Tadzhik, Kazakh, Kirgiz, or Uzbek. My question was invariably answered in the negative with a deprecating shrug, followed by "Why?"[19]

In the primary and less frequently the secondary schools as well, the problem of the native language versus Russian continues to be troublesome. At the Alma-Ata Conference, Candidate of Philological Sciences T. Z. Kozyreva, from Ordzhonikidze, spoke out for more attention to native-language study as a bridge to both a better knowledge of Russian and to native-language literature. In some schools the native language, Ossetic, was taught only one hour per week, she noted, while all instruction is in Russian from the first grade on. She adds:

> I will tell about the practice of the Ossetic schools. In the majority of the *raion* schools, instruction is carried on in Russian. It is poor pedagogy to teach the unfamiliar in a language that is not understood. The children mechanically memorize what they are taught.[20]

These digressions are necessary if one is to make any attempt at all to point out how actual practice may differ from theory, and from declarations intended to remind Soviet citizens of avowed ultimate goals in language policy.

One year after Gafurov's statement came another one, by N. Dzhandil'din, First Secretary of the Central Committee of the Communist Party of Kazakhstan, which also appeared in *Kommunist.* Speaking as a member of the Kazakh native elite—which appears to be unusually vigorous and articulate—Dzhandil'din, for one thing, emphasized the importance of struggling against that small minority of people who still thought narrowly with respect to nationality problems:

> There are people here and there who speak out against our rightful aspirations to acquire knowledge of the Russian language and culture, and who look disdainfully on those Kazakh children who wish to study and are studying in Russian schools. Some persons consider it necessary so to arrange things that Kazakh children should be able to attend only

> Kazakh schools. This sort of view is nothing more or less than a manifestation of bourgeois nationalism against which one must fight.[21]

Furthermore, Dzhandil'din lashed out against Kazakhs who protested against the borrowing of Russian words by the Kazakh language. One of these, he noted, was the young philologist Bodaubayeva, who had published an article in the journal *Leninshil Zhas* titled "The Corruption of the Language Through Foreign Words." He repeats the familiar refrain that "the mutual enrichment of one language by another through its lexical stock is a natural process. It is also characteristic for the development of the Russian language."[22]

Incidentally, a few pages later, however, he criticizes an art exhibit for its "ethnographic themes harkening back to the past," showing such scenes as "Evening on the Dzhaylau" (summer pasture) and "The Herd on the Dzhaylau"—all evocative of the nomadic days of Kazakh history. Dzhandil'din stresses that he would prefer to see examples of contemporary Soviet Kazakh realism. As is usual in discussions of this sort, there is very little if any enthusiasm expressed for borrowings from the minority languages by Russian.

As noted previously, Nikita Khrushchev discussed language policy only *en passant*. In the draft program of the Communist Party announced by him on July 30, 1960, for presentation to the Twenty-second Congress, he said:

> With the victory of Communism in the U.S.S.R., the nations will draw still closer together, their economic and ideological unity will increase, and the Communist traits common to their spiritual make-up will develop. However, the obliteration of national distinctions, and especially of language distinctions, is a considerably longer process than the obliteration of class distinctions. The Party approaches all questions of nationality relationships arising in the course of Communist construction from the standpoint of proletarian internationalism and firm pursuance of the Leninist nationality policy. The Party neither ignores nor exaggerates national characteristics.[23]

A bit later he describes existing policy as regards the languages of the U.S.S.R.:

> The Party will continue promoting the free development of the languages of the peoples of the U.S.S.R., and the complete freedom for every citizen of the U.S.S.R. to speak, educate, and teach his children in any language, with no special privileges, restrictions, or compulsions in the use of this or that language. By virtue of the fraternal friendship and mutual trust of peoples, national languages are developing on the basis of equality and mutual enrichment.

He then touched upon the all-important question of the position of Russian:

> The voluntary study of Russian, in addition to the native language, is of positive significance, since it facilitates reciprocal exchanges of experience and access of every nation and nationality to the cultural accomplishments of all the other peoples of the U.S.S.R. and to world culture. The Russian language has, in effect, become the common medium of intercourse and cooperation between all the peoples of the U.S.S.R.

There is really nothing new in these statements on language policy, nothing that has not been said over and over again, with minor modifications, since the 1930's. Kautsky, Lenin, Stalin, and Khrushchev have all repeatedly reaffirmed their belief and hope that once Communism reaches its ultimate goal, there would be one, and only one, common language. What this language will be, however, has been left rather vague—understandably so, since politicians must guard against being overexplicit and, above all, must not offend sensibilities, particularly nationalist ones.[24] Nevertheless, although Stalin expressed the view that the world language of Communism would not be any existing tongue, but a combination of several, it has by now become apparent that Russian is being groomed for this role, at least by Soviet Communist leaders.

Let us look at a few more programmatic statements made during the 1960's to ensure the continuity of Soviet language policy, kept fairly intact since the 1930's. Once more in the journal *Kommunist,* in 1962, we find an article by N. Gadzhiyev, Secretary of the Central Committee of the Azerbaidzhan Communist Party, entitled "The Cultures of the Socialist Nations, Their Present and Future." He repeats the Messianic ethnolinguistic goal of Soviet Communism as follows:

> The culture of the Communist society will come about not by means of a mere fusion of all the national cultures, not by means of administrative removal of national distinctions and national peculiarities, but in other ways. Gradually all those elements that separate the national cultures will die away, and those features that will form the international base of the culture of Communist society will become stronger.

He hastens to add, however, that:

> The development of the national cultures presupposes the further development of the national languages. Language is a most important form of national culture, which cannot flourish without the all-around development of language. V. I. Lenin defined language as the most im-

> portant means of human communication . . . and repeatedly indicated that the unity of language is one of the basic features of a nation, for it creates solid national bonds and is an inalienable condition for the formation of a community of economic life of national proportions as well as its psychological and cultural bases.[25]

Gadzhiyev goes on to quote Lenin's dictum that force should not be used to achieve linguistic aims: "We do not want to drive them into paradise with a stick."

There is need to comment on only one more thing regarding the above-cited article—i.e., that it is significant that an Azerbaidzhani Communist leader was picked to make this sort of statement, since trouble had occurred there regarding Thesis 19. Gadzhiyev in the course of the article observes, "It should be noted that in the recent past there have been violations among us [that is, the Azerbaidzhanis] of the voluntary principle in the study of languages."[26]

The most recent interpretation of language policy to appear in the authoritative Party journal *Kommunist,* as far as we know, is that by P. Rogachev and M. Sverdlin. The article bears the significant title "The Soviet Nation—A New Historical Community of Peoples." In emphatic terms the authors flail those who persist in adhering to narrow regionalistic ways and concepts and who resist joining the Soviet mainstream.

> In the spiritual *rapprochement* of nations, the spread of the inter-national language plays a great role. In effect, as is noted in the Program of the Communist Party of the Soviet Union, Russian has become that language. This is the tongue of a majority, or 54.7 per cent, of the population of the U.S.S.R.[27]

In conclusion, Rogachev and Sverdlin admit that fusion, *sliyaniye,* may take some time, but they serve notice that it is inadvisable to slow down or inhibit that process:

> The *rapprochement* [*sblizheniye*] of the Socialist nations is already evident even now, when we can only speak of fusion [*sliyaniye*] as a relatively distant prospect. On the other hand, it is just as incorrect to undermine these processes. The *rapprochement* of nations in the period of the advanced building of Communism is creating the conditions for their future fusion.

As far as purely linguistic and pedagogic journals are concerned, they largely, and quite understandably, echo the sort of statements found in *Kommunist* and other political sources. For example, an unsigned editorial of a 1962 issue of *Voprosy yazykoznaniya,* the official journal of Soviet linguists, is devoted to the status of the minority languages, calling for their continued development, as well as for the improvement of both their teaching and that of Russian, which is considered the "common language of inter-national communication and cooperation for all the peoples of the U.S.S.R."[28]

Lest it be thought that Soviet language policy is completely monolithic and that no opposition is expressed to official linguistic measures, let it be noted here that some disagreement has cropped up from time to time since Stalin's death. In general, this takes the form of protesting the reduced role of minority languages and the disproportionate elevation of Russian.

At the Alma-Ata Conference in 1962, Candidate of Philological Sciences N. A. Kolegova of Syktyvkar stated her opposition to the excessive borrowing of Russian loan words by the Komi language, lest the latter become a "Russo-Komi jargon." This is what she said:

> Some comrades think that the Komi language ought to be brought as close as possible to Russian, that is, that the greatest possible number of Russian words be introduced into it. Certainly one should not oppose those Russian words that have taken root and that in full measure enrich the Komi language. However, in order to master Russian culture, and the Russian language, it is necessary to study the native language and the native culture, and not to invent a Russo-Komi jargon.[29]

One of the most notable cases of opposition to complete acceptance of Russian as the sole medium of expression is the polemic triggered by Akhmed Agayev, a Dagestani poet, who wrote an unbridled paean of praise for Russian in his article in the December 5, 1961, *Izvestiya.* Not only did Agayev appeal to regional writers to utilize Russian, but he also asked them to eschew narrow local themes. He pleaded with them to direct their efforts into the Soviet Russian mainstream while creating works of an international character intended for all peoples.[30]

A lively discussion in the pages of *Izvestiya, Literatura i zhizn',* and *Literaturnaya gazeta,* which flared up in 1962 and afterward, showed that loyalty to the minority languages still existed. Thus, the February 6, 1962, issue of *Literaturnaya gazeta* contained an article by the poet Vladimir Soloukhin entitled "What Makes Us Kin?" Both subtle ridicule and frank resentment characterize this article. As for concentrating on "international" themes rather than those close to the writer, Soloukhin responds that, by this reasoning, Cervantes ought to have written about Persians, de Maupassant about Scandinavians, and Jack London about Italians. He speaks out unequivocally for writing in the language one knows best.

> The upshot of this is that A. Agayev espouses the gradual dying away of national literatures. Everyone writes in the language in which he wishes to write. But to advise writers to discard their own language, and to go about "declaring" and "decreeing" a rejection of their own language, I would consider, to put it mildly, simply absurd.[31]

Another bit of seeming opposition is worth noting, although our knowledge of it comes quite indirectly. On February 11–15, 1964, a Conference on Standards (Kul'tura) of the Ukrainian language was sponsored by the Ukrainian Academy of Sciences. According to a report by a Kiev educator in the March, 1963 (No. 3), issue of *Nasha kul'tura,* a monthly supplement to the Ukrainian-language newspaper *Nashe slovo* published in Warsaw, some surprisingly sharp exchanges took place at the meeting. In his article titled "Dolya ridnoyi movy" ("Fate of Our Native Tongue"), the author observes that complaints were voiced about limitations on the use of Ukrainian (with a suggestion that representations be made before the Ukrainian Communist Party Central Committee), about the extent of the use of Ukrainian in higher and specialized educational institutions, the publication of texts, public posters, and moving pictures. Wishes were supposedly also expressed for opening Ukrainian-language schools outside the Ukrainian S.S.R. Reportedly, participants "unanimously condemned the absurd theory that a nation has two languages."[32]

Finally, disagreement obviously exists regarding the need and desirability of developing and making official use of, as well as teaching, some of the minor languages, especially those of the Far North. At the Alma-Ata Conference, P. Ya. Skorik of the University of Leningrad made the following observations:

> Recently one has sensed a strong tendency to underrate the role of the native language of these peoples [of the Far North]. . . . Most often in veiled terms, and sometimes even openly, wishes are voiced to terminate publication in the languages of the small nationalities of the North of literature and periodicals, and to change over entirely to instruction in Russian. Some go as far as to suggest prohibiting students from using their native languages and thus "promote its dying off all the sooner." Such statements and wishes do not come from the small nationalities of the North themselves. They are expressed by local Russian officials, as a rule employees of the Ministry of Education of the R.S.F.S.R., and sometimes of the textbook publishers. The former do

so because teaching in the northern schools in both the native languages and Russian requires special care, and the latter because the publication of textbooks in the languages of the little nationalities of the North involves additional worries and losses.[33]

Everything considered, however, despite occasional divergent opinions, it would appear that prospects for the enhancement of the roles played by the minority languages are very slim. Nor is there much reason for assuming that such statements would fundamentally alter the direction of Soviet language policy.

Trends and Prospects

The preponderance of available evidence leads to the conclusion that the linguistic wave of the future will increasingly favor Russian to the detriment of the nationality languages.

This, however, does not signify that the main minority languages will not continue to play roles of varied significance in the Soviet communication network. As for the smaller languages—and this includes well over 100 of recent literacy and limited written traditions—these may well be the greatest losers, becoming primarily objects of linguistic analysis and reduced to use as a vernacular or medium of informal conversation with peer groups. At the same time, some sort of token official use of these minor languages is possible, to ward off accusations that the Leninist policy of ethnolinguistic self-determination has been scrapped.

There appears no real change in sight for the status of Yiddish, despite the publication in 1964 of two books in that language, and of the magazine *Sovyetish Heymland.*

It is not impossible that a third phase of language policy may be in the offing, with an abrupt elevation of the status of Russian. The regime may feel that after half a century of rule it can afford to reduce linguistic diversity and drive harder toward the goal of "Soviet nationality."

No timetable for such a "third phase" is apparent from the evidence available. Whether it has ever been discussed at the highest policy-making levels of the Kremlin is a matter of pure conjecture. Nevertheless, the constant promotion of Russian over minority tongues for the last thirty-five years or so has prepared the ground for such an eventuality.

Support for the belief that the role of Russian may be in for upgrading comes not only from the programmatic statements and the implications of Thesis 19, but also from the following other indicators:

1. *The far greater amount of attention devoted to the teaching of Russian than to the minority languages.* The last ten years have seen the proliferation of journals devoted to the improvement of Russian teaching in non-Russian areas. These include: *Russkiy yazyk v natsional'noy shkole* (Moscow); *Russkiy yazyk v nerusskoy shkole* (Baku); and *Russkiy yazyk v armyanskoy shkole* (Erevan). In addition, a large number of regional and interrepublic conferences have been devoted to this purpose, and in 1964 an institute was established in Tashkent for the improvement of the qualifications of instructors of Russian in non-Russian schools.

One thing is certain: The enthusiasm in the 1920's of many ethnic Russian leaders, eager to avoid the taint of "Great Russian chauvinism," for the minority languages is a thing of the past, and it has definitely not been revived by the post-Stalinist thaw and aftermath.

A corollary of the increasing official encouragement of Russian study is the praise lavished on those parents who, braving the disapproval or censure of their own ethnic groups, opt for the lingua franca as the language of instruction.

2. *Increased equating of career opportunities with Russian-language proficiency.* In contrast to the heyday of *korenizatsiya* during the first phase of Soviet language policy, increasingly greater stress is being placed on better knowledge of Russian by young people who will join the labor force and assume positions of leadership.

Thus, parents who do opt for Russian-language schools where there is a choice are not necessarily Russophiles. They may merely realize, quite realistically, that Russian rather than the local language affords the best, and sometimes the only, means of access to the power structure and to elite status, since the higher one goes on the educational and vocational ladder, the more important a command of Russian. In addition, facilities for instruction in their native language may not be available for children of many nationalities, and occasionally even for the larger ethnic groups, or there may not be enough students to make up the required minimum.

3. *Direct and indirect pressures to publish significant works in Russian.* Another indication of the shift toward Russian is that, with some exception made for Armenian, Georgian, Ukrainian, and the Baltic languages, less and less emphasis is being placed on the minority tongues for important scientific and sociopolitical writing.

True, the Laboratory of Physical Studies at the Yakut branch of the Academy of Sciences of the U.S.S.R. publishes the results of research on cosmic physics in Yakut,[34] but this is becoming the exception rather than the rule. The trend is toward using local languages merely for working-level technical, political, and administrative communication, as well as for studies in language, literature, folklore, and a certain amount of creative writing. Increasingly, however, Russian emerges as the medium assuring writers of a wide readership and even of possible international recognition. Allusions to Russian as the all-Union medium for science and scholarship are frequent.

These considerations, plus the constant danger of "bourgeois nationalism," have moved many members of the native elites to write in Russian, thus building up a growing body of Russian-language "Soviet literatures" by non-Russians. There is, however, some latent resentment and even overt hostility to this.

It is extremely difficult to form anything but general impressions on our limited evidence of the role that publications in the minority languages play in the reading patterns of the various segments of the population in non-Russian areas. Although for some of the languages the numbers of titles cited in statistics may sound impressive, we do not know how many of these books are actually purchased and read.

4. *Soviet work patterns in industry and agriculture tend to favor Russian as a lingua franca.* The economic methods of the Soviet system increasingly favor a lingua franca such as Russian, rather than the minority tongues. This is further reinforced by the unprecedented flow of Soviet citizens leaving their normal habitat for work at industrial enterprises or for agricultural projects in the virgin lands of Kazakhstan. Political resettlement also figures in this change of habitat.

The trend is indisputably for the non-Russian areas to become more Russian with the arrival of Russian (as well as Ukrainian and Belorussian) workers and specialists and settlers. Even official Soviet figures reveal that two Union republics, not to speak of the vast R.S.F.S.R., no longer have a majority of their "basic native population." For Kazakhstan, the figure is 30 per cent, for Kirgizia, 40.5 per cent; and 121.4 million of the 208 million Soviet citizens state that Russian is their native language—which does not necessarily mean that they speak Russian fluently or even very well. It signifies that many of them aspire to access to the dominant U.S.S.R. language, affording them maximum opportunities.

5. *Tendency to replace ethnically determined administrative units*

by larger ones drawn along economic and other lines. An example of this are the "economic councils" set up by Khrushchev, in which several republics, despite varying ethnolinguistic backgrounds, were joined into larger entities for the purpose of meeting common needs. Although these organizations are being eliminated, their planned successor units apparently show few indications of following purely ethnic lines.

From the linguistic viewpoint, administrative units of a higher type need a common over-all language if they are to function at all, and the language in these cases would without any doubt be Russian. This would mean that the local languages would be progressively reduced to simpler working level and local "grass roots" usages. Even here, however, the large proportion of monolingual Russian-speaking administrators, supervisors, and teaching and technical personnel assigned to non-Russian areas militates against the minority tongues.

6. *The loss in communication efficiency brought on by the use of such a multiplicity of regional languages favors a lingua franca.* The scholar, if he is to adopt a scientific approach to sociolinguistic problems, must avoid taking sides in the tremendously delicate matter of language choice and use. In the case of the Soviet Union, this would tend to show that, except for the larger languages, the problems of multilingual administration are exceedingly complex. For example, in Soviet educational literature complaints are endemic that not enough school texts are prepared in the minority languages.

Without going into the multifarious ramifications of this question and all the touchy issues that arise from it, the fact must be faced that the U.S.S.R., even after half a century of multilingualism, still has numerous unsolved problems in this area.

7. *Linguistic planning in this day of rapid telecommunications and transportation tends to emphasize languages of wider communications as linguas francas rather than diversity.* While ethnic aspirations and linguistic self-determination are still, and will continue to be, important, there is recognition of the need for "languages of wider communication."[35] This may be witnessed particularly in the new states of Africa, where despite the stigma attached to French and English as the language of former colonial masters, a majority of the governments have chosen either French or English as official languages as linguas francas.

The part played by the nationalities in the Bolshevik rise to power is well known.[36] However, that was half a century ago, and one could reasonably regard language problems in a somewhat different light today. Admittedly, this by no means implies that there is complete acceptance of official language policy in the non-Russian areas. Moreover, the increased emphasis by Soviet leaders on the concept of the "Soviet people" and the "Soviet nation" as a new, composite nationality is one that would seem to favor Russian rather than a multiplicity of languages.

On November 20–24, 1962, the previously mentioned All-Union Conference on the Principles of the Development of the Literary Languages of the Peoples of the U.S.S.R. in the Soviet Period was held at Alma-Ata. Sponsored by the Institute of Linguistics of the Kazakh Academy of Sciences and the U.S.S.R. Academy of Sciences' Institute of Linguistics and Institute of the Russian Language, this meeting heard talks and statements by a large number of prominent linguists, including the late V. V. Vinogradov, N. A. Baskakov, Yu. D. Desheriyev, and B. A. Serebrennikov, as well as experts on the main language families of the Soviet Union. The proceedings were published in Alma-Ata in 1964 in *Voprosy razvitiya literaturnykh yazykov narodov SSSR v sovetskuyu epokhu,* a volume containing a wealth of detail—all from the Soviet viewpoint, of course—of interest both to linguists and political scientists.

The meeting left no doubt that the status of Russian was, if anything, to be enhanced. At the same time, however, none of the participants went so far as to say (except about some tiny and "unstable" tongues) that the role of minority languages in the present and future was of no or little consequence. A recurrent leitmotif was that it was still necessary to utilize the native languages as a bridge to better knowledge of the inter-national medium, Russian.

One thing appears certain: the Soviets, after fifty years of multilingualism, are eager to take stock of their language situation. The results of the inventory called for in the ten recommendations of the Alma-Ata Conference, summarized below, would hardly be expected to alter the course of linguistic policy, since this is politically determined. Nevertheless, they do shed some light on what sort of operations the U.S.S.R. would like its language specialists to engage in and what sort of information it seeks from them.

Here is the gist of the ten recommendations:

1. Concentration of central and local linguistic research institutes on a study of the complex problems of the development of the national languages as they in turn relate to the development of socialist nations.

2. Study of the position of the Russian language in Soviet society by the country's foremost linguistic specialists.

3. More attention ought to be paid to improving the quality and standards (*kul'tura rechi*) of the Russian language, as well as to expanding its functions in Soviet society. The task of specialists in the other U.S.S.R. languages ought to be that of providing active support in the elaboration of the role of Russian as the language of inter-national communication in the life of the peoples of the U.S.S.R. At the same time, they ought to support the development of their own languages and their role in the enrichment of Russian.

4. Elimination of the consequences of Stalin's cult of personality.

5. Using the languages of the U.S.S.R. as the corpus to carry out linguistic studies of a comparative, descriptive, and structural nature to develop mathematical approaches to linguistics. Attention ought also to be devoted to the theory of lexicology, semasiology, typology, stylistics, style of belles-lettres, and the preparation of contrastive grammars.

6. Undertaking of a systematic program of field work, involving regional linguists and institutes, to study on the spot the interaction of the languages in the different areas of the country and the types of bilingualism[37] and to gather material for the investigation of inadequately studied languages and dialects.

7. Creation of a common lexical stock for the languages of the U.S.S.R. The further development of the literary languages requires increased attention to the standardization of scientific-technical and sociopolitical terminology. It is necessary to undertake the preparation of a lexicon of sociopolitical and scientific terms. In addition, it is necessary to study, examine, and improve the writing systems and orthographies of the various languages of the U.S.S.R.

8. Devotion of a special conference to the problems of the nature, types, and importance of Soviet bilingualism.

9. Organization of regional (inter-republic and inter-*oblast*) conferences of linguists, teachers, and education specialists to examine the interrelations of Russian and the native languages in the school, everyday life, and the activity of cultural-educational institutions in the national republics and *oblasts*.

10. Publication of the proceedings of the Alma-Ata Conference.[38]

The above points seem clear enough. The conference was held, one may suppose, to mobilize the best linguistic forces of the country to carry out the present linguistic intentions, or any future plans that the leadership may deem desirable. It cannot be emphasized too much that no linguistic decisions taken by a government can be implemented without the assistance of specialists at every rung of the central and regional administrative ladder. Perhaps, too, the Alma-Ata Conference is in the fullest sense a prelude to decisive action and a harbinger of new directions on the linguistic front.

Moreover, the amount of work done by Soviet specialists and their predecessors on the languages of the U.S.S.R. has been enormous, but much of it has not been systematized or made readily available. In addition, the contradictory guidelines given by the linguistic high priest Marr (later repudiated by Stalin), and conflicting practices at the local levels, have understandably created their share of confusion. For example, the question of whether Russian loan words should be taken into the respective languages in their Russian orthography or not was never clearly elucidated. This has given rise to numerous problems, especially where not even roughly similar units exist in the native-language phonemic inventories. All in all, the Soviets have everything to gain, no matter what course they may now take in linguistic policy, from a general stocktaking.

At any rate, most indications point to the real possibility of an impending third phase of language policy in the U.S.S.R. Unless we err greatly, this would bring sharp emphasis on the *sblizheniye,* or *rapprochement,* of the various nationalities and languages with a view to their eventual *sliyaniye,* or complete fusion. This would be in sharp contrast with the first period, with its accent on self-determination of the various ethnic groups, or to the second phase, with its striving toward maximum differentiation. A good case in point is the Turkic group of languages, whose differences since the 1930's have been stressed as much as possible. Now straws in the wind point to the reverse process.

At the Alma-Ata Conference, T. A. Bertagayev, of Moscow University, among other things, had these significant words to say about Turkic and other related languages:

> Without rushing headlong too recklessly, we ought now to pose the question of the *rapprochement* [*sblizheniye*] of the national languages of the Soviet Union, which ought to take two directions: (1) *rapprochement* of related languages, as, for example, the Turkic ones; (2) *rapprochement* of the national languages, with Russian as the second native language. In this connection I welcome the proposal to unify the writing systems of the Turkic languages.[39]

One wonders if Dr. Bertagayev also has in mind bringing Belorussian and Ukrainian closer together with Russian, since these belong to the Eastern Slavic group, as well as similar attempts for North and South Caucasian language families, and so on.[40] From the standpoint of linguistic intelligibility, the Soviets would probably have more to gain than to lose by reducing "language distances." From the sociolinguistic viewpoint, however, they would risk hurting ethnic sensibilities.

Be that as it may, it seems rather apparent from the declarations both of political leaders and scholars that all possible encouragement is to be given the processes that facilitate bringing the various ethnic groups closer together, linguistically and otherwise. One of the most revealing statements in this connection came to us from three members of the Academy of Science's Institute of Ethnography: V. K. Gardanov, B. O. Dolgikh, and T. A. Zhdanko. In their article "Fundamental Directions of the Ethnic Processes Among the Peoples of the U.S.S.R.," they state:

> The present historical period in the development of national interrelations in the Soviet Union is characterized by a progressively greater, deeper process of *rapprochement* of the Socialist nations, flourishing thanks to successes achieved on the road to the construction of Communism [*sic*].[41]

The authors then go on to talk about some of the practical ways in which *sblizheniye* is already being achieved on the regional level. It is to be noted that they speak not only of non-Russians who declare Russian to be their mother tongue (as has been the case in every census, most notably in that of 1959), but of the "fusion of the ethnic groups with the basic national group [*natsiya*]." Among the cases examined we may cite, by way of example, the Tadzhik Republic:

> The process of fusion of ethnic groups with the basic national group is going on also among the Tadzhiks, who have no clan-like divisions, but among whom small nationalities have lived for some time in the mountainous regions. The latter have conserved their languages, very different from the Tadzhik tongue, although the majority for a long time had known the former language, in addition to their own. A case in point are the Yaghnobi and the so-called Pamir peoples. . . . In the 1959 census they no longer figured as nationalities, since all declared themselves to be Tadzhiks, although many of the Shugni, Vakhi, and others, in response to the question about their mother tongue, gave their own language rather than Tadzhik.[42]

They quote similar cases from other parts of Central Asia and from the Caucasus. Quite understandably, the authors do not fail to emphasize that it is thanks to the Russian language that thirty national groups representing as many distinct languages and numerous dialects can speak to each other, including brides and grooms from different backgrounds.[43] And finally they repeat a refrain heard more and more frequently from Soviet commentators on the language problem: "The all-Soviet culture is inter-national. Before our very eyes there is taking place a unique and intensive process of the increasing *rapprochement* and mutual penetration of the national cultures of the large and small peoples."[44]

Another reflection of the rejection of linguistic diversity and the striving toward homogeneity is the tendency in non-Russian areas to reduce the number of languages of instruction. For example, a participant of the Alma-Ata Conference commented as follows on this trend in Uzbekistan, the most heavily populated republic after the R.S.F.S.R.:

> The organs of national education of Uzbekistan have consistently carried out a policy favoring the instruction of children in their native language or some other language, according to the wishes of the parents. As a consequence, during the period of developing Socialist construction, in the 1938–39 school year, instruction in Uzbekistan was conducted in twenty-two languages: Uzbek, Kazakh, Tadzhik, Russian, Ossetic, Armenian, Tatar, Yiddish, and so on. This was carried so far that when a Polish couple requested that their child study language and literature in his native tongue, that wish was granted.
>
> The policy of free choice by parents of the language of instruction in a society with our type of Socialist production relationships, nevertheless, has caused the former voluntarily and gradually to send their children to Russian-language schools. And now in Uzbekistan, instruction is carried on in seven instead of twenty-two languages—in the languages of the basic populations of Central Asia and Kazakhstan and in Russian. In the 1959–60 school year in Uzbekistan, children of non-Russian nationality (Ukrainian, Belorussian, Jewish, Armenian, Mordvin, Kazakh, etc.) constituted 50.2 per cent of the enrollment of Russian-language schools.[45]

The implications of such utterances seem fairly clear. Small ethnic groups can merge into the larger ones on a regional level, and the major ones can increasingly fuse with the still larger groups on the all-Union level. As the processes of *sblizheniye* and finally *sliyaniye* advance, it is difficult to see how the minority languages would not progressively lose the significance and number of their functions, and Russian, the lingua franca, gain continually at their expense.

A caveat is necessary, lest we become too hasty in underestimating the vigor of the minority languages of the U.S.S.R. They still continue to generate varying degrees of group solidarity and language loyalty among their respective speech communities. A historian, not a linguist, Hugh Seton-Watson, in numerous writings and talks, insists that language constitutes an enormous potential for maintaining and bolstering nationalistic feelings, passive though these may be. In his essay "Nationalism and Multi-National Empires," he has this to say: "The last category on which national consciousness has been based, and in modern times by far the most important, is language."[46] In discussing the non-Russian ethnic groups of the Soviet Union, he points to the experience of England with colonial India, demonstrating that there the fostering of native elites, who developed their own cultures and languages, was in the long run a divisive factor against loyalty to the British empire.[47]

Be this as it may, the possibility of a new phase of Soviet language planning is a real one. If it follows the lines suggested here, the Soviets will, of course, run the risk of creating a dilemma, in which the Leninist nationality policy, with its motto "national in form, socialist in content," would have to be reconciled with a situation in which Russian displaces the other languages for most purposes of serious written and spoken use in the Soviet linguistic communication model.

NOTES

1. See Jacob Ornstein, "Soviet Language Policy: Theory and Practice," *Slavic and East European Journal,* III (Spring, 1959), 1–24. This article also provides some basic bibliography on the subject.
2. See Heinz Kloss, *Die Entwicklung neuer germanischer Kultursprachen von 1800 bis 1950* (Munich, 1952).
3. For a Soviet discussion of this topic and standardization in general, see M. M. Guxman (ed.), *Voprosy formirovaniya i razvitiya natsional'nykh yazykov* (Moscow, 1960). This work is being translated and made available by Alfred Pietrzyk and others, at the Center for Applied Linguistics, Washington, D.C., with support from a National Science Foundation Grant.
4. See Karl W. Deutsch, *Nationalism and Social Communication* (New York: John Wiley & Sons, 1953), especially pp. 97–126, 204 ff.
5. Charles A. Ferguson speaks of the drawing up of "national sociolinguistic profiles," meaning the main features of the language communication network in a given country or place. See Charles A. Ferguson, "The Language Factor in National Development," in *Study of the Role of Second Languages in Asia, Africa, and Latin America,* ed. F. A. Rice (Washington, D.C.: Center for Applied Linguistics, 1962), p. 2.
6. A fine case in point here is the genesis of the language problem in Norway. See Einar Haugen, "Planning for a Standard Language in Modern Norway," *Anthropological Linguistics,* I (1959), 8–21.
7. Joshua Fishman, in his talk "Varieties of Ethnicity and Language Awareness," presented at Georgetown University, Sixteenth Annual Round Table Meeting on Linguistics and Language Studies, March 26, 1965. See also, Joshua Fishman, *Language Loyalty in the United States* (The Hague: Mouton, 1965).
8. See Felix Oinas, "Russian Calques in the Balto-Finnic Languages," in *Indiana Slavic Studies,* ed. Michael Ginsburg and Joseph T. Shaw (Bloomington, Ind.: Indiana University Press, I, 1956), 225–37.
9. It would be illuminating to apply Ferguson and Stewart's sociolinguistic classification systems to the languages of the U.S.S.R. See Ferguson, *op. cit.,* and William A. Stewart, "A Sociolinguistic Typology for Describing National Multilingualism," to be published in *A Reader on Sociolinguistics,* ed. Joshua Fishman. This is a revised version of Stewart's "Outline of Linguistic Typology for Describing Multilingualism," in *Study of the Role of Second Languages in Asia, Africa, and Latin America,* pp. 15–25.
10. *Voprosy razvitiya literaturnykh yazykov narodov SSSR v sovetskuyu epokhu* (Alma-Ata: Academy of Sciences of the Kazakh S.S.R., 1964), p. 18 (hereafter cited as *Voprosy razvitiya*).
11. A "pidgin" is a non-native language developed for trade, work, and other purposes between speakers of several languages, for example, "Melanesian Pidgin English in Southeast Asia."
12. Yaroslav Bilinsky, *The Second Soviet Republic: The Ukraine after World War II* (New Brunswick, N.J.: Rutgers University Press, 1964), pp. 141–85; also see pp. 16–35.
13. V. Danilov, "Problema izucheniya trekh yazykov v yakutskoy shkole" ("The Problem of Studying Three Languages in a Yakut School"), *Russkiy yazyk v natsional'noy shkole,* II (1959), 22.
14. Yaroslav Bilinsky, "The Soviet Education Laws of 1958–59 and Soviet

Nationality Policy," *Soviet Studies,* XIV (October, 1962), 138–57. See, also, his *The Second Soviet Republic,* pp. 29–32.

15. See Bilinsky, "The Soviet Education Laws of 1958–59 . . . ," pp. 146–47.
16. Bilinsky, *The Second Soviet Republic,* p. 31.
17. B. G. Gafurov, "Uspekhi natsional'noy politiki KPSS i nekotorye voprosy internatsional'nogo vospitaniya" ("Successes of the National Policy of the CPSU and Some Questions of International Education"), *Kommunist,* No. 11 (1958), p. 23.
18. *Ibid.*
19. "Some Impressions of the Central Asian Republics," *Central Asian Review* (London), XIII, No. 1 (1965), 12.
20. *Voprosy razvitiya,* pp. 348–49.
21. N. Dzhandil'din, "Nekotorye voprosy internatsional'nogo vospitaniya" ("Some Questions of International Education"), *Kommunist,* No. 13 (1959), p. 36.
22. *Ibid.,* p. 30.
23. "Program of the Communist Party," *Pravda,* July 30, 1961.
24. See Elliot R. Goodman, *The Soviet Design for a World State* (New York: Columbia University Press, 1960), pp. 264–84, and his "The Soviet Design for a World Language," *Russian Review,* XV (April, 1956), 85–99.
25. N. Gadzhiyev, "Kul'tury sotsialisticheskikh natsii, ikh nastoyashchee i budushchee," *Kommunist,* No. 1 (1962), p. 67.
26. *Ibid.,* p. 68.
27. P. Rogachev and M. Sverdlin, "Sovetskiy narod—novaya istoricheskaya obshchnost' lyudey," *Kommunist,* No. 9 (1963), p. 19.
28. "Za izucheniye i razvitiye natsional'nykh literaturnykh yazykov narodov SSSR" ("For the Study and Development of the National Literary Languages of the Nations of the USSR"), *Voprosy yazykoznaniya,* No. 4 (July–August, 1962), pp. 3–8.
29. *Voprosy razvitiya,* p. 355.
30. Akhmed Agayev, "V sem'e vol'noy, novoy" ("In the Free and New Family"), *Izvestiya,* December 5, 1961.
31. Vladimir Soloukhin, "Chto nas rodnit?," *Literatura i zhizn',* February 6, 1962. For a fuller discussion of "L'affaire Agayev," consult "The Nationalities Policy of the Soviet Union: A New Phase," *Central Asian Review,* X, No. 4 (1962), 330–31; and, particularly for rebuttals by Ukrainian authors, Bilinsky, *The Second Soviet Republic,* pp. 33–34, 322.
32. For a discussion of the conference, see S. Dovhal, "A Fight for the Language," *Problems of the Peoples of the USSR* (Munich), No. 18 (June, 1963), p. 47; and Bilinsky, *The Second Soviet Republic,* pp. 33–34. A great deal of information on language policy is available in the pages of *Problems of the Peoples of the USSR,* issued by the Institute for the Study of the USSR in Munich.
33. *Voprosy razvitiya,* pp. 320–21.
34. *Ibid.,* p. 215.
35. This phrase was coined by William E. Stewart. See his "Outline of Linguistic Typology. . . ."
36. A standard source for this is Richard E. Pipes, *The Formation of the Soviet Union: Communism and Nationalism, 1917–23* (Cambridge, Mass.: Harvard University Press, 1954).
37. It is clear from the context that the term "bilingualism" is here used to

include "multilingualism," a connotation becoming increasingly more widespread.

38. *Voprosy razvitiya,* pp. 373–76.
39. *Ibid.,* p. 224.
40. For an interesting and enlightening Western view of the *sblizheniye* of the Turkic languages, read "The Nationalities Policy of the Soviet Union: A New Phase," pp. 317–32.
41. V. K. Gardanov, B. O. Dolgikh, and T. A. Zhdanko, "Osnovnye napravleniya etnicheskikh protsessov u narodov SSSR," *Sovetskaya etnografiya,* IV (1961), 9.
42. *Ibid.,* pp. 13–14.
43. *Ibid.,* p. 18.
44. *Ibid.,* p. 28.
45. K. Kh. Khanazarov, in *Voprosy razvitiya,* pp. 340–41.
46. Hugh Seton-Watson, *Nationalism and Communism* (New York: Frederick A. Praeger, 1964), p. 7.
47. *Ibid.,* p. 18, *et passim;* see, particularly, pp. 24–30.

4

Assimilation and Ethnic Assertiveness Among Ukrainians of the Soviet Union

YAROSLAV BILINSKY

The Ukrainians in the Soviet Union present a paradox: Some of them occupy high positions in the Party, the secret police, and the armed forces in Moscow, while their fellow countrymen in Kiev have to struggle for such minimal needs as an adequate supply of books in good, unadulterated Ukrainian. Some share in ruling an empire, while many others find it hard to assert their cultural, let alone political, identity. Are the Ukrainians as a nation losing or gaining? The Ukrainian political elite in Moscow will be identified and their position discussed only briefly, for we know next to nothing about their attitude toward the Ukrainian cause in the Soviet Union. (The latter we arbitrarily define as the assertion of the cultural, socio-economic, and political interests of the Ukraine conceived *not* as a province of Russia but as the second most powerful member of the Soviet federation.) The bulk of our analysis will document the central government's attempts to break up the Ukrainian nation physically and morally—through population transfers and through cultural assimilation—as well as the Ukrainian reaction to that policy. Economic issues have been excluded.[1] So has all historical background.[2]

Under Khrushchev, a number of Ukrainians were given high positions in the Soviet armed forces. The late Minister of Defense, Rodion K. Malinovsky, who succeeded Zhukov in October, 1957, was officially listed as a Ukrainian, as was his deputy and successor, Andrey A. Grechko.[3] Another prominent Ukrainian is Marshal Kiril S. Moskalenko.[4] Specialists have identified them as members of the so-called Stalingrad group of officers who stood close to Khrushchev in World War II.[5] It is likely that all of these, with the possible exception of the somewhat independent-minded Malinovsky,[6] were personal protégés of Khrushchev. Their influence on Soviet nationality policy is problematical. The Party has done everything in its power to cut off the military from any access to political decision-making, quite apart from the delicate issue of nationalities. I would, therefore, estimate that Grechko, Moskalenko, and others are primarily so-called military specialists whose advancement largely was not related to their ethnic background. (I say "largely" because in the Soviet political climate it is highly unlikely that an Uzbek or a Jew, for example, would have been appointed Minister of Defense.) In any case, a Soviet military officer cannot—without running extreme risks—defend the cultural and political interests of his native people.

More could have been accomplished in that respect by Vladimir Ye. Semichastny, also a Ukrainian, and since November, 1961, head of the Soviet secret police. Semichastny is a professional politician put in charge of the Committee on State Security. But the secret police is now watched even more closely than the military. Its political moves can be gleaned only after a major upheaval (e.g., Beria's appeal to the non-Russian peoples in 1953).[7] Moreover, Semichastny, unlike his Russian predecessor Shelepin, does not appear to have the qualities of a major political leader. His links with the Ukrainian Party apparatus do not appear to be strong.[8] As this volume was going to press, it was announced that Semichastny had been replaced by Yuriy V. Andropov, a Russian, and since 1962 the Party Central Committee Secretary for relations with East European Communist parties. The immediate reason for Semichastny's removal appears to be a string of setbacks incurred by the KGB, not Semichastny's nationality or his political connections.[9]

More significant for Ukrainian national interests than either the high-ranking army or secret-police officials would appear to be top-ranking Party professionals, such as Kirilenko, Podgorny, Polyansky, Shelest, and Vitaly N. Titov. Kirilenko, admittedly, is officially listed as a Russian, but his name is typically Ukrainian, he was born in an ethnically mixed territory just outside the present border of the Ukraine, and more importantly perhaps, until 1955 he had held important posts in the Ukrainian Party apparatus.[10] Robert Conquest, a close student of Soviet affairs, flatly identifies him as a Ukrainian.[11] The first four are full members of the eleven-man Party Politburo. The fifth—Titov—was a member of the Secretariat, the executive arm of the Politburo. At first sight, the presence of four Ukrainians on that body—a third of its regular membership—would seem a major victory for the Ukrainians in the Soviet Union, who account for less than one-fifth of the total population.[12]

But what is their role on that body? To simplify our analysis, let us disregard the relative newcomer Shelest, who was appointed to alternate membership on the Presidium after Shcherbitsky's dismissal in December, 1963, and to full membership in November, 1964.[13] Possibly, as Conquest suggests, Shelest was made a full member on the initiative of other highly placed Ukrainians in order to counterbalance the appointment of Shelepin, who was granted full membership without going through the probationary stage of alternate as had Shelest.[14] Shelest's main qualification for the top post seems to lie above all in his control of the Ukrainian Party, whose First Secretary he has been since July, 1963. He thus appears to be a Politburo member ex officio. As soon as somebody else succeeds to his position in Kiev he will also take over his seat in Moscow. The other three Ukrainians on the Politburo, however, seem to have transcended this political limitation. Kirilenko was managing the Russian Republic Party organization immediately under Khrushchev; he appears to have maintained that position after his superior's fall;[15] Polyansky has apparently specialized in the supervision of agriculture;[16] Podgorny, the most senior of them, after Khrushchev's fall was involved in the very responsible, sensitive, and apparently thankless task of consolidating the industrial and agricultural branches of the Party throughout the U.S.S.R. This would indicate that Podgorny, who, alone among the four Ukrainians on the Presidium, was also a Secretary of the Central Committee, fulfilled the role of the Second Secretary in charge of cadres, or, in other words, was Brezhnev's immediate deputy in Party affairs.[17] Some years before Podgorny's assumption of power, from 1957 to 1960, the post of the Second Secretary in charge of personnel was held by another Ukrainian, Alexey I. Kirichenko. Kirichenko was dramatically demoted in January, 1960, and mysteriously disappeared from Soviet politics altogether in the summer of that year.[18] Until April, 1965, Podgorny and his predecessors were assisted in their work by the Ukrainian Titov, who since 1961 had been employed in the Central Committee's personnel administration, and had been a Secretary of the Committee since late 1962.[19]

These five Ukrainians are only the most well-known of their fellow countrymen to achieve high Party positions under Khrushchev. Professor Seweryn Bialer, who has very carefully investigated the composition of the All-Union Central Committees since 1939, contends that under Khrushchev there was a "Ukrainization" of the Central Committee.[20] Ukrainians were the only nationality other than the Russians whose members served in three major capacities: in their own republican Party apparatus (i.e., in the Ukraine), in the central Party machinery in Moscow, and in responsible posts in other republics.[21]

The rapid advancement of these Ukrainian Party cadres deserves careful examination. The suspicion is great that they were promoted because they were personally known and loyal to Khrushchev. This has been documented in some detail by Bialer.[22] Conquest adds two related negative considerations. As of November, 1964, the four Ukrainian Presidium members were the only ones who had not served on Stalin's last Central Committee in 1952. From the viewpoint of the regular Party organization they are upstarts. "Nor has their interim record been more than mediocre," he continues, "and certainly not so outstanding as to call for special promotion."[23] On the other hand, Bialer, though emphasizing the opportunistic reasons,[24] suggests that the Ukrainians might also have been advanced as a result of a conscious long-range policy decision:

> Ukrainians are not only the second largest nationality group in the Union, but the only group which can challenge Russian domination in the higher social and political strata in politically meaningful numbers. Moreover, the proximity of the Ukrainian language, cultural tradition, ethnic origin and characteristics make such a challenge less conspicuous and therefore more acceptable to the Russians.[25]

But Stalin thought otherwise, and during his life Ukrainians were discriminated against.[26] Before 1953, Party membership in the Ukraine was indeed disproportionately low. It was rapidly increased under, rather than because of, Khrushchev, and some but by no means all of the promotions may have been due to the regime's recognition of the new objective strength of the Ukrainian Party.[27] The corollary hypothesis that the Ukrainian appointees have overreached themselves, that after their protector's dismissal they have become very vulnerable,[28] has been lent new credence by Titov's mysterious assignment to the Second Secretaryship of the Communist Party of Kazakhstan.[29] In a non-Russian republic the Second Secretary may actually be the power behind the throne. Nor was it clear from the brief announcement in *Pravda* whether or not Titov has retained his Secretaryship of the Central Committee. It appears, however, certain that his position in drought-plagued Kazakhstan is less powerful than his old post in Moscow, where he headed the Central Committee Commission on Organizational Party Questions—a Party personnel agency.[30] The purge of Ukrainians from the highest Party offices had begun.

The main question that we have to ask ourselves is: "What benefits have nationally conscious Ukrainians derived from the positions of Kirichenko, Podgorny, and their like?" Are those men "plainly not at present to be considered as in any case representing anything more than one denationalized faction within the CPSU as a whole," as Conquest put it?[31] The published evidence indicates that on one occasion, so-called Ukrainian comrades were able to persuade Khrushchev to overrule a Gosplan decision that would have allotted a new hydroelectric plant to Siberia rather than to the Ukraine.[32] In other words, Ukrainian Party officials were not above some lobbying for the economic interests of their country. On the other hand, it is true that Kirichenko, although Khrushchev's first deputy, either could not or would not defend the Ukrainian language against the impact of the school reform of 1958–59. The highest Ukrainian Party leaders to speak up against certain provisions of the proposed reform were a junior secretary of the Kiev oblast committee (Tron'ko) and a junior secretary of the Central Committee of the Ukrainian Party (Chervonenko). Podgorny, who was then First Secretary of the Ukrainian Communist Party, kept silent.[33] Podgorny, not to mention Kirilenko and the considerably junior Polyansky and Shelest, also did not speak out against the pronounced assimilationist trend of the 1961 Party Program. Only the future will show for certain whether the four Ukrainians on today's Politburo are anything more than individual careerists who had survived the antinationalist purges of Stalin and been elevated by Khrushchev. Meanwhile, while their presence on that body is not a clear asset to the Ukrainian people, it does not appear to be a liability. There is the likelihood that at least Podgorny and Shelest will maintain contact with the Ukrainian Party organization and dispense some patronage.

But whatever influence these men yield, it is apparently not sufficient to prevent a falling-off in the hiring of Ukrainians for professional positions in the Ukraine, as happened between 1962 and 1964 (see Table I, below). The official statistics try to gloss this over by combining figures of professionals and semiprofessionals, which amounts to mixing college-educated engineers, e.g., with technicians from specialized high schools. Most meaningful are figures on professionals alone. They show, above all, that between 1957 and 1964, the share of Russian professionals in the Ukraine rose steadily (from 25.0 to 28.1 per cent)—*partly* at the expense of Ukrainians whose proportion since 1960 has been held down to about 58 per cent (58 in 1960, 58.4 in 1961, 58.5 in 1962, and 58.1 in 1964), but *mainly* at the expense of other nationalities whose share has fallen from 18.2 per cent in 1957 to 13.8 per cent in 1964. There is reason to believe that most of these other nationals are Jews.[34] The table shows clearly that the Ukrainians in the republic have not yet attained socio-economic parity with the Russians. The Ukrainian share in the total population, according to the 1959 census, was 76.8 per cent, that

TABLE I

ETHNIC COMPOSITION OF PROFESSIONALS AND SEMIPROFESSIONALS (GRADUATES OF COLLEGES AND SPECIALIZED SECONDARY SCHOOLS) EMPLOYED IN THE UKRAINIAN S.S.R., 1957–64

(December 1, except where indicated)

(*in per cent*)

	1957	1959	1960	1961	1962	1964[a]
Professionals						
(*Total in thousands*)	*534.6*	*625.4*	*685.9*	*742.5*	*789.8*	*883.8*
Ukrainians	56.8	57.9	58.0	58.4	58.5	58.1
Russians	25.0	26.3	26.7	26.8	27.0	28.1
Others	18.2	15.8	15.3	14.8	14.5	13.8
Semiprofessionals						
(*Total in thousands*)	*729.5*	*885.4*	*975.1*	*1,051.7*	*1,110.0*	*1,279.4*
Ukrainians	66.9	67.8	67.4	67.2	67.4	66.7
Russians	23.0	24.1	24.5	24.7	24.7	25.3
Others	10.1	8.1	8.1	8.1	7.9	8.0
Both categories						
(*Total in thousands*)	*1,264.1*	*1,510.8*	*1,661.0*	*1,794.2*	*1,899.8*	*2,163.2*
Ukrainians	62.6	63.7	63.5	63.5	63.7	63.2
Russians	23.9	25.0	25.4	25.1	25.7	26.5
Others	13.5	11.3	11.1	11.4	10.6	10.3

SOURCES: For 1959, see Tsentral'ne statystychne upravlinnya, *Narodne hospodarstvo Ukrayins'koyi RSR v 1959 r.: Statystychny shchorichnyk* (*National Economy of the Ukrainian SSR in 1959: A Statistical Yearbook*) (Kiev, 1960), p. 519. For 1961, see *Nar. hosp. URSR v 1961 r.* (Kiev, 1962), p. 533. For 1957, 1960, 1962, and 1964, see *Nar. hosp. URSR v 1964 r.* (Kiev, 1965), p. 476.

[a]As of November 15, 1964.

of the better paid professionals was, however, only about 58 per cent. Conversely, the figure of Russian professionals (about 28 per cent) is a much better indicator of Russian economic and political strength in the Ukraine than their share in the total population of the Republic (16.9 per cent in 1959).

One of the most difficult problems in this connection would be to ascertain whether the inferior Ukrainian position is still mostly due to their peasant past or whether this state is being artificially maintained by siphoning off trained Ukrainians to other republics. To give a practical example, in 1961, 63,224 professionals graduated from colleges in the Ukraine, of whom about 62.5 per cent, or 39,515, were Ukrainians.[35] In that year, only some 35,798 Ukrainians were hired for professional posts in the republic.[36] *Assuming that the graduates' training was such that they could have competently filled* the *existing vacancies,* we find a surplus of 3,717 Ukrainians who were assigned jobs outside the republic, mostly for political reasons.[37] That assumption, of course, is very difficult to prove, nor is it to be ruled out that some Ukrainians leave their republic of their own accord. The main point, however, is that except for a few careers, of which the military may be the foremost, Ukrainians as a national group are being discriminated against.

The basic centralizing, assimilationist policy of the government has not changed since Khrushchev's fall,[38] apart from the abolition of the Central Asian Economic Council, which hampered the powers of the republics involved.[39] The following general directive of the 1961 Party Program is still binding: "Full-scale Communist construction constitutes a new stage in the development of national relations in the U.S.S.R. in which the nations will draw still closer together until complete unity is achieved."[40] The Program also very usefully spells out the approach toward the achievement of complete unity:

1. The increased "mobility of the population and . . . greater intercourse between the peoples of the Soviet Union"; specifically, the "continuous exchange of trained personnel among nations."[41]
2. Administrative changes of republican frontiers and boundaries of economic regions. ("The boundaries between the Union republics of the U.S.S.R. are increasingly losing their former significance.")[42]
3. Further encouragement of the spread of Russian as a medium of access "to the cultural gains of all the other peoples of the U.S.S.R., and to world culture."[43]

It is to be taken for granted that all opposition to assimilation, such as the "idealization of the [national] past" and "manifestations of national aloofness in the education and employment of workers of different nationalities in the Soviet republics," is to be vigorously combated.[44]

The most dangerous ingredient of Soviet nationality policy from the viewpoint of Ukrainian ethnic interests is the planned exchange of population: immigration of Russians into the Ukraine and the emigration of Ukrainians into Kazakhstan, Western Siberia, etc. A recent scholarly article raises the specter of the resettlement in those areas of up to 16 million Ukrainians within the next twenty-five years, or as much as two-thirds of the normal population increase in the Ukraine.[45] This exchange is dangerous because the increased immigration of Russians, mainly into the cities, raises new demands for the provision of cultural services in Russian, such as schools, which are already very extensive in the Ukraine. The constant stream of Russian immigrants (between 1926 and 1959, the Russian minority in the Ukraine doubled, while the number of Ukrainians increased by 10 per cent)[46] helps to maintain the relative Russification of the cities. In the cities, ethnic Russians now form 30 per cent of the total population, as compared with 21.4 per cent in 1926. At first sight, the number of urban Ukrainians seems to have increased proportionately, from 40.3 to 61.5 per cent during the same period. But the Soviet Ukrainian demographer Naulko warns us that much of this latter increase may be fictitious: between 1926 and 1959, the city boundaries would often be expanded to include the suburban villages, most of which were predominantly inhabited by Ukrainians. This, in Naulko's words, "played a considerable part in increasing the percentage of the Ukrainian urban population."[47] The apparently disproportionate influx of Russians into the *old* cities had an impact not only on the ethnic composition as such but also on the pattern of ethnic intermarriages and on linguistic preferences among the urban Ukrainians.

The total number of Ukrainian emigrants has not been fully disclosed, though Naulko admits that "there is an annual planned voluntary resettlement of families and individuals from the densely populated Ukrainian regions to other regions of the country," meaning other areas of the Soviet Union.[48] In a long, incisive, and documented article on population exchanges, Stepan Y. Prociuk, a refugee scholar, has drawn our attention to some global figures contained in an inconspicuous Soviet article which allows us a rough estimate of the emigration from the Ukraine.[49] According to P. Kovalenkov, a bureau chief in the Ukrainian S.S.R. Gosplan, between 1946 and 1962, nearly 88,000 peasant families from the Ukraine were resettled, while during the same period about 810,000 workers left under the program of organized labor intake.[50] According to Soviet sources an average Ukrainian peasant family consists of four persons, which would mean an emigration of 352,000 peasants including dependents. The total population outflow would thus rise to 1,162,000 persons. On the basis of further official data, Prociuk obtains the number of Ukrainian emigrants: to wit, 920,000.[51]

This last figure is subject to the objection that according to Soviet law the "organized labor intake" (involving in our instance 810,000 men, Ukrainians and non-Ukrainians) is conceived as an assignment on a contractual basis: Once the contract expires—usually after three years—the worker is presumably free to move elsewhere, possibly return to the Ukraine.[52] Viewing the movement realistically, however, I think we would find that many Soviet workers are not likely to travel from the Ukraine to Central Asia and back again within the short span of a few years. I would therefore be inclined to accept Prociuk's figure as a maximum estimate as far as the workers are concerned. The peasants' figure is firm. Furthermore, Kovalenkov's figures do not include the emigration of Ukrainian professionals and semiprofessionals. Prociuk plausibly estimates that from 1946 to 1962, the figure of those who left the Ukraine amounted to some 400,000, over and above those 920,000.[53] In short, between 1946 and 1962, some 1,320,000 Ukrainians left the Ukraine.[54]

It is important to bear three major related considerations in mind. The exchange of population of different nationalities is an old established Soviet institution sanctioned by the 1961 Party Program. To take only its most sensitive aspect, viz., the intermixture of well-trained young professionals, we find that this is discreetly prescribed by Soviet administrative law. College graduates are obligated to work for three years at a job to which they are directed by special allocation commissions functioning under the Union-Republican Ministries of Higher Education.[55] Those Ministries in turn are expected to coordinate their plans of assignment of college graduates with the Gosplan of the U.S.S.R., *not* that of their republic.[56] In light of this and the general nationality policy, the existence of quotas for the assignment of college-educated professionals outside their native republics, though not clearly acknowledged, must be presumed.[57] These quotas are probably set by the U.S.S.R. Gosplan or by the U.S.S.R. Council of the National Economy (SNKh).[58]

Second, the policy of population exchange has continued to this day. According to the official Komsomol paper, *Molod' Ukrayiny,* of March 10, 1965, 110,000 "young patriots" left in 1964 to work on construction sites in Northern Siberia, Kazakhstan, and the Soviet Far East. On February 17, 1965, Radio Lutsk broadcast an appeal to the citizens of the Volhynia oblast by a resettlement agent from Kazakhstan.[59] The appeal was not without success: a group left for Kazakhstan early in April.[60]

Third, once Ukrainians leave their republic they are subjected to a concerted Russification drive. Though, according to the 1959 census, as many as 5.1 million Ukrainians live outside the Ukraine, frequently in compact groups, virtually no Ukrainian schools have been allowed outside the republic ever since Stalin had them closed down in 1933.[61] Practically no Ukrainian books or papers are published locally, and books and journals from the Ukraine arrive with great delays, if at all.[62] Only the most minimal and irregular forms of Ukrainian activities, such as amateur theaters, concerts by visiting artists from the Ukraine, are permitted outside the Republic.[63] As a result of being exposed to stronger assimilation pressures, in 1959 only 51.2 per cent self-declared Ukrainians living in the other republics of the U.S.S.R. gave Ukrainian as their "native" (actually, most frequently used) language, compared with 93.5 of their fellow countrymen in the Ukraine.[64]

What have the Ukrainian people and Ukrainian Party officials done to oppose the population transfers with their denationalizing effect? No published evidence of opposition against the influx of Russians has been found, though such evidence is available for Latvia, Kazakhstan, Uzbekistan, and Turkmenia.[65] Why did Ukrainians remain silent while their national substance was being undermined, particularly in the cities? Possibly they did so because the influx of Russians has not yet reached such critical proportions as in Kazakhstan, Latvia, or Estonia,[66] or possibly out of fear of severe reprisals, of which the Ukraine has had her share. Protests of this nature led to the removal of the Latvian Prime Minister, his deputy, and a Minister of Education, not to mention dozens of high Party and state officials; they also terminated the careers of the First Secretary of the Communist Party of Turkmenia and that of the Kazakh Prime Minister. Efforts, however, have been made to mitigate the denationalizing effect of emigration from the Ukraine. The most ambitious attempt in recent years was the demand made at a large republican conference of scholars, educators, and communication specialists, in February, 1963, to re-establish public education in Ukrainian outside the republic. But not only did the government reject that demand, it suppressed its publication in the Ukraine.[67]

The rate of ethnic intermarriages has gone up, partly as a result of increased population exchanges. Figures on this were released only some five years after the census of 1959, and they have not been included in the series of authoritative census publications, so that to this day they remain rather incomplete. We do not know, e.g., the number of ethnic intermarriages among the Ukrainians in the Soviet Union as a whole and in each of the fifteen republics separately: we have intermarriage rates only for the total population of the U.S.S.R., the total populations of the individual Republics, and a somewhat cryptic figure for ethnic intermarriages among the major nationalities of the Ukrainian S.S.R. The general intermarriage rate in the Ukraine is one of the highest in the U.S.S.R. (150 per thousand, compared with the Soviet average of 102); it is second only to that in the Latvian S.S.R. (158 per 1,000).[68] As was to be expected, the ethnic intermarriage rate in the Ukrainian cities (263 per thousand) is considerably higher than that in the Ukrainian countryside (58 per thousand). But how many ethnic Ukrainians are actually involved? Naulko offers this somewhat misleading comment: "According to the data of a 5 per cent reprocessing of the results of the All-Union census of 1959, mixed marriages constitute 26.3 per cent in the [Ukrainian] Republic today; 18.5 per cent among the Ukrainians, 40.6 per cent among the Russians, 10.3 per cent among the Jews, 51.8 per cent among the Poles, etc."[69] However, 26.3 per cent are 263 per thousand, the figure cited by Isupov, where it stood for intermarriages among the urban population only. If their figures are compatible, it would appear that Naulko's "5 per cent reprocessing" included urban responses only. This in turn means that out of the 263 per thousand ethnically mixed marriages in Ukrainian cities, only 185 involve Ukrainians and are thus pertinent to our concern. Nevertheless, compared with 1927, when only about 148 urban Ukrainians per thousand had married non-Ukrainian spouses, this is a considerable increase.[70]

One reason for the increase in intermarriages may be found in the pronounced demographic imbalance between the sexes caused by the Great Purges of the 1930's and, above all, by World War II. Also, fewer boys seem to have been born in the 1930's. Starting with the 25–29 age group, there is a definite surplus of women in the Ukraine.[71] In 1959, 820 out of 1,000 Ukrainian men, and only 727 Ukrainian women in that group were married. The disproportion grows with age: in the next age group (30–34), it is 934:750; among those 35–39 years old, whose men had been drafted into the Red Army, it is 962:692; among the next group the imbalance is 969:595.[72] It is most likely that the shortage of males is a powerful factor in ethnic intermarriages. The absence of sharp racial and cultural distinctions between Ukrainians and Russians is another. But whatever the cause, ethnic intermarriages are more conducive to assimilation to the politically dominant nationality (the Russians) than to the maintenance of the characteristics of the weaker nationality. No signs of opposition to this process have been observed among the Ukrainians.

The second major aspect of Soviet nationality policy delineated by the 1961 Party Program, to wit, changes in political and economic boundaries, has not yet impinged upon the Ukraine, although it has on the republics of Central Asia. On the contrary, in 1954 the Ukraine benefited from the Crimea being ceded to her by the Russian Republic. (Neither the Ukraine nor Russia has any moral or historical claim to the ancient home of the Crimean Tatars. But the administration of the Crimea by noncontiguous Russia was a distinct anomaly, and it was rectified in 1954.) Moreover, the Ukraine encompasses a relatively large territory and is comparatively self-sufficient economically, so that it is not so easy to manipulate her boundaries. But the Ukrainians are much more vulnerable to the third aspect of Soviet nationality policy: linguistic Russification.

The extent of that phenomenon can be gauged from the data of the 1959 census. The respondents were asked to state not only their nationality but also their "native language," the latter being apparently defined as the language of conversation (*Umgangssprache*) rather than their parents' language (*Muttersprache*).[73] During the census the Ukrainians thus had two opportunities to affirm their nationality: first, by declaring themselves Ukrainians, and, second, by giving Ukrainian as their native language. By comparing their responses with those in 1926 one could reach some cautious conclusions about the persistence of Ukrainian. The language in turn appears a powerful medium for the perpetuation of national culture.[74]

The linguistic Russification of Ukrainians proceeds apace. In 1926, 941 out of 1,000 self-declared Ukrainians in Eastern Ukraine (excluding Galicia, Volhynia, Bukovina, and Transcarpathia) gave Ukrainian as their native language. In 1959, *in the very same area* only 925 out of 1,000 Ukrainians did so. In 1926, 56 per thousand gave Russian as their native language, and in 1959, 75.[75] If the Western Ukraine is included, we obtain the figure of 935 (or 934) Ukrainian speakers per 1,000 of self-declared Ukrainians in 1959, which is most likely a decrease compared with 1926.[76] The linguistic Russification of the urban Ukrainians is more pronounced than that of rural Ukrainians (153 per thousand urbanites speak Russian compared with 13 per thousand rural dwellers);[77] the Russification of Ukrainians living outside their republic is even stronger, as has already been pointed out. On the other hand, on the all-union scale, more Ukrainian women retained their national language than did men; and—what is perhaps even more significant—it has been found that urban young male adults (age 20–34) and male children (age 0–19) tended to be a little less Russified than the middle-aged group that had undergone the terror of the 1930's. This might perhaps signify a countertrend toward linguistic Russification.[78]

In "Nationality and Language in the Ukraine: A Political and Demographic Analysis," a paper delivered on June 14, 1965, before the Canadian Association of Slavists, Professor John A. Armstrong offered a most valuable analysis of the data from the 1926, 1939, and 1959 censuses. He presented the following hypotheses: first, that there was very little correlation between the rate of urban growth and the proportion of Ukrainian speakers in the cities. My explanation of this is that the influx of Ukrainians from the countryside may be counterbalanced by an influx of Russians (Naulko, e.g., stresses non-Ukrainian immigration into the cities), or that the rural Ukrainians change their language upon immigrating into the cities, or both. Armstrong's second hypothesis is that the degree of linguistic Ukrainization of the urban areas is correlated to the compactness of the Ukrainian population. This correlation is not very close either. Professor Armstrong presents fascinating new data showing that outside the Ukrainian S.S.R., urban Ukrainian colonies of approximately the same relative size have different numbers of Ukrainian speakers. Thus use of Ukrainian is evidently minimal in Moscow and Voronezh (Russian S.F.S.R.) but quite prominent in the urban colonies in Kazakhstan. Almost as much Ukrainian is spoken by urban Ukrainians in Kazakhstan as in Odessa, Kiev, Nikolaev, and the Donbas. Many of the Ukrainians in Kazakhstan might possibly be relatively recent immigrants, and some even former political deportees who would continue to speak Ukrainian as a form of political protest. But the Ukrainians in Alma Ata, the old capital of Kazakhstan, tend to be more Russified. Professor Armstrong is led to refine his second hypothesis to state that "Russian has an attractive power in old urban areas of traditional Russian culture higher than would ordinarily result from the proportion of Russian speakers in the area." The greatest correlation has thus been established between urban Ukrainians speaking Russian and the number of Russian speakers in the city, whether ethnic Russians or not (hypothesis No. 3). Professor Armstrong finally notes in his general discussion that the *proportion* of Russian speakers among the self-declared urban Ukrainians in the Ukraine is far lower than it was a generation ago, but that in *absolute* terms the number of such Ukrainians speaking Russian has increased considerably, which reinforces the general impression of the continuing Russifying influence of the cities. There is little comfort in this for the Ukrainians, particularly in view of the fact that city boundaries have been manipulated so as to include Ukrainian workers from the suburbs, and the possibility that some of the most Russified Ukrainians by descent may have escaped our analysis by the simple expedient of giving Russian as their nationality.

Soviet Ukrainians realize the danger of linguistic Russification and it is in this area that they have made loud protests and waged an open polemic for years: for more teaching in Ukrainian at both higher and elementary-secondary schools, for the development of a Ukrainian scientific and technological terminology, for the cleansing of Ukrainian from alien Russian words and expressions. Recently an educator protested against the overloading of curriculums in Ukrainian-language schools with non-Ukrainian literary material; year in, year out, publication of Ukrainian books in inordinately small editions has been sharply criticized in the pages of Soviet Ukrainian newspapers; within the last two years, the work of a talented young poet has been thrown into the battle—illegally and posthumously.

In the long view, the program of elementary and secondary schools is the most important, for practically every Ukrainian now attends at least an eight-year school. In 1958, Ukrainian educators and parents, cautiously backed by some Ukrainian Party leaders, publicly opposed the intention of the regime to make Ukrainian an optional language in the Russian-language schools of the republic. They were defeated in 1959.[79] Not only was Ukrainian dropped from some schools as part of the school-reform of 1958–59, but more schools were set up in which all the instruction was in Russian. Before the reform, out of a total of 30,077 schools, 4,355 (or 14.5 per cent) were Russian. In the school year 1963–64, there were only 29,918 schools, of which "more than 4,500" (or at least 15 per cent) were Russian. The number of Ukrainian schools had meanwhile declined from 25,464 (84.7 per cent) in 1958 to 24,485 (81.8 per cent) in 1963.[80] Superficially this appears more than a fair proportion, the Ukrainians accounting for only 76.8 per cent of the republic's population in 1959. But the "catch" lies in the high probability that most of the Russian schools are large, well-equipped, and competently staffed institutions, whereas most of the Ukrainian schools are smaller and poorer rural units. I have been able to obtain an approximate breakdown of the schools in the city of Kiev, for which we possess nationality data from the 1959 census. According to these, the total city population consisted of 60.1 per cent Ukrainians, 23.0 per cent Russians, and 13.9 per cent Jews.[81] But the distribution of schools is an altogether different matter.

Out of a total of 171 schools that were accounted for in the year 1958–59, in only 70 (i.e., 40.9 per cent) was Ukrainian the language of instruction, and as in many as 101 (59.1 per cent) it was Russian. The comparison becomes even more invidious if we consider the quality of the schools involved. Of the 70 Ukrainian schools, 4 (5.7 per cent) were four-year elementary schools only; the Russian group did not contain any such schools. The Ukrainian schools further included 12 (or 17.1 per cent) so-called incomplete secondary schools (seven-year schools); there were only 8 such schools among the Russian (7.9 per cent of that group). But among the full ten-year schools, Russian schools outnumbered Ukrainian 93 to 54. In the nation's capital, only 77.2 per cent of Ukrainian schools had all ten grades, as compared to 92.1 per cent of the Russian schools.[82] The objection could be raised that a considerable number of Ukrainians in Kiev—28 per cent[83]—had given Russian as their native language. This would bring the distribution of schools more in line with the breakdown into Ukrainian- and Russian-speaking groups. But this in turn raises the question to what extent education influences the speaking habits: a portion of those 28 per cent self-declared Ukrainians may have adopted Russian after attending Russian-language schools. Nor is it to be excluded that a number of Ukrainian parents may welcome instruction in Russian which gives their children a better preparation for entry into the prestige universities of Moscow and Leningrad. Because of official pressure from above and partial acceptance from below, Ukrainians appear powerless to halt the steady expansion of Russian-language schools in the Ukraine: in 1955–56, there were only 4,008 of them, or 13.7 per cent of the total.[84]

The partial reversal of Khrushchev's school reform in August, 1964, providing for the abolition of the eleventh-school year by September, 1966, furnished educators and parents with an opportunity to insist on the advancement of their interests. The most skillful and energetic, not to say impassioned, representation was made by six well-known Estonian writers arguing that eleven-year education should be retained in their Republic. Their appeal was successful.

No similar protests apparently were made in the Ukraine. The reduction of the curriculum to ten years seems to have been accepted as a *fait accompli.*[85] To be fair, we should point out that before 1958, the schools in the Ukraine had operated on a ten-year program whereas an eleven-year curriculum had been traditional in the Baltic countries. Nevertheless, judging by a report published in the paper of the Writers' Union of the Ukraine, many Ukrainian educators are dissatisfied with the few hours allotted to the study of Ukrainian literature and language in the schools of the republic. The article refers to a conference that was recently held at the Ukrainian Scientific and Research Pedagogical Institute. "Public opinion [*hromads'kist'*], stated the participants, was disturbed by the fact that in the schools of the Republic the number of hours assigned to the study of literature, Ukrainian literature in particular, was slowly dwindling. This was an abnormal and illogical phenomenon. It contradicted the vital needs of a many-sided development of the individual."[86] As an official of the Republican Ministry of Education pointed out, only three hours a week were allotted to the study of Ukrainian literature in Grades IX and X. The correspondent found it to be "little, much too little." (For political reasons it was not mentioned that in Grade IX, Russian literature is assigned as many as four hours, in Grade X—three!)[87] As one of the conference participants remarked "wittily": "But even these 'positions' must be held." The correspondent added that "reserves" should be found not only to "maintain the positions," but also to increase the hours for literature, especially Ukrainian literature.

The very use of military terminology in the report would indicate that a continuing battle is in progress between the assimilators and the defenders of the Ukrainian national heritage. So far the assimilators have been winning ground, but not without stiffening opposition. A fascinating example of individual protests is a letter to the editor by a teacher from the Western Ukraine. He complains that the material of the anthologies is so arranged that Ukrainian schoolchildren are made to study the Ukrainian language on the basis of translations, presumably from the Russian. He had counted the pieces in the reader for Grade I and found two Ukrainian folktales, one single Ukrainian folksong, fifteen excerpts from Ukrainian classics, and as many as fifty-two translations. In the first four grades the schoolchildren read about 250 translations and only one-third as many Ukrainian folk-tales, songs, and classic excerpts. Contemporary Soviet Ukrainian writers had more of their works included, but often these were repetitious and poor.[88]

Of very great significance in the long run is also the ability of nationally conscious Ukrainian-speaking Ukrainians to enter higher Soviet schools. Unfortunately the most recent available data, those for 1963, are so summary that they show only the total number of Ukrainians studying in the U.S.S.R. as a whole, without a breakdown into republics. Even from these figures it would appear, however, that for whatever reasons (e.g., the comparatively high proportion of fairly immobile rural population in the Ukraine, political discrimination,[89] language difficulty) Ukrainians continue to suffer from a relative disadvantage in obtaining a college education. At the beginning of the academic year 1963–64, only 15.5 per cent of all Soviet college students were Ukrainians and as many as 64.7 per cent were Russians, compared with a Ukrainian share in the total population of 17.8 and a Russian share of 54.7 per cent (as of 1959).[90] These figures do not tell us anything, of course, about the extent of the students' assimilation to Russians in speech and outlook. If many of them study outside the Ukraine—and almost one quarter did in 1960–61[91]—they would be exposed to very strong assimilationist pressures. In this connection it might be worth noting that the establishment of a new university in the Ukraine has been authorized in Donetsk (Donbas).[92] The Donbas, however, is one of the more Russified regions of the Ukraine. Furthermore, courses in many colleges of the republic are taught in Russian. It is significant that no official statistics on the Russification of higher schools in the Ukraine have been published since the late 1920's.[93] Even today the language of instruction is apparently considered a state secret. A recent handbook for candidates for admission lists all kinds of information, except the language in which the prospective freshmen are to be taught.[94]

Friends of the Ukrainians cannot but hope that the situation in the colleges of their republic will not deteriorate as much as it apparently already has in Belorussia and Kirghizia. In Belorussia, all colleges, even teachers colleges, with the sole exception of *departments* of Belorussian language and literature, require candidates for admission to pass examinations in Russian language and literature, which seems to indicate that Russian is the language of instruction virtually everywhere.[95] In Kirghizian colleges all teaching is in Russian, with the result that the share of Kirghiz students has steadily declined because Kirghiz, who have difficulty in mastering Russian, are defeated in admissions competition by Russians.[96] According to private but authoritative sources, Ukrainian authorities are aware that the graduates of some Ukrainian rural schools, too, might not do so well in the countrywide entrance competition as some graduates from urban areas outside the republic. In 1963, at the Kiev conference on the "culture of the Ukrainian language," the demand was raised to conduct higher education in Ukrainian.[97] It went unheeded by the government. A few Ukrainian colleges have now taken to sending their faculty out on periodic inspection visits to relatively backward rural Ukrainian schools in an effort to bring them up to norm and increase their graduates' chances for admission to college.

The battle against cluttering up the Ukrainian language with borrowings from Russian is not new. It has been waged for at least a decade.[98] Recently the editors of *Literaturna Ukrayina* have urged periodic scholarly conferences on the culture of the Ukrainian language, the publication of appropriate yearbooks, the establishment of a special division within the Institute of Linguistics to watch over the quality of Ukrainian, and the public discussion of lexicographical materials.[99] But they seem to be fighting a hard battle, for the regime appears deliberately to encourage the wholesale borrowing of Russian words.[100] Valiant efforts are being made to establish a scientific and technological Ukrainian terminology, but the published dictionaries and handbooks somehow always happen to contain an overabundance of "carbon copies" from Russian terms.[101] The question of whether Ukrainian will be allowed to become a sociologically complete language or will be stunted in its development is not an unimportant one, but to my mind the more pressing problem (and one which lends itself better to analysis by a trained political scientist) is the extent of the Ukrainian language in print, in films, radio and theater performances. Let us start with the printed word.

The number of books published in Ukrainian in the Ukraine has steadily declined from a high point in 1958 (3,975 titles then, 3,321 in 1963), though it has not yet reached the low figures under Stalin (1,856 in 1950, e.g.).[102] But again, as under Stalin, more Russian books are published in the Ukraine than Ukrainian books (4,094, compared with 3,321 in 1963).[103] With respect to periodicals the situation is slightly better: In 1963, there were 130 periodicals in Ukrainian, 124 in Russian.[104] In 1963, 639 newspapers were printed in Ukrainian, compared with 365 in Russian;[105] but in 1956, there were as many as 979 in Ukrainian out of a total of 1,273.[106] In addition, numerous books, journals, and papers are, of course, imported from Russia. As if to add insult to injury, many Ukrainian books are published in surprisingly small editions and thus do not find their way to the bookstores and libraries.

In the wake of numerous complaints early in 1965, two Ukrainian newspapers—*Literaturna Ukrayina,* the organ of the Writers Union of Ukraine, and *Robitnycha hazeta,* the organ of the Ukrainian Trade Union Congress—sent their staffs on field trips to the bookstores and warehouses of the republic. The first report on bookselling in Kiev was given by L. Kovalenko, a doctor of philology. With appropriate restraint, he cited examples of booksellers ordering inadequate numbers of copies, which in turn results in the publication of insufficiently large editions of valuable works on Ukrainian culture and literature. Significant is a barbed paragraph in an otherwise academic report: "Some booksellers try to explain all this by chance. No, answer we, there are too many facts to believe in mere chance. This is clear from the cited figures, and we hope that the proper conclusions will be drawn."[107]

The most noxious aspect of the continuing battle of editions is that Ukrainian books for schoolchildren and teachers, unlike books in Russian, are extremely difficult to obtain. School library shelves bend under the weight of such fat but insubstantial volumes as S. P. Zhikharev's[108] *Zapiski sovremennika,* while at one school not a single copy of Sosyura's poems in the original Ukrainian was to be found. (The late Sosyura is a recognized Soviet Ukrainian poet, and his works are assigned reading in Ukrainian schools.) The librarian had to use a Russian translation of his poems and translate them back into the original as well as she could in order to acquaint the students at least with the contents of a poem.[109]

Surveys of the field of children's books—the most important area perhaps for the development of a broad Ukrainian culture—revealed a very discouraging state of affairs: in Kharkov, e.g., the schools were ordering Ukrainian books in dribbles of 250–500 copies to satisfy the needs of 1,638 school libraries in the province. Furthermore, the 1,975 public libraries also take a share of these quotas. School librarians assert that it is school administrators who are to blame for the paucity of children's books. Funds for books, they charge, have been merged with funds for visual aids. A recent survey of the holdings of school libraries in Kiev has revealed a catastrophic dearth of Ukrainian books.

> We visited school No. 118, considered the best in the Podilsky [Borough] of Kiev. There are 700 pupils in 17 classrooms. Of the 6,136 books in the school library, only 400 are Ukrainian classical and modern literature. The editions are old. This is for the higher grades. There is not a single Ukrainian book for the children of the intermediate and lower grades (this is an eight-grade school). School No. 20 has 600 pupils and a library containing 16,000 volumes, of which only 480 are Ukrainian classical and Soviet literature.[110]

The report blames the "thoughtless selection methods" of the school Ukrainians." The high point of the Congress undoubtedly was the

the failure of publishers of juvenile literature to print large enough editions. ("Can we condone the fact that for 30,000 schools with 7 million pupils in the republic books for children are published in editions of 30,000?") Nor are the holdings of Ukrainian books in college libraries much better. It was disclosed, e.g., that there were only three copies of the new Ukrainian translation of the Odyssey in the entire library of Kiev University.[111] Finally, the fact that the regime's Russification policy often reaches curious extremes is borne out by the complaint in the Komsomol paper of the Ukraine that the Ukrainian Concert Bureau's 1964–65 subscription series of readings for schoolchildren in Kiev did not include any of the literary works of Ivan Franko and Taras Shevchenko—two Ukrainian classics. Moreover, the works of Oles' Honchar—presently the chairman of the Union of Soviet Ukrainian writers—and the late O. Dovzhenko were given in Russian. The article ends with this: "It is, of course, very nice that our pupils are being acquainted with these works in Russian, but they would sound just as good in the original."[112]

In a limited area, almost as an act of desperation, Ukrainians have done more than merely organizing protests and making sarcastic comments. In December, 1964, the Writers Union of the Ukraine took over the sponsorship of 544 libraries in boarding schools. The writers donated part of their earnings and their own books to supply those schools with literature required by the curriculum, particularly modern and classical Ukrainian literature.[113] The chairman of the Union, Oles' Honchar, announced that he had donated all his Lenin Prize money to the project.[114] There is an interesting "dialectical" application of the assimilationist Lenin. We might also list complaints about the nonavailability of films in Ukrainian (it appears that almost all films produced in the Ukraine—even those on Ukrainian subjects—are made in Russian, and then Ukrainian is dubbed in),[115] complaints that too few Ukrainian songs are being played on the Soviet radio,[116] and that Ukrainian records are almost unobtainable.[117] But this only confirms the fact that there is considerable demand for Ukrainian culture and that the people will not quietly accept the deprivation.

Finally, I would like to introduce some new, possibly controversial material, which may shed light on the real feelings of prominent persons and on the bitterness and force with which the struggle for the preservation of Ukrainian national culture is now being waged. A good poet can often express in a few lines what a scholar feels requires volumes. The late Vasyl Symonenko was such a poet.

Symonenko was born in 1935 into a farmer's family in a village in the Poltava Province, the heartland of Ukrainian language and culture. He studied journalism at Kiev University, worked on the staffs of two provincial newspapers (traces of his journalistic training show in his literary work). In his spare time he wrote poetry and two children's tales in verse. A collection of his poems and the two tales were published during his lifetime. He died of cancer in December, 1963. In 1964, a second collection of poems was published, as well as a story in prose; a third volume of poems appeared in 1966. A collection of stories is being readied for publication.[118]

Symonenko's verse is highly melodious and easy to follow. Some of his poems have the beautiful ring of genuine Ukrainian patriotism. The Ukrainian youth could not resist his cheerful verse.[119] Symonenko's politics appeared orthodox enough: He had joined the Communist Party and had written some highly uncomplimentary and probably sincere lines about Ukrainian bourgeois nationalists in the West.[120] A good poet—if not quite the best—a tragic figure, extremely popular among his generation, and not objectionable to the political guardians of Ukrainian literature, Symonenko, in January, 1965, was posthumously recommended for the Taras Shevchenko Prize in literature, the highest literary award the republic can bestow.[121] Then the political scandal that has provided us with important revelations broke loose.

In its issue of January, 1965, the Ukrainian nationalist monthly *Suchasnist'* (*The Present*), which appears in Munich, published excerpts from Symonenko's diary and some unpublished poems by him that were said to be extracts from Symonenko manuscripts that were being circulated illegally in the Ukraine and in the satellites. Were they forgeries? On April 15, 1965, an indignant article in Kiev's *Radyans'ka Ukrayina* in effect allayed any possible suspicion. In a preface to that article, Symonenko's mother explained that after the poet's funeral several of his friends (two names were given) obtained her son's manuscripts from her and started circulating them without her permission. She also hints that her son might have erred in some respects. This admission is elaborated by a colleague of Symonenko's who tries to prove that small doubts and deviations notwithstanding, Symonenko had always been a loyal Communist. Neither his mother nor his colleague make any attempt to cast doubt on the authenticity of the materials published in the West.[122] In effect, Symonenko has provided us with one of the best authenticated examples of underground literature in the U.S.S.R. Except for possible misreadings of individual words that might have become illegible in the clandestine copies, the Western text is as perfectly rendered as that of Pasternak's *Doctor Zhivago*.[123]

Reading a few of his poems, even in a rather imperfect translation, we can understand not only why the poem could never appear in the Soviet Union, but we can also learn something of the true attitude of a young Ukrainian. I quote in its entirety the poem "To Our Kurdish Brother."

To Our Kurdish Brother

Struggle and you'll vanquish
—TARAS SHEVCHENKO

The mountains scream, blood streaming.
The stars, shot, fall down.
Into the fragrant valleys torn up with wounds
Breaks rapacious chauvinism.
  O Kurd, guard your bullets well
  But do not spare the killers' lives.
  Upon those rogues of wanton murder
  Fall like a bloody whirlwind, like a hurricane.
Talk to them with bullets:
Not only after goods have they come,
They have come to take away your name,
To turn your son into a bastard.
  You will not live in peace with your oppressor:
  His role is to be master, yours—the beast of burden.
  He waxes fat from the blood of tired peoples,
  Our most evil enemy—chauvinism.
Faithlessness to shame has married he,
He will do all to force you to your knees . . .
O Kurd, guard your bullets well,
Your clan'll be lost without them.
  Hate's force don't rock to sleep.
  Only then take kindness as your coat of arms,
  When into the yawning grave
  Will fall our planet's last chauvinist.[124]

Obviously Symonenko does not believe in eternally peaceful coexistence, and he may be guilty of using journalistic terms and phrases that purists will not hold welcome in poetry. As the motto from Shevchenko's "Caucasus" makes clear, the poem is actually addressed to his fellow Ukrainians. It is them he accuses of becoming too friendly with the chauvinistic intruders who are robbing them of their national self. The epithet "chauvinistic" clearly identifies them as Russians: Was it not Lenin himself who coined the expression of (Great Russian) imperial chauvinism?

Last but not least, I wish to alert the reader to some deliberate omissions and present a few tentative conclusions. I have purposely refrained from an analysis of Soviet religious policy; for unlike in the case of the Jews, to take only one example, it is very difficult to prove a link between religion and ethnic identity in the Ukraine, particularly in the Eastern Ukraine, where with the help of the regime the Russian Orthodox Church has become firmly entrenched. This difficulty does not apply to the crypto-Catholic Western Ukrainians; in a fuller study I would have mentioned the particular situation in that territory.[125] I have omitted the marginal but not totally insignificant activity of the Ukrainian S.S.R. in world affairs: In October, 1963, e.g., the republic, together with Belorussia, adhered to the partial nuclear test-ban treaty.[126] I have not analyzed an alleged Red Chinese intervention in the disputes among Ukrainians and Russians because the evidence does not appear conclusive.[127]

I have tried to show that Ukrainians are holding rather high but not necessarily secure positions in the All-Union Party hierarchy, the army, and the secret police. These men have not been able, or perhaps not willing, to help their fellow-countrymen assert themselves against the assimilationist pressures of the regime: the population exchange and the crowding out of the Ukrainian language, especially from the cities. Perhaps one of the reasons for their appointment was Khrushchev's desire to indicate to ambitious Ukrainians that they could make a good imperial career if they would cut their ethnic roots. I have an intuitive feeling, however, that the wiser among the Ukrainian elite will not fall into that trap, for a Shelepin will never accept a Podgorny in a top position in Moscow, nor a Kozlov a Kirichenko. But as long as the Podgornys and Shelests are insecure themselves they will not do much to help their fellow-countrymen in the Ukraine.

The measurable linguistic Russification among the latter is not conclusive evidence of a total change in cultural and political outlook, but it does come very close to it. The greatest weakness of the Ukrainians in my mind is the persistence of the semi-Russian and substantially Russifying character of the larger cities in the Ukraine. The regime reinforces this weakness by its population exchange and its school policies. It is helped by some assimilated Ukrainians. They gloss over any differences between the Ukrainians and Russians that are not so great as those between Estonians or Georgians and Russians. Against the assimilators and the assimilated, however, are ranged the articulate Ukrainian cultural elite. They in turn are backed up by the overwhelming majority of originally rural Ukrainians who not only have retained their native language but acquired at least a secondary and in some cases a higher education. The war continues to be waged mostly in the cultural field, but it is a grave struggle, for language may control the educational and thus the economic opportunities of many an individual. Despite the defeat of 1958–59, which seriously undermined the position of Ukrainian in the Republic, the war is not yet lost. Compared with 1926, the relative proportion of Russian-speaking Ukrainians in the cities has decreased rather than increased. The manipulation of city boundaries had something to do with this, but this does not seem to have been the only reason. Above all, the regime has not been able to break the spirit of some of the young Communist-educated intellectuals. Symonenko may be exceptionally outspoken, but he is not unique in his thinking, as is attested to by his wide acceptance. In their struggle for ethnic self-assertion the Ukrainians also seem to be helped by the factor of mass. Stalin allegedly wanted to deport all Ukrainians but found that even he was not able to move some 40 million people. It is not easy to assimilate such a large number if a substantial minority are opposed to assimilation. Nor would I completely write off Ukrainian political leaders as assimilated careerists: Tito did not start out as a Yugoslav nationalist. As Conquest observed wisely:

> There are potentials within the Party for a breakup of the U.S.S.R. into national Communist states—just as . . . the Soviet empire in Eastern Europe crumbled in an earlier decade. . . .
>
> [The colonial problem] is one of the elements in the present general crisis of the Soviet system, and one that could lead to future changes which may now appear remote and extravagant. Here, again, we should remember that the Soviet future is unlikely to comprise an easy and evolutionary development, and that any too cautious or conservative view of its potentialities is certain to be wrong.[128]

In the last months of 1965 and in 1966 occurred several events that shed further light on our topic: the publication of a lengthy polemic with Ukrainian nationalists on the pages of *Pravda,* the discovery of stealthy arrests of Ukrainian students and intellectuals, the political infighting prior to the Twenty-third congresses of the Ukrainian and Soviet Parties, and some fascinating and significant statements from the tribune of the Fifth Congress of the Writers of Ukraine. On December 16, 1965, V. Malanchuk, a historian and a Secretary of the Lviv obkom of the CPU published a lengthy attack on Ukrainian nationalists under the title "The Power of Great Friendship: Notes on International Education." Lenin, he writes, had already predicted that socialism could completely internationalize the economic, political, and intellectual life of mankind, but "sometimes" we find ourselves among "immature people who oppose the local interests against the interests of the entire country, who try to 'grab' as much as possible from the common resources, who want to participate as little as possible in common undertakings and select responsible officials [*kadry*] primarily according to their nationality. It is to be understood that the number of such people is insignificant [*nichtozhno malo*]."[129] Dr. Malanchuk proudly admitted that many graduates of Lviv colleges were being sent to other republics and tried to convey the impression that only Ukrainian nationalists in the United States deplored this exchange of talent. Certain Ukrainian writers in Lviv, however, had strayed from the ideological line. Furthermore, in the Turkiv boarding school, Ukrainian history had "to a significant extent been taught from bourgeois-objectivist positions." The Lviv Province Party organization was well advised not ever to diminish their alertness against recidivist manifestations of Ukrainian nationalism. The recentralization of economic controls including the abolition of local economic councils would undercut the roots of nationalistic localism.

Where there is this much smoke there must be fire. In April, 1966, Ukrainian circles in New York began to receive reports of the arrests and subsequent trials—or, occasionally, release—of at least seventy fairly prominent Ukrainian writers, scientists, teachers, and other intellectuals who had engaged in such anti-Soviet propaganda as copying and spreading officially censored literary works, articles, and pamphlets relating to the state of the Ukrainian language and culture in the U.S.S.R. The Ukrainian refugees were able to list only seventeen names of persons who had received prison sentences ranging from eight months to as much as twelve years (the average being five years).[130] These rumors, however, were partly confirmed by two Soviet Ukrainian poets, Ivan Drach and Dmytro Pavlychko, at two literary evenings in New York. On November 11, 1966, Ivan Drach, speaking for Pavlychko and himself, at the Overseas Press Club, confirmed the arrests and admitted that among those arrested were friends (he named three he knew personally and referred to "quite a few" [*chymalo*] whom he did not know). Drach also expressed his personal opinion that some of those arrested had been given too severe a sentence.[131] Earlier, on September 24, 1966, at a meeting arranged by pro-Communist Ukrainian circles at the Ukrainian Workers' Home in New York, Pavlychko confirmed that twenty-three persons had been arrested for anti-Soviet activity, including Karavansky, a former "Gestapo agent in Odessa."[132] Thus the arrest of at least four persons was confirmed specifically, and that of nineteen others in general terms.

The political infighting preceding the Twenty-third Party Congress in Moscow (March 29–April 8, 1966) and the earlier Ukraine Party Congress in Kiev (March 15–18, 1966) may be even more significant in the long run. Recent events have borne out that a purge of Ukrainians from the highest Party offices is under way. In July, 1965, the Kharkov Party organization was severely reprimanded for not being properly selective in the admission of new members.[133] The maneuver was ultimately directed against Titov and Podgorny, both of whom had been First Secretaries of the Kharkov Province Party Committee before being promoted to full-time personnel(!) work in Moscow. The September plenum of the CPSU Central Committee formally released Titov from his Secretaryship—an obvious demotion.[134] It was not until early December, however, that his successor, the well-known Russian *apparatchik* Ivan V. Kapitonov, was formally appointed.[135] The same December Central Committee plenum that appointed Kapitonov reappointed Vladimir V. Shcherbitsky, a Ukrainian, as alternate member of the Party Presidium, a position from which he had been dislodged in December, 1963.[136] Shcherbitsky has been identified as an associate of Brezhnev rather than Podgorny.[137] Within a few days, Mikoyan resigned the nominal Presidency of the U.S.S.R. and Podgorny took over the post—an honorific, but nonetheless clear demotion.[138] The Twenty-third Party Congress in Moscow formally relieved Podgorny of the Secretaryship of the Central Committee, though he kept his seat on the Presidium, renamed the Politburo. On the other hand, Kirilenko, who is officially listed as a Russian although possibly of Ukrainian origin and who had been Brezhnev's successor as Party leader in Dniepropetrovsk, was newly elected as Secretary.[139] Altogether this seems to be a reverse for the Ukrainian Party elite, for they have lost two Secretaries dealing with crucial—and possibly thankless—personnel affairs and have gained a doubtful one (since 1955, Kirilenko has not been identified with the Ukrainian Party organization), together with a junior Politburo member (Shcherbitsky, who was re-elected at the Congress).

At the preceding republican Party Congress in Kiev, the most revealing speech was not that of Shelest, CPSU Presidium member and First Secretary of the CPU, but that of the veteran writer Korniychuk, who praised the achievements of Ukrainian culture, notably of literature and language, paying only a perfunctory tribute to the Russian language. But the real point of his speech was a sharp warning to a "few isolated [*poodynokykh*] young people whose ears had swollen from listening at nights to the clever and subversive anti-Soviet propaganda broadcasts" not to spread "all kinds of lies fabricated in Western Germany." He threatened them with people's courts and expulsion from the Soviet Union,[140] an oblique reference to the trials in progress at the time of the Congress. Surely "a few isolated" individuals would not warrant so much attention from a Party Congress. In contrast to the practice under Khrushchev, but in accordance with Stalinist tradition, the Twenty-third Congress of the Ukrainian Party elected two non-Ukrainians to its Presidium: the Belorussian general I. Yakubovsky as full member, the Russian V. I. Degtyarev as an alternate member.[141]

But the most significant event by far proved to be the Fifth Congress of the Writers of Ukraine, which was convened in Kiev in mid-November, 1966. Shelest's address on behalf of the Party included one very cautious commitment:

> The development of the socialist Ukrainian culture and language in many respects depends on people who have gathered here today; and it depends, in the first place, not on talks about the necessity of such development but on your creativity. We must treat our beautiful Ukrainian language with great care and respect. . . . Your efforts in this direction always were and will be supported by the Communist Party.[142]

The writers themselves were much more outspoken. Oles' Honchar, the Chairman of the Writers' Congress, in his report incidentally condemned the despoliation of Ukrainian forests (beechwood from Carpathia was being given away as firewood in Siberia [*sic*])[143] and the second-class status of the Ukrainian language in schools ("Due to certain conditions, our native language often fares worse in school [at the university and secondary school level] than foreign languages").[144] But speaker after speaker, from Honchar and Usenko, who gave the report of the auditing commission,[145] to ordinary discussants, the writers deplored, as one of them put it, "the paper bed of Procrustes . . . the ridiculously and criminally pitiful edition[s]."[146] The alleged reason was lack of paper. The most extreme of the discussants called for saving paper by publishing fewer political pamphlets addressed to the campaigns of yesterday,[147] the less radical darkly hinted "at some kind of subjective considerations" in the minds of the officials distributing paper.[148] Honchar himself diplomatically mentioned that the publishers in the (small) Baltic states were putting out their books in larger editions than the houses in the large Ukrainian Republic.[149] A noteworthy corollary demand voiced by Smolych was the resumption of publication in the Ukraine of works in the minority languages, including Yiddish.[150]

But most important was another theme of the Writer's Congress, voiced by several discussants, though not by Honchar: the explicit, detailed denunciation of the theory of the fusion of national cultures under Communism, which would have entailed the disappearance of the Ukrainian language, a theory that had been propagated in the last years of Khrushchev's rule. One discussant called it "paper Communism . . . garrison Communism . . . the direct descendant of a dogmatic, or to use today's terminology, 'Red Guards' muse."[151] A more reasoned attack by the literary critic Novychenko explicitly took issue with a 1962 editorial in a Moscow linguistic journal in which by implication the Ukrainian (and the Belorussian) languages had been condemned to extinction. Novychenko clearly warned that

> in some readers [those tendencies] call forth an [equally] one-sided reaction, blocking from their view the real splendor of our lives, and forcing them to see and feel only their own "national grievances." These tendencies put such people in the unhealthy position of eternal complainers, of the perennially hurt. And frequently, they simply lead them astray into an ideological jungle where the so-called "national consciousness" becomes the alpha and omega of human wisdom.[152]

Another writer quoted the Russian Kalinin against certain Russian nationalists:

> To be an internationalist means to respect every nationality, and that is the heart of the matter. If you treat all nationalities with respect you are an internationalist, but if you are, for instance, a Russian who feels that only what is Russian is good, then you are a backward Russian chauvinist [rusotyap] and not an internationalist, you are a limited person, who does not see beyond his own nose.[153]

He also said, "Though we are internationalists, we always remain Ukrainians." The high point of the Congress undoubtedly was the admission by Sergey Baruzdin, the visiting Secretary of the Writers' Union of the Russian Federated Republic: "I, as a Russian, could not always understand the haste with which we suddenly began to talk about the merging of cultures."[154] Shortly after the Congress, another Ukrainian writer publicly called upon his countrymen to show "at least a drop of national pride" in approaching their past: instruction of history in schools was cluttered up with the campaigns of ancient Egyptians and the detailed habits of individual Russian Czars, while Ukrainian national heroes were being slighted. Why should Potemkin's portrait be prominently displayed in a historical museum collection entitled "The Zaporozhe Sich"? Was not Potemkin the "errant one-eyed lover of a dissolute empress, the vengeful and cruel hangman of the Ukrainian working people"? Communist progress, in his opinion, leads to "the development and strengthening of national feelings"; it definitely does not require kowtowing before a Potemkin because he was a Russian.[155]

The basic policy of the regime aiming at an eventual assimilation of the Ukrainians does not appear to have changed as of the end of 1966, and the "intolerably low"[156] output of Ukrainian books is being justified by spurious arguments, such as lack of paper. The battle between the assimilationists and the loyal, Communist nationalists continues as well, the assimilationists being equated with the notorious Chinese Red Guards and attacked with the help of Kalinin and Lenin, of course. The regime has put dozens of the most ardent nationalists in jail and has quietly removed Podgorny and Titov—Ukrainians by origin rather than conviction—from levers of power in Moscow. The present Ukrainian Party leader Shelest is understandably cautious, even though he holds a full seat on the new Politburo. It is the Ukrainian writers who have stepped into the forefront of the battle against cultural *Gleichschaltung,* but they keep referring to the political importance of the question. How many persons are there in the Ukraine today, for whom " 'national consciousness' has become the alpha and omega of all human wisdom"? Our evidence does not permit a precise answer, but the indication is that the assimilators face serious and possibly growing resistance.

NOTES

1. See Vsevolod Holubnychy, "Some Economic Aspects of Relations Among the Soviet Republics," above, pp. 50–120.
2. See Yaroslav Bilinsky, *The Second Soviet Republic: The Ukraine after World War II* (New Brunswick, N.J.: Rutgers University Press, 1964), chap. i (hereafter cited as *Second Soviet Republic*).
3. The most reliable evidence on the nationality of Soviet leaders is contained in the latest biographical directory of the U.S.S.R. Supreme Soviet, *Deputaty Verkhovnogo Soveta SSSR: Shestoy sozyv* (Moscow: *Izvestiya,* 1962). This and all the following identifications are based on that source. A goodly number of high Ukrainian officers in the Soviet Army are also listed in K. Dubyna, "Vklad trudyashchikhsya Ukrainy v razgrom nemetsko-fashistskikh zakhvatchikov," *Kommunist Ukrainy,* No. 5 (May, 1965), p. 29. During World War II, 285 Ukrainians served as general officers.
4. He took over the crucially important command of the Moscow Military District in 1953, when Khrushchev was rising in the Party hierarchy.
5. See the brief but substantial memorandum by Roman Kolkowicz, *Conflicts in Soviet Party-Military Relations: 1962–63* (RAND memorandum RM-3760-PR, August, 1963), pp. 37–45.
6. Cf. his speech in January, 1960, discussed in Merle Fainsod, *How Russia Is Ruled* (2d rev. ed.; Cambridge, Mass.: Harvard University Press, 1963), p. 488.
7. See John A. Armstrong, *The Politics of Totalitarianism: The Communist Party of the Soviet Union from 1934 to the Present* (New York: Random House, 1961), pp. 239 ff.; and *Second Soviet Republic,* pp. 237–40.
8. He served as First Secretary of the Ukrainian Komsomol from 1947 to 1950. Since 1950 he has served almost exclusively in Moscow, never in the Ukraine.
9. *The New York Times,* May 20, 1967, p. 8. For Andropov's biography, including his nationality, see *Deputaty Verkhovnogo Soveta SSSR: Sed'moy sozyv* (Moscow, 1966), p. 23.
10. See *Second Soviet Republic,* pp. 242–43. See also below, pp. 172–73, for more recent changes.
11. Robert Conquest, *Russia After Khrushchev* (New York: Frederick A. Praeger, 1965), p. 153.
12. According to the 1959 census, Ukrainians constitute 17.8 per cent of the total population of the Soviet Union.
13. *Second Soviet Republic,* p. 240; and *Pravda,* November 17, 1964, p. 1. From February, 1956, to April, 1966, the Politburo was called the Presidium.
14. Conquest, *op. cit.,* p. 154.
15. See the analysis in *Ezhednevniy Informatsionniy Byulleten'* (*Daily Information Bulletin,* hereafter abbreviated as *DIB*) (Radio Liberty, Munich), March 23, 1965.
16. According to *Time* (October 30, 1964), p. 38, it was Polyansky who denounced Khrushchev's agricultural policies at the Presidium session at which the latter was deposed. See also the detailed analysis of Polyansky's concern with agriculture in *DIB,* April 12, 1965.
17. *Pravda,* November 17, 1964, p. 1.
18. *Second Soviet Republic,* pp. 236–37 and 245.
19. See *ibid.,* pp. 243–44, for his background. From November, 1962, until

April, 1965, Titov was chairman of the Central Committee Commission for Organizational-Party Questions (see Fainsod, *op. cit.*, p. 221, for a brief discussion of this office). In early April, 1965, Titov was elected Second Secretary of the Communist Party of Kazakhstan without formally resigning from his job as Central Committee Secretary (*Pravda*, April 6, 1965, p. 2; *The New York Times*, April 6, 1965, p. 2; and analyses in *DIB*, April 13, June 3, and June 11, 1965).

20. Seweryn Bialer, "How Russians Rule Russia," *Problems of Communism*, XIII, No. 5 (September–October, 1964), 47.
21. *Ibid.*, p. 52. This can be seen more clearly in Bialer's paper presented at the 1964 American Political Science Association annual meeting, "Notes on the Study of Soviet Elites," pp. 32–33 (mimeographed).
22. Bialer, "How Russians Rule Russia," p. 52, and Table IV on p. 51.
23. Conquest, *op. cit.*, p. 153.
24. "It is thus at least possible that personal connections have played an even greater part in the rise of Ukrainians than have policy considerations," Bialer writes. ("How Russians Rule Russia," p. 52.)
25. *Ibid.*, p. 51.
26. *Ibid.* For further evidence of Stalin's animosity, see *Second Soviet Republic*, pp. 9, 232, 333 n. 17.
27. *Second Soviet Republic*, chap. viii, especially pp. 247–49.
28. Bialer, "How Russians Rule Russia," p. 52; and Conquest, *op. cit.*, p. 153.
29. See note 19, above.
30. He reportedly also managed the Central Committee Division of Party Organs. See *DIB*, June 11, 1965.
31. Conquest, *op. cit.*, p. 214.
32. *Pravda*, November 20, 1962, p. 5.
33. See Yaroslav Bilinsky, "The Soviet Education Laws of 1958–59 and Soviet Nationality Policy," *Soviet Studies*, XIV (October, 1962), 143, 144.
34. Apart from Ukrainians and Russians, the highest number of professionals employed in the Ukraine in 1960 were Jews, with 83,689. They were followed by the Belorussians, with 6,272. See Tsentral'noe statisticheskoe upravlenie, *Vysshee obrazovanie v SSSR: Statisticheskiy sbornik* (*Higher Education in the USSR: A Statistical Handbook*) (Moscow, 1961), p. 70.
35. For the number of graduations, see Tsentral'ne statystychne upravlinnya, *Narodne hospodarstvo Ukrayins'koyi RSR v 1961 r.: Statystychny shchorichnyk* (*National Economy of the Ukrainian SSR in 1961: A Statistical Yearbook*) (Kiev, 1962), p. 644. The nationality breakdown for all students during 1960–61 is in *Vysshee obrazovanie v SSSR* . . . , p. 130.
36. There were 433,620 Ukrainian professionals employed in December, 1961 (58.4 per cent of 742,500), and 397,822 employed a year before (58.0 per cent of 685,900)—see Table on p. 152, above. This gives a net increase of 35,798. Admittedly, I have not made any allowance for mortality, which would have increased the number of vacancies by a small amount. Turnover in jobs, however, can be disregarded because the employee would stay in the same occupational class.
37. Actually the situation is even more complex, for a considerable number of Ukrainians are studying in other republics—82,673, or 24.1 per cent, of all Ukrainian students in 1960–61; see *Second Soviet Republic*, p. 77. Some of those may have obtained jobs in the Ukraine. Those 3,717 stand for the *net*, not the actual, outflow of professionals.
38. See G. Zimanis, "Kul'turnoe sotrudnichestvo narodov SSSR—vazhnoe

uslovie ikh dal'neyshego sblizheniya," *Kommunist* (Vilnius), No. 11 (November, 1964) (or *DIB,* December 8, 1964), which reaffirms the old line.

39. *The New York Times,* December 23, 1964, p. 2.
40. Section IV of the Party Program; cited in Herbert Ritvo (comp.), *The New Soviet Society* (New York: The New Leader, 1962), p. 192.
41. *Ibid.,* pp. 190, 200.
42. *Ibid.,* p. 191.
43. *Ibid.,* p. 198.
44. *Ibid.,* pp. 200–201.
45. See V. V. Pokshishevsky, "Perspektivy migratsii naseleniya v SSSR," in Akademiya nauk SSSR, Sibirskoe otdelenie, Institut geografii Sibiri i Dal'nego Vostoka, *Geografiya naseleniya Vostochnoy Sibiri* (*Geography of the Population of Eastern Siberia*) (Moscow, 1962), pp. 68, 75–76.
46. See V. I. Naulko, "The Nationality Composition of the Population of the Ukrainian SSR (According to Census Data)," *Narodna tvorchist' ta etnohrafiya,* No. 3 (May–June, 1964), p. 24; or *Digest of the Soviet Ukrainian Press* (hereafter abbreviated as *DSUP*), VIII, No. 10, 9.
47. Naulko, *op. cit.,* p. 25; or *DSUP,* VIII, No. 10, 10.
48. Naulko, *op. cit.,* p. 27; or *DSUP,* VIII, No. 10, 12.
49. Stepan Yu. Prociuk, "Shlyakhy i metody peremishannya naselennya v SRSR (Na prykladi Ukrayiny)," *Suchasnist'* (Munich), No. 7 (July, 1965), pp. 104–13, and No. 8 (August, 1965), pp. 94–112. All subsequent references are to the second installment of the article, which is more pertinent to this paper.
50. P. Kovalenkov, "Pro polipshennya vykorystannya trudovykh resursiv," *Ekonomika radyans'koyi Ukrayiny,* No. 6 (November–December, 1963), p. 83; and Prociuk, *op. cit.,* pp. 94–95.
51. Prociuk, *op. cit.,* p. 107.
52. See article "Pereselennya," in *Ukrayins'ka Radyans'ka Entsyklopediya* (Ukrainian Soviet Encyclopedia) (Kiev, 1963), XI, 63. Zh. A. Zayonchkovskaya and V. I. Perevedentsev, "K voprosu o sovremennykh migratsionnykh svyazyakh naseleniya Krasnoyarskogo kraya," in *Geografiya naseleniya Vostochnoy Sibiri,* p. 91, complain that many settlers try to flee Siberia at the first opportunity.
53. Prociuk, *op. cit.,* pp. 105 and 107. This author has adapted Prociuk's method for the calculations on p. 153, above. See also earlier calculations by Holubnychy, cited in *Second Soviet Republic,* p. 52.
54. Prociuk, *op. cit.,* p. 107. A more recent article indicates that both original immigration and emigrants' returns to the Ukraine run high. V. I. Tovkun writes in "Peculiarities of Migration of the Population of the Ukrainian SSR in the 1959–1963 Period," *Ukrayins'ky istorychny zhurnal* (Kiev), No. 4 (April, 1966), pp. 49 ff.: "As a result of intra-union migration, the Ukraine increased its population. Only the Kazakh and Moldavian Union Republics had a mechanical population increase at the expense of the Ukraine. All other republics and economic regions lost populations as a result of migratory connections with the Ukraine. . . . The Urals, Siberia and the Far East needed a considerable increase of the population, but at the same time they lost population as a result of contacts with the Ukraine." (See *DSUP,* X, No. 7, 14.) Unfortunately, the *nationality* of the immigrants and the returnees is not revealed.
55. See the Soviet decree of October 1, 1963, summarized in detail in *Sotsialis-*

ticheskaya zakonnost', No. 4 (April, 1964), pp. 70–73, and analyzed by A. Bil, "Novoe polozhenie o raspredelenii molodykh spetsialistov," in *DIB*, July 8, 1964. A brief description of the machinery for implementing this decree will be found in Alfred Oxenfeldt and Vsevolod Holubnychy, *Economic Systems in Action* (3d ed.; New York: Holt, Rinehart and Winston, 1965), p. 129.

56. See the decree of the U.S.S.R. Council of Ministers of June 17, 1959, No. 671, "O perestroyke rukovodstva vysshimi i srednimi spetsial'nymi uchebnymi zavedeniyami SSSR," in A. G. Khazikov (comp.), *Sbornik normativnykh aktov po sovetskomu administrativnomu pravu* (*Collection of Normative Acts in the Field of Soviet Administrative Law*) (Moscow, 1964), p. 412. (The author is indebted to Dr. Andreas Bilinsky, of Munich, for supplying this source.)
57. As far as graduates of ordinary vocational (Labor Reserve) schools are concerned, the existence of out-of-Republic assignment quotas is explicitly acknowledged. See the joint decree of the CPSU Central Committee and the U.S.S.R. Council of Ministers of July 11, 1959, No. 844, "Ob uluchshenii rukovodstva professional'no tekhnicheskim obrazovaniem v SSSR," Art. 2, Para. (*v*), in Khazikov, *op. cit.*, p. 406. (The author is indebted to Dr. Andreas Bilinsky for supplying this source.)
58. There are such plans for *commodity* supplies that are drawn up and supervised by the office of the Inter-Republic Exchange of the SNKh of the U.S.S.R. Hence, it is also plausible that there is a plan for exchange of the labor force. (The author is indebted to Vsevolod Holubnychy for supplying this information.) The SNKh was abolished in late 1965; its functions reverted to Gosplan.
59. *DIB*, February 19, 1965.
60. Radio Lutsk, April 2, 1965; and *DIB*, April 8, 1965.
61. See Prociuk, *op. cit.*, p. 97. Pokshishevsky, *op. cit.*, p. 79n., suggests that they be reopened again. Professor Harry Lipset informed me that—exceptionally—there were Ukrainian-language schools in the Moldavian S.S.R.: 38 out of a total of 1,756 in 1957–58, and 28 out of 1,804 in 1962–63. (See *Narodnoe khozyaystvo Moldavskoy SSR v 1962 godu* [*National Economy of the Moldavian SSR in 1962*] [Kishinev, 1963].)
62. Witness the touching complaint in *Literaturna Ukrayina* (hereafter abbreviated as *Lit. Ukr.*), April 3, 1964, p. 4, cited in *Informator* (*Newssheet*) (hereafter abbreviated as *Inf.*) (Radio Liberty Committee, New York), No. 6, pp. 3–4:

> When Ukrainian books arrive in the transpolar zone, beyond the 68th latitude, this is a great joy for us who live and work here (Ukrainians and non-Ukrainians alike). We were overjoyed when we obtained the first volume of M. Stelmakh's subscription edition. Unfortunately, books stopped coming from the Ukraine after that. The subscription series of the works of T. H. Shevchenko, Lesya Ukrayinka, . . . arrive here very irregularly. As many as fourteen volumes of the Ukrainian Soviet Encyclopedia have been published to date, but we have received none.—Dear comrades from the Ukraine, what is the matter?

Not so long ago, a bookstore in Krasnodar (Kuban, R.S.F.S.R.), where Ukrainians live in a compact mass, could not offer its customers any Ukrainian publications, except in Russian translation (V. Orel, in *Lit. Ukr.*, October 2, 1964, p. 4; or *DSUP*, VIII, No. 11, 20).

63. See, e.g., Radio Kiev report, on February 8, 1965, on such a concert in Norilsk (Northern Siberia), in *Inf.*, No. 27, p. 11. V. Orel, in *Lit. Ukr.*, May 14, 1965, p. 2, hints that the touring Ukrainian theater in Krasnodar, which was founded in the first years of the Soviet regime and in 1946 counted forty-six members, was dissolved. Since 1952 there have been annual performances by theaters from the Ukraine, though.
64. A. A. Isupov, *Natsional'niy sostav naseleniya SSSR—po itogam perepisi 1959 g.* (*Ethnic Composition of the Population of the USSR—According to the 1959 Census*) (Moscow, 1964), p. 33.
65. Conquest, *op. cit.*, pp. 209–12; and *Second Soviet Republic,* pp. 60 and 373 n.106 (the Babayev affair).
66. *The New York Times,* July 20, 1965, p. 2. Russians already accounted for about 40 per cent of Tallinn's total population of 300,000. In Estonia as a whole Russians constituted 20.1 per cent; in Latvia, 26.6 per cent; and in Kazakhstan, 42.7 per cent (a plurality). See Tsentral'noe statisticheskoe upravlenie, *Itogi vsesoyuznoy perepisi naseleniya 1959 goda: SSSR* (*Results of the All-Union Population Census of 1959: USSR*) (Moscow, 1962), pp. 208 and 206 (hereafter cited as *Itogi perepisi 1959: SSSR*).
67. *Second Soviet Republic,* p. 34. Nor was this proposition published in the proceedings of the conference; see Akademiya nauk Ukrayins'koyi RSR, Instytut movoznavstva im. O. O. Potebni, *Pro kul'turu movy* (*About the Culture of the Language*) (Kiev, 1964).
68. Isupov, *op. cit.*, p. 38.
69. Naulko, *op. cit.*, p. 28; or *DSUP,* VIII, No. 10, 13.
70. *Second Soviet Republic,* p. 54.
71. See Tsentral'noe statisticheskoe upravlenie, *Itogi vsesoyuznoy perepisi naseleniya 1959 goda: Ukrainskaya SSR* (Moscow, 1963), Table 13, pp. 30–31 (hereafter cited as *Itogi perepisi 1959: UkrSSR*).
72. *Ibid.*, Table 56, pp. 192–93. A more general discussion and a useful diagram can be found in Isupov, *op. cit.*, pp. 26–27.
73. See the discussion in *Second Soviet Republic,* p. 422.
74. *Ibid.*, chap. v and pp. 423–26.
75. Naulko, *loc. cit.*
76. *Second Soviet Republic,* p. 149; and Naulko, "Sovremenniy etnicheskiy sostav naseleniya Ukrainskoy SSR," *Sovetskaya etnografiya,* No. 5 (September–October, 1963), p. 59. This is based on the assumption that Ukrainians in the Western Ukraine would speak almost exclusively Ukrainian; a small minority might speak Polish, or a local dialect far removed from standard Ukrainian, but only in very rare cases would they be Russified.
77. *Itogi perepisi 1959: UkrSSR,* pp. 170 and 172.
78. *Second Soviet Republic,* p. 423. Regrettably, such correlations have not been released for the Ukrainian Republic alone, but only for the U.S.S.R. as a whole. Professor Richard Pipes, in his challenging article "The Forces of Nationalism," *Problems of Communism,* XIII, No. 1 (January–February, 1964), 1–6, has found that "the proportion of those who consider Ukrainian . . . their native [tongue] has actually *increased.* In 1926, 87.1 per cent of the Ukrainians spoke their native language; in 1959, 87.7 per cent" (p. 5). These figures are compatible with those presented here and with my analysis if it is borne in mind that (1) they refer to all Ukrainians in the Soviet Union, and (2) that an increase of Ukrainian

speakers was to be expected after the incorporation of the Western Ukraine.

79. Bilinsky, "The Soviet Education Laws of 1958–59 . . . ," *passim.*
80. For 1958, see the statement by Ukrainian S.S.R. Minister of Education Bilodid, in *Pravda Ukrainy,* February 1, 1958, p. 2; or *Second Soviet Republic,* p. 163. For 1963–64, see the statement by his successor, Alla Bondar, in *Radyans'ka Ukrayina,* December 5, 1964, p. 3; or *DSUP,* IX, No. 1, 13. In the year 1966–67, Ukrainian-language schools numbered 23,900, or 82 per cent of the total. See Bondar, in *Pravda Ukrainy,* November 3, 1966, p. 2; or *DSUP,* X, No. 12, 13.
81. *Second Soviet Republic,* p. 57.
82. Based on the schematic map "Popular Education in the Kievan Oblast of the Ukrainian SSR in 1958–59," in Ministerstvo vyshchoyi i seredn'oyi spetsial'noyi osvity UkrSSR and Kyyivs'ky ordena Lenina Derzhavny Universytet im. T. H. Shevchenko, Heohrafichny fakul'tet, *Heohrafiya Kyyivs'koyi oblasti: Atlas* (*Geography of Kiev Oblast: An Atlas*) (Kiev, 1962), p. 66. (The author is indebted to S. Yu. Prociuk for supplying this source.) Six boarding schools on the elementary-school level have been excluded from the calculation, since no data is available on their language of instruction. Because of the difficulty of interpreting the map, the data does not quite agree with the data in the statistical handbook, Statystychne upravlinnya m. Kyyeva, *Narodne hospodarstvo m. Kyyeva: Statystychny zbirnyk* (*National Economy of the City of Kiev: A Statistical Handbook*) (Kiev, 1960), p. 123. But the total number of schools—171 plus 6, or 177, on the map and 180 in the statistical handbook—are close enough.
83. *Itogi perepisi 1959: UkrSSR,* p. 182.
84. *Second Soviet Republic,* p. 163. According to private information, the regime is also increasing the number of bi-lingual Russian–Ukrainian schools. For a similar development in Latvia, see *Sovetskaya molodëzh',* February 2, 1965; or *DIB,* March 11, 1965.
85. See the interview with Ukrainian S.S.R. Minister of Education Alla Bondar, in *Molod' Ukrayiny,* September 1, 1964, p. 1; excerpts translated in *DSUP,* VIII, No. 10, 14.
86. *Lit. Ukr.,* March 30, 1965, p. 4, for this and the following quotations in the paragraph.
87. *Radyans'ka osvita,* August 19, 1964; or *DSUP,* VIII, No. 10, 16.
88. "Pershoknyhy ridnoho slova," *Lit. Ukr.,* May 21, 1965, p. 1.
89. *Second Soviet Republic,* p. 290. See also the anonymous account "With French Students in the Ukraine" (in Ukrainian), *Suchasnist'* (Munich), No. 8 (August, 1965), pp. 114—a girl student had not been admitted to a university because of Ukrainian patriotism.
90. See Tsentral'noe statisticheskoe upravlenie, *Narodnoe khozyaystvo SSSR v 1963 g.: Statisticheskiy ezhegodnik* (*National Economy of the USSR in 1963: A Statistical Yearbook*) (Moscow, 1965), p. 579 (such yearbooks hereafter cited as *Nar. khoz. SSSR* plus the year covered). No data for the Ukrainian S.S.R. are given in the companion volume for that Republic. Census data from Isupov, *op. cit.,* p. 14.
91. See *Vysshee obrazovanie v SSSR . . . ,* pp. 128–57; or *Second Soviet Republic,* p. 77.
92. *Radyans'ka osvita,* May 26, 1965, p. 2; or *DSUP,* IX, No. 7, 15.
93. See Table V-7, in *Second Soviet Republic,* pp. 170–71.
94. See *Dovidnyk dlya vstupnykiv do vyshchykh uchbovykh zakladiv Ukra-*

yins'koyi RSR na 1965 rik (*Handbook for Those Entering Higher Educational Institutions of the Ukrainian SSR in 1965*) (Kiev, 1965).

95. *Znamya yunosti,* May 14, 1965; and *DIB,* June 3, 1965.
96. P. Pakhutkin, in *Komsomolets Kirgizii,* February 26, 1965; and *DIB,* March 10, 1965.
97. *Second Soviet Republic,* p. 34.
98. See *ibid.,* pp. 28–29.
99. See, for example, M. Pylyns'ky, in *Lit. Ukr.,* March 30, 1965, p. 3.
100. See the protest in *Lit. Ukr.,* June 4, 1965, p. 3, against the "seventh, uncorrected" edition of a spelling dictionary for elementary school students.
101. See the complaints in *Lit. Ukr.,* October 27, and November 13, 1964; and in *Robitnycha hazeta,* February 24, 1965, p. 2. M. Chaykovs'ky, in *Lit. Ukr.,* March 2, 1965, p. 3, writes: "The basic shortcoming of the entire series of academic terminological dictionaries is that they were conceived and realized as translations of Russian terminological material, thus becoming more or less skillful carbon copying. . . ."
102. Gosudarstvenniy komitet Soveta Ministrov SSSR po pechati, Vsesoyuznaya Knizhnaya Palata, *Pechat' SSSR v 1963 godu: Statisticheskie materialy* (*Printed Publications in the USSR in 1963: Statistical Materials*) (Moscow, 1964), p. 90; and *Nar. khoz. SSSR 1958* (Moscow, 1959), pp. 872–73.
103. *Pechat' SSSR v 1963 g. . . . ,* p. 90.
104. *Ibid.,* p. 93. In 1958 there were 214 Ukrainian-language periodicals out of a total of 488. See *Nar. khoz. SSSR 1958,* pp. 874–75; and *Nar. khoz. SSSR 1963,* pp. 616–17.
105. *Pechat' SSSR v 1963 g. . . . ,* p. 96.
106. *Nar. khoz. SSSR 1958,* p. 876. Note that *Nar. khoz. SSSR 1963,* pp. 618–19, presents misleading data due to the inclusion, since 1958, of small kolkhoz newspapers.
107. *Lit. Ukr.,* February 2, 1965, p. 2; excerpts in *DSUP,* IX, No. 3, 22. See also a second report on Kiev booksellers, in *Lit. Ukr.,* February 19, 1965, p. 2.
108. He is identified as a relative of Count S. S. Baratynsky.
109. *Lit. Ukr.,* November 20, 1964, p. 1; or *Inf.,* No. 22, pp. 3–4.
110. *Lit. Ukr.,* October 23, 1964, p. 1; or *DSUP,* VIII, No. 12, 24, for this and the following quotes.
111. *Lit. Ukr.,* June 15, 1965, p. 4.
112. *Molod' Ukrayiny,* February 28, 1965, p. 2; or *DSUP,* IX, No. 4, 27.
113. *Lit. Ukr.,* December 1, 1964, p. 1; or *DSUP,* IX, No. 1, 14–15.
114. *Lit. Ukr.,* May 14, 1965, p. 4.
115. *Kul'tura i zhyttya,* April 1, 1965; or *Inf.,* No. 31, p. 2.
116. *Radyans'ka kul'tura.,* February 11, 1965, p. 3; or *Inf.,* No. 27, p. 7.
117. *Lit. Ukr.,* April 3, 1964, p. 4; or *Inf.,* No. 6, p. 3.
118. See the biographical note in *Suchasnist'* (Munich), No. 1 (January, 1965), pp. 3–4.
119. *Lit. Ukr.,* December 15, 1964, p. 3; or *Inf.,* No. 24, p. 3.
120. Some examples have been reproduced in an article by Mykola Nehoda, "Everest pidlosty" ("The Mt. Everest of Vileness"), *Radyans'ka Ukrayina,* April 15, 1965, p. 3.
121. *Lit. Ukr.,* January 8, 1965, p. 2. His candidacy had been endorsed by the Central Committee of the Ukrainian Communist Party; see the enthusiastic endorsements in *Radyans'ka Ukrayina,* February 17, 1965; *Molod'*

Ukrayiny, February 21, 1965; and *Robitnycha hazeta,* March 7, 1965. See also the glowing tribute in *Dnipro,* No. 3 (March, 1965), p. 151; or *Inf.,* No. 32, pp. 4–5.

122. See the article by Nehoda, *loc. cit.*
123. Also, some of Symonenko's poems published in Munich were printed in the Ukraine under the title *Zemne tyazhinnya* (*Earthen Gravity*) (Kiev, 1964). There are significant omissions in the more political of them. Cf. the versions of "Duma pro shchastya" and "Zadyvlyayus' y tvoyi zinytsi," in *ibid.,* p. 60 and p. 66, respectively, with those in *Suchasnist'* (Munich), No. 1 (January, 1965), p. 5 and pp. 10–11, respectively.
124. *Suchasnist'* (Munich), No. 1 (January, 1965), pp. 9–10; translated with permission. This poem was omitted from *Poeziyi,* a collection of Symonenko's poems, published in Kiev in 1966.
125. See, however, *Second Soviet Republic,* pp. 95–109; and Bohdan R. Bociurkiw, "The Uniate Church in the Soviet Ukraine: A Case Study in Soviet Church Policy," *Canadian Slavonic Papers,* VII (1965), 89–113, as well as his mimeographed paper "The Orthodox Church in the Ukraine since 1953," presented at the Annual Meeting of the Canadian Association of Slavists in Vancouver, June 14, 1965.
126. *Lit. Ukr.,* October 11, 1963, p. 1. (The author is indebted to O. Zinkevych for supplying this source.)
127. *Der Spiegel* (Hamburg), March 31, 1965, pp. 112 ff., reported the contents of a Peking broadcast to Soviet Ukrainian soldiers stationed in Siberia. That broadcast accused the Soviet regime of dangerous Russification, pointing out that Ukrainian troops were sent to the Far East, while Russian troops were stationed in the Ukraine. The editor of *Der Spiegel* informed the author that the source of the report was a Ukrainian news service in Munich (incidentally, *not* the publishers of *Suchasnist'*).
128. Conquest, *op. cit.,* pp. 215–16.
129. *Pravda,* December 16, 1965, p. 2.
130. *Visti z Prolohu* (*News from Prolog*) (New York), September 16, 1966, pp. 1–3. See also *The New York Times,* April 7, 1966, pp. 1+.
131. *Visti z Prolohu* (New York), November 23, 1966, p. 5; abbreviated in English edition of *News from Prolog,* November 18, 1966, p. 1. Substantially the same account, omitting one name, appears in *Ukrayins'ke zhyttya* (Chicago), November 22, 1966, p. 5. The latter account by an independent source is a very detailed but not verbatim report on the evening at the Overseas Press Club.
132. *Visti z Prolohu* (New York), November 23, 1966, p. 5; and *News from Prolog,* November 18, 1966, p. 1.
133. See *Partiynaya zhizn',* No. 15 (August, 1965), pp. 24–25; and commentary in *DIB,* September 15, 1965 (by Dr. Duevel).
134. *Pravda,* September 30, 1965, p. 1.
135. *Ibid.,* December 7, 1965, p. 1. It is noteworthy that in his official biography *Pravda,* departing from its usual custom, did list his nationality.
136. *Ibid.,* together with biography including nationality.
137. By Dr. Duevel, in *DIB,* December 14, 1965.
138. *Izvestiya,* December 10, 1965, p. 1.
139. *Ibid.,* April 9, 1966, p. 2.
140. *Radyans'ka Ukrayina,* March 17, 1966, p. 2.
141. *Ibid.,* March 19, 1966, p. 1; and Duevel's commentary in *DIB,* March 29, 1966.

142. *Radyans'ka Ukrayina,* November 17, 1966, p. 2; or *Lit. Ukr.,* November 17, 1966, p. 2; translated in *DSUP,* XI, No. 1 (January, 1967), 2. See also *The New York Times,* January 29, 1967, p. 13. For background, see Jaroslaw Pelenski, "Recent Ukrainian Writing," *Survey,* No. 59 (April, 1966), pp. 102–12.
143. *Lit. Ukr.,* November 17, 1966, p. 4.
144. Honchar, in *ibid.,* p. 5; or *DSUP,* IX, No. 1 (January, 1967), 7.
145. *Lit. Ukr.,* p. 6; or *DSUP,* IX, No. 1 (January, 1967), 9.
146. Yuriy Smolych, in *Lit. Ukr.,* November 20, 1966, p. 4. See also Dmytro Tkach, in *ibid.,* p. 5.
147. Smolych, *loc. cit.;* also *DSUP,* IX, No. 1 (January, 1967), 12.
148. Victor Korzh, in *Lit. Ukr.,* November 22, 1966, p. 3; also *DSUP,* IX, No. 1 (January, 1967), 17.
149. Honchar, in *Lit. Ukr.,* November 17, 1966, p. 4; or *DSUP,* IX, No. 1 (January, 1967), 5.
150. Smolych, *loc. cit.* See also the commentary by *The New York Times,* January 29, 1967, p. 13.
151. Vasyl Kozachenko, in *Lit. Ukr.,* November 20, 1966, p. 2.
152. Leonid Novychenko, in *Lit. Ukr.,* November 25, 1966, p. 2; or *DSUP,* IX, No. 1 (January, 1967), 15.
153. Korzh, *loc. cit.;* or *DSUP,* IX, No. 1 (January, 1967), 17.
154. Baruzdin, in *Lit. Ukr.,* November 22, 1966, p. 3; or *DSUP,* IX, No. 1 (January, 1967), 16.
155. Serhiy Plachynda, ". . . and a Drop of National Pride," *Lit. Ukr.,* December 29, 1966, pp. 1–2. The last quotation is taken by Plachynda from Ye. Bagramov's article "Leninist Teaching on the National Question and Our Times," *Pravda,* October 17, 1966.
156. Honchar, in *Lit. Ukr.,* November 17, 1966, p. 4.

5

Communist Rule and the Changing Armenian Cultural Pattern

MARY KILBOURNE MATOSSIAN

Chouruh knatsadz jampan chi mornar.
Running water does not forget its course.

Meg kaghak muh g'ertas, guh desnas vor kdagneruh dzour en trer, toun al dzour tir.
If you go to a town and you see that the inhabitants have put on their hats crooked, you do the same.

—Armenian Proverbs

Are the Armenians being assimilated into Soviet Russian society? Clearly, the Armenians as a group have survived under Soviet rule: Indeed, they have flourished, both in numbers and achievements. Two Soviet Armenian names—Anastas Mikoyan and Aram Khachaturian —are well known even in the West, and scores of others are well known to the ordinary Soviet citizen.

In discussing the resistance of the Armenians to assimilation, at least three issues are to be considered:

1. How many persons continue to regard themselves as Armenians?
2. To what extent have these people preserved the characteristics of traditional Armenian culture?
3. Do Soviet Armenians have ethnic loyalties that bring them into conflict with the authorities in Moscow?

1. Numbers of Armenians

The 1959 Soviet census provides a great deal of information about the Armenians today as well as material on long-term trends. In January, 1959, there were 2,786,912 Armenians in the Soviet Union, of whom only 55.7 per cent lived in the Armenian S.S.R. Another 15.9 per cent lived in Soviet Georgia, 15.9 per cent more in Azerbaidzhan, and the rest in scattered localities. Of those who considered themselves Armenian by nationality, 89–95 per cent (depending on age) gave Armenian as their mother tongue (or were children for whom the parents designated Armenian as the mother tongue). A total of 232,695 gave Russian and 45,098 gave Georgian as their mother tongue.[1] Continued assimilation of Armenians in Tbilisi (Georgia) and the large cities of Russia seems likely, but assimilation of the Armenians in the countryside of Georgia and Azerbaidzhan does not.

In this paper I have restricted myself to the subject of Armenians living in the Armenian S.S.R. According to the 1959 census, of the total population of 1,763,000 in that republic, 1,552,000 are Armenians, or 88 per cent of the total. Thus, Armenia has one of the most homogeneous and "rooted" populations in the Soviet Union. Further, the trend has been toward greater homogeneity: In 1939, Armenians constituted only 82.8 per cent of the total population of the republic.[2] This is not simply a case of numerical predominance: Armenians hold virtually all important positions in Soviet Armenia.

Not only has the proportion of Armenians in the population of Soviet Armenia grown, the total population has grown as well. Between the census of 1926 and that of 1959, the population doubled.[3] This growth may be accounted for in large part by the high birth rate and, in recent years, the low death rate, in Soviet Armenia.

TABLE I

POPULATION GROWTH BY NATURAL INCREASE IN SOVIET ARMENIA

(*per 1,000 population*)

	1914	1926	1940	1955	1959
Births	34.8	54.2	41.2	38.0	41.0
Deaths	18.6	17.3	13.8	8.8	7.9
Net Gain	16.2	36.9	27.4	29.2	33.1

By comparison, in 1961, the following rates held for the Soviet Union in general: births, 23.8; deaths, 7.2; net increase, 16.6. In 1926, the average Armenian family had 4.08 members; in 1931, 4.45; in 1939, 4.9; and in 1959, 4.8 members.[4]

Another source of population growth is immigration of Armenians from abroad to Soviet Armenia since World War II. Exact data are unavailable, but according to a Soviet source well over 100,000 came between 1946 and 1948.[5] Large-scale repatriation resumed in 1962, and 4,149 came during 1962–64. The official policy today is to accept repatriates only as fast as adequate housing and schools can be prepared for them; but the doors of the homeland remain open.[6] Many Armenians from abroad, and perhaps also from other parts of the Soviet Union, come to Soviet Armenia for higher education; some may stay.[7]

In trying to understand the reasons for the high birth rate in Soviet Armenia and the return of Armenians from abroad, it seems useful to recall the recent history of the Armenian people. The Armenians, like the Jews, have been victims of genocide. Perhaps as many as 1.5 million were massacred in the Ottoman Empire during World War I. Many fled eastward into what is now Soviet Armenia, the eastern half of the land traditionally inhabited by Armenians. The Armenians are now recouping the losses suffered in a demographic catastrophe. To have a large family is, in a sense, patriotic.

2. To What Extent Have Armenians Preserved Traditional Armenian Culture?

The unique marks of Armenian culture in the past have been the use of the Armenian Language and membership in the Armenian Church. Armenian family, housing, dress, food, work, and play patterns to various degrees resemble those of other peoples of Transcaucasia.

Language. Armenian is the official language for everyday business, government operation, and instruction in Soviet Armenia. There are some exceptions: Dealings with the post office are generally in Russian and Russian literature courses are in Russian. Although Armenian children begin studying Russian in elementary school, Armenian remains the primary means of communication. Armenian is spoken at home by college graduates, except for some natural scientists, who use Russian as the basic language in their work.

The Armenian language itself has been undergoing certain changes in Soviet Armenia. Changes in phraseology and vocabulary reflect the influence of Russian and other European languages. Russian influences were already evident in the second half of the nineteenth century. Specifically, Soviet Russian influences are reflected in:

1. The tendency to borrow political terms from the West via Marxism, even when adequate Armenian equivalents exist: *partia* for political party, instead of *kousaktsoutiun; respublika* for republic, in-

stead of *hanrapetoutiun; sotsialistakan* for socialist, instead of *unkervarakan; kultur* for culture, instead of *mshakuit.*

2. The tendency to form new words from syllables of two or more words in typical Soviet style: *zhoghkomkhor,* derived from *zhoghovrtaken komisarner khorhourd*—Council of People's Commissars; *pethrat,* derived from *petakan hratarakchoutiun*—State Publishing House.

3. The tendency for the Armenian language to become standardized and for local dialects to disappear under the influence of centralized Soviet administration and mass media of communication.[8]

The Armenian Church. That unique institution, the Armenian Church, apparently still functions. Its services are well attended and many babies are baptized. But since one cannot "succeed" in the Soviet Union if one is openly active in any religious organization, the Armenian Church lacks intelligent local support and must rely heavily on the diaspora for funds and leadership. The Armenian Church is not trying to widen its appeal by "modernizing" its theology (which would probably upset the Communist authorities). Its appeal is rooted in a strong and widespread sentiment, namely, that to be a "good" Armenian one must be a member of the Armenian Church; to be baptized and attend church on festive occasions is to confirm one's identity as an Armenian. In the past, when Armenians were under the rule of Turks and Persians, the church was a substitute for the secular state. Now that Armenians have the trappings of political autonomy and a measure of cultural autonomy, the church plays a more marginal role. At the moment it seems to be trying simply to survive.

Social Stratification. At the beginning of the twentieth century, Russian Armenia was primarily an agrarian country, with over 80 per cent of its population classified as rural. Most of the big landowners were Turks. Although foreign private investors had initiated modern copper mining operations in Armenia, in 1913 there were only 5,000 workers in a large-scale industry, out of a population of about 1 million. Perhaps 5 or at most 10 per cent of the population was sufficiently educated for white-collar jobs. Thus, conditions in 1917 were hardly suitable for a national class struggle between Armenian peasants and Armenian landlords, Armenian proletarians and Armenian bourgeoisie. The net effect of the Revolution and Civil War in Armenia was to give power locally to those educated few who had not compromised themselves politically.

Under Soviet rule Armenia has become urbanized. An estimated 54 per cent of the population lived in towns in 1963.[9] The proportion of the population engaged mainly in mental rather than physical work increased from 15.7 per cent in 1939 to 21.8 per cent in 1959.[10]

The allocation of work between men and women has greatly changed. Apart from domestic work and agriculture, women traditionally worked at rug-making, weaving, and ceramics. Now women generally avoid jobs involving heavy physical labor, such as construction and reaping, but they perform a great many of the white-collar jobs formerly monopolized by men. As elsewhere in the Soviet Union, it is now customary for married women with young children to work outside the home. In 1959, 69.1 per cent of all doctors in Soviet Armenia and 59.7 per cent of teachers and other "cultural workers" with college degrees were women. The preponderance of women in the lower levels of the teaching profession and in nursing was even greater. However, they were not prominent in political and administrative positions. Only 4 out of 790 collective farms had women chairmen, and female political and industrial administrators were rare.[11] In short, the division of labor between the sexes is similar to that of the West (except for women doctors), and it is more common for the young mother to work outside the home in Armenia.

The Family. The Armenians traditionally preferred the large extended family embracing three or more generations and including all married sons and their wives. Toward the end of the nineteenth century, large families tended to split up into smaller units encompassing parents and unmarried children only. For a time this trend continued in the Soviet period, but in 1939 it was reversed. Today the Armenian family averages just under five members (slightly higher in the villages), an increase not due only to the high prevailing birth rate. Soviet ethnographers report that there has been a significant increase in the number of "undivided families" (encompassing parents and several married sons with children). In the countryside, such families often consist of seven to ten persons. It has also become fairly common for a married couple to live with the wife's relatives, although the husband's parents are preferred.[12]

So far I have used the word "family" to designate all persons living under one roof. However, among the Armenians this word often has a much broader significance. Some relatives who live away from "home" (because of jobs or other reasons) contribute part of their earnings to the family budget. Even relatives who live apart and do not contribute regularly to the budget may send money for special occasions, e.g., for weddings or funerals.[13]

The resurgence of the "undivided" Armenian family needs explanation. Family members may prefer to gather under one roof because of the housing shortage, or because they may find it more economical to share household appliances and other goods, or they many tend to form large units in localities with desirable educational facilities. However, tradition may also be a factor in the Armenians' preference for large family units.

The functions of the Armenian family have changed markedly under Soviet rule. The family is no longer a productive unit. Even in villages each working member of a family is paid as an individual and directed in his work by an appointed superior (who of course may be a relative). Although the working members of the family may still pool their resources and the father as a rule has remained the family head, Soviet ethnographers report that relationships within the family are growing less authoritarian. The head of family, who may be a woman, is usually chosen by agreement of its adult members. In the villages a man with advanced education—e.g., a teacher, doctor, or agronomist—in practice becomes head of family regardless of his age. The opinion of an elder who is not head of the family is still greatly respected, especially in family matters.[14]

Most marriages today are based on the free choice of the partners. In some peasant circles the boy's parents still select the bride, but the choice must be approved by both prospective bride and groom. Girls generally marry after the age of twenty, boys after twenty-five (somewhat earlier in the country).[15] Marriages between urban and rural Armenians, and between Armenians and non-Armenians, seem to be fairly common, but no precise data are available.[16]

In the Soviet period, Armenian wedding ritual has become simpler and at the same time has tended to lose its serious "religious" content among those who still observe it in form, according to Soviet Armenian ethnographers. However, the customary betrothal ceremony, the ritual of dressing the bride, and many other traditional forms are intact, at least among the peasants.[17]

The newly wed Armenian woman is no longer under the tight restrictions of the past. She may now speak with her husband's father and his other male relatives and she may sit at the table with men, but in some villages the old customs persist. Armenian women do all the housework and care for the children, although in the cities husbands occasionally help.[18]

On the whole, the birth of a girl has ceased to be a disappointment to the parents. In villages babies are born at home with the help of an accoucheur.

Housing. There has been a great deal of construction since World War II throughout Soviet Armenia. Stone is replacing clay as the basic construction material. Many village parks have monuments of Lenin and other political leaders, of Armenian writers, and of Armenian Civil War and World War II heroes. Some villages have been electrified.[19]

Traditionally Armenian meals are cooked in a *tonir,* a brick-lined hole in the ground in the middle of the main room of the house, around which the family gathers for warmth in the winter. *Lavash,* the fine flat bread of the Armenians, is cooked in the *tonir*. The tendency now is to move the *tonir* out of the main room to a special shed. Some homes have castiron stoves for heating, especially in the forested mountain areas, but the *tonir* survives where dried dung is still the basic fuel. The peasants no longer eat while sitting on the floor, using their fingers or a piece of bread to pick up food; instead, they use chairs, tables, and cutlery, Western style. They furnish their homes with ready-made furniture and utensils, such as kerosene and primus stoves, electric hot plates, electric irons and teakettles. Almost every peasant home has a radio and some have television sets.[20]

Dress. Armenian men used to wear a variation of the traditional Caucasian costume; women wore flowing long pants under a kind of serafan and a high headdress with scarves. The older villagers still wear the traditional costume, particularly the headdress.[21] Rather shabby Western dress is typical. Western-style clothes for men are universal in Erevan and the more prosperous (such as research workers at the Academy of Sciences) look well dressed.

Education. In traditional Armenian society only the clergy and nobility were literate. The Armenian Church was the chief educational institution. There is still a seminary of Echmiadzin, the seat of the Catholicos (head) of the Armenian Church, not far from Erevan. But the Church is permitted to train only a limited number of clergy there. Apparently some zealous laymen have made efforts to spread the faith, but under Soviet conditions these efforts cannot be systematic or continuous.[22]

The Soviet school system is probably the most effective agent for changing the Armenian cultural pattern. It also serves to promote social mobility, equality of the sexes, and Soviet Armenian achievements in science, scholarship, and the arts.

Armenia in 1959 had one of the highest percentages of university graduates in the Soviet Union: Georgia, with 38 per 1,000 was first; Armenia, with 28, was second; the average for the U.S.S.R. was 18 per 1,000. Armenia also ranked second (after Georgia) in the proportion of persons with an incomplete higher, secondary, or seven-year education. Almost every Soviet Armenian between the ages of nine and forty-nine is literate. In 1926 only 53.7 per cent of Soviet Armenian males and 22.7 per cent of the females in this age group were literate.[23]

The Soviet school system has produced a large number of skilled "brain" workers each year, especially since 1958. As of 1964 there were 58 academicians, 208 persons with doctoral degrees, 1,718 with candidate degrees, and 6,489 scientific workers in Armenia. A substantial number of these are full-time professionals engaged in the study and preservation of the Armenian cultural heritage. As of 1962, the list of scientific workers included the following workers in the humanities at the Academy of Sciences of the Armenian S.S.R.[24]

Institute of History	57
Institute of Language	62
Institute of Literature	54
Government Historical Museum	20
Museum of Literature and Art	25
Matenadaran (depository for ancient documents)	22
	240

Not all of these people are currently studying Armenian problems, but a majority seem to be, judging from publications received from Soviet Armenia.

The Soviet school system has also been important in changing the role of Armenian women. Practically all Armenian girls are literate. As of December, 1959, women accounted for half of the 35,100 specialists in state employment who had higher or specialized secondary education.[25]

3. Do Soviet Armenians Have Ethnic Loyalties That Bring Them into Conflict with the Soviet Authorities in Moscow?

How do the Armenians feel about the distinctive cultural pattern in Armenia? Do they take pride in being different from the Russians and other peoples of the Soviet Union? I believe they do. And if this is so, does their ethnic loyalty come into conflict with their loyalty as Soviet citizens?

We can only guess at the answer. The politically conscious adults of Soviet Armenia might be divided into these four groups:

1. The Communists of Armenian birth. This group, probably relatively small, includes the hard core of active members of the Com-

munist Party of Armenia who feel little or no preference for Armenians or Armenian culture as such and may even prefer living in Russia or elsewhere in the Soviet Union.

2. The Soviet citizen of Armenian birth. This is a non-Party man or inactive Party member. He is neither a militant Communist nor a militant Armenian nationalist. He may be critical of one or more aspects of Soviet life, but he is satisfied, or unconcerned, with the status of the Armenians. Many artists, natural scientists, and other highly educated Armenians may be said to fall in this group.

3. The Armenian Communist. He has a particular stake in the progress of Soviet Armenia, for his power base lies there. Soviet Armenia is the club of which he is an officer. However, he believes that the progress of Armenia would have been impossible without sovietization and that the Soviet system only needs time and some minor repairs to overcome existing "deficiencies" in its operations. This view is of course a "safe" position. How many hold it sincerely?

4. The fellow-traveling Armenia nationalist. He may be a non-Party man or inactive Party member, and he cares little for the Russians or the Soviet system. He attributes the economic and cultural achievements of Soviet Armenia to the talent and hard work of the Armenians themselves. Nevertheless he believes that Armenia is better off as part of the Soviet Union: at least, no more desirable alternative seems available at present. He believes that nowhere else can Armenians achieve first-class citizenship without assimilation. The fellow-traveling nationalist hates and fears the Turks of Turkey and dreams that the traditional Armenian parts of Anatolia will someday be annexed by Soviet Armenia.[26] But he sees little chance of realizing these without Russian help.

In the postwar years the fellow-traveling nationalists of Soviet Armenia have frequently come into conflict with the Communist authorities. They have been publicly censured and expelled from the Party for a "narrow nationalist viewpoint."[27] But at present the Party is very tolerant of Armenian nationalism. Meetings were held in Erevan in April, 1965, in commemoration of the fiftieth anniversary of the 1915 Massacre of the Armenians in the Ottoman Empire. A meeting held in the House of Art Workers was attended by Armenian students from abroad studying in the higher educational institutions of Erevan. At this meeting the Soviet Armenian poet Kevork Emin said:

> The rulers of Sultanist Turkey destroyed the peaceful population of the towns and villages of western Armenia, spilling the blood of innocent people. But our people came back to life. Modern towns grew, villages

were reorganized. The new, well-constructed settlements of Zeitun, Kilikia, Aresh, and Adzhin came into being. And now we proclaim with pride: Our people were, are, and will be.[28]

What is most striking about this passage is the use of the term "western Armenia," instead of "Ottoman Empire," "eastern Anatolia," or "eastern Turkey."

An editorial in *Kommunist* (Erevan) on April 24, 1965, likened the Armenian Massacre to Nazi genocide. Further, it quoted Lenin as demanding complete freedom "for *all* Armenia" (original italics).[29] On the same day, a relatively mild editorial by M. Nersesian, Academician of the Armenian Academy of Sciences, and N. Ushakov, Doctor of Juridical Science, appeared in *Pravda* entitled "Genocide—Gravest Crime Against Humanity." It condemned the Armenian Massacre by the "Young Turk Government" but put in a kind word for "new Turkey."[30]

It appears that Moscow is going as far in tolerating Armenian nationalism as is possible without causing a rupture with Turkey. The tolerance is greater than ever shown before in the Soviet period. There can be little doubt that such a policy, if continued, will increase Soviet popularity not only in Soviet Armenia but in the Armenian diaspora.

Conclusion

Under Soviet rule the Armenians are leading a more and more secular life, similar to that of the contemporary industrial West. However, they themselves have provided most of the local leadership and some of the national leadership in this movement. They continue to speak and write mainly in the Armenian language. Although their political, economic, and educational institutions have been formed in the Soviet mold, the Armenians have used these institutions to produce wealth, discover truth, and create beauty that bring credit to themselves. The Armenian cultural pattern is being modernized, and the Armenians are the modernizers.

If the case of the Armenians shows anything, it is that the Soviet leaders find it expedient on occasion to encourage nationalism not only abroad in former colonial countries, but also within the Soviet Union. Why do they show favor to the Armenians?

To be sure, the Armenians as a people are high achievers. They may even be more loyal than the average Soviet ethnic minority. But it seems doubtful that the Soviet leaders favor them out of gratitude for these qualities. Rather, the Moscow elite realizes that Soviet Armenia serves as a magnet within the Soviet container pulling Armenians abroad back to their homeland. Such Armenian visitors might return to their diaspora communities singing the praises of the Soviet Union and might even become Soviet agents abroad. Further, the Soviet leaders might someday wish to use Armenian claims to eastern Anatolia as a lever for further Russian expansion at the expense of Turkey. In this case, a persisting minority nationalism within the Soviet Union would serve Soviet policies abroad.

In promoting non-Russian nationalism, the Soviet leadership is going against its ideological grain. Nationalism emphasizes the values of group spontaneity and variety as ends in themselves. The nationalist leader says, "Be glad you are different!" But Marxism emphasizes uniformities in universal processes of social evolution. "Be glad you're progressive," says the Marxist, seeing a uniform type as the goal of progress.

Despite his ideological discomfort, however, the Soviet leader who encourages non-Russian nationalism may in the end find peace of mind. He may find that unity within diversity is not always precarious politically, especially if one ethnic group constitutes a clear majority. He may even find that the persistently different ethnic minority can enrich the culture of the majority by being pleasantly strange, and strangely pleasant.

NOTES

1. Tsentral'noe statisticheskoe upravlenie, *Itogi vsesoiuznoi perepisi naseleniia 1959 goda: SSSR,* pp. 184–85, 210, 222–23 (hereafter cited as Russia, 1959 Census); and *Itogi vsesoiuznoi perepisi naseleniia 1959 goda: Armianskaia SSR,* pp. 102–3 (hereafter cited as Armenia, 1959 Census).
2. Armenian S.S.R., Tsentral'noe statisticheskoe upravlenie, *Sovetskaia Armeniia za 40 let: Statisticheskii sbornik* (also published in Armenian), p. 17. The total population as of January 1, 1965, was estimated at 2,134,000 by *Kommunist* (Erevan), February 3, 1965.
3. Armenia, 1959 Census, p. 11.
4. *Sovetskaia Armeniia za 40 let,* p. 8; Armenian S.S.R. Tsentral'noe statisticheskoe upravlenie, *Sovetskaia Armeniia v tsifrakh: Statisticheskii spravochnik, 1923–27* (Erevan, 1928), p. 21; Russia, 1959 Census, p. 280; Armenia, 1959 Census, p. 110; and Z. Korkotian, *Khorhrdayin Hayastani bnakchoutiune verchin haryouramiakoum (1831–1931).*
5. Armenian S.S.R., Gitoutiunneri akademia, patmoutian institut (Academy of Sciences, Institute of History), *Haikakan SSR-i patmoutiun,* p. 306.
6. *Kommunist* (Erevan), March 11, 1965.
7. *Ibid.,* April 22, 1965.
8. Akademiia nauk S.S.S.R., Institut etnografii, *Narody Kavkaza,* II, 438.
9. *Kommunist* (Erevan), April 7, 1965.
10. Armenia, 1959 Census, pp. 11, 28–29, and 53.
11. *Sovetskaia Armeniia za 40 let,* p. 170; and S. A. Tovmasian, *Otchetnyi doklad Ts. K. Kommunisticheskoi Partii Armenii XXI s"ezdu K. P. A., 10 fevralia 1960 goda,* p. 85.
12. D. Vardoumian and E. Karapetian, *Hayastani koltntesakanneri untanikuh ev untanekan kentsaghuh,* pp. 122–23 (hereafter cited as Vardoumian, *Kolkhoz Family*).
13. D. Vardoumian, *Loretsineri nor kentsaghuh,* p. 95; and Vardoumian, *Kolkhoz Family,* pp. 123–24.
14. Vardoumian, *Kolkhoz Family,* pp. 118 and 123; and *Narody Kavkaza,* pp. 534–35.
15. Armenia, 1959 Census, p. 19.
16. Vardoumian, *Kolkhoz Family,* pp. 124–25; and *Narody Kavkaza,* p. 535.
17. *Narody Kavkaza,* pp. 535–36.
18. *Ibid.,* p. 534.
19. *Ibid.,* pp. 502–4.
20. *Ibid.,* pp. 506, 508–9, and 523.
21. *Ibid.,* pp. 513–20.
22. Tovmasian, *op. cit.,* p. 97; and *Kommunist* (Erevan), January 13, 1965, and February 19, 1965.
23. Russia, 1959 Census, p. 85; and Armenia, 1959 Census, p. 27.
24. Armenian S.S.R. *Kul'turnoe stroitel'stvo Armianskoi SSR: Statisticheskii sbornik,* pp. 7, 82–83, and 92–93; and Ya. Zarobian, *Hayastani komunistakan partiai kentkomi hashvetou zekoutsoumuh Hayastani kompartiai XXIII hamagoumarin* (1964), p. 68.
25. Armenia, 1959 Census, p. 90; and *Sovetskaia Armeniia za 40 let,* p. 170.
26. Vahakn Dadrian, "An Appraisal of the Communist Formula, 'National in Form, Socialist in Content,' with Particular Reference to Soviet Armenia," *Armenian Review,* XVI (1963), 11–12.

27. Edward Alexander, "The Ferment in Soviet Armenian Literature," *American Slavic and East European Review,* XXIII (December, 1958), 506; and Zarobian, *op. cit.,* p. 103.
28. *Kommunist* (Erevan), April 22, 1965. He was referring to new settlements built in Soviet Armenia for Turkish Armenian refugees. Various settlements were named after the locality in western Armenia from which their inhabitants came.
29. *Ibid.,* April 24, 1965.
30. Reprinted in *ibid.,* April 25, 1965.

6

Nationalism in the Soviet Baltics

JAAN PENNAR

In July, 1965, the Soviet Union celebrated the twenty-fifth anniversary of the Soviet Socialist Republics of Estonia, Latvia, and Lithuania. These three Baltic states were incorporated into the U.S.S.R. in 1940. The constant theme of the celebrations, which included native dancing and singing, speeches about past glories under the Soviets, promises for the Communist future, and keynote addresses by Suslov, Kosygin, and Mikoyan in Vilnius, Riga, and Tallinn—the capitals of the three republics—was nationalism.

Pravda set the tone on the eve of the celebrations. The culture of the Baltic countries, "national in form, socialist in content," is becoming increasingly richer as the result of the "creative Leninist national policy," it said on July 17, 1965. These and other well-worn phrases were echoed locally, with appropriate acknowledgments of assistance to the Balts from "our older brother, the great Russian people." Most of what was said can be traced directly to passages in the 1961 Communist Party program calling for "unity and affinity" in the nationality relations of the peoples of the U.S.S.R. and looking toward "an international culture common to all the Soviet nations." The importance attached to these guidelines is underlined in an article by Vaino Valjas, First Secretary of the Tallinn City Party Committee: "The ideas of educating the toilers in the spirit of the friendship of the peoples run through all economic and cultural efforts like a red thread. These problems are central to the work of primary Party organizations." Valjas adds that the local Party organizations, together with the Estonian Academy of Sciences, had conducted a "sociological" poll in the field of nationality relations and were processing 2,500 questionnaires.[1]

The keynote addresses by Suslov, Kosygin, and Mikoyan were very much alike, with only minor variations. All three emphasized the "restoration" of Soviet rule in 1940, the solidarity of the Baltic revolutionary struggle with that of Russia, the dark days of independence in the clutches of "international imperialism," the harsh years of war, fraternal "victory over the fascist invaders," and, finally, the alleged achievements under the Soviet regime. The talk about "restoration" of Soviet rule is based on the claim by local Communists in 1917–18 that they, and not the nationalist parties who proclaimed independence, represented Estonia, Latvia, and Lithuania. Although some claims about early Soviet rule in Latvia might be made, based on election results in the eastern districts in November, 1917, this situation later was reversed in countrywide elections, and the great majority of Latvians, as well as the Estonians and the Lithuanians (among whom the Bolsheviks were less significant), rejected Communist rule after World War I.[2]

Mikoyan, in his address at the celebrations in Tallinn, called the annexation of the Baltic states by the U.S.S.R. "a model of the peaceful transfer of power into the hands of the working class."[3] He added that the elections to the National Assembly in Estonia were by secret ballot, and that Estonia and, similarly, the other Baltic countries had thus legitimately entered the Soviet fold. Mikoyan, however, qualified some of his observations. "Under the [then] existing alignment of forces and thanks to the correct tactics of the Communist Parties, the possibilities of the bourgeoisie to oppose the revolutionary populace [in 1940] were reduced to a minimum." Mikoyan's "correct tactics" are better explained by *Kommunist Estonii:*

> The elections to the State Duma [National Assembly] took place under conditions of sharp class struggle. The bourgeoisie also attempted to put its candidates into the new State Duma. The district commissions, however, composed of representatives of toilers, annulled the electoral lists of the bourgeoisie.[4]

In concluding his keynote address, Mikoyan showed good Armenian sense by playing up to local national sensitivities: "Elagu Kommunism!" he shouted in Estonian, "Long live Communism!" This, according to official reports, was greeted by "stormy, prolonged applause," and a little later, when Mikoyan announced the award of the Order of Lenin to the Estonian republic, he went even one better: "Elagu Eesti!"—"Long live Estonia!" Neither Kosygin in Riga nor Suslov in Vilnius showed a similar concern for such niceties.[5]

The Baltic nations are both similar and different. The Latvians and Lithuanians belong to the Baltic subgroup of the Indo-European language family. The Estonians speak a language closely akin to Finnish and thus belong to the Finno-Ugric language family. Occasional campaigns to beautify and purify these languages are encouraged, judging from articles on the subject in the local press. Religious practices, on the other hand, are discouraged. Latvia and Estonia are predominantly Lutheran; Lithuania is Catholic. The Baltic countries have always had significant ethnic minorities.

TABLE I
NATIONAL COMPOSITION OF LITHUANIA

	1936		1959	
Ethnic Groups	Number (*in thousands*)	Per Cent	Number (*in thousands*)	Per Cent
Lithuanians	2,000	80	2,151	79.3
Russians	—	—	231	8.5
Germans	100	4	—	—
Poles	75	3	230	8.5
Belorussians	—	—	30	1.1
Jews	175	7	25	0.9
Ukrainians	—	—	18	0.7
Others	150	6	26	1.0
Total population	2,500	100	2,711	100.0

SOURCES: *Bolshaya sovetskaya entsiklopediya* (1938), XXXVII, 103; Tsentralnoe statisticheskoe upravlenie, *Itogi vsesoyuznoi perepisi naseleniya 1959 goda: SSSR* (Moscow, 1962), p. 207.

In 1940, after Vilnius and its environs had become part of Lithuania, the total population increased to 2.9 million, a figure surpassed only in 1964.[6] By 1959, the number of Lithuanians in Lithuania had not reached the 1940 total, which, according to Soviet sources, was 2.32 million.[7] The largest single minority group in prewar Lithuania, the Jews, has all but disappeared. The table above does not include Vilnius, which had a Jewish population estimated at 80,000, of whom only 15,000 now remain in that city.[8] During the war, according to Antanas Snieckus, First Secretary of the Lithuanian Communist Party, "the Hitlerites liquidated a total of 700,000 Soviet people on the territory of Soviet Lithuania."[9] Lithuanian *émigré* sources agree with this estimate, but they do not place all the blame on the "Hitlerites." The accuracy of these figures cannot be determined because many Lithuanians were also deported to the East, or drafted into the warring armies, and many others fled to the West. But the population loss dur-

TABLE II
NATIONAL COMPOSITION OF LATVIA

	1935		1959	
Ethnic Groups	Number (*in thousands*)	Per Cent	Number (*in thousands*)	Per Cent
Latvians	1,463	75.5	1,298	62.0
Russians	234	12.0	556	26.6
Belorussians	—	—	62	2.9
Poles	49	2.5	60	2.9
Jews	94	4.8	37	1.7
Germans	62	3.2	—	—
Lithuanians	23	1.2	32	1.5
Ukrainians	—	—	29	1.4
Estonians	16	0.4	5	0.2
Others	15	0.4	14	0.8
Total population	1,951	100.0	2,093	100.0

SOURCES: *Bolshaya sovetskaya entsiklopediya* (1938), XXXVI, 22; *Itogi vsesoyuznoi perepisi naseleniya 1959 goda: SSSR,* p. 208.

ing the past twenty-five years has indisputably been substantial and was only partially counterbalanced by the Russians, who now constitute the largest minority group in Lithuania.

The changes in the Latvian population over the past quarter-century follow the Lithuanian pattern. The native Latvians have suffered a considerable population loss, which has been more than compensated for by the increase in the local Russian population. If the Ukrainian and Belorussian minorities are counted with the Russian, as they were in the 1935 table, the Slavic component (excluding the Poles) in the present Latvian population would amount to one-third. The Jewish minority has also suffered a considerable loss. The Germans of Latvia, as well as those of Estonia and Lithuania, were all evacuated to Germany in 1939–41. "We are proud of the fact," noted Arvids Pelse, former First Secretary of the Latvian Communist Party, "that the national composition in our republic is international."[10] This statement was paraphrased by Ilmars Iverts, editor of *Cina,* the official Communist Party paper, speaking to foreign journalists visiting Latvia during the anniversary celebrations. He applied it to Riga, the capital of Latvia, where the native Latvian component now constitutes a minority of 45 per cent.[11]

Here again the same basic pattern of population change prevails as in Latvia and Lithuania. The population losses suffered by native Estonians have been more than counterbalanced by migrants from

TABLE III
NATIONAL COMPOSITION OF ESTONIA

	1934		1959	
Ethnic Groups	Number (*in thousands*)	Per Cent	Number (*in thousands*)	Per Cent
Estonians	992.5	88.10	893	74.6
Russians	92.5	8.20	240	20.1
Germans	16.5	1.50	—	—
Swedes	7.5	0.65	—	—
Finns	—	—	17	1.4
Ukrainians	—	—	16	1.3
Belorussians	—	—	11	0.9
Latvians	5.5	0.50	3	0.2
Jews	4.5	0.40	5	0.5
Others	7.5	0.65	12	1.0
Total population	1,126.5	100.00	1,197	100.0

SOURCES: Karl Inno and Felix Oinas, *Eesti—Eesti Entsüklopeedia Andmeil,* Vol. II; *Rahvas ja Riik* (Geislingen, 1949), pp. 7–8; *Itogi vsesoyuznoi perepisi naseleniya 1959 goda: SSSR,* p. 208.

other parts of the U.S.S.R., particularly Russia. The Swedes and Germans were evacuated to their respective countries during the war. The new Finnish minority represents largely Karelians who were settled in Estonia after World War II. Moreover, there were Finnish settlements in and around Leningrad between the wars, some of which were resettled in Estonia. Although it might appear as if the small Jewish community in Estonia managed to survive all trials of the past quarter century, this is not the case. Soviet sources, citing German documents, indicate that 2,000 of the 4,500 Estonian Jews remained in Estonia when German troops occupied the country in 1941.[12] This, of course, sealed their fate.

The population dynamics since the 1959 Soviet census indicate that by January 1, 1965, the population of Lithuania had increased by 8.8 per cent, of Latvia by 7 per cent, and of Estonia by 6.35 per cent. Since the prewar growth rates, particularly for Latvians and Estonians, were much too low to account for such a rapid increase, it can be assumed that settlers from elsewhere continue to enter the Baltic countries.[13] It is fairly certain, however, that the influx of Russians and other non-Baltic nationalities was much larger immediately after the war. This is confirmed by a Soviet Estonian demographer who writes that during the years 1945–50, "quite a few people came to us from fraternal republics." And he continues:

According to the reports of the All-Union Research Institute of Labor, the unoccupied working force from the R.S.F.S.R. European and Belorussian oblasts will be sent to the eastern regions of our country. The Baltic republics must [therefore] orient themselves on the local labor force.[14]

The above quotation fits neatly into a remark to visiting journalists by Arnold Veimer, then chairman of the Estonian Sovnarkhoz, quoted in *The New York Times* of July 24, 1965: "I can assure you that no more Russians are being settled in Estonia under Government plans." Since there are certain residence restrictions in the U.S.S.R., this should pretty much slow down migration into Estonia.

The current problem confronting the Baltics is perhaps urbanization rather than immigration. The population of Latvia and Estonia is now more than 60 per cent urban, and that of Lithuania, 43 per cent. These percentages are almost double the prewar rates. Tallinn, for instance, has grown to twice its size. Unlike the Letts in Riga, the Estonians still retain a clear majority in their capital city—60 per cent.[15]

Not all Balts live in their own republics in the U.S.S.R. Even during the period of independence, substantial colonies of Estonians, Letts, and Lithuanians were to be found in all parts of the Soviet Union. Many had migrated to Russia proper in the late nineteenth and early twentieth centuries. It has been alleged that St. Petersburg (now Leningrad) had a larger Estonian population than Tallinn.

TABLE IV
THE BALTS IN 1939 AND 1959

Nationality	Number (*in thousands*) 1939	1959	Percentage Decrease	Percentage in Own Republic 1959	Percentage Speaking Russian in Own Republic 1959
Estonians	1,143.6	988.6	13.5	90.3	0.5
Latvians	1,628.3	1,399.5	14.1	92.7	1.4
Lithuanians	2,352.3	2,326.1	1.1	92.5	0.1

SOURCES: Akademiya nauk S.S.S.R., *Chislennost i rasselenie narodov mira* (Moscow, 1962), p. 64; *Itogi vsesoyuznoi perepisi naseleniya 1959 goda: SSSR*, p. 210; P. G. Podyachikh, *Naselenie SSSR* (Moscow, 1961), p. 110; A. Ya. Boyarskii and P. P. Susherin, *Demograficheskaya statistika* (Moscow, 1955), p. 80; *Bolshaya sovetskaya entsiklopediya* (2d ed.; 1964), XXV, 251; *Sovetskaya etnografiya,* No. 5 (1965), p. 11.

Although large numbers returned to their native countries after the Revolution, many remained. The 1926 Soviet census lists 154,700 Estonian and 151,400 Latvian residents in the U.S.S.R.[16] By 1939, these figures had decreased to 142,500 and 126,900, respectively.[17]

The above table also bears out the substantial population losses of the Balts. It has been estimated that about a quarter of a million Estonians, Letts, and Lithuanians have fled to the West.[18] This estimate still leaves a large number unaccounted for. Russification in the Baltics, however, still has quite a long way to go. As a matter of fact, one might even say that there has been a Balticization of the Russians. In Estonia, 2 per cent of the local Russians regard Estonian as their native language; in Latvia, the parallel percentage is 1.5; and in Lithuania, 0.15.[19] These percentages are higher than those in the above table for Russian-speaking Lithuanians, Latvians, and Estonians. But as was noted, a significant number of Balts reside outside their republics. The Russian republic alone accounts for 8.6 per cent of all Estonians, 5.9 per cent of all Letts, and 5.3 per cent of all Lithuanians. Other Balts are found in Belorussia, the Ukraine, and Georgia, as well as in other parts of the U.S.S.R. Taking into account all Balts in the Soviet Union, the Russian-speaking element in their midst reaches almost 5 per cent among the Letts and Estonians and more than 1 per cent among the Lithuanians. These figures still compare favorably with the 12.2 per cent Ukrainians on an all-Union scale who do not speak Ukrainian.[20]

The national composition of the Baltic Communist parties is reflected in the table below. The figures are based on the Nineteenth Latvian Communist Party Congress, which took place December 24–25, 1963; the Fourteenth Lithuanian Congress, held January

TABLE V

NATIONALITY OF DELEGATES TO BALTIC PARTY CONGRESSES 1963–64

Republic	Delegates of Own Nationality	Per Cent	Russians	Per Cent	Delegates of Other Nationalities	Per Cent
Estonia	468	60	255	33	55	7
Latvia	310	55	196	35	53	10
Lithuania	580	67	180	20	104	13

SOURCE: "Die Baltischen Sowjetrepubliken," Forschungsdienst *Osteuropa,* BA/11/64 (February, 1964), p. 13.

9–10, 1964; and the Fourteenth Estonian Congress, on January 7–8, 1964.

As the figures above indicate, the proportion of Russians among Communist Party delegates is greater than that in the local population (see Tables I, II, and III). And this proportion is even higher in the ruling Central Committees of the Communist parties of Lithuania and Latvia. It has been estimated that the Russian component in the Central Committee of the Estonian Communist Party is about 25 per cent, that of Lithuania, 32.5 per cent, and that of Latvia, 40 per cent.[21] Moreover, a significant number of the ruling Party elite claiming local nationality was either born or brought up in Russia and therefore might consider themselves more Russian than Estonian, Latvian, or Lithuanian.

TABLE VI
COMMUNIST PARTY MEMBERSHIP

Republic	January 1, 1961	January 1, 1965
Estonia	37,848	54,836
Latvia	72,519	95,742
Lithuania	60,551	86,366

SOURCE: *Partiinaya zhizn,* No. 10 (May, 1965), p. 8.

It is difficult to determine the exact proportion of Balts in the republics' Party membership rosters. An approximation, however, can be made. As of January 1, 1965, the CPSU membership included 61,500 Lithuanians, 44,300 Latvians, and 33,900 Estonians.[22] This would seem to indicate that Lithuanians make up about 70 per cent, Letts about 45 per cent, and Estonians about 60 per cent of their respective republics' Party membership rosters. It also would seem to indicate that the ratio of Balts in the CPSU membership is smaller than their total population ratio. This is especially evident in the case of the Lithuanians, who constitute 1.1 per cent of the total Soviet population but whose Party membership amounts to only 0.5 per cent.

The local Party elite has been most stable in Lithuania. The First Secretary of the Party, Antanas Snieckus (born 1903), has held the post as an underground leader since 1936, and openly since 1940. Justas Paleckis (born 1899), Chairman of the Presidium of the Supreme Soviet, has also held his post since 1940, the year he joined the Party. The Chairman of the Council of Ministers, Motiejus Sumauskas (born 1905), is an old Lithuanian Communist who was active in the clandestine Party organization in independent Lithuania. He has been in his present post since 1956, after a two-year term as Second Secretary. The latter post has since reverted to a Russian, B. Popov, who has held the post since 1961. In the Secretariat, I. Maniusis (born 1910) has held his own since the mid-1950's.[23]

The Latvian Party leadership underwent a major shakeup in 1959. It is "the duty of every Communist . . . to struggle relentlessly against all signs of nationalism," stated a Party journal in an article on the problem, and went on to cite "localist" tendencies in Latvia in the late 1950's, "where some leading elements showed a tendency to create in their republic a closed economy under the pretext of aiming at a complex development of the administrative economic sector."[24] The Deputy Chairman of the Latvian Council of Ministers, an old Latvian Communist by the name of Eduards Berklavs, was dismissed from his post for advocating national isolation and economic self-sufficiency, thus weakening "the bond of friendship" between the Russian and Latvian peoples.[25] The purge encompassed the entire Party leadership. Janis Kalnberzins (born 1893), First Secretary since 1940, was released "at his own request" and was kicked upstairs to the post of Chairman of the Latvian Supreme Soviet. Vilis Lacis (1904–66), Chairman of the Latvian Council of Ministers from 1940 on, was also dismissed from his post, but unlike his immediate subordinate, Berklavs, retained his seat in the Latvian Central Committee, perhaps because he had distinguished himself more as a writer and novelist than as a government official. The shakeup affected the whole Latvian Party apparatus, and shifts continued for several years after 1959. The present Party leadership consists of several Latvians who were born or trained in Russia. Among them was the former First Secretary, Arvids Pelse (born 1899), and at least one more member of the Secretariat, Elmars Bemanis (born 1926 in Moscow). Pelse was elevated to Politburo membership at the Twenty-Third Party Congress in April, 1966. August E. Voss replaced him as First Secretary of the Latvian Communist Party. The Second Secretary is a Russian, N. A. Belukha.

In Estonia a purge similar to that of Latvia took place in 1950, when the Central Committee of the CPSU adopted a resolution "concerning mistakes and shortcomings in the work of the Central Committee of the Communist Party of Estonia." This resolution, dated February 20, 1950, raised such points as slow collectivization and bourgeois nationalism, which allegedly had infiltrated the Party.

After a brief interregnum, Ivan Kabin (born 1905), an Estonian who had spent the formative years of his life in Russia, became First Secretary and has continued in this post ever since. (Ivan Kabin apparently prefers to be referred to in the local Estonian press as Johannes Kabin.)[26] Leonid Lentsman, another Estonian from Russia (born 1915 in the Crimea), was Second Secretary from 1954 through 1963, when he became a Secretariat member in charge of ideological work. Lentsman once taught school in Murmansk. The Second Secretary since 1964 is another Estonian, Artur Vader (born 1920 in Belorussia). Vader was first assigned to Estonia in 1948 and has received considerable training in Party work, including a period of service in the Central Committee apparatus in Moscow between 1959 and 1963. Before becoming Second Secretary, Vader was Chairman of the Estonian Party-State Control Committee. The only Russian in the Secretariat, Fyodor Ushanev, has been there since at least 1955, and according to the latest information is in charge of agricultural affairs. Still another Estonian from Russia, Aleksei Muurisepp (born 1902), is Chairman of the Estonian Supreme Soviet. He was Chairman of the Estonian Council of Ministers from 1951 to 1961, when he was replaced by Valter Klauson, also a Russian Estonian. In 1965, the only top post occupied by an Estonian of non-Russian background was the chairmanship of the Estonian Sovnarkhoz, which was held by Arnold Veimer (born 1903). Veimer, incidentally, was purged in 1951, when he lost his job as Chairman of the Estonian Council of Ministers to Muurisepp.[27] After the recent abolition of the sovnarkhoz system, Veimer became Deputy Chairman of the Council of Ministers. Aside from Russian Estonians, there is another group in the Estonian Communist Party which might be referred to as Estonian Russians. One high official in this category is Dmitriy Kuzmin, Deputy Chairman of the Party-State Control Committee, who was active in the Estonian Communist Party underground between the wars.[28] Kuzmin's knowledge of Estonian is apparently better than that of some of the Estonians in the Party hierarchy.

In contrast to the tight control over national ratios in the Party, the ceremonial republican Supreme Soviets, as well as local Soviets, are not bound by such restraints. Here the nationalist *garnitura* reigns: the percentage of native Estonians in the Estonian Supreme Soviet has been as high as 86.4, leaving the Russians 11.2 per cent and the remainder 2.4. On the local Soviet level, the Estonian percentage has reached 88.25.[29] Roughly the same proportions apply to deputies to the U.S.S.R. Supreme Soviet. In 1962, the Estonian four-member delegation to the Council of the Union did not include a single Russian. There were three Russians (or 12 per cent) in the twenty-five-member delegation to the Council of Nationalities. The Latvian and the Lithuanian delegations to the Council each had one Russian, and the Latvian an additional Belorussian. The Latvian delegation to the Council of Nationalities included at least six Russians. The composition of the Lithuanian delegation to the Council of Nationalities paralleled the Estonian.[30]

Between 1939 and 1965, Estonian industrial output increased thirteen-, eighteen-, or nineteen-fold, depending on the Soviet source used.[31] During the same period, industrial production in Latvia increased twelve-fold, and in Lithuania eleven-fold.[32] These increases are higher than the All-Union average and indeed represent a considerable investment in the Baltic area, but probably not at as high a percentage as the Soviets indicate. Nevertheless, the Baltic area is considered to have "suitable conditions for industrial development."[33]

Although the Baltic republics have been relatively efficient in farming, agricultural developments have not matched those in industry. Forced collectivization has taken its toll. In Lithuania, the process spurred partisan warfare, which was to be found in all Baltic countries shortly after the war, and which was sufficiently serious for the Soviets to acknowledge its existence: "During the first postwar years," noted Antanas Snieckus, "bands of bourgeois nationalists attempted to frighten toilers of the village by killing innocent people, thus interfering with the building of socialism."[34]

At present, Estonia appears to rank first in the U.S.S.R. in many areas of agriculture, not least because it instituted, in 1963, payments to kolkhoz farmers on a physical-day rather than the old workday unit basis.[35]

The churches in the Baltic states continue to function, but roughly half of them were either destroyed during the war or closed by the Communists and put to other uses. During the period of independence, Lithuania was predominantly Roman Catholic: 85.5 per cent of the Lithuanian population was Roman Catholic; 7.6 per cent Jewish; 4.2 per cent Protestant; 2.5 per cent Greek Orthodox; and 0.2 per cent other. It has been estimated that about 600 Catholic priests continue in office and about 500 churches remain open, about half the number of both priests and churches before the war.[36]

Latvia was 75 per cent Lutheran during its period of independence, the remainder being mainly of the Orthodox, Catholic, and Jewish faiths. Archbishop Turs, currently the primate of the Latvian Lutheran Church, claims that there are 300 churches now open in Latvia.[37] According to the *Christian Science Monitor* of December 2, 1964, there were "formerly . . . about 130 operating churches in Riga . . . now there are 25. The others have been locked up or converted to concert halls, museums, and the like."

Estonia also was a predominantly Protestant country; 78.2 per cent of its populaton was of the Lutheran denomination. Of the remaining 22.8 per cent, 19 belonged to the Greek Orthodox Church. According to Jaan Kiivit, Archbishop of the Evangelic Lutheran Church of Estonia, there is currently a total of 170 churches and chapels in Estonia, with the same number of clergymen attending to them.[38] When a delegation of the World Union of Lutherans visited Estonia in 1964, they noted that there were "many people" attending churches.[39]

Osgood Caruthers of *The New York Times* reported on September 26, 1959, that "the lone synagogues in Tallinn, Riga, and Vilna had been restored after wartime damage. They were newly painted and were open for worship to the remnants of what were once large Jewish communities."

As shown by Tables VII and VIII, Lithuanians still lag far behind in higher education and the number of scholars, as well as in Lithuanian-language materials. Estonians are ahead in the volume of journals and newspapers published and slightly behind in all other areas examined in the table. Latvians are not up to par in specialist training and the volume of Latvian books.

Educational statistics can also be viewed from a different point of view with the same results. For instance, a few years ago the Soviet average of people with higher and specialized secondary education was 384 per 10,000 of population. This figure was higher for the Russians—439—and higher still for the Georgians—542. The statistics for the Balts were as follows: Estonians—457; Latvians—413; Lithuanians—284. In the process of "building Communism," notes *Voprosy filosofii,* "this relative lag will be eliminated."[40]

Like so many other things Khrushchev initiated, the 1958 school reform was thrown out the window, officially and irrevocably, in 1965. This gave rise to a debate in the Baltics on the length of secondary education. A somewhat unusual lead article appeared in the March 12, 1965, issue of *Sirp ja Vasar* (*Sickle and Hammer*), a weekly literary journal issued in Tallinn. Six well-known Estonian authors signed an article entitled "Ten or Eleven Grades?" on behalf of a theoretical seminar of the Union of Writers of the Estonian

TABLE VII

THE BALTS IN RELATION TO THE RUSSIANS IN EDUCATION[a]

Nation-alities	POPULATION 1959		STUDENTS IN SECONDARY SPECIAL SCHOOLS 1963–64		STUDENTS IN INSTITUTIONS OF HIGHER EDUCATION 1963–64		SCHOLARS AND SCIENTISTS 1963		PARTY MEMBERS AND CANDIDATES January 1, 1965	
	Number (*in thousands*)	Ratio to Russians (*in per cent*)	Number (*in thousands*)	Ratio to Russians (*in per cent*)	Number (*in thousands*)	Ratio to Russians (*in per cent*)	Number (*in thousands*)	Ratio to Russians (*in per cent*)	Number (*in thousands*)	Ratio to Russians (*in per cent*)
Russians	114,114	100.0	1,910.0	100.0	1,988.0	100.0	373,498	100.0	7,335	100.0
Estonians	989	0.9	16.6	0.8	16.6	0.8	3,039	0.8	34	0.4
Latvians	1,400	1.2	20.5	1.0	20.8	1.0	3,837	1.0	44	0.6
Lithuanians	2,326	2.0	43.2	2.3	36.2	1.8	4,645	1.2	62	0.8

SOURCES: *Itogi vsesoyuznoi perepisi naseleniya 1959 goda: SSSR,* pp. 209–10; Tsentralnoe statisticheskoe upravlenie, *Narodnoe khozyaistvo SSSR v 1963 godu* (Moscow, 1965), pp. 579, 591, 613; *Vestnik statistiki,* No. 7 (1965), pp. 94–95; *Partiinaya zhizn,* No. 10 (May, 1965), p. 12.

[a] The assistance of Ivan Bakalo, of the Institute for the Study of the USSR, in the preparation of this table is gratefully acknowledged.

TABLE VIII

THE BALTS IN RELATION TO THE RUSSIANS IN NATIONAL-LANGUAGE PUBLICATION[a]

Language	VOLUME OF BOOKS PUBLISHED 1963		VOLUME OF JOURNALS PUBLISHED[b] 1964		VOLUME OF NEWSPAPERS PUBLISHED[b] 1964	
	Yearly Number (*in millions*)	Ratio to Russian (*in per cent*)	Yearly Number (*in millions*)	Ratio to Russian (*in per cent*)	Number per Edition (*in thousands*)	Ratio to Russian (*in per cent*)
Russian	1,026.9	100.0	979.2	100.0	59,464	100.0
Estonian	7.8	0.7	12.8	1.3	639	1.1
Latvian	9.1	0.8	22.4	2.2	717	1.2
Lithuanian	9.8	0.9	13.0	1.3	1,081	1.8

SOURCES: *Narodnoe khozyaistvo SSSR v 1963 godu,* pp. 579, 591, 613; *Vestnik statistiki,* No. 7 (1965), pp. 94–95; *Partiinaya zhizn,* No. 10 (May, 1965), p. 12.

[a] The assistance of Ivan Bakalo, of the Institute for the Study of the USSR, in the preparation of this table is gratefully acknowledged.

[b] Figures refer to the Baltic republics only.

S.S.R. The article was an impassioned plea for the retention of the eleven-year system of education in Soviet Estonian schools using Estonian as the language of instruction. It asked where the study of the Estonian language and literature can be fitted in if the length of study in the Estonian S.S.R. were to be leveled to the ten-year system of the R.S.F.S.R. In part the article read as follows:

> With good will one could digest the same material in ten years as in eleven and, moreover, a ten-year [system] will release in the republic approximately 4,000 young people a year, and a year earlier, for industry. True. The question arises, however, whether industry today requires workers in general or whether it requires people with a better general education?

The plea was heeded, and the Estonian Supreme Soviet issued a decree on August 18, 1965, retaining the eleven-year system in secondary schools with Estonian-language instruction. A few days earlier, the Presidium of the U.S.S.R. Supreme Soviet had granted "a partial exception" to the Soviet school regulations to institute eleven years of secondary schooling in all Baltic schools using local languages as their language of instruction (including Polish in Lithuania).[41] One of the reasons for the exception apparently was that the extra year would help the Balts to improve their command of Russian.

Schools in the Baltic countries are encouraged to set up parallel classes for instruction in Russian and the native language. This is particularly prevalent in Latvia, where there are at least 200 schools of this nature, providing "the most favorable conditions for bringing up children in the spirit of friendship of the peoples of the U.S.S.R."[42]

At the university level something similar is being accomplished by having Baltic universities specialize in different fields, so that students can be sent from one Baltic republic to another for study. The instruction in these special fields is in Russian, of course. This innovation, however, has not been too successful. For instance, during the academic year of 1964–65, the Tartu State University had an average of 195 Estonian daytime study groups and only 11 in the Russian language. The Tallinn Polytechnicum had 130 day lectures in Estonian, as against 30 in Russian. The proportions are no different for evening study.[43] Considerable effort is made to facilitate the transfer of students to other republics. Entrance examinations for study outside of Estonia, for instance, are given in the country in Estonian. When the students reach their destination they are matriculated *hors concours.*[44] In 1964, 190 young Estonians were sent to higher educational institutions in other republics, and 600 students came to Estonia. Students in Estonia wear caps similar to those worn in the Scandinavian countries and by the German corporations. This is a concession to a tradition more nationalistic than anything else; it was reinstituted in 1957. At Tartu University, moreover, a student club was established for the extracurricular study of the Estonian language.[45]

Student caps and clubs are manifestations of a nationalism that can be controlled. The Soviets really quarrel with what they refer to as "bourgeois nationalism." This expresses itself most obviously in anti-Russian feelings and yearnings for the past independence of the Baltic states. It exists. "One of the most repulsive survivals of the past," writes *Kommunist* (Vilnius), "is bourgeois nationalism, which in different aspects still seeps through to our youth."[46] It would appear that "bourgeois nationalist" feelings are more prevalent in Lithuania and Latvia than in Estonia, since the Lithuanian and Latvian press and Party journals devote much more space to the problem. In general, however, the Baltic republics are more inclined to show their separateness from the Soviet Union in trying to be more *avant-garde* and up to date with regard to the latest Western developments. This may express itself either in furniture design or architecture, which attempts to copy the modern Scandinavian trends, or in the restoration of medieval city centers, in the choice of theater materials, in the selection of Western authors for translation, or in music. It is even evident in the choice of sports, such as the preference for tennis and regattas. Bertolt Brecht is frequently performed. The Estonian Drama Theater performed his *Mother Courage* at a guest appearance in Finland in 1965. A young Estonian composer, Arvo Part, has been taken to task for his twelve-tone compositions. Camus' *Plague* has been published in Tallinn in Estonian, whereas a Russian edition is still to appear. Kafka was also published in Tallinn before it appeared in Moscow. *My Fair Lady* was in its third year in 1965, and *West Side Story* played for a whole season at the Estonian State Theater that same year. *My Fair Lady* subsequently opened also in Kaunas. A singular development has been the republication of anti-Communist *émigré* Estonian authors now resident in Sweden. The best-known Estonian composer, Eduard Tubin, also living in exile in Sweden, was invited to Estonia to conduct one of his ballets, and, having done this, he returned to Sweden. When the Estonian State Publishing House issued a book of reproductions of Eduard Wiiralt, a well-known Estonian artist who died in exile, *Sovetskaya kultura* could not contain itself and noted:

> The awarding of diplomas for this book to the Estonian State Publishing House seems a sad misunderstanding. . . . The works of this artist have deservedly been criticized in the press; many of them are nefarious in content, poisoned by the venom of Expressionism and sometimes bordering on pornography.[47]

The Soviets speak softly on the subject of nationalism. "Bringing closer the culture of socialist nations," writes Genrikas Zimanas, "does not mean the leveling of national culture, nor its elimination as long as there exist nations."[48] Professor Kammari, corresponding member of the U.S.S.R. Academy of Sciences, comments:

> According to Leninist theory the adoption by all peoples and nations of one of the languages of a culturally powerful nation as an international world language in no way means their confluence with this nation (or these nations), for every nation also continues to use freely its national tongue.[49]

And, he adds, the future fusion of languages was nothing but an "abstract Stalinist scheme." Finally, an Estonian historian warns that "any attempts to hasten these processes artificially can only bring about a revival of remnants of nationalism which slow down the *rapprochement* between the nations."[50]

Where, then, does Baltic nationalism stand?

It is obvious from this short survey that the Soviet leadership pays considerable attention to the Baltic states. It almost seems as if it had certain guilt feelings about their annexation to the U.S.S.R. at a time in history when colonial empires were falling apart. The twenty-fifth anniversary celebrations were therefore conceived as a propaganda spectacle in an attempt to assure the world that everything was in perfect order. But as the celebrations unfolded, pride at times caused the performers and the audience to forget their roles. At the song festival in Tallinn, people stood up and men bared their heads during the singing of a patriotic song which has almost become a substitute national anthem.[51]

The Baltic nations are small and their populations have become even smaller during the past quarter of a century. But if further migration into their countries is cut back, as would seem to be the case, there is a good chance that the Estonians, Latvians, and Lithuanians may survive as nations for some time to come. To be sure, the Slavs comprise one-third of the population of Latvia. The Baltic nations, however, have always had significant minorities in their midst. The issue is not the obvious one of Russification but that of assimilation. Russification connotes force, and this on the whole is being abandoned. Assimilation, which is voluntary, is potentially much more dangerous from a Baltic nationalist point of view. For the present, however, it does not constitute a danger. The Baltic countries are culturally and economically more advanced than Russia proper. Migration from the Baltics, so prevalent during the Czarist times, holds little if any attraction. The Balts prefer to remain in their native lands.

Baltic Communist Parties are led by people who are Russian-oriented, if not outright Russians. The national component in these parties is underrepresented. This is being corrected. As past purges have shown, however, local nationalism can corrupt a Communist as well. In many instances the local Party apparatus relies upon local and nationalist pride for teamwork and efficiency. This, naturally, feeds further the fires of nationalism.

In some ways, Estonia is in a more favored position than the other two republics, due mainly to an affinity with Finland. The Finns speak a language closely related to Estonian, and this has created certain ties that set the two nations apart from others. Both the Soviets and the Finns have encouraged mutual contacts for different reasons. The ones to benefit have been the Estonians, who are being given increasing exposure to Finnish and Scandinavian ideas and to Western cultural developments. And because of these contacts, they are also enjoying greater tolerance for their nationalist tendencies.

NOTES

1. *Sovetskaya Estoniya,* July 16, 1965.
2. Cf. Stanley Page, *The Formation of the Baltic States* (Cambridge, Mass.: Harvard University Press, 1959), and a critique thereof in the *Latvian Information Bulletin* (Washington, D.C.: Latvian Legation), No. 1/60 (March, 1960).
3. *Pravda,* July 18, 1965. See also *Current Digest of the Soviet Press,* XVII, No. 29 (August 11, 1965).
4. *Kommunist Estonii,* No. 7 (July, 1965), p. 30.
5. *Sovetskaya Estoniya,* July 18, 1965.
6. According to Lithuanian *émigré* sources, the 2.9 million in 1940, based on Soviet statistics, should actually read 3.2 million. (ELTA, Information Service of the Supreme Committee for Liberation of Lithuania, No. 9, [September 20, 1965], p. 9.)
7. *Bolshaya sovetskaya entsiklopediya* (2d ed.; 1964), XXV, 251.
8. *The New York Times,* July 26, 1965. Vilnius remains international. The Lithuanians themselves compose 34 per cent of the population. See *Sovetskaya etnografiya,* No. 5 (1965), p. 9.
9. *Kommunist* (Vilnius), No. 8 (August, 1964), p. 6.
10. *Sovetskaya Latviya,* October 14, 1964.
11. *The New York Times,* July 24, 1965, and *Sovetskaya etnografiya,* No. 5 (1965), p. 9.
12. *Kommunist Estonii,* No. 5 (May, 1965), p. 30.
13. See "Population Changes in the Baltic States," *East Europe,* XIV, No. 4 (April, 1965), 19.
14. *Kommunist Estonii,* No. 12 (December, 1964), pp. 16, 18.
15. *The New York Times,* July 24, 1965, and *Sovetskaya etnografiya,* No. 5 (1965), p. 9.
16. Akademiya nauk S.S.S.R., *Chislennost i rasselenie narodov mira* (Moscow, 1962), p. 64.
17. A. Ya. Boyarskii and P. P. Shusherin, *Demograficheskaya statistika* (Moscow, 1955), p. 80; *Bolshaya sovetskaya entsiklopediya* (2d ed.; 1964), XXV, 251.
18. Aleksander Kaelas, *Baltikum i Sovjetsfären* (Stockholm, 1960), p. 9.
19. *Sovetskaya etnografiya,* No. 5 (1965), p. 11.
20. *Ibid.,* and Tsentralnoe statisticheskoe upravlenie, *Itogi vsesoyuznoi perepisi naseleniya 1959 goda: SSSR* (Moscow, 1962), p. 184.
21. *Osteuropa,* No. 10 (1964), p. 760; *Osteuropa,* No. 6 (1964), p. 476; Vytautas Vaitiekunas, *Lithuania* (New York, 1965), p. 35, and own estimate for the Estonian Communist Party.
22. *Partiinaya zhizn,* No. 10 (May, 1965), p. 12.
23. Biographic data from *Who's Who in the USSR,* compiled by the Institute for the Study of the USSR (Montreal: Intercontinental Book and Publishing Co., Ltd., 1962).
24. A. M. Gindin and S. G. Markin, "Certain Characteristics of the New State in the Development of the Friendship of the Peoples of the USSR," *Voprosy istorii KPSS,* No. 2 (1965), p. 24.
25. *Padomju Latvijas Kommunists* (*Soviet Latvian Communist*), No. 9 (September, 1959), cited in *Latvian Information Bulletin,* No. 1/60, p. 1.
26. Cf. *Sirp ja Vasar* (*Sickle and Hammer*), January 10, 1964.

27. Aleksander Kaelas, *Das Sowjetisch Besetzte Estland* (Stockholm, 1958), p. 10.
28. *Sovetskaya Estoniya,* June 25, 1965.
29. *Ibid.*, December 19, 1959, p. 3.
30. Cf. *Deputaty Verkhovnogo Soveta SSSR* (Moscow, 1962).
31. The lowest growth figure comes from *Soviet Life,* July, 1965; the figure 18 was supplied by Mikoyan, speaking in Tallinn at the anniversary celebration (*Pravda,* July 18, 1965); and the highest figure can be found in *Pravda,* July 16, 1965, p. 2.
32. *Soviet Life,* July, 1965.
33. G. Zimanas, "Strength of Leninist National Policy," *Kommunist* (Vilnius), No. 4 (April, 1965), p. 33.
34. *Kommunist* (Vilnius), No. 8 (August, 1964), p. 11. V. Stanley Vardys, writing in *Foreign Affairs,* XLIV, No. 3 (April, 1966), notes that the guerrilla war of 1944–52 caused at least 40,000 casualties, half of them guerrilla and half Communist. These are Soviet figures and probably should be revised upward.
35. Cf. Elmar Jarvesoo, "Agriculture in Estonia," *East Europe,* XIV, No. 7 (July, 1965), 20–22.
36. "Conditions in the Baltic States and in other Countries of Eastern Europe," Hearings before the Subcommittee on Europe, Committee on Foreign Affairs, House of Representatives, 89th Cong., 1st sess., May 17 and 18, 1965, pp. 33–34.
37. *Soviet Life,* July, 1965, p. 14.
38. *Native Land—Kodumaa* (Published in English in Tallinn), 1964, p. 11.
39. TASS, June 10, 1964.
40. *Voprosy filosofii,* No. 11 (1962), pp. 36–48.
41. *Sirp ja Vasar,* August 20, 1965, and *Pravda,* October 3, 1965.
42. *Sovetskaya Latviya,* March 18, 1965.
43. *Sovetskaya Estoniya,* January 25, 1964.
44. *Kommunist Estonii,* No. 7 (July, 1965), p. 19.
45. *Sovetskaya Estoniya,* November 18, 1964.
46. *Kommunist* (Vilnius), No. 2 (February, 1965), p. 41.
47. *Sovetskaya kultura,* June 2, 1960.
48. *Kommunist* (Vilnius), No. 11 (November, 1964), p. 15.
49. *Kommunist Estonii,* No. 7 (July, 1964), pp. 68–69.
50. *Sovetskaya Estoniya,* August 6, 1965, p. 2.
51. Cf. *Vaba Eesti Sona* (*Free Estonian Word*) (New York), September 23, 1965, p. 5.

7

The Belorussian People Between Nationhood and Extinction

NICHOLAS P. VAKAR

The view that the Belorussian people is an established nation has been losing ground lately; the view that it is a national minority doomed to extinction in our time has gained ascendancy. Either view can be supported by various facts or by the same facts seen in a different light or presented in different terms. It is the purpose of this paper to sum up the ambiguities and uncertainties of the Belorussian situation today.

Generally, the political, economic, and social issues on the Belorussian scene are not viewed on their own merits but through the glass of either Russian or Belorussian nationalism on one hand, and pro-Communist or anti-Communist bias on the other. Indeed, the very idea of "nationhood" under the Soviet system and, for that matter, of "Belorussian people" has different meanings for the parties involved. Discussion requires not only a detached view but caution in the use of even the most common words.

When we say "Belorussia," do we mean the Belorussian Soviet Socialist Republic or do we also include the lands ethnographically Belorussian and partitioned between Poland, Lithuania, Latvia, Russia, and the Ukraine? The ethnographic maps were drawn in 1915–17, and political claims are still made today on the same old basis.[1] And when we say "Belorussian people," do we refer to all Belorussian-speaking inhabitants of the Soviet Union and Poland or only to the population of the Belorussian Soviet Socialist Republic? Shall we include those who claim to be Belorussians but say that their language is Russian? How shall we relate linguistic usage and national consciousness? We may count 12 million Belorussians (as the nationalists-in-exile do) or 8 or 6 million (as the last Soviet general census stated) or even less, according to some more recent estimates. Which information shall we trust?

Those Belorussians living outside the political boundaries of the Belorussian Soviet Republic, approximately 1.5 million scattered throughout the Soviet Union and the eastern provinces of Poland, do not enjoy national-minority status. Since many of them will probably lose the awareness of their separate identity within a generation or two, we will limit our discussion to the Belorussian Soviet Socialist Republic and the people living within its political boundaries.

The Belorussian Soviet Socialist Republic is by definition a sovereign political nation within the Soviet Union. It has its own territory, its own government, and such formal attributes of independent statehood as a national flag and a national seal. Should the Belorussian people find membership in the Soviet Union no longer desirable, they have the formal right to secede at any time, presumably to form new alliances or stand on their own feet. A member of the United Nations since 1945, the republic enjoys equal status with other nations of the world, including the Soviet Union itself. Indeed, the Belorussian Ministry of Foreign Affairs has published a large collection of treaties, conventions, and agreements concluded since World War II between the Belorussian S.S.R. and foreign powers.[2] Nominally independent in international relations, the republic has delegated to the Soviet Union —which it formed with other Soviet republics in 1922—its powers to print national currency and maintain a national army. This proved to be a wise measure. Had it not been for the joint Soviet effort, the Belorussian people would not have been able to free their land from the Poles and the Germans, nor to rehabilitate their economy after the devastation of war, nor to see their political territory increased sixfold since the founding of the republic in 1919.

The Belorussian and Ukrainian republics enjoy a privileged status among the nations of the Soviet Union. In other words, Belorussia's nationhood would be indisputable were it not for the fact that the country is both "socialist" and "soviet." The Belorussian situation is better understood when it is examined in the common context of blending a multinational community into a larger nation of a new and special design.

The Belorussian nationalists in exile contend that Soviet Belorussian nationhood has been a fraud and a sham from the first day. It is a fraud because the Bolsheviks did not, as they claim, found the Belorussian state. They captured it. Less than a year after the Soviet

Revolution, they invaded the republic established by the Belorussian Declaration of Independence on March 25, 1918. With the help of a few Belorussian collaborationists, the Bolsheviks proceeded to establish their own "Belorussian Republic" on January 1, 1919, to disguise the fact of military conquest and occupation. Since then, the nationalists insist, Belorussia has been a captive nation—first partitioned between the Poles and the Russians, then occupied by the Germans, then again by the Russians. And the Belorussian Soviet Republic is a fraud also because it does not include all the ethnographically or historically Belorussian lands. Sizable parts were handed over by Moscow to Poland, Lithuania, Latvia, Russia, and the Ukraine.[3]

Soviet Belorussia is a sham republic, it is claimed, because, like any other province of the Soviet Union, it is governed from the Kremlin. The name and symbols of Belorussian statehood are used to conceal the planned and directed process of forcible denationalization, assimilation, and gradual extinction of the Belorussian people.

There is, of course, no lack of evidence that politically and economically the Belorussian S.S.R. is simply an administrative unit of the larger Soviet state.[4] There is nothing uniquely Belorussian about the governing Belorussian Communist Party; indeed, its very name, "Communist Party *of* Belorussia," puts emphasis on region, not on nation. The First Party Secretary may at times be a native, but he and his deputies are executive officers of the Communist Party of the Soviet Union (CPSU). They run the sovereign Belorussian Republic as they would the Yakut Autonomous Republic or, for that matter, the Stavropol or Kuybyshev *oblast*. But politically and economically, the national symbolism of the Union republics has proved useful, indeed indispensable, in building "socialism in one country" (Stalin); and it is still useful, if only because it can disorient and disarm the "bourgeois-nationalist" opposition at home and abroad. Symbols deprived of all substance may generate difficulties, and the state has let national cultures develop and thrive on condition that they be "socialist in content, national in form" (Stalin). Belorussian culture, limited as it is to formalization of the Soviet way of life, has been the last stronghold of Belorussian patriots, their last hope that the people will remain Belorussian.

They seem to be losing this battle, too. Belorussian is still formally the language of the Belorussian Republic, but it is seldom heard in the streets and in the offices of Minsk. Higher education in the republic has been conducted in Russian for some time; now the native idiom is being banned from secondary and elementary schools. Complaints are heard that bookstores have been unable to fill orders for Belorussian literature because the government drastically reduces or cancels print orders, especially for school texts in the Belorussian language. The Belorussian press reports that regional school libraries are unable to obtain works of a number of Belorussian writers, though they are still included in the lists of recommended reading. On the other hand, Russian books, including translations from the Belorussian, are readily available. Indeed, some Belorussian writers prefer to publish their works in Russian rather than in the national idiom.[5] The two-volume *History of the Belorussian S.S.R.* is the collective work of forty-five Belorussian scholars, written in Russian for the Belorussian Academy of Sciences.[6] The Academy apparently publishes all scholarly works in Russian without indicating that at least some of them might be translations from the original Belorussian. A periodical entitled *Holas Radzimy* (roughly, *The Old Country Speaks to You*), is sent to Belorussian exiles and urges them to return to their now prosperous homeland. Only about one-half of the articles in this publication are in Belorussian.

According to Soviet statistics, questionable though they may be, the general census of January 15, 1959, counted 8,054,648 people in the Belorussian Republic. People were asked to state their nationality and to tell what language they considered their native tongue (*rodnoy yazyk*).[7] In all, thirteen nationalities were registered. People who called themselves Belorussians made up 81.1 per cent of the total; Russians, 8.2 per cent; Poles, 6.7 per cent; Jews, 1.9 per cent; and Ukrainians, 1.7 per cent. All others combined made up less than 1 per cent (0.6). More than 1 million persons (16.2 per cent of the population), including half a million Belorussians, called Russian their language.[8]

It appears that by "nationality" some meant their ancestry, others their place of birth, and still others their mother tongue or even their religion; and by "language," some meant the linguistic group to which they belonged by birth, and others the language they actually use. For example, one-half of the people who registered as Polish stated that their language was Belorussian (254,860) or Russian (21,732); one explanation given is that those who thought of themselves as Poles were born in western Belorussia (in the part under Polish rule) and were probably Roman Catholics. The mother tongue of the 150,000 people registered as Jewish was Russian (114,225) or Belorussian (2,815); only 33,000 said it was Yiddish. About

8,000 people listing either Belorussian (3,862) or Russian (3,609) as their language identified themselves as Tatars—descendants of families that settled in Belorussia after the Mongol invasion; and of the 1,276 Mordvins, whose ancestral home is Central Russia, 400 said that Mordovian was their "native tongue," though probably only a few could speak it.

The government decided to allow publications in only two languages, Belorussian and Russian. Statistically, Russian-speaking people made up 46 per cent of the urban and only 5 per cent of the rural population. In fact, the Russian language prevailed in most cities. In the countryside, too, Russian was becoming the second language of more and more people. Only five years before the general census, 60 per cent of all books and pamphlets published were in Russian, and 40 per cent in Belorussian. Five years after the general census, 78 per cent of all books and pamphlets published were in Russian, and only 22 per cent in Belorussian. The figures for 1965 are 80 per cent for Russian, 20 per cent for Belorussian. Belorussian newspapers outnumber Russian papers (eighty-seven Belorussian; thirty-five Russian), but most Belorussian papers are small provincial and rural bulletins. For years, the Belorussian press has been losing ground in both city and village.[9] The contrast with other Union republics is striking. All are exposed to the tremendous pressures, both natural and coercive, of the federal language—Russian. But all the other republics managed to hold their own more readily than Belorussia. Even in the Kazakh and the Moldavian republics, three Russian books are published for every two in the vernacular, whereas in the Belorussian Republic the ratio is four to one. The ratio in the Ukrainian Republic is even, one to one. In all other Union republics, publications in the vernacular still outnumber those in Russian. The Belorussians are the third largest linguistic group in the Soviet Union. Why should they show so little resistance to systematic Russification?

Resistance in Belorussia is centered around a few literary periodicals, such as *Litaratura i Mastatstva* (*Literature and the Arts*) or *Moladz* (*Youth*), cultural agencies such as Narodna Asvieta (Popular Education), choirs, dramatic and folklore clubs. The leaders are dedicated men and women, struggling desperately for the survival of the national idiom and customs, who decry the incursions of Russian in Belorussian homes, schools, and offices. They find only divided support in the country. The growing new Belorussian intelligentsia holds that the use of the Russian language is necessary and beneficial for the people and that it does not by any means make them less Belorussian.

The spread of Russian has been linked to the economic rehabilitation of the country, the social mobility and technological progress since World War II. For the new Belorussian intelligentsia, there is every indication that the long doctrinal battle which took up the energies of a whole generation of nationalists has been lost. They know that the Irish speak English but are yet aware of their separate identity. They know that the community of language did not prevent the American Declaration of Independence. Why should the Russian language be a threat to Belorussian independence? The real and, indeed, age-old problem is the Belorussian will to be, or become, a nation.

I asked that question of a Russian-speaking young Belorussian, a Soviet exchange student in the United States. I believe he considered me a fascinating relic of the Russia of the past. Moved by mutual curiosity, we became quite friendly. He was, of course, a Communist Party member ("A great honor," he said), but he did not try to hand me the Party line. Indeed, he showed little interest in Marxism-Leninism; but was firm on one point: "Get rid of the Communist Party, and the whole country will go to hell; nothing else can hold it together." He meant not only the Soviet Union but Belorussia as well. "There will be hell in every town and in every home," he said. "The people are not ready for freedom." I was not surprised when he said that only under the Soviet system could the Belorussians maintain their full status as a nation, but I wanted him to explain.

He did not deny that the Russian language had made deep inroads into Belorussian life, but insisted that this was as it should be. "I am a Belorussian and so is my wife," he said, "but we speak Russian most of the time." Why? For many reasons. First, he said, what education can you get in Belorussian? With Belorussian alone, you cannot go beyond secondary school. The efforts to translate more sophisticated literature into Belorussian proved costly and utterly worthless. Even professors were unable to understand some of the new Belorussian texts. "Our fathers," he said, "wasted two precious decades before common sense compelled them to adopt Russian books. Everybody found it easier to learn Russian than to sweat over translations in the clumsy academic Belorussian." Besides, the Russian language had opened up for him a whole world of higher culture, made world science and world literature at once accessible. This, according to him, was only one reason for the dominance of Russian in the field of education.

"Take my case," he said. "I was brought up speaking the dialect of the southwest, my wife the dialect of the north, and we had to learn still another brand of Belorussian in school. To be sure, there must be a standard, but the one we have does not derive from a long and independent literary tradition. It has some of that dead academic weight which makes it acceptable for print but not for life. People speak the dialects at home, and the educated naturally switch to Russian." O yes, he said, he loves the Belorussian language, he loves Belorussian folklore, and enjoys the new Belorussian poetry and novels, but "we also aspire to the higher culture which we can get through Russian—and many of us also study English, French, or German. We are fortunate that linguistically Russian and Belorussian are so close."

Would not the Belorussians lose their sense of separate identity if they became a Russian-speaking nation? Not at all, he said. The Russian language did not make him any less Belorussian than his old, stubborn father, who would not touch a Russian newspaper or book. On the contrary, he felt that he was a better Belorussian, more useful to his land and people. "For us," he said, "Russian is the Soviet language, not just the language of the Russians. It is a world language like English or French. Through it, we are participants in world history and culture. Without it, we would have been a semiliterate nation of workers and peasants as, indeed, most Belorussian people are."

No, he said, answering my other question, Russian is not a mark of social distinction as French was in prerevolutionary Russia, though, he conceded, in a way it is. Perhaps more than in any other Union republic, it is a matter of practical necessity. Since the last war, skilled labor has been coming to Belorussia from all parts of the Soviet Union; a command of Russian is necessary in order to communicate with engineers, foremen, or economists in the growing Belorussian industries, or with mechanics, agronomists, or veterinarians on a large collective farm. Some old rural customs and traditions still linger, but not as vital parts of community life. Belorussian songs still can be heard in the fields, but one has to go to a pageant or a theater to see Belorussian dances and the Belorussian national dress. The dialects are widely spoken in the countryside, but, my friend insisted, all young people in secondary schools are bilingual.

I remarked that Belorussian might well become a dead language within a few generations. Possibly, he conceded, though some people will always stick to local dialects. At any rate, he said, Belorussian is no longer needed to remind us that we are a people.

The young man was of course largely restating the Communist

Party policy toward nationalities. But I was struck by the low esteem in which this peasant's son held Belorussian culture and language. It was the first time I had met a native Belorussian who professed to love his land and people and yet scorned their customs and speech. He sounded much like the educated Belorussians of a century and more ago: Under Poland, they turned Polish, and under Russia, Russian; in both instances they abandoned the people. The term "Belorussian" was then synonymous with "peasant," and the peasantry began to form its own educated class only at the beginning of this century. All the Belorussian nationalists of our time came from that stratum. Today, this new Belorussian intelligentsia seems to be taking the old route—with one difference: in turning Russian, they want to take their people along.

I do not know how typical my young Belorussian was. Many observable facts bear him out. He is, or at least wants to be, a man of Russian culture. And he pointed out that this was a general trend in his generation, not only in Belorussia but throughout the Soviet Union.

There is no question about the ultimate aim of the Soviet Government to make the Soviet Union a homogeneous nation.[10] The question is the national minorities' will and ability to resist. The situation may differ from one Union republic to another. Some are protected by their geographic position, others draw strength from historical memories, still others can take refuge in their old cultural heritage. The Belorussian position is weak in all respects—geographically, historically, and linguistically.

The people realize that even under ideal conditions they could not hope to stand alone. Their land lies on the historical invasion route. They must seek protection of the stronger neighbor and accept his terms or perish.[11] The people have a long history, but they must go to Polish or Russian sources for any record of it. Their past gave them no heritage other than the soil their forefathers tilled since prehistoric times. To be sure, they now have their historical pedigree, conveniently remodeled and rewritten, but they know that they have to build from scratch. Their only treasure was the language of their peasantry—an old idiom considered variously a Polish or a Russian dialect. They have organized, unified, and refined it into an effective tool of statehood.[12] They have created a literary standard, but one that still has many limitations. It has not taken root among the people, nor can it meet all the requirements of modern science and advanced education. It is not unnatural that they should seek to supplement their national resources with what their stronger neighbors can offer them. They may not be aware of the price exacted. Striving to become "better Belorussians," they are in danger of defining themselves out of existence.

My young man insisted that the formal symbols of nationhood had real meaning for him, that even if the Belorussian language were to become extinct, there would always be a Belorussian people and a Belorussian state, its national home. He declared that it was not the Belorussian culture and language (for which he has little use) but the Belorussian political state that made him feel Belorussian.

Can it be said that there is a Belorussian nation *because* there is a Belorussian state? References in Soviet literature to Belorussians are beginning to sound like references to the inhabitants of a region rather than a people. They sound exactly like the references to Siberia and Siberians or to any other geographical division of the country—the Urals, the Crimea, the Arctic, the Caucasus—and its inhabitants, or, in American terms, much like our own references to the Midwest, New England, or a particular state.

In the case of Belorussia today, we cannot speak of either nationhood or extinction. The people have their special ethnic characteristics, but the trend is to preserve them merely for their historical and sentimental value.

NOTES

1. N. Durnovo, N. Sokolov, and D. Ushakov, "Opyt dialektologicheskoy karty russkogo yazyka v Evrope s prilozheniem ocherka russkoy dialektologii," *Russkii filologicheskii vestnik,* IV (Moscow, 1915). This journal was edited by E. Karski and published by the Moscow Dialectological Society. See also N. P. Vakar, *Belorussia: The Making of a Nation* (Cambridge, Mass.: Harvard University Press, 1956), pp. 7–8.
2. S. P. Margunskii and A. S. Zaitsev (eds.), *Belorusskaya SSR v mezhdunarodnykh otnosheniakh. Mezhdunarodnye dogovory, konventsii i soglashenia Belorusskoy SSR s inostrannymi gosudarstvami 1944–1959 gg.* (Minsk: Belorussian Academy of Sciences, 1960). These international agreements were negotiated at the United Nations.
3. The Belorussian nationalists claim not only the Brest and Belostok regions (Poland), Vilna (Lithuania), Pskov, Smolensk, and Briansk (Russia), but also the Kalinin (Koenigsberg) province of the R.S.F.S.R. "in compensation for our losses in World War II." (*Nash sciag* [Toronto], No. 1 [May, 1965].)
4. The political claims that a Union republic should plan its own national economy are branded "criminal nationalism." (See *Voprosy istorii,* No. 4 [1964], p. 60.)
5. This has increasingly been the practice since the late 1950's. See the article by A. Adamovich, in *Studies on the Soviet Union* (Munich), No. 2 (1963).
6. Akademia nauk Belorusskoy S.S.R., Institut istorii, *Istoria Belorusskoy SSR* (2 vols.; 2d rev. ed.; Minsk: Belorussian Academy of Sciences, 1961).
7. The Russian term is ambiguous and can be interpreted as "mother tongue," "native language," or "habitual language." My children were born in France of Russian parents and moved to the United States at the ages of ten and twelve. I do not know how they would have answered the questionnaire, but their language is English.
8. As of June 1, 1941, the Soviets estimated the population of the Belorussian S.S.R. at 10,525,511, of which 80.6 per cent were Belorussian, 8.2 per cent Jewish, and 7.2 per cent Russian. Cf. Vakar, *op. cit.,* p. 6.
9. According to the general census of January 15, 1959, the population of the Belorussian S.S.R. was 30 per cent urban and 70 per cent rural. The total population has grown 5 per cent in the last five years (*Ezhegodnik bolshoy sovetskoy entsiklopedii* [Moscow, 1964]), but the proportion of urban to rural population has been changing rapidly by migrations from the village, as well as by urbanization of the new industrial sites. In 1957, the Belorussian Republic counted sixty-nine cities and ninety-eight towns (*poselki gorodskogo tipa*); by January 1, 1964, their number had increased to 74 and 124.
10. "Mutual assimilation is, in substance, denationalization of the autonomous national territories, even of the Union Republics; the Soviet society is thus approaching the point where a complete national fusion can be seen as a matter of the near future." *Sovetskoe gosudarstvo i pravo* (Moscow), No. 12 (1961), p. 25.
11. Professor V. Krutalevich, member of the Belorussian Academy of Sciences, reminded the Belorussian "bourgeois-nationalists" that they "never dreamed of Belorussian political independence before the Bolshevik Revolution, and would have been satisfied with some kind of autonomy within

the old Russian empire. . . . Belorussian nationhood was, in fact, a Bolshevik idea and accomplishment. It was, however, necessary to devise a practical form of Belorussian statehood in harmony with the natural trend toward unity of the Belorussian and the Russian peoples, and in union with other peoples of old Russia." *Voprosy istorii,* No. 4 (1964), p. 64.

12. The first Belorussian grammar was compiled by Br. Tarashkevich in 1918. Cf. Vakar, *op. cit.,* p. 78.

8

*The "Nationality" Idea in Czarist Central Asia**

EDWARD ALLWORTH

Coupling the rise of the "nationality" idea in Central Asia with the coming of European civilization to the area via Russia, beginning early in the nineteenth century, is a tempting proposal offered by Czarist and Soviet political writers.[1] Testing the premise requires, first of all, an understanding of Central Asian attitudes toward the changes in their own situation and toward foreign thinking about "nationality." Then, the shape of existing Central Asian communities must be explored, for some kind of union, if not unity, constitutes either the basis or the expression of nationality.

Associating the emergence of "nationality" ideas in Central Asia directly and affirmatively with the early Czarist presence in the region is risky, because Russian moves at the outset argued against the notion that St. Petersburg wanted to bring unity to the northern plains of Central Asia. In 1801, the Czar had hastily approved a plan to create another major Kazakh division, the Bokey Ordasi (*Ish Jüz,* or Inner Horde), from among those peoples nominally subject to his empire under earlier treaties negotiated between the Kazakh khans and the Russian Government. As a result of this new measure, a fourth "horde" was carved out of the flank of the old *Kishshi Jüz* (Little Horde) Kazakhs. This action further fragmented a population already badly split by local dissension. Consequently, these Kazakhs lacked that sense of nationality sometimes generated through political unification. Moreover, commencing about 1820, when the Russians actually started to occupy Kazakh lands south of the Orenburg-Omsk-Semipalatinsk frontier, and until the end of the century, the Czarist Government continually redrew internal administrative boundaries

* "Central Asia," as used here, designates Western Turkistan, or approximately the area presently called "Soviet Central Asia and Kazakhstan" in the U.S.S.R.

between Kazakh groups in order to weaken their traditional political organization.[2] Progress toward Central Asian "nationality" formation, under the circumstances, was hardly discernible during the sixty-five years following the occupation. Russia's aim appeared, rather, to discourage any Kazakh inclination to become a single corporate entity. Had this trend continued, the vast Kazakh area on the Central Asian map might look different today, but several actions, more a reaction against than a response to Russian initiatives, checked the tendency toward disintegration and provided the initial steps that eventually readied the area for a reversal of its self-image.

Czarist measures contributed directly to this alteration. The government, for political reasons, had been encouraging Kazakh membership in the Muslim religious community. Then, the Czar decreed Kazakh language unity and at the same time urged vigilance against the seductions of outside cultural influences, particularly those from the Tatars of Kazan. Most important, Russian armies had taken control of the entire Kazakh expanse. By 1864, the Russian Government, regardless of its intent, had changed the Kazakhs' situation in Western Turkistan by reuniting them all under one, albeit foreign, rule for the first time since the Kazakh khanate was shattered into three separate *jüzes* (in Russian, "hordes") in the seventeenth century.

Kazakh reunification through Czarist military action was accomplished at the substantial cost of provoking desperate struggles with whole groups of tribes that had previously maintained fairly amicable relations with Russia. For the moment, these strong anti-Russian surges remained too scattered to bring the Kazakhs together for self-preservation, and in 1864, a vision of Kazakh unity was still largely unperceived by a population clinging to tribal loyalties. From this time to 1900, some educated Kazakhs became conscious of an idea of Kazakh oneness that presaged the nationality idea. Foremost among these recorded early prophets was Shokan Shingis-uli Valiqan-uli (Valikhanov) (1835–65), who near the end of his active life proudly enunciated in Russian the prospect of the Kazakhs as a distinct, homogeneous group:

> Russia has in the number of her sons not a few peoples [*narodnosti*] of foreign faiths and foreign tribes who carry on a way of life diametrically opposed to the way of life of the native Russian population. . . . Out of all the foreign tribes [*inorodcheskie plemena*] making up the Russian empire, first place in numerical strength, in wealth, and, perhaps, in hopes for development in the future belongs to us—the Kazakhs. We occupy one spacious, continuous territory, whereas other aliens [*inorodtsy*]

are scattered among the Russian population. . . . Our people [*narod*], finally, are not so wild and crude as Russian society thinks them.[3]

The reality of Kazakh agony behind this noble dream had shown Central Asians that physical similarities and homogeneity by themselves do not automatically create national awareness among a people. In the proper context, these two factors supply the raw material for the making of a group, but the master key to the phenomenon called nationality is intricate, though it fits a variety of situations. Valiqan-uli measured the resemblances apparent throughout the Kazakh plain in the anthropological, geographic, and demographic elements that he believed unique to his people, and he also hinted at their separate (religious) ideology. Yet the nearly unanimous self-awareness characteristic of a true nationality, often stimulated by foreign conquest such as that undergone by the Kazakhs, was absent. Valiqan-uli simply failed to discover what tie the Kazakhs lacked in his day, namely, the spiritual linkage essential to binding people together in a nationality. If peoples themselves cannot recognize the presence of this intangible element, if they cannot identify its essence, their unification as a nationality remains in doubt.

Aside from common language, territory, or ethnic origin, the one constant indispensable to the nationality condition is an idea of it. Moving much closer to this realization late in the nineteenth century came other thoughtful Kazakhs, such as the poet Ibrahim (Abay) Qunanbay-uli (Kunanbaev) (1845–1904), who expounded the gist of their idea concerning "national" unity at that time. In 1891, employing a Kazakh proverb ("The beginning of understanding lies in unity and the beginning of abundance in work") as the starting point of his discussion, Qunanbay-uli identified the Kazakh dilemma. "But," he said, "what unity is and how to achieve it the Kazakhs do not know. Thus, among the Kazakhs it turns out that unity is the community of cattle, provisions and dress. . . . But unity lies in a community of thought, in common intentions, not in an imaginary community of wealth."[4]

The old habit among Kazakh tribesmen of referring to themselves in the presence of outsiders as members of one of the *ush jüz* (three hordes) rather than of a single Kazakh society continued into the twentieth century, a symptom of perennial disunity. The peculiar Czarist insistence, at the same time, on referring to the Kazakhs as "Kirgiz" further helped to confuse their self-identification. Similarly, Russians and Tatars lumped the settled people of the south together under one, somewhat pejorative, misnomer, "Sart," regardless of their real political or ethnic affiliations.

While the Kazakhs in northern Central Asia fell under a single rule, the Central Asians of the south continued to experience the very antithesis of union. Like the Kazakhs before Russian occupation in the nineteenth century, the people of southern Central Asia were divided into four major political groupings, but only one, the Turkmens of the Transcaspian wastes, had any distinct homogeneity. The Khivan and Khokandian khanates and the Bukharan emirate represented what might later have been called "multinational" states, for under their rule each dominated members of most principal groups in Central Asia. Notwithstanding the pulls of Islam, which held the south together more firmly than the nomadic north, no political figures in the sedentary areas had the strength and the requisite willingness to unite the area under one government. The major ethnic and linguistic obstacle to harmony seemingly came from the presence of an Iranian (Tajik) minority comprising perhaps as much as 10 per cent of the mainly Turkic local population.[5]

The southerners may have enjoyed little political unity, but they were not without enlightened men who saw the advantage of modern, combined effort. A few were able to see the great potential of unification that lay beyond the constant petty infighting. Intellectuals like the Bukharan diplomat Ahmad Mahdum (Dānish) (1827–97) betrayed no insight into nationality ideas, but their cognition of the Central Asian Muslim *millat* (religious community) as a perfectible spiritual entity distinct from the Bukharan *dawlat* (state) provided a fresh foothold for the newly rising old idea of a meaningful human grouping distinguishable from the state structure.[6] Nevertheless, these individuals, like their Kazakh relatives, were unable to persuade the people to join together in permanent union, despite the direct threat of foreign aggression. But in 1885, with the conquest of Turkmen territory completed by Czarist armies, perhaps coincidentally to certain other sections of the south already under Russian control, came a moment for ending the undeclared moratorium on local opposition to the Slavic governors. Feelings of resistance gave birth to embryonic local unity. Sporadically, opposition crystallized around militant religious leaders and, after almost twenty years of passivity, stirred people to re-examine their anonymous condition and to think of effecting a change.[7]

None of the spiritual and physical forces urging the integration of southern Central Asia was to be more potent in this new era than two intensified and rechanneled ancient drives, both of which pressed for union, each of a different kind. Predictably, the sustained, old vitality of Muslim concord retained its strength, but for the future the more dynamic seemed to be a resurgence of a conception whose origins predated even the tenth-century conversion of the numerous Turkic Qarakhanids of the area to Islam.[8] This conception was "Turkistan" unity. The Turkistan idea, dormant during the Mongol period, had been revived by the Uzbeks in the fifteenth and sixteenth centuries to designate the prairieland north-northwest of the ancient Transoxianian cities.[9] The surprisingly tenacious Turkistan conception had not disappeared by the nineteenth century, perhaps in part because it could not be comprehended in any exact territorial, historical, or political context of the past. By 1864, when the Czarist Army took the town of Turkistan and in 1865 named the environs of Tashkent "Turkestanskaia Oblast'," the Russian notion of Turkistan had long since been attached to southern Central Asia. Thus, a modern Turkistan was delineated only when the Russian regime gave that name to the first southeastern section deep in Central Asia to come under its control. This version of Turkistan excluded most of Central Asia north of the Syr Darya and Lake Balkhash that Sultan Babur (1482–1530) had called Turkistan.[10]

The revival of the latent Turkistan idea may therefore be credited to the Russian Government. The Czarist leadership here reversed the technique it employed in organizing the Kazakhs, and in the south chose, in the main, to unify rather than divide the people, doubtless because the area already possessed several pronounced, visible state structures. In order to dilute the appeal exerted by the old khanates, the Russians widened the confines of the Turkistan Oblast' to the larger "Turkistan Wilayati" (Turkistan Governor Generalship; in Russian, General-Gubernatorstvo) in 1867. When Khokand fell, in 1876, that domain, too, swelled the Turkistan Wilayati. By 1898, the already large Wilayat had expanded to include a broad band of territory between the Caspian Sea and eastern Turkistan, minus the Bukharan and Khivan enclaves, and extending some 800 miles up from the Persian and Afghan borders.

To impress this new territorial designation upon the southern Central Asians outside Bukhara and Khiva, Russian military commanders gave the name *Turkistan wilayatining gazeti* to the official bulletin that began to circulate in 1870 from Tashkent. For twelve years, the regime published it alternately in Kazakh and Chaghatay-Uzbek. This had the effect of reinforcing the newly created Turkistan unity while bolstering the nearly nonexistent Kazakh written language and literature, distinguishing it from the powerful Chaghatay literary heritage that in the past had dominated Kazakh, Tatar, Uzbek, and related writings. The selection of the languages used by the government's Central Asian publications constituted the Russian authorities' principal overt move to divide the local population officially, without regard to oblast or wilayat jurisdictions. After 1888, the administration went still further in this process, completely dropping Kazakh editions or articles from the Tashkent bulletin and initiating a separate Kazakh publication at Omsk. Thereafter, Turki (Chaghatay-Uzbek) remained the official written language throughout the south, so far as state publishing was concerned, though a minor deviation from this pattern developed quite late at Ashkhabad, then also within the Turkistan Wilayati. There, the Persian- and Turkmen-language government bulletins, published sporadically between 1904 and 1917, probably reflected the vicious bureaucratic rivalries within the colonial mechanism rather than indicating a refinement in Czarist language or nationality policy.[11]

The introduction of periodical publishing, like earlier practical demonstrations of modern arms, the building of railroads and other innovations, it is generally agreed, prompted significant local responses. How to classify the positive and negative effects of these innovations on the idea of nationality, their importance in comparison with previous influences, to which later tendencies they must be related, and what motivated them are questions that have never been settled to everyone's satisfaction. Controversy has persisted because the two main conflicting points of view concerning them seem to be irreconcilable. On the one side, there are those who classify nearly everything on the local scene that reveals resentment against the Russians, reflects Western practices and technology, or represents cultural, social, and artistic modernization in nineteenth-century Central Asia, as a manifestation of a "national (liberation) movement." Such a movement was said to be strictly a middle-class phenomenon, a manifestation of "the epoch of rising capitalism," as the Marxists described it. The nation itself was considered by them as a product of that period. Since Lenin and Stalin, according to the same scheme, held that Central Asia's peoples never went through the capitalist phase of development, it might seem that a contradiction would arise if "national movements" were to be discerned in Central Asia. Real doubts could also be raised about the existence in Muslim Asia of a genuine bourgeoisie, necessary to the functioning of those European theories. The first danger was skirted by allowing that the *beginnings* of capitalism had been seen in southern Central Asia after the Russian conquest and parallel with them had started a rudimentary but of course incomplete national movement. The equivalence of Western and Eastern class structures remained an article of Marxist faith.

Flatly opposed to that analysis of affairs or even to the very idea of the existence of such movements stand some suspicious scholars who base their case upon a simple reading of the Central Asian spokesmen's expressed or demonstrated intent. The anti–"national-movement" group fail to fit their studies into a rigidly formulated pattern or to find the historical imperative dictating a particular sequence of events, such as the appearance of "national movements" during a time of "feudal" breakdown and rise of capitalism in Czarist Asia. The debate, therefore, pits mainly Russian Marxists against European authors. It is joined over the interpretation of events like the Kazakh attacks between 1836 and 1838 led by Isatay Tayman-uli against the Russians' puppet Khan Jangir and his followers in the Bokey (Inner) Horde. Termed an insurrection in contemporary Czarist documents,[12] the accompanying flare-up between Russian troops and Isatay's band was in fact admittedly prompted by the incursion of Russian punitive detachments into the open plains in support of their docile Kazakhs. Though it could be considered an indirect protest against Russian authority, Isatay's struggle involved no "national" aims, for there was as yet no modern Kazakh nation or nationality, nor was the Kazakh chieftain represented as speaking or striving for one. On the more peaceful side of the transformation of Central Asians from isolated Easterners to people in contact with the West, the Marxists often said that this process of change, too, embodied a "national movement": "The *narodnyi* [national, people's] teachers turned out to be organizers and leaders of the *natsional'noe dvizhenie* [national movement] . . . among the more enlightened tribes like the Kazakhs and even the Kazan Tatars."[13] Such a national movement, the Marxists asserted, consisted of a national consciousness awakened first by the persecution of the Russian Government and later by the Russian "liberation movement" of 1905. It was made up, they contended, "of interest aroused for the first time in questions concerning the state in general, and the onset for the first time of the well-known type of spiritual *sblizhenie* [*rapprochement*] with the *kul'turnye elementy* [leftist politicians] of Russia."[14]

Besides holding such a view of Central Asian happenings, believers in the reality of national movements have also arrived at a restrictive usage of the adjective "national," which removes, for them, most of the difficulties ordinarily met in discussing the nationality idea said to have prevailed in the nineteenth century. In that context, "national" becomes a synonym for "anti-Russian," and it has continued for Soviet Marxists to mean "non-Russian," just as "the nationalities" are the non-Russian peoples in the U.S.S.R. Central Asians also occasionally subscribed to this interpretation. Thus, "national" resembles the terms "minority" or "nonwhite" in our Western discussions of religious or racial inequality and, similarly, the word has acquired a pejorative connotation. The special reading of "national," finally, permits actions construed as protests against the Russian authorities to be classified as elements in a "national (i.e., anti-Russian) movement."

Additional arguments against the existence of national movements in pre-Soviet Western Turkistan cast doubt upon the very "nationality" of the Central Asians. Evidence like that supplied by Shoqan Valiqan-uli in 1864 generally shows that nationality in the accepted sense (corporate awareness urging allegiance to a supreme rather than a subgroup) in the 1800's remained quite undeveloped among the emirate and khanates or within Kazakh, Uzbek, and similar divisions in the area. Without such consciousness, opponents of the national-movement theory can insist, you may not have a coherent national tendency of any kind. Since few people of Central Asia had any concept of the nation-state or the nationalism generating one, and an awareness of nationality has its corollary in the urge to nation statehood, neither of these can be said to have existed in that region, at least up to 1917.[15] Moreover, the use of "movement" in this connection, with its unspoken attributive "mass" also comes into question, because the forces of the hypothetical movement failed to unify the leadership, much less the ordinary men. In most cases events which might have constituted such a movement were neither contingent upon one another nor connected by a common, ideological basis. There was, therefore, no concerted move.

Proponents of the national-movement theory found themselves on surer ground when discussing the situation developing in Central Asia at the start of the twentieth century, because then the local intellectuals were beginning to speak more and more frequently about their religious *millat,* sometimes in the sense of "nation." For the indigenous leaders, the obvious alternatives appeared to be these: the majority of Central Asians, and particularly those in Turkistan Wilayati, might begin to regard themselves as one nationality if they could overcome their tribal or dynastic fealty; otherwise, they might finally secularize the concept of the Muslim *millat* then much talked of in that connection in Ottoman Turkey, for example.[16] If these were not the paths, another route remained: the emerging Kazakh pattern could be generalized also in the south to split the whole area down into ethnic, linguistic units.

A three-way collision on the course toward a solution occurred just at that moment in southern Central Asia between the old drive of the Muslim *millat* converging with thoughts of "Turkistan" unity and the new Jadid (reformist) ideas, which had come in from the Crimea and Kazan. Untangling the confusion required more time than the people involved were likely to have if a strong unifying leadership could not be found. At first, this phase of the search for identity was less the creation of a conscious program with which a particular, organized group set out to propagandize the idea of separateness than a subtle infiltration of assumptions that came into people's thinking almost unnoticed. This proceeded fairly rapidly under the twin pressures applied by fresh legions of Russian immigrants flowing daily to the plains (though less to the south), and the influx of Azeri, Tatar, and Turkish missionaries bringing reforms to Central Asia.

Younger southern leaders, especially outside the khanates, seized upon old Turkistan as an inspiration for their new identity, an impulse to be realized within two decades in the first separate Turkistan state. But even as early as 1900, this optional identity had already allowed them to slough off the spirit of the past characterized by the enfeebled but persistent dynasties, while it offered union still under Islam upon specific terrain to Turkic men of good will. Moreover, Turkistan, then recently sanctioned by the Russians, by analogy legalized Kazakhstan as a counterpoise to it in Central Asia. Many Kazakh intellectuals had moved into the twentieth century virtually unencumbered by the ingrained habits of Islam and seemingly quite without traces of the ancient Turkistan outlook. This occurred principally because nearly all of the Kazakh leaders to emerge in the new times matured far from the southern periphery. Educated mostly in the towns along the northern fringe of the plains like Orenburg or Semipalatinsk, they also associated constantly with Turkic (Tatar) Jadids from Kazan.

This polarization of Central Asia's northern and southern zones, perceptible in the early 1900's, seemed to segregate its people so thoroughly that reunion in the near future was extremely unlikely. In each section, however, separatist ideals progressed at first almost exclusively among a select portion of the small, educated circle. The traditional clergy, making up the largest literate body, could not countenance such a schism within the Muslim community. Moreover, the local Jadid knew that he could hardly be granted the right to speak for the old religious *millat*. To call this widening gap between Kazakhstan and Turkistan a national movement could not be justified by the halting, often blind, Jadid steps in either area toward social change. Without a recognized nationality to invoke or defend, the Jadid could not be considered a nationalist in the usual sense of the term. Given the Czarist police surveillance, understandably he declined to call for "national" political independence before 1917. But notwithstanding such serious disqualifications as a leader, the Jadid, because he brought new intellectual life to the area in a familiar religious form, became the catalyst that hastened the precipitation of national elements in Central Asia. The Jadid at best enjoyed little political liberty, so he acted through schools, social organizations, literature, and the press to institute changes. Whichever of these media he employed forced the selection of the target audience and a modern language of communication. Making each of these choices raised various aspects of the nationality question, and, in a few years, awkwardly settled some of them.

Turkistan could not stand mute if it were to become a popular modern concept. If it was to communicate efficiently it had to have a common language. None of the traditional literary languages (Arabic, Chaghatay, and Persian) of the area, being archaic and complex, was adequate to the new need. Escape from this dilemma lay either through (1) updating one or more of the old mediums, (2) generalizing a selected modern tongue, (3) creating an artificial Turkic "Esperanto," or (4) developing a number of vernacular dialects into written languages. While conservative Central Asians stubbornly clung to the old, some local Jadids, choosing the third solution, worked to popularize an innovation borrowed from Ismail Bey Gaspirali (1851–1914) of the Crimea, the popularizer of the Jadid idea in the Russian empire. To facilitate intercourse among all Turkic populations, Gaspirali in the 1880's had created a simplified general Turkic language based on Turkish, called the *tawhid-i lisan* (unified language) or *lisan-i umumi* (common language). Backers of this special language in Central Asia, named here *ortä shiwä* (middle dialect), included outstanding reformist figures, like the Uzbek writer Mahmud Khoja Behbudiy (1874–1919) and Uzbek-Tajik essayist 'Abdalra'uf Fitrat (1886–1947). As authors and editors of hundreds of books, articles, newspapers, and magazines, they commanded for their time, a wide audience. Nevertheless, they failed to secure universal adoption of the common language in their area, just as Gaspirali faltered among the Tatars, because both the reasoned and emotional opposition was too great. Despite the joint effort of the third All-Muslim Congress of Russia and the Ittifaq-i Muslimin (Muslim Union) in August, 1906, for the introduction of "the common language" in schools serving Central Asians, among others,[17] the Kazakhs of the plains countered the thrust of the new language into Central Asia. They insisted upon their right to develop a distinctive Kazakh language. The very existence of a Kazakh nationality, so said Kazakh reformers, led by Aqmet Baytursin-uli (1873–1937), hinged upon having their own language.[18] Their attitude had been conditioned by alarm over the stifling influence of Tatar and Russian schooling which had driven out the local language and substituted those two languages among educated Kazakhs.

The fight for national survival that sparked northern Kazakh resistance to the middle dialect would seem to have had no pertinence for the situation in southern Central Asia where literate men generally did not write in their spoken tongue. Nevertheless, opposition to *ortä shiwä* broke out there almost at the same time as it did in Orenburg and Troitsk. In the south, people expressed concern over infiltration of foreign words, particularly Russian, Arabic, and Tatar into local composition and speech: "If our language and literature are not defended and if we join a foreign vocabulary and terms to them, in a little while we shall very likely destroy our language and our *millat.*"[19] Before long, Baytursin-uli and Behbudiy both admitted that educated persons in both Kazakhstan or Turkistan would have to learn more than one language.[20] The northerners, it was said, needed a "Muslim" tongue as well as the Russian language, and people in the south required Turki (Chaghatay-Uzbek), Farsi (Persian), Arabic, and Russian. It was realized that using a foreign tongue as a second language did not necessarily nullify the modern group integrity of those in other unities who employ it. Gradually, the southerners found, too, that using literary languages closer to the vernacular did not automatically diffuse the *spirit* of their larger *millat.* So, the Kazakhs held to their language, and the Turkistan Jadids struggled with *ortä shiwä,* but this did not conclusively establish the people's primary written language throughout the area and its relation to nationality. Because this competition between local and area-wide mediums for Turkistan Wilayati and the khanates throughout the last of the Czarist period never came to an end, language reform remained a troublesome issue, and nationality questions connected with it naturally were left half open.

Although language remained an inextricable part of the nationality problem, literature enjoyed a kind of vague neutrality for the moment. Therefore, didactic writings, especially the newer genres, served as the most accessible arena in which to debate the question of the Muslim *millat*. The initial local drama published and performed at Samarkand during 1913–14, advertised as "Turkistan's first *milliy* tragedy," pleads for educating the youth in the language of "their own *millat*."[21] Likewise, one of the earliest substantial pieces of modern fictional prose in Uzbek, *Yanghi sa'adat: Milliy roman* (*New Happiness: A "National" Novel*) (1915), by Hamza Hakim Zada Niyaziy (1889–1929), climaxes in a peroration demanding the preservation of the *millat:*

> So it is evident that even if we cannot be superior to the [other] *millats* on the face of the earth, the degree to which we do not remain trampled under their feet [will depend on] seeking out certain measures! Uniting our men and women who are in the entire *millat* of Islam by entering together into the solution of the problem (studying and teaching), which is the Lord God's repeated command, doubtless we shall be able to attain this second, new happiness.[22]

The author's scheme for escaping foreign domination by means of education and internal union in order to achieve the equality of all *millats* mirrors the standard Jadid attitude. But this *millat* invoked by the novelist Niyaziy and the dramatist Behbudiy differed to no significant extent from that amorphous ghost addressed by the Khivan poet 'Awaz Otar-oghli (1884–1919) in his poem *"Millat,"* which appeared in a liberal magazine at the time,[23] or by the Khokand writer Ahmad 'Ali Yoldash-oghli Khoqandli in his verses *"Millatdan rija"* ("Request from the *Millat*"), circulated in a conservative Tashkent periodical the very same year.[24] Thus, all across southern Central Asia the *millat* in literature at one turn looked like our subjective "nationality" and at the next breath returned momentarily to the concrete old "Muslim religious community." Such wild vacillation made it impossible to tell positively which "nationality" or what group of Muslims was meant, for the writers themselves appeared unwilling or, more likely, unable to specify.

Unexpectedly, writings like "Request from the *Millat*" raised arguments over nationality, not because the poem dealt directly with the meaning of *millat* but because the language and grammar were Ottomanized beyond the tolerance of Central Asian localizers, who now demanded a home-style literary product. This in itself was revolutionary. Deep in the Farghana Valley, that receptacle of purest Uzbek speech, within half a century after Russian troops had overpowered Tashkent, grew up the conviction among local intellectuals that literature should reflect one's group identity. They felt that this required the use of a morphology and phraseology characteristic of the area represented by the author and his readers who employed that language as their written one. Localizers rejected poetry such as Ahmad 'Ali Yoldash-oghli Khoqandli's "Request from the *Millat*" or whatever Jadid writer Abdullah Awlaniy (1878–1934) composed in the "common language" or "language of Turkism," and the cry went out for a true "native" medium:

> No *millat* can read a poem which has been written in a *til* [tongue] not understandable for itself, and thus it is only natural if the name of such a [non-national] poet fades and disappears throughout the *millat*. Let us come now to our own *milliy* poets and we shall see that within our *millat* our *milliy* poets also have no influence. What is the reason for this? The reason is that our esteemed poets have not written poems in our *shiwa* [dialect]; the majority of their poems are combinations of Ottoman and Tatar.[25]

Among the northern Central Asians, too, the spectacle of their most prominent rising poets, the Kazakh Maghjan Jumabay-uli (1896–*ca.* 1938) and the Kirgiz Qasim Tinistan-uulu (*ca.* 1900–32), resorting to the Tatar and Kazakh written languages, respectively, proved too much for the intellectual leadership to bear.

Controversies over language and literature reflected the general tension between urges toward Central Asia's larger or smaller, linguistic or spiritual unities. But important as they were, the debates on the critical problem of language and literature in nationality by no means pre-empted the thoughts of local Jadid leaders in the period. Their almost total concern for many other aspects of reform early in the 1900's received a boost that stimulated them to begin the pursuit of national political integrity in earnest. The shock came from the revolution of 1905 in Russia proper, not so much from the upheaval itself, which barely touched Central Asians, as from its political and journalistic aftermath. Modern parties and indigenous newspapers or magazines, which had not previously existed in Central Asia, suddenly appeared there late in 1905.

In this altered situation, the question of Turkistanian or Kazakh nationality became obscured momentarily by a drive, initiated outside

Central Asia, to create a league of all Muslims in the Russian Empire. The busy Tatars of Kazan organized the move, acting through the apparatus of several congresses called in 1905 and 1906. Kazakhstan was the only part of Central Asia directly represented in these meetings by a local delegate, and that solely at the last of the congresses.[26] Similarly, participation in the State Dumas of 1906–7, again mainly involving Central Asia's few Kazakh deputies, whose constituency was separated by law from that of Turkistan Wilayati, nevertheless blunted the point of ethnic nationality by combining all Muslims into one caucus of the representation along with the dominant Tatars of Kazan, the Azerbaijanians and the like. Nonetheless, the consequences of this very limited activity were not completely insignificant. A flimsy alliance between the Muslim faction from Central Asia and the Muslim Union formed in January, 1906, grew out of the Muslim congresses of that period in the empire. Through this channel the Central Asian parliamentary deputies linked themselves tenuously with the Russian Constitutional Democratic Party (Kadets), and its programs, to which the Muslim Union also adhered.

On the surface, the Kadets' views concerning the question of nationality, compared with the announced policies of the other parties, hardly seemed likely to attract Central Asian support. In this field the Kadets then cautiously offered no more than "free cultural self-determination . . . of each *narodnost'* [people]," and in the future some sort of vague local autonomy,[27] without saying a word about regional political independence for the Central Asians. Rival programs advertised at the same time by Russian Socialist Revolutionaries and Social Democrats promised language and cultural freedom plus outright political self-determination to each *natsiia* (nation) or *natsional'nost'* (nationality) of the empire.[28]

In spite of this appeal, both the conservative and Jadid leadership of Central Asia initially rejected the socialist parties. Kazakhstan's intellectuals moved together in late 1905 to work with the Russian Kadets. Aliqan Nurmuhammad Bokeyqan-uli (1869–1932), himself a Kadet party member, was chosen as a deputy to the first State Duma in 1906, and Muhammadjan Tanishbay-uli (1879/80–192[?]), also a Kadet, won a place in the second, in 1907.[29] Within a very few years, this promising political beginning seemed to be establishing a belief in political nationality throughout ever wider Kazakh circles:

> . . . the spreading of revolutionary ideas, that is, rather, the ideas of national equality and liberation, was observed especially among the

> student young people from 1912 on. Those who inspired the awakening of the young Kazakh *intelligentsiia* were "revolutionary" Kadets prominent at that time, the journalists Bokeyqan-uli [Mir Jaqib] Duwlat-uli [1885–1937], and Baytursin-uli.[30]

These leaders of Kazakhstan did not possess an ideological monopoly any more than their counterparts in Turkistan. Politics divided the Kazakhs between a national-religious wing advocating union with other Muslims led by Kazan's Tatars, and a Westernizing tendency inclined to follow the Russian political opposition parties, particularly the Kadets.[31] Both of these currents had also flooded areas in southern Central Asia.

In the south almost no one outside the Russian colony joined any of the Russian parties, but a few Jadids of Turkistan Wilayati like Ubaydullah Khoja-oghli at Tashkent centered their interest upon the Socialist Revolutionaries,[32] and Behbudiy at Samarkand on the Constitutional Democrats. Behbudiy, always concerned with order, concluded in October, 1906, that regardless of religious and ethnic differences, everyone active in the Empire's politics should belong to one universal party.[33] Moreover, he called on all Muslims of Turkistan to join a single party which would enter into the Muslim Union and then, presumably, into the one great party of Russia that he proposed. The Jadids' future party would base its economic, ideological and scientific planks on the platform of the Muslim Union, which in 1906 had come out for regional, cultural-religious autonomy within Russia's Muslim population. As for political solutions, the Central Asians should, thought Behbudiy, look to the Kadet program.[34]

Thus, most startling in the new season among southern Central Asian leaders was their surprising indifference to the possibility of relying upon the formidable potential strength in ethnic units or regional politics. Behbudiy's predilection for one-party rule had not, however, blinded him to the realities of Czarist Russia. Listing what he saw as the four most prominent existing political currents (monarchists or bureaucrats, Kadets, Socialist Revolutionaries or Social Democrats, and Pan-Islamic movements), Behbudiy passed over the Muslims without comment, probably because they exercised too little influence in Russia proper and were in any case dominated by the Tatars and tended to work with the Kadets, to show why he favored the Kadets in politics. Kadet de-emphasis of the importance of ethnic-linguistic differences within the future state accorded with his ideas. Their guarantees of civil and personal rights and government through a constitutional monarchy held in check by a parliament, he felt, would provide better opportunities for individual liberty and equality and more protection for the status of all classes and *millats,* including the Muslims, than the other parties could promise. Like his Kazakh contemporaries, he properly held the monarchists responsible for the government's execrable record in dealing with the Central Asians and for the other excesses of the autocracy.

Finally, Behbudiy dispensed with the socialist parties, not necessarily in this way applauding the absence in the Kadet nationality program of specific provisions for Central Asia's political autonomy or independence, but because the Social Democrats, in particular, deeply offended him by threatening to tamper with fundamental aspects of Muslim life, such as private property.

The lively political journalism of which Behbudiy's article was one of the earliest Central Asian examples soon disappeared. The Russian reaction after 1907 not only blocked further Central Asian participation in the State Duma, but it deprived the area of its local periodical press. In the north of Central Asia the blackout lasted until 1911 and in the south up to 1913; during that time the dissemination of Central Asian literature of Jadid ideas was also inhibited but not cut off. After the hiatus, Central Asian newspapers and magazines returned more effectively than ever to the fight for their own public. The press became an obvious choice to lead in establishing the nationality idea, but found itself torn between tame and independent-minded editors, between arch-conservative and moderate contributors or readers, between Kazakh, Tajik, and Uzbek language groups, between pro- and anti-Russian views. Ideological uniformity was out of the question. Union appeared doubtful.

The very names of newspapers or periodicals confirmed the persistence of the divergence of ideas in the area. Both before and after the newspaper drought, the names of papers in northern Central Asia tended to stress the respective languages or ethnic groups. Before 1920, this had not been the case in the south, and probably was unique among Muslims anywhere in the Russian empire. Thus, during a short span of time, readers in the plains received, among others, these newspapers in their language: *Qazaq gaziti* (1907), *Qazaqstan* (1911–13), *Qazaq* (1913–18), *Qazaq mungu* (1918), *Qazaq 'agli* (1919), and *Qazaq sozu* (1919).

In contrast with this display of Kazakh ethnocentrism, the press in the south generally circulated either under names known to newspaper readers the world over, like *Khurshid* (*Sun*) (1906) and *Ayinä* (*Mirror*) (1913–15), or became identified with cities and larger places, as in the case of *Asiya* (*Asia*) (1908), *Samarqand* (*Samarkand*) (1913–14), and *Sada-i farghana* (*Voice of Farghana*) (1914, 1915). The seemingly innocuous procedure of naming these ephemeral Jadid newspapers emphatically demonstrated the state of nationality development in the south in its final pre-Soviet form. For lack of a consensus, the Turkistan idea had become the Turkistan dilemma by the end of the Czarist tenure.

A most significant revelation in this crisis came with the christening of two late-Jadid newspapers shortly before and after the 1917 Bolshevik takeover: *Sada-i Turkistan* (*The Voice of Turkistan*) (1914–15) and *Ulugh Turkistan* (*Great Turkistan*) (1917–18). Neither acknowledged allegiance purely to the Turkistan Wilayati, so long represented by the Chaghatay-Uzbek-language government bulletin *Turkistan wilayatining gazeti* (1870–1917). In fact, both private papers eagerly reached out from Tashkent for a much wider readership. Each, in its own way, was highly political. *Sada-i Turkistan* aimed for a pan-Turkistanian constituency concentrated mainly in the southern portions of Central Asia. Going far beyond this, *Ulugh Turkistan*'s slogan was *"Yashasun millatlar mukhtariyati"* ("Hail to the Autonomy of the Millats"). The paper's policy was set by a cosmopolitan staff of Kazakhs, Tatars, and Uzbeks, who plagiarized the earlier aims of both pan-Turkists and pan-Islamists by presuming to bring the millions of Turkic and other Muslims of Russia into one grand union boasting a common language. Now their gigantic combine was to be proclaimed "greater Turkistan."[35]

When deflated, such grandiose visions, which never were fulfilled before 1917, left the idea of Turkistan as flabby as an empty camelskin. Even so, most Central Asians had some sense of the physical limits represented by both legendary and contemporary Turkistan. For anyone with doubt about its geographical reaches, Behbudiy in 1913 had provided a fairly definite description of both the traditional and Czarist versions:

> Turkistan is made up of Central Asia, or the country of Turan, and is inhabited by various branches of the Turkic *qawm* [people, race]. Today it is divided into the Russian and Chinese parts, and one [other] portion, in the Afghan government's domain, is called Turkistan or "Chahar wilayat." Kirgiz Kazakhstan, or the land of the plains, is also considered part of Turkistan. . . . Present political borders of the Russian Turkistan *muzafat* [province] are, in the west, the Caspian Sea; to the north the Ural lands and Aral Sea and a vast portion of Kirgiz Kazakhstan; to the east, Chinese Turkistan, and to the south it adjoins the Afghan

> and Iranian countries. The Bukharan and Khivan khanates fall within these limits, and exist on the south side of Turkistan.[36]

Though Bukhara and Khiva remained technically outside modern Turkistan because of Russian treaty arrangements, local politicians in the twentieth century often specified a Turkistan which included the khanate and emirate.[37] Thus, the geographical and political variants of Turkistan needed no further debate. They urgently required stabilization if they were to become meaningful in organizing society into nationalities and nations.

The homeland upon which men lavished their patriotic feelings began to take on the dimensions of this modern Turkistan not by local agreement but under the pressure of foreign cultural, colonial domination. In one manifestation, the southern Central Asians who rebelled at this time against the unwanted name "Sart" indiscriminately applied to them by outsiders, now started to insist upon their right to be called, instead, *Turkistanlilar* (Turkistanians).[38] Generally, however, local groupings in the years immediately preceding the demise of the Czarist regime retained their attachment to smaller rather than larger divisions within the area. Sections of what later were called the Uzbeks, for example, continued to separate themselves into "Turks," "Uzbeks," "Kipchaks," "Kuramas," and even "Sarts," so that among them there could be no feeling of belonging to a common Uzbek unity or territory.[39]

Because the idea of nationality itself remained too vague, the idea of Turkistan nationality had still to come fully in focus. For the Central Asians, a major difficulty in comprehending it lay in the lack of an obvious example, best shown by nation statehood, in either the Ottoman or Russian empires through which they borrowed so much. In any case, European models of nationality, linked inseparably as they seemed to be with ethnic and language clusters in independent countries, could hardly be applied appropriately to most of these eastern population mixtures.

When the first political upheavals of 1917 hit Central Asia, theoretical details regarding group identity did not greatly trouble the Kazakhs in the north. To them the nationality question by that time seemed clear, and their nation definable in concrete terms. Immediately after Czarism collapsed, leading Jadids founded an all-Kazakh political party called Alash Orda, a name peculiar to the Kazakh heritage. Three months later one of the dynamic Alash Orda leaders, Jihanshah Dosmaghambet-uli, commenced publicly shattering with ethnic, racial arguments the fragile Tatar notions of Muslim religious-cultural unity advocated at a congress in Moscow: "[the Pan-Islamist] intends to create one Muslim *millat* by joining together the [various] Muslim *millats*. . . . Generally, is it possible to unite the *millats?* No! . . . In the body of the *'millat'* there is one group of people possessing common blood; to create a *millat* in an artificial form is impossible."[40] These convictions found their logical fulfillment within the year, when Dosmaghambet-uli and his associates rose to the executive committee of the first separate Kazakh national government of modern times, the Alash Orda Government, which declared its independence from Russia on December 10, 1917.[41] The precedent for this had been set two weeks earlier, when a representative council of southern Central Asians meeting at Khokand formed the Autonomous Provisional Government of Turkistan and declared its independent status in federation with a democratic republic of Russia.[42] This short-lived government embraced a constituency ethnically and linguistically as mixed as the Alash Orda people were homogeneous. By chance, two Kazakhs in turn also headed the Autonomous Provisional Government of Turkistan, and this, also, was peculiarly characteristic of a state populated by Kirgiz, Tajiks, Turkmen, Uzbeks, and Kazakhs.

Both new governments were manned by persons who had but recently acquired a "national" outlook, and that self-identification in most cases had yet to spread to a substantial part of their followers. Central Asia thus faced the new Communist era completely divided, north and south, so far as the tenuous new nationality arrangements were concerned. This logically followed from the colonial administrative policy pursued by the Russian Government since the early nineteenth century as well as the natural divisions in this great area. Tentatively, the 1917 actions suggested that either the ethnic-linguistic-geographic or the subjective-personal-political nationality system was viable in modern Central Asian circumstances. It said nothing concerning their ability to survive under adverse conditions, but that test was soon to come.

NOTES

1. A. I. Kastelianskii (ed.), *Formy natsional'nogo dvizheniia v sovremennykh gosudarstvakh. Avstro-Vengriia; Rossiia; Germaniia* (St. Petersburg: Izdanie T-va "Obshchestvennaia Pol'za," 1910), p. 546; M. G. Vakhabov, "O formirovanii uzbekskoi burzhuaznoi natsii," *Voprosy istorii,* No. 7 (1954).
2. Mikhail A. Terent'ev, *Istoriia zavoevaniia Srednei Azii* (St. Petersburg: Tipo-Litografiia V. V. Komarova, 1906), III, 343.
3. Ch. Ch. Valikhanov, "Zapiska o sudebnoi reforme," in *Sobranie sochinenii* (Alma-Ata: Izdatel'stvo Akademii Nauk Kazakhskoi S.S.R., 1961), I, 494, 497.
4. Abai Kunanbaev, "Shestoe slovo," in *Sobranie sochinenii* (Moscow: Gosudarstvennoe Izdatel'stvo Khudozhestvennoi Literatury, 1954), p. 330.
5. Counted in the earliest census to list them separately for all Central Asia, in 1920, were between 1,240,000 and 1,584,000 Tajiks. See Edward Allworth, *Central Asian Publishing and the Rise of Nationalism* (New York: New York Public Library, 1965), Table I, ff.; cf. M. Nemchenko, *Natsional'noe razmezhevanie Srednei Azii* (Moscow: Litizdat NKID, 1925), end sheet.
6. Ahmad Mahdum, "Navādir ul-vaqāe'," MS. of the Tajik State University, I, 221, cited in Z. Radzhabov, *Iz istorii obshchestvenno-politicheskoi mysli tadzhikskogo naroda vo vtoroi polovine XIX i v nachale XX vv.* (Stalinabad: Tadzhikskoe Gosudarstvennoe Izdatel'stvo, 1957), p. 190.
7. Edward Allworth (ed.), *Central Asia: A Century of Russian Rule* (New York: Columbia University Press, 1967), pp. 163–68.
8. V. Bartol'd, "Turkestan," in *Entsiklopedicheskii slovar'* (St. Petersburg: F. A. Brokgauz, I. A. Efron, 1902), XXXIV, 203.
9. Allworth, *Central Asia: A Century of Russian Rule,* p. 60.
10. Zahiru'd-din Muhammad Babur, *The Babur-nama in English* (*Memoirs of Babur*), trans. Annette Beveridge (London: Luzac and Co., 1922), I, 73–75, 135.
11. M. D. Annagurdov, *Sovet Türkmenistaninin metbugat tarikhidan ocherkler* (Ashkhabad: Türkmenistan Dövlet Neshriyati', 1962), II, 12; and M. D. Annakurdov, *K istorii kommunisticheskoi pechati v Turkmenistane* (Ashkhabad: Turkmenskoe Gosudarstvennoe Izdatel'stvo, 1958), p. 16.
12. *Kazakhsko-russkie otnosheniia v XVIII–XIX vekakh* (Alma-Ata: Izdatel'stvo "Nauka," 1964), pp. 280–82.
13. K. Zalevskii, "Natsional'nye dvizheniia," in *Obshchestvennoe dvizhenie v Rossii v nachale XX-go veka,* ed. L. Martov, P. Maslov, and A. Potresov (St. Petersburg: Tipografiia Tovarishchestva "Obshchestvennaia Pol'za," 1910), IV, Part I, 235–36.
14. *Ibid.,* p. 235.
15. G. E. Wheeler, *The Modern History of Soviet Central Asia* (New York: Frederick A. Praeger, 1964), pp. 52–53, 65; and Hans Kohn, *The Idea of Nationalism. A Study in Its Origins and Background* (New York: The MacMillan Company, 1961), pp. 12–19.
16. Ziya Gökalp, "Millat ve vatan," *Türk yurdu,* VI, No. 66 (Istanbul, 1914); an English translation appears in *Turkish Nationalism and Western Civilization* (New York: Columbia University Press, 1959).
17. A. V. Piaskovskii, *Revoliutsiia 1905–1907 godov v Turkestane* (Moscow: Izdatel'stvo Akademii Nauk, 1958), p. 564.

18. Aqmet Baytursin-uli, in *Qazaq,* No. 1 (1913), quoted by M. Dulatov, "Akmed Baitursunovich Baitursunov (Biograficheskii ocherk)," *Trudy Obshchestva Izucheniia Kirgizskogo Kraia,* No. 3 (1922), p. 22.
19. S. A., "Har millat oz dili ila fakhr etar," *Ayinä,* No. 35 (June 21, 1914), p. 838.
20. Mahmud Khoja Behbudiy, "Iki emas, tort tili lazim," *Ayinä,* No. 1 (August 20, 1913), pp. 12–13; and Aqmet Baytursin-uli, "Jazu tartibi," *Ay qap,* No. 4 (1912), p. 84.
21. Mahmud Khoja Behbudiy, *Padarkush yakhud oqumaghan balaning hali* (Samarkand: Tipo-litografiia T-va B. Gazarov i K. Sliianov, 1913), pp. 1, 6–7.
22. Hamza Hakim Zada Niyaziy, *Yanghi sa'adat: Milliy roman* (Khokand: [publication of the author], 1915), p. 45.
23. 'Awaz Otar-oghli, "Millat," *Ayinä,* No. 12 (April 16, 1915), p. 333.
24. Ahmad 'Ali Yoldash-oghli Khoqandli, "Millatdan rija," *al-Islah,* No. 19 (October 15, 1915), p. 578.
25. Rasuli, "Sha'ir wa milliy shi'rlarimiz," *Ayinä,* No. 9 (February 14, 1915), pp. 213–14.
26. Allworth, *Central Asia: A Century of Russian Rule,* p. 186.
27. N. I. Astrov, *et al.* (eds.) *Zakonodatel'nye proekty i predpolozheniia Partii Narodnoi Svobody 1905–1907 gg.* (St. Petersburg: Tipografiia "Obshchestvennaia Pol'za," 1907), pp. xii–xiv.
28. *Vtoroi ocherednoi s"ezd Ross. Sots.-Dem. Rabochei Partii. Polnyi tekst protokolov* (Geneva: Izdanie Tsentral'nogo Komiteta [1903]), pp. 3–4; Kh. Korobkhov, "Sotsial-demokratiia i pravo kazhdoi natsii na samoopredelenie," *Studenchestvo* (St. Petersburg), No. 3 (November 20, 1906), pp. 29–32; and *Programma i organizatsionnyi ustav Partii Sotsialistov-Revoliutsionerov, utverzhdennye na pervom partiinom s"ezde* (n.pl.: Izdanie Tsentral'nogo Komiteta P. S.-R., 1906), p. 24.
29. A. Arsharuni and Kh. Gabidullin, *Ocherki panislamizma i panturkizma v Rossii* (Moscow: Izdatel'stvo Bezbozhnik, 1931), p. 120.
30. Manab Shamil, "O kirgizskoi intelligentsii," *Zhizn' natsional'nostei,* No. 37 (November 25, 1920), pp. 2–3.
31. A. Bukeikhanov, "Kirgizy," in Kastelianskii, *op. cit.,* p. 599.
32. A. Zeki Velidi Togan, *Bugünkü Türkili (Türkistan) ve yakin tarihi* (Istanbul: Arkadash Ibrahim Horoz ve Güven Basimevleri, 1942–47), p. 355.
33. Mahmud Khoja Behbudiy, in *Khurshid* (October 11, 1906), cited in *Ozbekistan SSR tarikhi* (1-vol. ed.; Tashkent: Ozbekistan S.S.R. Fanlar Akademiyasi Nashriyati, 1958), pp. 380–81.
34. *Ibid.,* p. 382.
35. Piaskovskii, *op. cit.,* p. 563; and Ziya Sa'id, *Ozbek waqtli matbu'ati ta'rikhiga matiriyallar, 1870–1927* (Tashkent-Samarkand: Ozbekistan Dawlat Nashriyati, 1927), pp. 67, 70.
36. Mahmud Khoja Behbudiy, "Turkistan," *Ayinä,* No. 1 (August 20, 1913), p. 2.
37. 'Abdalra'uf Fitrat, "Himmat wa sabati bolmagan millatning haqq-i hayati yoqdur," *Ayinä,* No. 7 (January 14, 1915), p. 164.
38. Bayrambeg Dawlat Shah, "Sart mas'alasi," *Ayinä,* No. 17 (February 19, 1914), p. 300.
39. M. G. Vakhabov, *op. cit.,* p. 115.
40. *Butun rosiya musulmanlarining 1917nchi yilda 1–11 mayda maskawda*

'umumi isyezdining protaqollari (Petrograd: "Amanet" Shirkati Matbu'asi, 1917), p. 197.

41. Joseph Sastagné, "Le Bolchevisme et l'Islam" (Part 1), *Revue du Monde Musulman,* LI (October, 1922), 173–75; and A. Zeki Velidi Togan, *op. cit.,* p. 369.
42. Joseph Castagné, "Le Turkestan depuis la Révolution Russe (1917–1921)," *Revue du Monde Musulman,* L (June, 1922), 46–47.

9

Demographic and Cultural Trends Among Turkic Peoples of the Soviet Union

GARIP SULTAN

INTRODUCTION

Ethnographers usually classify peoples according to their languages. Thus classified, the Turkic peoples are the second most numerous group in the U.S.S.R., after the Slavs. The 1959 census showed that there were more than 23 million persons of Turkic stock in the U.S.S.R., or 11 per cent of the population. This group comprises twenty different nationalities occupying vast areas in both the Asian and European parts of the U.S.S.R.[1]

Whereas the Slavic peoples live contiguously in their ethnic territories in the European parts of the U.S.S.R., the Turkic peoples do not live in a compact geographical area. The main national divisions of the Turkic peoples, in both numbers and culture, are the Uzbeks, the Tatars, and the Azerbaidzhanis. The Uzbeks, together with the Kazakhs, the Turkmen, the Kirghiz, and the Kara-Kalpaks, are the indigenous peoples of Central Asia. More than half of the Turkic-speaking population lives in Central Asia. Azerbaidzhan is in Transcaucasia, while the North Caucasus is inhabited by small Turkic peoples such as the Kumyks, the Karachai, the Balkars, and the Nogai. The middle Volga-Ural area is the home of the Tatars, the Bashkirs, and the Chuvash. In Siberia live such small groups as the Yakuts, the Tuvinians, the Altais, the Khakass, and the Shors. Another geopolitical area of Turkic settlement, Crimea, was lost to the Slavs as a result of the deportation of the Crimean Tatars and the liquidation of their autonomous republic in 1944.[2]

Aside from the Turkic-speaking peoples of Siberia, who have no territorial contiguity with one another, the chief Turkic national groups form a territorially united historical and ethnographic area in

TABLE I
Turkic Population in the U.S.S.R.

Nationality	Total Number in the U.S.S.R. (*in thousands*)	Percentage of Entire Soviet Population	Political Status
Central Asia (Turkestan)			
Uzbek	6,015.4	2.88	Uzbek S.S.R.
Kazakh	3,621.6	1.73	Kazakh S.S.R.
Turkmen	1,001.6	0.48	Turkmen S.S.R.
Kirghiz	968.7	0.46	Kirghiz S.S.R.
Kara-Kalpak	172.6	0.08	Kara-Kalpak A.S.S.R. (Uzbek S.S.R.)
Uighur	95.2	0.05	None
Total	11,875.1	5.68	
Central Volga-Ural			
Tatar	4,967.7	2.38	Tatar A.S.S.R.
Chuvash	1,469.8	0.70	Chuvash A.S.S.R.
Bashkir	989.0	0.45	Bashkir A.S.S.R.
Total	7,426.5	3.53	
Caucasus			
Transcaucasia			
Azerbaidzhani	2,939.7	1.41	Azerbaidzhani S.S.R.
North Caucasus			
Kumyk	135.0	0.06	Daghestan A.S.S.R.
Karachai	81.4	0.04	Karachai-Cherkess Autonomous Oblast
Balkar	42.4	0.02	Kabardino-Balkar A.S.S.R.
Nogai	38.6	0.02	Daghestan A.S.S.R.
Total	3,237.1	1.55	
Siberia			
Yakut	236.7	0.11	Yakut A.S.S.R.
Tuvinian	100.1	0.05	Tuva A.S.S.R.
Khakass	56.6	0.03	Khakass Autonomous Oblast
Altai	45.3	0.02	Gorno-Altai Autonomous Oblast
Shorian	15.3	0.007	None
Total	454.0	0.217	
Other Areas			
Gagauz	123.8	0.06	None
Turkish	35.3	0.02	None
Grand Total	23,151.8	11.057	

Source: Tsentral'noe statisticheskoe upravlenie, *Itogi vsesoiuznoi perepisi naseleniia 1959 goda: SSSR* (*Results of the All-Union Population Census of 1959: U.S.S.R.*) (Moscow, 1962).

Central Asia, the Caucasus, and the Volga-Urals. The Turkic peoples are also notable in that their political and administrative status is not everywhere the same. Only five of the twenty Turkic-speaking nationalities and ethnic groups in the U.S.S.R. have the political subdivision "Union Republic": Uzbeks, Kazakhs, Turkmen, and Kirghiz in Central Asia, and the Azerbaidzhanis in the Caucasus. Six of them have the status of "autonomous republic," the largest of which is the Tatar A.S.S.R., while the rest are "autonomous *oblasts*" within the R.S.F.S.R.

The eastern regions, particularly Central Asia, have undergone an economic expansion during the last twenty to twenty-five years. Today, the Turkic republics constitute important economic-geographical areas of the Soviet Union. The Tatar and Bashkir Autonomous Republics of the Volga-Ural area and Azerbaidzhan in Transcaucasia are major oil centers. Uzbekistan is the main producer of cotton, ranking third in the world after the United States and China. Kazakhstan has become one of the most important grain producers, with well-developed animal husbandry. It is natural that this economic development, which has also been responsible for major population shifts, had a strong impact on the demographic situation of the Turkic peoples.

Patterns of Growth

The 1939 and 1959 census figures show that two factors determine the changes in the size of the principal Turkic nationalities. These are (1) the high rate of natural increase in comparison with the average rate of increase of the U.S.S.R. population in general and with the rate of increase of the Slavic groups, and (2) the substantial population growth in their autonomous and Union republics as a result of the organized immigration to these regions of Slavic-speaking "foreign elements," chiefly Russians.

During the twenty-year period between the above-mentioned two censuses, the population growth of the U.S.S.R. was low owing to World War II and the forced-labor camps. During this period, the population increased by 9.5 per cent (18.1 million people), the average annual increase being 900,000 people. But the Turkic-speaking sector increased by 3.5 million, or 18 per cent. Of the principal Turkic groups, the Uzbek population has increased by 24 per cent, the Tatars by 15, the Azerbaidzhanis by 29, the Kazakhs and Bashkirs by 17, the Turkmen by 23, and the Kirghiz by 9.5.[3]

Soviet authors claim that the rapid rate of growth of the Turkic population proves (1) "that Leninist policy ensures extensive possibilities for the development of nationalities,"[4] and (2) that the assertions of Western Sovietologists concerning the Russification and denationalization of the peoples of the Soviet East has no validity.[5] True, the increase in the last twenty years of people who consider themselves as Uzbeks or Tatars does not bear out the Western experts. However, the rapid rates of growth cannot serve as an argument in favor of the so-called Leninist nationality policy either. The fact that the growth rate of the main Turkic peoples is higher than that of the Slavic peoples (in the Ukraine the growth amounted to a mere 3.5 per cent) is due to a large extent to the relatively high Turkic birth rate in the period between the two censuses. The Russians, the Ukrainians, and the Belorussians were directly affected by the war. Not only were millions killed at the front, but the Ukraine, Belorussia, and some Russian regions were occupied by the Germans. The Slavs constituted the bulk of the slave laborers deported to Germany. Consequently the death rate among the Slavs was extremely high. But the population losses among the Turkic nationalities of Central Asia and Transcaucasia, which were not occupied, were not so great. The difference in the birth rate is due also to climatic factors. In Central Asia and Transcaucasia, women mature at a younger age and marry earlier. The 1959 census showed that while the percentage of married women aged sixteen to nineteen amounted to 9.3 among the Russians, 10.1 among the Ukrainians, and 7 among the Belorussians, the percentage for Turkmen women in this age group is 32; for the Uzbeks, 31.8; for the Kazakhs, 28.7, and for the Azerbaidzhani, 27.8.[6] Unfortunately, we have no data on the Turkic nationalities of the autonomous republics.

TABLE II
THE NUMBER OF MARRIED RUSSIAN AND TURKIC WOMEN PER 1,000 POPULATION IN THE U.S.S.R.

Nationality	Age 16 and Over	16–19	20–24	25–29	30–34	35–39
Russian	512	93	482	761	776	720
Azerbaidzhani	602	278	686	841	856	808
Kazakh	619	287	784	905	904	862
Kirghiz	669	442	878	921	903	873
Turkmen	673	320	894	952	924	838
Uzbek	666	318	837	929	916	886

SOURCE: *Itogi vsesoiuznoi perepisi naseleniia 1959 goda: SSSR*, p. 232.

Whereas the comparatively high rate of natural increase of the principal Turkic groups may be explained by the aforementioned objective factors, which have no direct relationship to the government's nationality policies, the low rate of increase among some of the smaller Turkic nationalities may indeed be attributed to the nationality policies. Among the North Caucasian groups that were exiled as a body from their national home, because of their nationalism, the natural increase is either nil—as in the case of the Balkars—or else lower than the rate of increase for the rest of the Soviet Union: only 7.5 per cent, for example, for the Karachai. The rate of increase among the Chuvash in the Volga region was only 7 per cent, which is also lower than the average for the Soviet Union, and some Soviet authors themselves attribute this fact primarily to "closer ties and mingling of nations," in other words, Russification.[7]

Another factor affecting the demographic situation of the Turkic peoples was the automatic over-all growth of the population, resulting from immigration of people from the Slavic-language group, mainly from the Russian regions. The resettlement of populations, especially in the Turkic republics of Central Asia in the last twenty to twenty-five years, occurred during World War II (evacuation of populations and the moving of industrial enterprises) in connection with the industrial development of eastern regions and the development of virgin and idle lands in Kazakhstan. As a result of this, the population in the five republics of Central Asia (including the Iranian-speaking Tadjikistan) increased by 38.1 per cent; this includes an increase of 28 per cent for the Uzbek S.S.R., 53 per cent for the Kazakh S.S.R., 21 per cent for the Turkmen, and 42 per cent for the Kirghiz. But in spite of substantial natural growth and an increase in actual numbers, the proportion of the Turkic peoples in their own republics has decreased, while the proportion of Russians has increased. Whereas, in 1939, the Russians comprised 11 per cent of the population, in 1959 their percentage rose to 13.5 per cent in Uzbekistan; from 40 to 42 per cent in Kazakhstan; from 20 to 30 per cent in Kirghizia; and from 42 to 43.1 per cent in the Tatar Republic. Moreover, the multinational diversity of the population of the republics has also increased.[8] Whereas, in 1897, the number of various nationalities in the territories of the Kazakh and Uzbek republics was about 70, in 1959 it was more than 113.[9]

The resettlement of other nationalities in small groups essentially has had no effect on the demographic situation of the indigenous Turkic population, since they are distributed in a scattered manner

TABLE III
NATIONALITY GROUPS IN THE

Nationality	Total in Central Asian Republics (*in thousands*)	UZBEK S.S.R.		KAZAKH S.S.R.	
		Number (*in thousands*)	Percentage of Republic's Population	Number (*in thousands*)	Percentage of Republic's Population
Azerbaidzhani	101	40	0.5	38	0.4
Bashkir	17	13	0.2	...	...
Belorussian	116	9	0.1	107	1.2
Chuvash	11	...	...	11	0.1
Dungan	10	...	...	10	0.1
Jewish	146	94	1.2	28	0.3
Kara-Kalpak	168	168	2.1	...	...
Kazakh	3,233	335	4.1	2,795	30.0
Kirghiz	956	93	1.1	...	...
Korean	138	138	1.7	...	...
Russian	6,215	1,091	13.5	3,974	42.7
Tadzhik	1,377	311	3.8	...	...
Tatar	780	445	5.5	192	2.1
Turkmen	979	55	0.7	...	...
Uighur	91	19	0.2	59	0.6
Ukrainian	1,035	88	1.1	762	8.2
Uzbek	5,973	5,038	62.2	137	1.5
Others	1,632	169	2.0	1,197	12.8
Total	22,978	8,106	100.0	9,310	100.0

SOURCE: *Itogi vsesoiuznoi perepisi naseleniia 1959 goda: SSSR.*

and not in compact formations. These non-Russian groups are themselves victims of planned migration, since their children are deprived of an opportunity to study in their own language and are forced to attend schools with a Russian curriculum. As a result of this, according to the 1959 census, 50 per cent of the Ukrainians, Mordvins, and Estonians, more than 60 per cent of the Belorussians, and more than 25 per cent of the Georgians, Lithuanians, Armenians, and Latvians in the Uzbek S.S.R. named Russian as their native language.[10] The main threat to the integrity of the ethnic territory of the Turkic peoples comes from the Russians, who are the "assimilating," "ruling" nation. Although the Russians are still a minority in the total population of Central Asia, in Kazakhstan and Kirghiza they have become a majority. In other words, the migration of the Russians to Central Asia is actually extending the borders of ethnic Russia to the East through the appropriation of Turkic lands. To be sure, migration is not due entirely to a deliberate policy of Russification. Industrialization and the economic development of sparsely populated regions of Central Asia, rich in natural resources, have resulted in a need for

UNION REPUBLICS OF CENTRAL ASIA

TURKMEN S.S.R.		KIRGHIZ S.S.R.		TADZHIK S.S.R.	
Number (*in thousands*)	Percentage of Republic's Population	Number (*in thousands*)	Percentage of Republic's Population	Number (*in thousands*)	Percentage of Republic's Population
13	0.8	10	0.5	. . .	. . .
. . .	. . .	. . .	. . .	4	0.2
. . .	. . .	. . .	. . .	. . .	. . .
. . .	. . .	. . .	. . .	. . .	. . .
. . .	. . .	. . .	. . .	. . .	. . .
4	0.3	8	0.4	12	0.6
. . .	. . .	. . .	. . .	. . .	. . .
70	4.6	20	1.0	13	0.6
. . .	. . .	837	40.5	26	1.3
. . .	. . .	. . .	. . .	. . .	. . .
263	17.3	624	30.2	263	13.3
. . .	. . .	15	0.7	1,051	53.1
30	2.0	56	2.7	57	2.9
924	60.9	. . .	. . .	. . .	. . .
. . .	. . .	13	0.7	. . .	. . .
21	1.4	137	6.6	27	1.4
125	8.3	219	10.6	454	23.0
66	4.4	127	6.1	73	3.6
1,516	100.0	2,066	100.0	1,980	100.0

skilled workers and technicians from the densely populated industrial and agricultural centers of the European area of the Soviet Union, primarily Russians and Ukrainians. The densely populated regions of Turkestan lacked the skilled labor force necessary for the functioning of modern industrial enterprises. Moreover, the specialized economies of the individual republics, e.g., cotton growing in Uzbekistan, also made "internal migration" impossible, i.e., the transfer of workers from agricultural areas to industrial production either within the individual Turkic republics or from one Turkic republic to another.[11] Soviet students of Central Asian demography describe the migration of European Russians to Asian republics as a "means of efficiently utilizing natural resources and ensuring a work force for the expanding industry."[12] Of course, it is hard not to agree with this argument. Without resettlement it would hardly be possible, say, to develop idle and virgin lands in Kazakhstan on such a large scale.

However, official Soviet documents do not deny the political purpose of organized migration, primarily of Russians, to Central Asia.

TABLE IV
Chief Nationality Groups in the Turkic Autonomous Republics of the Volga-Ural Region

Nationality	Total in Volga-Ural Republics (*in thousands*)	TATAR A.S.S.R.		CHUVASH A.S.S.R.		BASHKIR A.S.S.R.	
		Number (*in thousands*)	Percentage of Republic's Population	Number (*in thousands*)	Percentage of Republic's Population	Number (*in thousands*)	Percentage of Republic's Population
Bashkir	737	...	...	...	...	737	22.1
Belorussian	21	...	...	...	...	21	0.6
Chuvash	1,024	144	5.0	770	70.2	110	3.3
Jewish	17	10	0.4	...	...	7	0.2
Mari	108	14	0.5	...	...	94	2.8
Mordvin	100	33	1.2	24	2.2	43	1.3
Russian	2,933	1,252	43.9	263	24.0	1,418	42.4
Tatar	2,144	1,345	47.2	31	2.9	768	23.0
Udmurt	48	23	0.8	...	...	25	0.8
Ukrainian	103	16	0.6	4	0.3	83	2.5
Others	53	13	0.4	5	0.4	35	1.0
Total	7,288	2,850	100.0	1,097	100.0	3,341	100.0

SOURCE: *Itogi vsesoiuznoi perepisi naseleniia 1959 goda: SSSR*, pp. 202–8.

TABLE V
NATIONALITY GROUPS IN THE AZERBAIDZHAN S.S.R.

Nationality	Number	Percentage of Republic's Population
Azerbaidzhani	2,494,381	67.5
Russian	501,282	13.6
Armenian	442,089	12.0
Daghestan nationalities (including Turks)[a]	121,442	3.3
Jewish	40,204	1.1
Tatar	29,552	0.8
Ukrainian	25,778	0.7
Georgian	9,526	0.3
Tati	5,887	0.2
Others	27,576	0.5
Total	3,697,717	100.0

SOURCE: *Itogi vsesoiuznoi perepisi naseleniia 1959 goda: SSSR,* p. 207.
[a] Of the Daghestan nationalities, the Lezghians number 98,211 and constitute 2.7 per cent of the Republic's population.

What Western Sovietologists call a typical act of colonialism, the Soviet leadership calls a policy of "economic internationalization" and "socialist division of labor" in a multinational society.[13] The basic political purpose of "economic internationalization" was clearly reflected by the fact that skilled Tatar workers of the Volga area were transferred to Turkestan, and Russian replacements from neighboring regions were moved to Tatarstan at a time when Tatarstan itself (especially its oil industry) was expanding economically and in need of workers. Such a shuffling of the labor force does not correspond to the concept of "economic purposefulness." Rather its aim is a political one: to give the Russians a position of dominance in the Turkic republics. Whereas, according to the 1939 census, there were 158,000 Volga Tatars in Uzbekistan, in 1959 their number had increased to 400,000.[14] And yet, the proportion of Tatars in their native Tatar A.S.S.R. decreased while the proportion of the Russians increased.[15] Here we come to still another aspect of the resettlement policy, one which does not stem directly from the needs of economic expansion and takes the form of organized resettlement (emigration) of members of the indigenous Turkic population beyond the borders of their republic or ethnic territory. This method was used with the Volga Tatars. As a result, of the 5 million Tatars in the Central Volga–Ural area, 1 million found themselves outside the borders of their national territory. Of this 1 million, more than 700,000 now live in kindred

Turkestan, but the rest live in Russian cities and regions (Moscow, Leningrad, Rostov-on-Don).[16]

The Impact of Immigration on Language

"Linguistic Imperialism." Hugh Seton-Watson considers the immigration of Europeans to Central Asia as a form of Russification and imperialism that, simultaneously with the annexation of the ethnic territory of the Asians, created more favorable conditions for the wider diffusion of the Russian language.[17] In the early 1960's, the number of Russians in Kazakhstan exceeded the entire European population of Africa, including the Union of South Africa, Algiers, Kenya, and the Central African Federation.[18] The Russian "newcomers" to Central Asia have settled mainly in cities and other industrial centers, where they usually constitute the majority of the population as well as of the administrative and technical cadres. The Kazakhs, Uzbeks, and Kirghiz are compelled to communicate with them in Russian. Moreover, as Seton-Watson has noted,[19] nationality personnel cannot hope to obtain responsible posts and good jobs unless they master Russian. The introduction by administrative fiat of the Russian script and of Russian words into Turkic-language dictionaries during the period of the personality cult, i.e., "linguistic imperialism," as Walter Kolarz calls it,[20] undoubtedly was intended to prepare the ground for the Russification of the Turkic-language group. However, the last census shows that "linguistic assimilation" among the Turkic peoples is insignificant. Whereas 2.9 per cent of the entire Turkic population of the U.S.S.R. named Russian as their native language, only 1 per cent of the Central Asian and Azerbaidzhani Turks consider Russian their native language; 91–99 per cent of the population of the principal Turkic peoples of the U.S.S.R. and 97–99 per cent of Turkestan have retained their native language. Only among the Tatars, who have been under Russian domination and influence for more than 400 years, and under the Soviets for more than 45 years, has the percentage of persons who consider Tatar their native language decreased, and even there only from 98.9 per cent in 1926 to 92 per cent in 1959.[21] While the number of Tatars who consider Russian their native language rose from 2.6 per cent in 1939 to 7 per cent in 1959, this figure includes mainly those Tatars who live among Russians outside their own national territory in the Central Volga area and the Urals, and therefore cannot receive education in their own language. Mixed marriages between Tatar men and Russian women in this group apparently also favor "linguistic assimi-

lation." Tatar women very rarely marry Russians. It is mostly Tatar men who marry Russian wives. During the 1959 census, in families where the father and mother were of different nationalities, the nationality and language of the mother as a rule were used to determine the nationality and language of their children; for children who were not yet able to speak, the language usually spoken in the family was given.[22] As regards Tatars married to Russians, this method, undoubtedly, had a negative effect on Tatar statistics. Moreover, the group of Tatars who consider Russian their native language includes the Kreshen (Tatars who have been baptized Russian Orthodox). They number about 250,000 and have been linguistically assimilated since before the Revolution.

The reason that the extent of "linguistic Russification" has remained limited, in spite of the harsh measures taken to bring it about (imposition of the Cyrillic alphabet, persecution of national leaders, and intensified teaching of Russian in the schools), may be in the complexity of the cultural development process among the Turkic peoples in the last fifty years. The cultural revolution (*djadidism*), which began at the end of the nineteenth century among the Tatars of the Volga area, who organized their own European school system in their native language and who were the first reformers in the Moslem world,[23] penetrated into Turkestan at the beginning of this century. However, the main process of the cultural revolution—i.e., the transformation of the semifeudal and partly nomadic peoples of Central Asia into modern nations—occurred during the Soviet period. What took place before the 1939 census was the elimination of almost total illiteracy, the construction of schools conducting studies in the native language, including higher educational institutions, the introduction of literary speech into the administration, the theater, and the press, and the training of nationality cadres. The postwar period up to the 1959 census marked the phase of the development of linguistics, science, the organization in the republics of such learned institutions as the Academies of Sciences, and the building up of scientific and technical cadres. Although the persecution of the nationality intellectuals and of the literary and artistic heritage during the personality cult era impeded the rate of development,[24] it could not weaken the sense of national individuality and distinction, or the resistance to linguistic assimilation.

"Linguistic Nationalism." It is too early to determine what effect the policy of a "second native language" will have on the languages of the Turkic peoples in the future. Russian is taught in the national schools of all the republics beginning with the second grade, and ex-

TABLE VI

PERCENTAGE OF POPULATION AMONG CHIEF TURKIC GROUPS CONSIDERING NATIONAL LANGUAGE OR RUSSIAN AS NATIVE TONGUE

Nationality	Percentage Considering National Language as Native Tongue	Percentage Considering Russian as Native Tongue	
	1959	1939	1959
Azerbaidzhani	98.0	0.5	1.2
Bashkir[a]	62.0	0.6	2.6
Chuvash	91.0	3.1	9.0
Kara-Kalpak	95.0	0.5	2.4
Kazakh	98.0	0.4	1.2
Kirghiz	99.0	. . .	0.3
Tatar	92.0	2.6	7.0
Turkmen	99.4	. . .	0.5
Uzbek	98.4	0.05	0.5
Yakut	97.0	0.5	2.4

SOURCE: *Itogi vsesoiuznoi perepisi naseleniia 1959 goda: SSSR,* pp. 181–201.
[a] 35.4 per cent of the Bashkir consider Tatar as their native tongue.

tensive propaganda is being conducted to enroll children "voluntarily" in schools in which Russian is the language of instruction. About 30 per cent of all Kazakh students and almost 24 per cent of all students in the Uzbek S.S.R. attend such schools, whereas students of Russian nationality comprise only 11 per cent of the school children of the Uzbek Republic.[25] Instruction in 317 schools in Kirghizia is conducted in Russian, while in 280 schools children are taught in two languages. And yet many of these schools are in regions inhabited mainly by the Kirghiz.[26]

On the other hand, public opinion in Turkic autonomous and Union republics has expressed dissatisfaction with the trend imposed by the "administration" from above to make Russian the language of instruction in national schools.[27] Debates on this matter have been held in Kazakhstan and the Tatar Republic, and parents who enrolled their children in Russian schools were criticized. The consensus was that the teaching of children in their native languages should be made compulsory.[28] The Ministry of Education of the Tatar Republic was compelled to issue a decree on the teaching of the Tatar language and literature to Tatar children being educated in Russian schools, from grades one to ten, and to Tatar students in higher educational institutions.[29]

Khanazarov, member of the Academy of Sciences of the Uzbek S.S.R., has protested in writing against the "narrow linguistic" interpretation of the expression "second native language," believing that this term does not mean the "equally fluent knowledge of two languages," i.e., that the mastery of the Russian language by the masses should not be "equal to their mastery over their own native language." In his words, a considerable number of non-Russian nationalities "have an insufficient knowledge of the Russian language, while some of them actually do not have any knowledge of it at all."[30] R. Bikmukhametov, the young Tatar literary critic, wrote in 1963 in the Moscow periodical *Voprosy literatury* (*Problems of Literature*) at the time of the debates concerning the role of language in culture: "It is still too early to speak about making Russian the native language of all the Soviet peoples. . . . Facts show that the growth curve of other national languages at the present time is going up. . . . The inculcation of the Russian language often gives rise to the mistaken opinion that it is the only language of the arts."[31] What I would call signs of "defensive linguistic nationalism" also became manifest during discussions on problems of Turkic linguistics when linguists, writers, and teachers spoke out against the Russian words where they were not needed, believing that this artificial cluttering up of the language was introduced during the personality cult under the pretext of "friendship of peoples."[32] Representatives of the Kazakh intelligentsia even came forward with the demand that only "persons conversant with the Kazakh language" hold responsible posts in Kazakhstan, since today "as a result of socialist development" there is a sufficiency of trained, indigenous personnel,[33] and that entrance examinations for Kazakhs to the higher educational institutions be given in the Kazakh language.

Statistics and Cultural Trends

Professor Pipes believes that modernization and economic development in the Soviet Union have intensified national differences and national consciousness.[34] To be sure, this is also related to the over-all cultural development. Indeed, statistical data show that among the Turkic peoples, especially in Central Asia, industrialization, which touched off the influx of the European population, was accompanied by a rise in the cultural level.

To begin with, the general education level of the population became higher. Whereas, according to the 1939 census, only 15 out of

1,000 Uzbeks had either a higher, a secondary, or an incomplete secondary education, in 1959 their number rose to 208; among the Kazakhs this number increased from 22 to 182 per 1,000; among the Turkmen, from 14 to 242; among the Kirghiz, from 9 to 199; and among the Azerbaidzhani, from 49 to 242.[35] Though the number of persons with a higher, secondary, or incomplete secondary education among the Turkic nationalities per 1,000 persons is lower than the average in the U.S.S.R. (281 in the U.S.S.R. and 295 among the Russians), the educational level has, nevertheless, gone up substantially, if we consider the fact that before the Revolution virtually no Uzbeks, Kazakhs, Kirghiz, and Turkmen had a secondary or higher European education.

Great progress has been noted in the number of students enrolled in higher educational institutions and the secondary special schools. Whereas in 1927–28, only 500 Uzbek students were enrolled in higher educational institutions (excluding correspondence courses), at the beginning of the 1960–61 school year, their number was in excess of 53,000; the total number of Uzbek students attending higher educational institutions in the U.S.S.R. in the 1963–64 school year was 79,000; a similar trend is found among other Turkic peoples as well.[36] If we make a comparison of the proportion of students of every people, however, we find that among the Turkic peoples of Central Asia the proportion continues to be lower than among the peoples of the European part of the U.S.S.R.

Moreover, with the development of industry and agriculture in Central Asia, the population's social and professional composition and the proportion of manual and white-collar workers has increased. Whereas in 1939 18 per cent of all employed Uzbeks were blue- and white-collar workers, in 1959 there was an increase to 36 per cent; among the Kazakhs, from 37 per cent to 60 per cent; among the Kirghiz, from 12 to 30 per cent; and among the Turkmen, from 19 to 32 per cent. In addition to the working class, there arose a nationality technical intelligentsia, virtually nonexistent forty years ago, and whose ranks continue to grow. The number of Tatar specialists with a higher or a secondary special technical education employed in the national economy of the U.S.S.R on December 1, 1962, was about 153,000; of Uzbeks, about 119,000; of Azerbaidzhani, about 110,000; and of Kazakhs, about 90,000. Whereas on January 1, 1941, there were only 2,900 Uzbek specialists with a higher education, in 1962 their number was about 59,000.[37] Nevertheless, the proportion of Turkic specialists with a higher and secondary special technical education in the total number of Soviet specialists is lower than the proportion of the Turkic population in the total population of the U.S.S.R. Moreover, not all of them work in their republics. For political reasons, a portion of these technical

TABLE VII

SPECIALISTS WITH HIGHER EDUCATION AMONG THE TURKIC NATIONALITY GROUPS

Nationality	As of January, 1941	As of December, 1960
Azerbaidzhani	8,000	47,900
Kazakh	1,800	34,800
Kirghiz	100	9,400
Turkmen	200	10,400
Uzbek	2,900	46,500

SOURCE: Tsentral'noe statisticheskoe upravlenie, *Vysshee obrazovanie v SSSR* (*Higher Education in the USSR*) (Moscow, 1961), p. 69.

TABLE VIII

SPECIALISTS (EXCLUDING MILITARY PERSONNEL) WITH HIGHER OR SPECIALIZED SECONDARY EDUCATION AMONG THE TURKIC NATIONALITY GROUPS (AS OF DECEMBER 1, 1962)

(*in thousands*)

Nationality	Total	Higher Education	Specialized Secondary Education
U.S.S.R.	9,955.8	4,049.7	5,906.1
Altai	1.2	0.5	0.7
Azerbaidzhani	109.6	52.9	56.7
Balkar	1.1	0.3	0.8
Bashkir	18.9	7.4	11.5
Chuvash	39.9	15.0	24.9
Daghestan nationalities (including Kumyks and Nogai-Turks)	21.9	8.5	13.4
Karachai	2.0	0.9	1.1
Kazakh	89.7	40.8	48.9
Khakass	1.7	0.7	1.0
Kirghiz	22.7	11.6	11.1
Tatar	152.9	59.7	93.2
Turkmen	24.2	12.4	11.8
Tuvinian	2.2	0.7	1.5
Uzbek	118.9	58.9	60.0
Yakut	10.3	3.8	6.5

SOURCE: Tsentral'noe statisticheskoe upravlenie, *Narodnoe Khoziaistvo SSSR v 1963 godu* (*The USSR National Economy in 1963*) (Moscow, 1965), p. 493.

and scientific workers is sent to other republics to keep their proportion in the governments of the republics lower than that of Russian personnel. For example, in 1960, of more than 46,000 Uzbek specialists with a higher education, only 40,000 were employed in the economy of their own republics; and yet the total number of specialists with a higher education in the Uzbek S.S.R. was almost 109,000. The distribution of Kazakh, Turkmen, and Kirghiz specialists with a higher and a secondary special education follows a similar pattern.[38]

The last twenty to twenty-five years have also seen the emergence of creative and scientific intellectuals. Whereas in 1958 there were only 2,666 Uzbek scientists, in 1963 their number rose to 5,990; the number of Tatar scientists grew from 2,899 in 1958 to 6,251 in 1963.

TABLE IX
SCIENTISTS AMONG THE TURKIC NATIONALITY GROUPS

Nationality	1958	1963
U.S.S.R.	284,038	565,938
Altai	13	33
Azerbaidzhani	3,855	7,209
Bashkir	334	676
Chuvash	498	963
Kara-Kalpak	102	198
Karachai	11	48
Kazakh	1,966	3,793
Khakass	29	46
Kirghiz	456	834
Tatar	2,899	6,251
Turkmen	539	1,011
Tuvinian	13	38
Uzbek	2,666	5,990
Yakut	135	315

SOURCE: *Narodnoe khoziaistvo SSSR v 1963 godu,* p. 591.

Before the Revolution only the Tatars of the Volga area and the Azerbaidzhani had their own professional and national theater; today, the Turkic peoples of Central Asia have their own composers, playwrights, and motion picture directors, who create ballets, operas, and films on national, historical, and epic themes, which are permitted as long as they are not contrary to the Party line in art. Ballets and operas by Farid Yarullin and Nadjip Djihanov (both Tatars) and Karaev (an Azerbaidzhani), all of whom have a nationwide reputation, are included in the repertories of Moscow's Bolshoi Theater. At the same time, the theaters of Kazan, Tashkent, Baku, Ufa, Alma-Ata, and Ashkhabad produce the works of Shakespeare in the native languages, and the ballets of Tchaikovsky.

The cultural trend is also reflected in the publication of books in the native languages. Before the Revolution only the Tatars of the Volga area (and to some extent, the Azerbaidzhani) were active in book publishing. Back in 1913 they published more books than in 1957. At present all the peoples of Central Asia publish native-language books in millions of copies. The fields covered, especially in Tatar languages,[39] in addition to political propaganda, include literature, science, the arts, and linguistics, as well as textbooks for the nationality schools.

The cultural and technical development of a nation brings about heightened intellectual activity. De-Stalinization created more or less favorable conditions for the discussion of problems of national culture. As a result, there was an intensified interest and research into the national literary and artistic heritage, called *miracism* (the word

TABLE X
BOOK PUBLISHING IN TURKIC LANGUAGES IN THE U.S.S.R.

	Number of Titles			Number of Copies (*in thousands*)		
Language	1913	1957	1963	1913	1957	1963
Azerbaidzhani	91	832	976	112	7,411	8,357
Bashkir	—	105	150	—	478	909
Chuvash	56	187	153	93	1,014	905
Kazakh[a]	40	496	518	40	6,990	7,026
Kirghiz	—	434	393	—	2,905	2,317
Tatar	340	322	262	1,671	3,483	3,847
Turkmen	—	392	365	—	2,728	2,626
Uzbek[a]	37	699	1,039	86	14,074	16,949
Yakut	1	94	117	2	399	435

SOURCES: *SSSR v tsifrakh* (*The USSR in Figures*) (Moscow, 1958), p. 375; *Narodnoe Khoziaistvo SSSR v 1963 godu,* p. 613.
[a] Printed in Tatar publishing houses.

miras means heritage). During the Stalin period, the Uzbek and Tatar linguists, historians, and literary scholars were not allowed to make objective comments, or any kind of comment at all, on monuments of literature and the arts, since the heritage of the past was considered to be a bearer of a "reactionary East" and of "Islamic scholasticism." Also, outstanding writers and poets who are considered literary classics—such as the Tatar novelists and playwrights G. Ibragim, Fatikh Amirkhan, Fatkhi Burnash, and K. Tinchurin; the Uzbeks' A. Fitrat, Abdulla Kadri, and Cholpan; the Kazakhs' B. Maylin and Saken Seyfullin; as well as many others—were killed, or their writings banned, during the era of the personality cult. In recent years, considerable work has been done in Tashkent, Kazan, and Alma-Ata to make possible the publication of their works and of monographs devoted to the study of the literary heritage. Anthologies of ancient Tatar and Uzbek poetry, textbooks on the history of literature for secondary and higher educational institutions, and books on the history of national architecture and of Turkic linguistics have been published.[40] Before de-Stalinization, it was officially held that the Russian influence played the most important role in the cultural development of the Turkic peoples; today Turkic scholars stress the influence of the Turkic peoples themselves on the development of their literature, linguistics, education, and the theater, and of the influence of Turkic literature on Turkmen writers.[41] The Bashkir folk poet Mustai Karim, criticizing the "cult of the Russian influence" on the cultural development of the Turkic peoples, established during the period of Stalinism, writes: "Deep national historical roots and distant sources of poetry refute the falsehood that in the past small nations used to approach their old and new friends empty-handed, that they were not able to lay claim to any creative achievement. The socialist culture of peoples has not sprung out of nothing. We must not turn away in shame from the sacred tombs holding the remains of our ancestors—the wise thinkers and fiery bards."[42]

Another cultural trend that must be considered a good thing in the life of the Turkic peoples is the elimination of their "internal isolation." Stalin, pursuing the policy of linguistic and national differentiation of the Turks under the pretext of struggle with "Pan-Turkism," barred free contacts not only with the outside world but also between the Tatars and Azerbaidzhani and Turkestan, especially after the discovery of the movement of national opposition of the Turkic members of the Russian Communist Party under the leadership of the Tatar Sultan Galiev at the end of the 1920's. Today, cultural exchange between the Turkic republics has been revived. They arrange conferences on literature and the arts where linguists, literary men, and historians can exchange views on the standardization of the orthography of the Turkic languages, disrupted during the personality cult.[43]

Some improvement in the position of the Turkic intellectuals with respect to national culture and education obviously has occurred. We know, however, that historians and men of letters are still barred from studying their cultural heritage and history if this conflicts with Russian national feelings. For example, the Tatars are not permitted to study or print the epic work *Edegi,* which is a masterpiece of fourteenth-century Tatar folklore. The CPSU Central Committee decree of 1944, "On the condition of, and measures for, the improvement of mass political and ideological work in the Tatar Party organization," that banned this epic work, states that it idealizes the Emir of the Golden Horde, who subjugated the Russian principalities. However, Russian writers, dramatists, and composers may, without any restriction, write novels, plays, and cantatas glorifying Ivan the Terrible, who set up his harsh rule over the Tatar Khanates. Turkic historians may not study their past history objectively if this in any way deals with Russian history. The official theory that the subjugation of the Turkic peoples by the Russian Czars was not imperialism but a "progressive phenomenon," advanced during the period of Stalinism, is still in force. As a result, the Turkic teachers in the schools are obliged to laud Russian conquests and inveigh against their own empires, which had subjugated the Russians. This fact, of course, contradicts the arguments of the Soviet critics of the Chinese nationality policy in East Turkestan, who maintain that the Chinese great-power chauvinists are following a policy of discrimination and forced assimilation toward other nationalities.[44]

Conclusions

1. The influx of the Russian population into Central Asia, whatever its motivations, may be viewed as appropriation of the territory of one people by another, since it occurs without the consent of the indigenous population. Hence, it is nothing but an act of colonialism. Apparently, with greater economic expansion, this immigration will continue, creating (1) greater opportunities for diffusion of the Russian language among the native population and (2) increasing the number of Russian personnel controlling the economy and the administration of the Turkic republics. Lenin wrote: "The demands of economic turnover always force the nationalities living within one country (as long as they wish to live together) to study the language of the majority."[45]

2. As for Russia's economic expansion in Central Asia, essentially

a beneficent phenomenon insofar as it increases the "utilization of natural resources" for the purpose of raising the living standard of the population, would be still more beneficial for the entire Soviet society if it were not tied to "linguistic Russification," implemented through the transfer of Kazakh, Kirghiz, and Uzbek children to Russian-language schools.

3. Further modernization of the nationalities will at the same time strengthen their national consciousness. Significantly enough, even those Tatars who consider Russian their native language do not repudiate their nationality. The nationality cadres, who are more numerous today than in the past and whose educational level is now equal to that of the Russians, will demand more important roles in their own republics. The Sino-Soviet conflict may foster a liberalization of the Soviet nationality policy in regard to the Turkic peoples, especially in the Central Asian areas bordering on China, and I believe that this would also have a favorable effect on the future of the native languages in the republics.

NOTES

1. All-Union Census, 1959, in *Ekonomicheskaia gazeta,* No. 27 (July, 1966), p. 27. During the seven years that followed the census of 1959, the Turkic peoples increased by 28 per cent, while the Slavs increased by only 11 per cent. The present total number of Turkic peoples may, therefore, be estimated at 25 million.
2. *Genocide in the USSR* (New York: The Scarecrow Press, 1958), pp. 20–35; The Turkic peoples of the North Caucasus were deported in 1944. The Balkars and the Chechen-Ingushes were rehabilitated in 1957. See the decrees of the Supreme Soviet on the recall of various deported peoples and on the restoration of their republics, in *Pravda,* February 12, 1957.
3. P. G. Pod'iachikh, *Naselenie SSSR* (*The Population of the USSR*) (Moscow, 1961), p. 106.
4. *Ibid.,* p. 47.
5. E. Bagramov, "The Character of Nationality Relations in the USSR and the Fabrications of Bourgeois Propaganda," *Politicheskoe samoobrazovanie* (*Political Self-Education*), No. 8 (August, 1965).
6. Tsentral'noe statisticheskoe upravlenie, *Itogi vsesoiuznoi perepisi naseleniia 1959 goda: SSSR* (*Results of the All-Union Population Census of 1959: USSR*) (Moscow, 1962), p. 232; and A. A. Isupov, *Natsional'nyi sostav naseleniia SSSR—po itogam perepisi 1959 g.* (*Ethnic Composition of the Population of the USSR—According to the 1959 Census*) (Moscow, 1964), p. 25.
7. Isupov, *op. cit.,* p. 29.
8. *Narody Srednei Azii i Kazakhstana* (*Peoples of Central Asia and Kazakhstan*), I (Moscow: U.S.S.R. Academy of Sciences, 1962), 13; and Isupov, *op. cit.,* pp. 29–31.
9. K. Kh. Khanazarov, *Sblizhenie natsii i natsional'nye yazyki v SSSR* (*Rapprochement of Nations and Nationality Languages in the USSR*) (Tashkent: Academy of Sciences of the Uzbek S.S.R., 1963), p. 102.
10. Tsentral'noe statisticheskoe upravlenie, *Itogi vsesoiuznoi perepisi naseleniia 1926 goda: Uzbekskaia SSR* (*Results of the All-Union Population Census of 1926: Uzbek SSR*), XV (Moscow, 1928); and Tsentral'noe statisticheskoe upravlenie, *Itogi vsesoiuznoi perepisi naseleniia 1959 goda: Uzbekskaia SSR* (*Results of the All-Union Population Census of 1959: Uzbek SSR*) (Moscow, 1962). Includes data on the distribution of the male and female, urban and rural population by nationality and native language in the Uzbek S.S.R.
11. Khanazarov, *op. cit.,* pp. 101–5; and Isupov, *op. cit.,* p. 45.
12. Khanazarov, *op. cit.,* p. 100; and Bagramov, *op. cit.,* p. 14.
13. F. Tabeev, "International Education of Workers and Political Education," *Politicheskoe samoobrazovanie,* No. 1 (January, 1963), pp. 76, 79; and Khanazarov, *op. cit.,* p. 109.
14. Khanazarov, *op. cit.,* p. 106; Tsentral'noe statisticheskoe upravlenie, *Itogi vsesoiuznoi perepisi naseleniia 1939 goda: Uzbekskaia SSR* (*Results of the All-Union Population Census of 1939: Uzbek SSR*), on nationality composition; and *Itogi vsesoiuznoi perepisi naseleniia 1959 goda: SSSR,* which provides data on the distribution of the most numerous nationalities of the Soviet Union by autonomous republics, autonomous oblasts, and national okrugs.
15. Isupov, *op. cit.,* p. 30.

16. Tsentral'noe statisticheskoe upravlenie, *Itogi vsesoiuznoi perepisi naseleniia 1959 goda: RSFSR* (*Results of the All-Union Population Census of 1959: RSFSR*) (Moscow, 1962); and *Itogi vsesoiuznoi perepisi naseleniia 1959 goda: SSSR.*
17. Hugh Seton-Watson, "Moscow Imperialism," *Problems of Communism,* XIII, No. 1 (January–February, 1964), 16–19.
18. Walter Kolarz, *Communism and Colonialism* (New York: St. Martin's Press, 1964), p. 46.
19. Seton-Watson, *loc. cit.*
20. Kolarz, *op. cit.,* p. 35.
21. Richard Pipes, "The Forces of Nationalism," *Problems of Communism,* XIII, No. 1 (January–February, 1964), 5.
22. Isupov, *op. cit.,* p. 34; and *Itogi vsesoiuznoi perepisi naseleniia 1959 goda: SSSR,* pp. 184–89, which provides data on the distribution of the population by nationality and native language.
23. Hugh Seton-Watson, *Neither War Nor Peace* (New York: Frederick A. Praeger, 1960), p. 297.
24. Khanazarov, *op. cit.,* p. 11.
25. *Ibid.,* p. 176.
26. Isupov, *op. cit.,* p. 50.
27. Khanazarov, *op. cit.,* p. 202.
28. M. Valiev, "Rapprochement of Nationality Languages in the Struggle for the Construction of Communism," *Sovet edelbiaty,* No. 5 (1962), pp. 141–43 (in Tatar).
29. M. Makhmutov (Minister of Education of Tatarstan), "Reorganization of Tatar Schools," *Sovet edebiaty,* No. 5 (1959), pp. 75–82.
30. Khanazarov, *op. cit.,* p. 202.
31. See R. Bikmukhametov, "New Prospects," *Voprosy literatury,* No. 1 (1963), pp. 68–69.
32. S. Faizulin, *The Treasure of Two Languages* (Kazan, 1964), pp. 14–15, 59–60 (in Tatar); B. Kerbabaev, "Culture of Language—Culture of the People," *Edebiat va sungat* (*Literature and Art*), February 6, 1963 (in Turkmen); R. Mustafin, "One Hundred Literatures," *Literaturnaia gazeta,* December 22, 1966; and M. N. Khydyrov, *Materials on the History of the Turkmen Language* (Ashkhabad, 1962), p. 6 (in Turkmen).
33. N. Dzhandildin, "Some Problems of International Education," *Kommunist,* No. 3 (1959), pp. 34–36; "Communist of Kazakhstan," in *Kazakhstan Kommunisi,* No. 7 (1957) (in Kazakh); and A. Karybaev, "Appetite Comes While Eating," *Komsomolets Kirgizii,* May 16, 1965, and "About Language, One's Own and Foreign," *Komsomolets Kirgizii,* February 26, 1965.
34. Pipes, *op. cit.,* p. 3.
35. *Itogi vsesoiuznoi perepisi naseleniia 1959 goda: SSSR,* p. 234.
36. Tsentral'noe statisticheskoe upravlenie, *Vysshee obrazovanie v SSSR* (*Higher Education in the USSR*) (Moscow, 1961), pp. 84–85.
37. Tsentral'noe statisticheskoe upravlenie, *Narodnoe khoziaistvo SSSR v 1963 godu* (*The USSR National Economy in 1963*) (Moscow, 1965), p. 493; and *Vysshee obrazovanie v SSSR,* p. 69.
38. *Vysshee obrazovanie v SSSR,* pp. 60, 67, 70.
39. In 1964, 270 books were issued for 5 million Tatars in their native language; the total edition was 3,978,000. In 1965, 230 additional books with a total edition of 3,365,000 were issued. In 1950, relatively more books came out in the Tatar language—385 titles with a total edition of

4,770,000. See *Narodnoe khoziaistvo SSSR v 1963 godu,* p. 723; and Tsentral'noe statisticheskoe upravlenie, *Narodnoe khoziaistvo SSSR v 1965 godu* (*The National Economy of the USSR in 1965*) (Moscow, 1966), p. 701.

40. See *Antologiia tatarskoi poezii* (*Anthology of Tatar Poetry*) (Kazan, 1956 and 1958) (in Tatar and Russian), beginning from the thirteenth century; *Antologiia uzbekskoi poezii* (*Anthology of Uzbek Poetry*) (5 vols.; Tashkent, 1961–62) (in Uzbek); and *Tatarskaia literatura* (*Tatar Literature*) (Kazan, 1963) (in Tatar).
41. Seiit Garryev, "Some Problems of Mutual Literary Influence," *Sovet edebiaty,* No. 2 (1965), pp. 82–90 (in Turkmen); and P. Azimov, "Eminent Turkmen Linguist," in *Izvestiia Akademii Nauk Turkmenskoi SSR* (*News of the Academy of Sciences of the Turkmen SSR*) (Social Science Series, No. 4 [Ashkhabad, 1965]) (in Turkmen).
42. Mustai Karim, "The Life of Sutia," *Literaturnaia gazeta,* November 15, 1962.
43. "Conference of Turkologists," *Qazan ultary* (*Lights of Kazan*), No. 1 (1966), p. 141 (in Tatar); and *Muallimnar gazeti* (*Teachers Paper*), October 22, 1965 (in Turkmen).
44. See the speech by Kuzhamyarov in *Kazakhstanskaia pravda,* April 5, 1964, at the plenum meeting of the Central Committee of the Kazakhstan Communist Party.
45. V. I. Lenin, *Sochineniia,* XIX, 317.

10

Sovyetish Heymland—An Analysis

JOSEPH BRUMBERG AND ABRAHAM BRUMBERG

I

1961–64: The Early Years

In August, 1961, a Yiddish periodical appeared in the Soviet Union for the first time in thirteen years. It was called *Sovyetish Heymland* (*Soviet Homeland*), and its editor-in-chief was one Aaron Vergelis, a comparatively unknown Yiddish poet, writer, and stanch Communist Party member. Its editorial board announced that *Sovyetish Heymland* would appear every two months and that it would publish the works of the more than one hundred Yiddish writers and poets of the Soviet Union, as well as contributions from Yiddish writers in the neighboring "people's democracies."

What is *Sovyetish Heymland* like? Who are its contributors? How good is their writing? How much "Jewish content" does it have? For years the Soviet regime had denied that there was any demand for Yiddish literature in the Soviet Union. Why then did it suddenly reverse itself by sanctioning this magazine and predicting that its circulation would grow by leaps and bounds? Indeed, why did Soviet authorities, who had for many years suppressed almost all manifestations of Jewish cultural and religious life, suddenly provide their Jewish citizens with a cultural forum—and one with nationalist potential?

According to the population census taken in Czarist Russia in 1897, Yiddish was the mother tongue of 97 per cent of the Jews of that country. Yiddish was the language of instruction in all Jewish-sponsored schools, the overwhelming majority of which were religious

Part I of this article was written by Joseph Brumberg and Part II by Abraham Brumberg.

—i.e., the *khedorim* (ungraded one-room schools) and the *yeshivos* (talmudic academies). Czarist Russia had very few secular Yiddish schools.

The 1917 Revolution promised to realize the cultural aspirations of Russia's numerous nationality groups. When the Bolshevik government established a Commissariat for Nationalities, it included a special department for Jewish affairs, a seemingly favorable sign for the cultural aspirations of Russian Jewry. By the school year 1932–33, 137,212 children were attending 1,201 Yiddish primary and secondary schools in the Soviet Union. There were twenty-five Jewish teachers' institutes, departments for Jewish studies at the Universities of Moscow, Kiev, and Minsk, a number of university chairs in Yiddish linguistics and literature,[1] as well as four Yiddish periodicals and seventeen state-financed theaters.

The special department for Jewish affairs within the Commissariat for Nationalities was abolished in 1924, and Jewish cultural activities were entrusted to the repressive Jewish Section of the Communist Party (Yevsektsia). The latter, in turn, was abolished in 1930.[2] The liquidation of the Yevsektsia coincided with the beginning of the decline of Yiddish cultural institutions in the Soviet Union. During the great purges of 1936–38, three Yiddish dailies (*Emes, Shtern,* and *Oktiabr*) were closed and former leaders of the Yevsektsia, together with a number of Jewish intellectuals, were arrested and never heard from again.[3]

World War II witnessed an almost complete decimation of Jewish cultural institutions, and after the end of hostilities, Soviet authorities refused to permit their revival.[4] Early in 1945, a number of Soviet Yiddish writers pleaded with local government officials in Lvov, Bialystok, and Vilna to sanction the continuation of the few Yiddish schools and other cultural institutions that had been reopened. Their pleas were in vain. Almost all of these establishments were liquidated within the year.

Hundreds of writers, journalists, and educators were sent to labor camps, where many of them perished. In 1948, all the remaining Yiddish cultural institutions—including the Moscow Yiddish Theater—were closed down. The height of Stalin's persecution of the Soviet Jewish intelligentsia on the grounds of "cosmopolitanism" was reached on August 12, 1952, when twenty-three Yiddish writers and intellectuals were executed.

How important was the role of "popular" anti-Semitism in the suppression of Jewish culture in the Soviet Union? It was probably as widespread during the 1920's as it had been under the Czars. During the 1920's, however, it was a source of embarrassment to Soviet leadership, which considered any manifestation of chauvinism and nationalist animosity to be contrary to the revolutionary and internationalist principles of Marxism—and therefore suppressed it.

But as Stalin eliminated his rivals for power, a new spirit began to pervade the Communist Party. In keeping with the new slogan of "Soviet patriotism," national minority groups were forcibly Russified. The steady growth of Russian chauvinism was accompanied by its traditional concomitant—anti-Semitic prejudice—extending from the benighted masses to the "enlightened" Communist Party leaders.

The strains of World War II and the influence of the Nazi occupation of large parts of the Soviet Union accelerated the spread of popular anti-Semitism. When the war ended, the Soviet authorities took no steps to combat it. On the contrary, as one perceptive observer noted:

> After the war, the government quite consciously and deliberately sought to exploit this new anti-Semitism, at first only indirectly and to a limited extent under Zhdanov from 1946–48, then much more markedly and explicitly in the "anti-cosmopolitan" campaign launched in 1949. [It finally became] a major and inseparable ingredient of Stalinism . . . [partly] designed to mobilize support for Stalinist policies as a whole.[5]

There is considerable evidence that Stalin personally had always been anti-Semitic, even if his prejudices lay rather dormant in the 1920's and 1930's. Now, as the tension of the cold war mounted and antagonism toward the West became almost an obsession with him, his anti-Jewish phobia deepened: he saw Soviet Jewry as the hidden ally of Western democracy, the new state of Israel as an "agent of imperialism." Stalin mounted a "vigilance campaign" which many Soviet Jews at the time regarded as the ominous prelude to a massive attack on Soviet Jewry as a whole.* The country was rife with rumors that several million Jews were to be evacuated to distant Siberian regions, when Stalin's death on March 5, 1953, put an end to the most frightening chapter of anti-Jewish repression in the Soviet Union.

Under Khrushchev, the lives of Soviet Jews became considerably more secure. The most harrowing manifestations of officially inspired anti-Semitism came to an end. It soon became clear, however, that the new leadership had not abandoned its classic policy of singling

* This has since been confirmed by many sources. See, for instance, the memoirs of Ilya Ehrenburg, *Post-War Years, 1945–1954* (Cleveland, 1967), chap. XV, and his novel *The Thaw* (Chicago, 1955).

out the Jews as scapegoats for its own endemic shortcomings and failures. Nor did it intend to grant its Jewish subjects the same cultural and religious rights enjoyed by other minorities in the U.S.S.R. The 1962–63 campaign against "economic crimes," with its transparent emphasis on *Jewish* "criminals," clearly illustrates the former. The continued proscription of Yiddish schools, theaters, and other cultural activities—with the exception of the *Birobidzhaner Shtern,* a thrice-weekly bilingual sheet published in the "Jewish Autonomous Oblast"—underscores the latter.

How, then, is one to explain the sudden appearance, in September, 1961, of a Yiddish journal, complete with an editorial board and office, and accompanied by a flurry of official statements, interviews, and promises of more publishing ventures in the future? Above all, did the launching of *Sovyetish Heymland* signify a basic change in the Soviet attitude toward Jews and Jewish culture?

The answer to the last question is, alas, No. There is no evidence that Soviet ideological tenets on "the Jewish question" have undergone any change whatsoever. These tenets are almost as old as Marxism itself. According to Karl Kautsky, leader of the German Social Democratic Party before World War I, "The Jews are an appreciable revolutionary factor, whereas Jewry is a reactionary one." This simplistic formulation came to be challenged by other Social Democratic theoreticians (especially in Austria), but never by the Leninist wing of the Marxist movement. As early as 1903, Lenin criticized the nationalist ideology of the revolutionary Russian Jewish Labor Bund, the first workers' party in Russia: "The idea of a separate Jewish people, which is utterly untenable scientifically, is reactionary in its political implication. . . . The whole idea of Jewish 'nationality' is manifestly reactionary."[6]

Ten years later, on the eve of World War I, Lenin returned to the attack: "Anyone directly or indirectly putting forward the slogan of Jewish 'national culture' is an enemy of the proletariat, a partisan of the *old* and the *caste-like* in the Jewish group, an accomplice of the rabbis and bourgeoisie. . . . Jews carry on the best Jewish tradition when they combat the slogan of 'national culture.' "[7]

Thus, when in the same year Stalin in his *Marxism and the National Question* opposed any form of autonomy for "a nation whose future is denied and whose present existence remains to be proven," he was merely following in Lenin's footsteps.

To be sure, with the establishment of a Bolshevik government in Russia, the Jews (like other ethnic minorities) were granted cultural and to some extent even territorial autonomy—by none other, incidentally, than the first Commissar of Nationalities, Stalin. The motives, however, were purely practical: first, to satisfy the needs of thousands of Jewish Communists who, while Marxists to the core, remained emotionally committed to the secular Yiddish tradition; and second, to channel the Jewishness of the Jewish masses away from religious "clericalism" and nationalism with Zionist overtones, into a "socialist" Jewish culture, whose sole form of expression was to be the Yiddish language.

The discrepancy between Communist theory and Soviet practice produced an inevitable internal contradiction. For Yiddish culture was bound to engender some kind of Jewish nationalist sentiment, and this the Soviet ideologists could not accept. Consequently, the ban on Yiddish culture in the 1940's as "bourgeois," "chauvinistic," "clerical," and "counterrevolutionary."

There is no reason to believe that this contradiction between Communist ideology and Soviet expedience has been resolved with the publication of *Sovyetish Heymland.* In July, 1956, Mikhail Suslov, then a member of the Presidium of the Central Committee of the Communist Party, told a delegation of visiting Canadian Communists, "We have no intention to call back a dead culture." Yekaterina Furtseva, Soviet Minister of Culture, as well as former Premier Nikita Khrushchev himself, delivered themselves of similar sentiments. On April 9, 1958, Khrushchev told Serge Groussard, correspondent of *Le Figaro:* "A genuine cultural community of Jews is not more practicable than a political community: the Jews are interested in everything, discuss everything, and finally end up with profound cultural divergencies among themselves."[8]

Sovyetish Heymland was preceded between 1959 and 1961 by the publication in the Soviet Union of six Yiddish books, the first time since 1948 that any Yiddish books were published at all. Significantly, none of these books was by a living Yiddish author: Three were selected works by the classic writers Mendele Mocher Sforim, Sholom Aleichem, and I. L. Peretz, one was by David Bergelson (one of the writers executed on August 12, 1952), one by Osher Schvartsman, and one an anthology of works previously published in Birobidjan. Clearly, this was not the harbinger of a renaissance of Yiddish culture but a polite bow to the past.

To a certain extent, *Sovyetish Heymland* represented a similar act of Soviet expediency. Soviet anti-Jewish policies have had a bad press throughout the Western world. A number of leading intellectuals

—some, like Bertrand Russell, friends of the Soviet Union—have protested directly to the Soviet Government for its suppression of the rights of the Jewish national minority. Even more important, leading Communists in the United States, Canada, Great Britain, France, and Italy, both Jewish and non-Jewish, have strongly criticized the Soviet Union's discrimination against the Jews in general, and their cultural life in particular. Thus, the American Communist party, though never noted for its independence vis-à-vis Moscow, declared that the Soviet Government, if it were to honor the principle of the cultural equality of all national groups in the Soviet Union, was duty-bound to grant the cultural demands of the Jews.

It may thus be assumed that foreign pressures—both from the so-called progressive camp as well as from non-Communist quarters—have had some effect on Soviet policy. Yet it is doubtful whether, taken by themselves, these pressures would have had a decisive influence on Moscow's policy vis-à-vis the Jews. In this author's view, another more potent—or at least equally potent—factor has been at work, namely, the cautious yet nevertheless very substantial emergence of public opinion *within* the U.S.S.R.

The term "public opinion" in this context is not to be taken as embracing all strata of the Soviet population. True, with the abandonment of mass terror the man on the street has to some extent shed the stifling fear and suspicion that were so characteristic of the Stalin era and has frequently dared to express opinions not in accord with the official Party line. With regard to the position of Jews in the Soviet Union, however, as well as any important *political* issue, it is the voice of the intellectuals that counts. It has become increasingly evident over the past few years that many Russian intellectuals have been articulate in associating the struggle against manifestations of anti-Jewishness with the general struggle against the Stalinist heritage. And it is this association that codetermined the emergence of *Sovyetish Heymland*—the single official concession to Soviet Jews, of whom, according to the last Soviet census, conducted in 1959, one out of five still claimed Yiddish as his mother tongue.

Ever since Stalin's death, the cultural scene has been divided into, roughly speaking, two camps: a liberal and a conservative one. Alexander Tvardovski, poet and editor in chief of the monthly *Novyi mir* (*New World*), may be said to represent the liberals; N. Kochetov, editor of the monthly *Oktiabr,* is undoubtedly the spokesman of the conservatives. The latter include some of the most vicious and vocal contributors to the "anticosmopolitan" campaign directed against

Soviet Jews in the last years of Stalin's life—e.g., Nikolai Gribachov, who greeted the arrest of the nine Jewish doctors accused of conspiring against Stalin's life in January, 1953, with these memorable words:

> There is weeping by the rivers of Babylon—the most important of which is the Hudson. The Joint [Distribution Committee] has been plucked—that vulture dressed in the pigeon feathers of charity and philanthropy. . . . The bourgeois newspapers are shedding inky crocodile tears. From Jerusalem to London stretches the perplexed mutter of the Zionist leaders.[9]

The liberals, on the other hand, feel a tremendous sense of revulsion at Stalin's crimes against the Jews, as well as the continuation of anti-Jewish policies under Khrushchev and his successors.

Yevgeni Yevtushenko's moving poem "Babi Yar," commemorating the twentieth anniversary of the German slaughter of 100,000 Jews in a ravine near Kiev, was greeted with sympathetic approval by the liberals, and by all of Soviet youth, when it was published in *Literaturnaia gazeta* in 1961. The poem's reception dramatically pointed up liberal Russian sensitivity to the Jewish tragedy, and their willingness to express it. The reaction is all the more important in that it is so strikingly reminiscent of the sensibility of the pre-1917 Russian intelligentsia, so much a part of the liberal Russian tradition.

There is also considerable evidence that the group around, and to the left of, Tvardovski has been deeply disturbed by the total destruction of Soviet Jewish culture. The Khrushchev regime must have carefully noted and reflected on these aspects of public opinion at home. Unlike Stalin, whose actions were frequently distorted by paranoiac hatred, Khrushchev was always more practical, rational, and willing to compromise. Common-sense evaluations of domestic public opinion, together with a sensitivity to his public image, are quite likely to have impelled Khrushchev to consent, or at least not to object, to the publication of *Sovyetish Heymland* so long, of course, as it conformed to party policy.

All of these factors played a part in the decision to publish *Sovyetish Heymland.* It represented a compromise with public opinion by the Khrushchev regime, but one which did not alter the over-all Soviet approach to the Jews. To ensure that nothing politically embarrassing crept into the pages of this new Yiddish bimonthly, the job of editor was entrusted to Aaron Vergelis, a man who could be expected to make *Sovyetish Heymland* another reliable Soviet magazine, different from others of its kind only in that its language was Yiddish. He was expected to prevent it from becoming in any way specifically *Jewish.* We shall see how successful Vergelis has been.

The name of Aaron Vergelis is little known to the Jewish literary world outside of the Soviet Union. Professor Max Beloff of All Souls College, Oxford, in a letter to the London *Jewish Chronicle,* published on November 22, 1963, wrote:

> American Jews are presumably aware that Vergelis' name has been associated in a circumstantial way with the purge of the Soviet Jewish intelligentsia between 1948 and 1953, of which he is one of the few survivors. . . . Students of the Soviet Jewish scene are seemingly convinced of the truth of these allegations, and they would be consistent with Vergelis' own attacks upon the poets Haim Grade and Israel Emiot in *Literaturnaia Gazeta* on August 8, 1959, and subsequently, in the *Morning Freiheit* [Communist Yiddish daily, New York] on September 1, 1959. . . . Vergelis himself opposed the revival of Jewish literature after the end of the purge, and in his limited edition of some Yiddish classics he went so far as to state in his introduction to Sholom Aleichem that this writer's main characteristic was Russian patriotism.[10]

Little is known of Vergelis' biography from official sources. He was born in the Ukraine in 1918. Ten years later, his parents moved to the abortive Jewish Autonomous Province of Birobidjan. Later he studied linguistics and literature at the University of Moscow. He served in the Soviet Army during World War II and was wounded several times. Subsequently, he became associate editor of a military front newspaper. In 1945, he returned to Moscow. Three years later he turned up again in Birobidjan, publishing essays and poems in the Soviet Union's sole Jewish periodical at the time, the *Birobidzhaner Shtern.* A few years later he returned to Moscow. His first Russian-language book was published there, in 1956.[11]

When Vergelis visited the United States, no representative of an American Jewish organization would consent to meet with him, with the sole exception of the editor and staff of the *Morning Freiheit.* Asked by a reporter for *The Day-Morning Journal* to comment on anti-Jewish propaganda in the Soviet Union, Vergelis vigorously denied its existence. He also denied that German nationality groups were being granted the kind of cultural facilities not available to Soviet Jews.

(The truth is that the 1,620,000 Germans in the Soviet Union have two weeklies: *Neues Leben,* published in Moscow, and *Rote Fahne,* published in the Altai territory, as well as a literary magazine, *Hand in Hand.* In addition, there is a regular German-language broadcast over the Soviet radio, and a number of schools have German as their language of instruction. Soviet Jewry, with a population of almost 3 million, have, in *Sovyetish Heymland, one* literary journal and nothing else.)[12]

In view, then, of the singular circumstances surrounding the publication of *Sovyetish Heymland*—the fact that it is the *only* Yiddish periodical in the Soviet Union, and that it was published after a lapse of thirteen years of cultural barrenness—its appearance was greeted with general approval in the West: *The New York Times* went so far as to underline it as a "significant fact—a change in Soviet policy." In the Soviet Union itself, *Sovyetish Heymland* was prominently mentioned in numerous Russian magazines. The illustrated weekly *Ogoniok* featured a photostat of *Heymland*'s first page and the table of contents of its first issue.[13] Under a banner headline, *Literaturnaia gazeta* published on August 31, 1961, an interview with Vergelis, listing the contents of the first issue and stressing hopeful prospects. *Sovyetish Heymland*'s arrival was prominently announced by *Sovietskaia kultura* on the same day, and many other Soviet magazines followed suit.

Sovyetish Heymland is, of course, under official auspices, being published by the Soviet Publishing House; like *Novyi mir,* it is an official organ of the Union of Soviet Writers. The physical surroundings in which it is edited are lavish. To quote an eye-witness account:

> The first impression is very favorable. A building on Kirov Street in downtown Moscow . . . eight room office . . . soft chairs, desks, telephones. Placards on each door, with the name of the room's occupants in both Russian and Yiddish. Newspapers from foreign countries available (which I unfortunately did not see—they are kept in a closet). I asked one of the staff whether I could read them. The answer was that only editors are permitted to read the foreign press.[14]

The announcement that *Sovyetish Heymland* was to be published released a remarkable outpouring of Yiddish manuscripts: according to Vergelis, there were close to 1,000. The first issue listed 110 Yiddish writers who were to contribute. At the end of 1964, the number of Soviet contributors rose to 142. In addition, there were 24 authors living ouside the Soviet Union (13 in Israel, 7 in the United States, 2 in France, 1 each in Canada and Argentina).

Taking into consideration the fate of so many Yiddish writers in the Soviet Union, the fact that the most talented of them had perished during Stalin's reign of terror in the 1940's and early 1950's[15] and the official persecution of Jewish culture in general, the number of

Sovyetish Heymland's contributors is indeed impressive. Apparently, there were many comparatively young Yiddish writers, still unpublished, who had been writing for themselves and a small circle of friends.[16]

Biographical material for many of the Soviet Yiddish writers is lacking. But it is noteworthy that of those for whom information is available, more than sixty were university graduates, almost all served in the Soviet armed forces during World War II, and quite a number earned military awards.

The *Heymland* has also published the work of ten Yiddish writers who died before 1961 of natural causes, and of eleven who perished in the purges but were later rehabilitated. There are also pieces by fifteen authors who survived the labor camps, jail, and banishment, though, understandably, the editors do not always mention this fact. According to the writer and literary critic Alexander Pomerantz, the great majority of the forty-eight authors who participated in the first issue of *Sovyetish Heymland* had spent years in confinement.[17]

The informed Western Jewish press had expected *Sovyetish Heymland* to be used as a Soviet propaganda weapon to refute the widespread charge of the persecution of Jewish culture in the Soviet Union. Within a few months after the periodical began appearing, this expectation seemed confirmed officially by Minister of Culture Furtseva, and by General David Dragunski, who is a Jew. (His "Three Journeys to Paris" was printed in the January–February, 1962, issue.) These two public figures in effect admitted that *Sovyetish Heymland* was being published mainly for foreign consumption, and for purely political purposes.[18] Paradoxically, however, this prognostication was to prove only partly true.

It is important to understand that *Sovyetish Heymland* could not be *essentially* different from any other literary magazine published in the Soviet Union. These may differ somewhat in their approach to works of art, may be more flexible or less flexible in interpreting "partymindedness" (*partiinost*) as reflected in literature, may exhibit divergent attitudes toward "formalism" or "naturalism." Some may open their pages to younger poets, such as Yevtushenko, who write honestly about the crimes of the past and the shortcomings of the present, others may attack these same poets for "slandering Soviet reality." Yet basically all Soviet literary journals are expected to adhere to the principles of "socialist realism," and none can afford the luxury of honesty in the sense in which these terms are understood in any democratic society. In the past few years, the Communist

Party has tolerated a more heterogeneous situation in the literary field than it did under Stalin. (The journals *Novyi mir* and *Oktiabr* are cases in point.) But it always reserves the right to prescribe the limits of what is and what is not permissible, esthetically as well as politically.

This being so, it was to be expected that a new magazine in the Yiddish language would never defy the dictates of the Communist Party. In fact, given the special sensitivity and past history of Jewish literary activity in the Soviet Union, one might have expected it to be "more Catholic than the Pope." The surprise is that *Sovyetish Heymland* has over the years succeeded in injecting a certain amount of specifically Jewish content into a Yiddish Communist publication.

This author has carefully examined all issues of *Sovyetish Heymland* up to and including the November–December, 1964, issue.*

The very first issue, published in September, 1961, is prefaced by a lengthy excerpt from the Draft Program of the Communist Party of the Soviet Union, entitled "The Bright Future of Mankind," and this "Letter to the Subscribers":

> Dear Readers:
> We transmit into your hands the first issue of the *Sovyetish Heymland*. Here you will feel the breath of our times, be informed of our literary life, hear the voice of the multinational Soviet literature. Being a part of this literature will bring honor to the names inscribed on the title page. We are living in a time when the whole Soviet literature is animated with the ideas with which our whole nation is preparing itself for the Twenty-second Party Congress. . . . [A quotation from one of Khrushchev's speeches about art follows.] Events of gigantic proportions are taking place over the vast expanses of our country. . . . It is [therefore] the holy duty of our writers to find the warm words and lofty feelings appropriate to these historical events.
>
> Solemn are the tasks facing our journal, *Sovyetish Heymland*. It has to illuminate all the aspects of the life of the Soviet nation. . . . The works already submitted to us by Soviet Yiddish writers give us the assurance that this journal will be able to reflect most of the important problems of our time on a high artistic level. The voice of the Soviet Yiddish writers will resound vigorously in the chorus of brotherly literature. . . . The hero of our works is the man who long ago discarded the heavy burden of the past and who is living a creatively productive life together with all builders of Communist society. . . . The fact that Yiddish poets are still deeply interested in poetry is completely in ac-

* Part II of this study, by Abraham Brumberg, contains an analysis of the 1965 issues of *Sovyetish Heymland*.

cord with the experience of the multi-language Soviet literature, which teaches us that great journals flourish in great times. We believe that our critics will pay special attention to the new generation of writers who are now active in Soviet Yiddish literature. These, dear readers, are the immediate goals of the journal *Sovyetish Heymland.*

These opening lines do not clarify whether *Sovyetish Heymland* intends to be a "Jewish" magazine. Its avowed aim is to serve the Soviet nation, to be a part of Soviet—i.e., Communist—literature. It offers its readers "a broad picture of Soviet life"—but what about Jewish life? Judging from the opening statement, one would expect to find nothing in the magazine even remotely connected with Jewish interests. Nevertheless, even the very first issue does contain works of meaningful Jewish content.

The first issue contains contributions by twenty-six Yiddish writers. One of these, L. Vaserman, lives in Birobidjan.[19] One died shortly before the appearance of this issue. Thirteen of the twenty-six were unknown to Yiddish readers in the West. Almost all of them were brought up under Soviet rule. The first issue also includes a fine poem by Alexander Tvardovski called "Siberia," as well as poetry by Alexander Prokofiev and Chingiz Aytamatov from Dagistan—all in Yiddish translation, thus setting a precedent that was to be followed in all subsequent issues. Finally, there is a long article devoted to Vissaryon G. Belinski, the prominent nineteenth-century Russian literary critic and militant liberal, on the occasion of his one hundred fiftieth anniversary.

Most of the writing shows no special tendency to glorify Soviet achievements. On the other hand, there are no themes that may meaningfully be called Jewish. Some are the usual "construction" stories so abundant in Soviet literature during the 1930's and 1940's. Then there are topical contributions, e.g., Dora Haikin's "To the Widow in the Congo" (about Lumumba's widow), Motl Gruvman's poem "Leningrad," an ode to the cosmonaut Yuri Gagarin, and similar contemporary verse about Cuba and the Congo, by Motl Grubyan. The veteran poet Samuel Halkin, who died in 1960, is represented by only one poem, *"Gut Yomtev, Mayn Land"* ("Happy Holiday, My Country"), whose title speaks for itself. Like other Jewish writers, this talented Yiddish poet (born 1897) started his literary career in Hebrew and later turned to Yiddish. Halkin was noted for his deeply Jewish national feelings. Arrested during Stalin's reign of terror, he was released after the dictator's death and allowed to live out his life in comparative peace. According to the editors, Halkin composed "*Gut Yomtev, Mayn Land,*" together with other patriotic poems, shortly before his death.

Then there are some—unfortunately few—honest pieces dealing either with Jewish life before the Revolution, or with the destruction of the Jews during World War II. Outstanding is a poem by Moyshe Teyf, "Song of My Brothers," mourning the fate of East European Jewry. Interestingly enough, the poem contains a reference to Babi Yar, epitomized in the famous poem by Yevgeni Yevtushenko, which has never appeared in translation in *Sovyetish Heymland.* Several other pieces make reference to Babi Yar and similar places of mass execution; there is also a sketch by the non-Jew Boris Prorokov of three women lamenting at a grave. Yet there is no mention made of the fact that Babi Yar was a specifically *Jewish* tragedy. To do so would presumably not have been in accord with the principles of the "multinational" literature of the Soviet Union.

The first issue's literary quality is mediocre. The stories glorify the "positive hero," single-minded in his devotion to Communism. The style is generally in the manner of the stereotyped and tendentious writings of the 1930's and 1940's. The stories sound like translations of Russian stories about collective farms, the Russian names of the heroes simply having been replaced by Jewish ones. The poetry is archaic, rhetorical, and declamatory.

Still, not everything published in the first issue is inferior. Abram Gontar, though writing the usual Soviet platitudes, shows genuine talent in his story "*A Geveynlikhe Mishpokhe*" ("An Ordinary Family"); the same is true of Yosef Rabin in his "Rachel and Her Children." There is also a competent literary essay by Elie Falkovich, a lengthy analysis of the writings of the Yiddish classicists.

A section chronicling the events in Soviet and Yiddish culture—which was to become a regular feature of the magazine—reports on the successful concert tours of the talented Yiddish singer Nehama Lifshitz, which were attended by over 300,000 people, and the tremendous success of the play "*Tevye der Milkhiker*" by Sholom Aleichem, directed by Vladimir Schvartser. We are told of the more than 125 concerts performed all over the Soviet Union by the chorus of Emil Horevits, and of the "cultural exchange" with Israel (limited to concerts performed by Jewish musicians in Israel).

We also find announcements about the antireligious works published in Russian in 1961. One, by the "great atheist" Khivi Habalkhi, which saw the light of day no less than 1,000 years ago, contains sixty-six "scientific" theses denying the divine origin of the Bible. Another book highly praised by the editors of *Sovyetish Heymland,* both for its rich language and erudition, is M. Altshuler's *A Discussion on the Day of Rosh Hashanah,* 100,000 copies of which were published.

With minor exceptions, then, the first issue proved to be a disappointment. As it turned out, the subsequent one was not much better. Again, the lead article was propaganda—this time a greeting to the Twenty-second Congress of the Communist Party of the Soviet Union held in October of that year, followed by Haim Baider's poem "My Party":

> Say but a word, and I am ready again,
> I hear your call and stride toward you.
> Whatever I do, whatever your orders,
> I shall accept them with a serene conscience. . . .

Khrushchev's 1962 campaign to raise more pigs as an inexpensive means of producing more meat is faithfully reflected in a short story by Haim Melamud, "Visiting the Brigade Leader." It tells of an old Jew on a collective farm who, "though not born a Communist," is enthusiastic over his job as a pig-breeder. Max Riant from Birobidjan is poetically proud as he "carries with love the lofty name of the Soviet man."

So it goes, the theme of love and loyalty to the Soviet homeland repeated again and again by the more or less talented contributors. Then, for a fillip, we are given something different, namely, the first part of a hitherto unpublished novel by Sholom Aleichem called *The Mistake*. According to N. Oyslander, one of the editors of the *Sovyetish Heymland,* this novel was never published in full by the Yiddish newspapers in the United States because of Sholom Aleichem's sharply critical attitude towards what he called "the country of business" and the upper strata of American society.[20]

The second issue also contains "Toward New Yiddish Artistic Heights" (*"Tsu Naye Yidish Kinstlerishe Hoykhn"*), an essay by Moshe Notovich. "Partisanship in artistic creation is the basis of Soviet literature," Notovich asserts, and then goes on to praise the first issue of *Sovyetish Heymland* for having clearly shown its devotion to the Communist cause.

An important feature is a list of forty-one Yiddish writers who were killed at the front by the German Army in World War II. (One is thankful to the editors for publishing these names—thus we know that at least these forty-one writers did not simply "disappear.") The second issue's current events department is disappointing. Most of the items bear no relation to Jewish life or culture. Two items are of interest: an announcement of the publication of a book of seventy songs, with lyrics in Russian and in Yiddish; and information about a Yiddish amateur theatrical group organized by the Council of Trade Unions in Vilna five years earlier. The troupe, the magazine informs us, had been enthusiastically received. Its most successful production, *Freylakhs,* devoted to the Twenty-second Congress of the Communist Party, had been performed in Riga as well as Vilna.

Of the issues that followed, the March–April, 1963, issue of *Sovyetish Heymland* deserves special mention in that it devotes an entire section to the twentieth anniversary of the Warsaw Ghetto uprising—in other words, to a singularly *Jewish* event.

The March–April, 1963, issue of *Sovyetish Heymland* is unique in that it devotes an entire section to the twentieth anniversary of the Warsaw Ghetto uprising—in other words, to a singularly *Jewish* event.

Yet, lest there be any misunderstanding, let us point out, first of all, that the section on the uprising is very small indeed. The tone of the issue, which one might have hoped would be *entirely* devoted to this tragic yet heroic chapter in contemporary Jewish history, is introduced by a picture of Lenin on page 1. This is followed by a thirty-page translation of Khrushchev's speech of March 1, 1963, delivered at a meeting of Party and Soviet Government officials with representatives of the Soviet literary and artistic world. Next comes a number of "programmatic" poems, including six by Vergelis, entitled "The Beginning and the End." ("The Beginning" refers to the October Revolution, "The End" to the victory of the Revolution.)

In the *Sovyetish Heymland* version, the uprising was led exclusively by Communists, with Polish workers rendering incalculable help to their Jewish comrades. "The Great Battle Behind the Walls of the Ghetto," by the editor of the Warsaw *Folksshtime,* Hersh Smolyar, manages to mention the name of one non-Communist leader—Mordecai Anilevich, the commander in chief of the Jewish Fighters Organization, and a member of the left-Zionist youth group Hashomer Hatzair. Other political groupings, such as the Socialist Bund, are not only not given credit for their part in the uprising but are maliciously slandered. Smolyar's more remarkable historical reconstructions include the assertion that Polish Communists not only provided the Jewish fighters with ammunition, but actually engaged the Nazis in several diversionary battles near the ghetto walls. He also reports that the Soviet Army helped the Jews by bombarding Warsaw on the night of May 13. (Smolyar seems to have forgotten that the uprising was already over by that time.)

All in all, *Sovyetish Heymland*'s "tribute" to the Ghetto fighters is in incredibly poor taste, mitigated only by the late Peretz Markish's moving poem *"Der Trot fun Doyres"* ("The March of Generations").

The first few issues described above are representative of the bulk of the contributions to *Sovyetish Heymland.* Yet with each successive issue there has been an increase of poems, stories, and novellas bearing little relation to the tedious, stereotyped, and mendacious examples of "socialist realism." Among the authors in this category the following are most prominent: Yosl Rubin, Note Lurye, Shmuel Gordon, Aaron Guntar, Moyshe Teyf, Irme Druker, Shike Druz, Rokhl Boymvol, and Roze Baliasne. The poems by Shike Druz and Rokhl Boymvol, especially those written for children, are particularly impressive.

Two of the stories deserve special mention. Y. Rabin's *"Nit Haynt Gedakht"* ("Heaven Forbid!") describes the fate of a Jewish Communist girl who fled from Poland to the Soviet Union before the war, only to be accused of spying for Poland. The other, by Irme Druker, called *"Der Vilner Balebesl"* ("The Householder from Vilna"), is remarkable for its nostalgic evocation of the Jewish past. The hero, a young cantor with an extraordinarily beautiful voice, makes the acquaintance of a Catholic organist. Through his new friend, he falls under the spell of the "gentile" music of the nineteenth-century Polish composer Stanislaw Moniuszko. Gradually, his cantorial melodies take on the tonalities of the Polish composer, much to the horror of the pious Jews, who eventually oust him from the synagogue. With the help of his organist friend, the cantor obtains a job at the Warsaw Opera House—there to be rejected for "Judaizing" the arias of Moniuszko and other Polish composers. Spurned by both Jew and gentile, the cantor finds himself in a limbo of alienation.

Occasional stories and poems on Jewish themes apart, *Sovyetish Heymland* fulfills its role as a specifically *Jewish* journal by providing its readers, through its regular section on current events, with some information about Jewish cultural life both inside and outside the Soviet Union. We find in this section regular reports on the activities of several choral and dramatic groups in the Soviet Union, mostly itinerant, who draw large and enthusiastic audiences wherever they go, information about translations from the Yiddish that appear in the Soviet Union, and so forth. In addition, "Chronicles" reflects the changing attitude of the editors of *Sovyetish Heymland* toward "bourgeois" Yiddish writers abroad. While the editorial reports are highly selective and hardly give the reader a balanced picture of Yiddish cultural life outside the Soviet Union, they do indicate that it is no longer obligatory for Soviet Yiddish writers to reject out of hand the works of their "capitalist" brethren.

Thus, the editors noted the death in New York of the "great Yiddish poet" H. Leivick (author of *The Golem*) on October 23, 1963; the one hundredth anniversary of the birth of the playwright S. An-sky (author of *The Dybbuk*); the eightieth anniversary of the noted literary critic S. Niger (pejoratively characterized as a "typical representative of Yiddish bourgeois critics in the United States"); and the anniversaries of the novelist I. J. Singer and the poet Mani Leyb (the latter, as "one of the most prominent representatives of American Yiddish poetry"). All of these authors are "safely" dead.

Of particular interest was the observance of the ninetieth anniversary of the outstanding Hebrew-Yiddish poet and dedicated Zionist Haim N. Bialik, previously vilified as a "reactionary nationalist." The fact that *Sovyetish Heymland* now pays its respects to Bialik, rationalizing his writing in Hebrew as "just a question of language," may be a straw in the wind. Another, even more startling example of the same "liberalism" was the noting of the recent seventieth birthday of "the philologist and literary critic" Max Weinreich, the founder of the renowned YIVO Institute for Jewish Research, now living in New York.

In its capacity as the only "representative" of secular Jewish culture in the Soviet Union, *Sovyetish Heymland* plays an important public relations role vis-à-vis the outside world and the non-Jewish public within the Soviet Union. Ever since its inception in 1961, its offices have been the second biggest attraction, after the Moscow synagogue, for the large number of Jewish tourists visiting the Soviet Union. Throughout the year visitors from the United States seek interviews with Vergelis. The latter has shown himself very obliging in this respect, if not always equally candid.

Occasional meetings with Russian writers have been very positive indeed. The editors proudly report: "How well we are accepted by the Russian literary world may be deduced from the number of meetings with Russian authors in the offices of *Sovyetish Heymland*"

(January–February, 1962, and November–December, 1963, issues). The November–December conference with Russian musicians was presided over by no less a personage than Dmitri Shostakovich. At one of the meetings reported in the January–February, 1963, issue, Konstantin Fedin, renowned Russian writer and chairman of the Union of Soviet Writers, offered his congratulations to the editors of, and contributors to, *Sovyetish Heymland.*

Exactly how the Jews in the Soviet Union regard the new Yiddish magazine is hard to tell. One can only surmise that they have accepted it as the best that could be expected under existing circumstances. The serious reservations of one Soviet Jew may be gleaned from "Diary of a Soviet Jew," published anonymously in the May–June, 1963, issue of the American Yiddish monthly *Di Zukunft,* and whose authenticity was vouched for by the editors. A few passages are revealing:

> The office of the editor is a very useful showplace for tourists—Jews and non-Jews alike. Important visitors are told: "Here you have a Yiddish publication. Here you have Jewish editors.". . . Occasionally, a few Yiddish writers and their wives get together, drink tea, and talk about the state of Yiddish literature, etc. . . . I asked one of the editorial staff whether they intended to publish a primer to teach our children to read Yiddish. For we do have many children who would like to learn to read the language. The answer was: "This is not a subject for discussion." . . . I left the office of *Sovyetish Heymland* with a broken heart. I saw there soft chairs, beautiful rooms, but unfortunately, neither Jews nor Jewishness.

Whatever the services *Sovyetish Heymland* performs for the Jews in the Soviet Union, they are inconsequential compared to the services it performs for the Soviet authorities. One of them is undisguised propaganda—wholesale defense of Soviet Jewish policy, and attacks on the "calumnies" printed in the "vicious foreign press." Thus, the November–December, 1963, issue contains a lengthy report of a meeting held at the offices of *Sovyetish Heymland,* attended by "dozens of people, men and women of various occupations, Jews and non-Jews." Here, Aaron Vergelis spoke about the many letters the editors had received from abroad decrying "the great wave of anti-Semitism and racism . . . in West Germany, the United States, Argentina, and other countries." The audience, mostly readers of *Sovyetish Heymland,* expressed its indignation at these deplorable events, then went on to inveigh against the "slanderous campaign directed at the Soviet Union"—that is, the Western press reports of anti-Semitism in Russia. How sensitive the editors of *Sovyetish Heymland,* and, of course, the Soviet authorities, are to this campaign may be gauged from the fact that this gathering was attended by Roman Rakhumov and Gennadli Terakhov, two high officials from the office of the R.F.S.F.R. Procurator (more or less equivalent to the Attorney General's office in the United States). In a speech, Rakhumov referred to Article 123 of the Soviet Constitution as incontrovertible proof that anti-Semitic propaganda was not tolerated in the Soviet Union.[21] Lieutenant-General Hirsh Plaskov, speaking at the same meeting, denied the existence of anti-Semitism by referring to the large number of Jews in high positions in such institutions as the armed forces.

As might be expected, *Sovyetish Heymland* goes to great lengths to "refute" allegations of Soviet anti-Semitism. The September–October, 1963, issue, for example, reports on an article that appeared in the Russian-language publication *Znamia kommunizma* (*Flag of Communism*), attacking Israeli "spies" and tourists who spread "ideological poison" in the Soviet Union. One year later, the editors replied to Bertrand Russell, who had asked the magazine to publish a letter from a Soviet Jew which he had received some time before, apparently containing incriminating information about the situation of Soviet Jews. Since the letter was unsigned, the editors informed Russell they could not publish it. They took advantage of the opportunity to lecture the noted British philosopher (generally well-disposed to the Soviet Union) on the dangers of giving credence to anti-Soviet propaganda. "The real needs of Soviet Jews and Jewish culture," Russell was assured, "are fully satisfied."[22]

Vergelis does not confine himself to the pages of *Sovyetish Heymland*. His articles have appeared in Russian, Ukrainian, and Moldavian newspapers and magazines. To mention two examples:

The October 10, 1963, issue of *Literaturnaia gazeta* printed Vergelis' "New York Lament on the Day of Atonement." In this piece, Vergelis assails the "impudent campaign in the reactionary press abroad" that misrepresents Soviet life, and in particular, the plight of Soviet Jewry. He castigates by name the two largest Yiddish newspapers in New York, the *Jewish Daily Forward* and *The Day-Morning Journal,* as well as Moshe Decter, author of an article in *Foreign Affairs* entitled "The Status of the Jews in the Soviet Union." These "spokesmen" of the Jewish "bourgeoisie," asserts Vergelis, wish "to preserve national identity through a return to the ghetto," allegedly claiming "that the situation of Jews in the Soviet Union is bad because they cannot create the style of life of New York's Williamsburg."

Again, in an article published in the May 16, 1964, issue of *Sovietskaia Moldavia,* submitted at the request of the editors, Vergelis asserts with pained naïveté: "We, Soviet persons of the Jewish nationality, are bewildered when asked to 'prove with facts' that we enjoy the same rights as Russians, Ukrainians, Moldavians, Azerbaijanians, etc."

Given Vergelis' obvious role as propagandist-at-large for the Soviet regime in regard to its Jewish policy, it is not surprising that he was sent on a tour of the United States.

As noted earlier, representatives of the American Jewish community flatly refused to meet with Vergelis in his capacity as "representative of Soviet Jewry"; Vergelis blamed the American rabbinate for his failure to establish a line of communication. The fact is that Vergelis quickly undermined his own mission by a categorical denial of the existence of any Jewish problems in the Soviet Union. Immediately upon arrival in New York, he publicly charged that a campaign was being waged in America over the "so-called Jewish question" in Russia. He then summarized the life of Jews in the Soviet Union as "in a single sentence, the normal life of people in Soviet society."

A reporter from the *New York Herald-Tribune* asked Vergelis why there were no cultural facilities for Jews in the Soviet Union outside of *Sovyetish Heymland*. Vergelis' answer was disingenuous: "They are already integrated. They are satisfied with general Russian culture." Why *Sovyetish Heymland,* then? "There is still an element that reads and loves Yiddish." Apparently, Vergelis did not realize that these two statements were not quite reconcilable.

On his return home, Vergelis wrote a long, largely offensive account of his visit to the United States. "Twenty Days in America" appeared in four successive issues of *Sovyetish Heymland*. Jewish life in America, the editor reported to his Soviet readers, is controlled by rabbis, Zionists, and Jewish capitalists.

As might be expected, *Sovyetish Heymland* follows an explicitly antireligious line. Thus, the March–April, 1962, issue highly recommends Hillel Lifshitz's book *Religion and Church Past and Present,* which devotes a separate, defamatory chapter to Judaism. The magazine has nothing but praise for such books that endeavor to "help those who are still believers to rid themselves of the dangerous influence of religion." The January–February, 1963, issue carries a short story by M. Shulman, *"Untervegs"* ("En Route"), in which the author expresses his distaste for informers—such as the Jew who showed him a number of documents proving the existence of speculation and thievery in the local synagogue. Shulman does not need this evidence; "the facts" are generally widely propagated in the Soviet press: Jewish religious leaders are "money grubbers, parasites, thieves . . . using 'the Temples of God' to hide foreign currency. . . . Yes, we must admit that these 'thieves of God' have made considerable progress in the art of swindling."

Nearly four years of publication of *Sovyetish Heymland* yield a clear picture of the position of Yiddish literature in the Soviet Union. Essentially another Soviet publication wholly dedicated to the Communist cause, it was intended to prove conclusively to the world that Jews and Jewish culture were not being persecuted in the land of "freedom and equality." This was the official line to which staff and contributors had perforce to hew. Yet, despite the controls exerted by the editor, despite the fears that any deviation must surely arouse in every Yiddish writer in the Soviet Union, despite all the ideological exhortations and indirect threats, one finds in the pages of *Sovyetish Heymland* occasional startling passages suffused with longing for a more positive form of Jewish self-identification, lines that bespeak the authors' nostalgia for the Jewish past, for heroes and attitudes that have nothing in common with the stereotyped concepts of "socialist realism." Such are the stories of Jewish martyrdom during the last World War, the descriptions of Jewish heroism in the ghettos and forests of Poland and the Ukraine (though the fighters are always identified with the Communist Party).

It is not difficult to understand the *authors'* fears to write the truth about contemporary Jewish life in the Soviet Union. Yet one wonders whether the *editors* are not perhaps too cautious and oversensitive to possible reprisals from on high. After all, Yevtushenko's "Babi Yar" did appear in a Russian magazine—why not publish it in a Yiddish translation as well? If *Novyi mir* could print such shattering descriptions of Stalinist prison camps as Solzhenitsyn's *One Day in the Life of Ivan Denisovich,* why cannot *Sovyetish Heymland* do the same—especially since so many of the Yiddish writers associated with the magazine have spent a good part of their lives in such camps?

One answer may be that there are few Yiddish writers talented enough to deal with so large a theme. But this, of course, hardly goes to the root of the problem, which is psychological rather than artistic. As many travelers to the Soviet Union have reported, the Soviet Jewish community is perhaps the most cowed national minority in the Soviet Union. Besides the universal scars of Stalinist repressions that disfigure the Soviet people as a whole, the Jews bear the special scars of specifically anti-Jewish repressions. Soviet Jewry lives in constant fear of the revival of those horrors.

The literary value of *Sovyetish Heymland,* as pointed out before, is largely negligible, both for political reasons and because the flower of the Jewish intelligentsia in Russia has been decimated by Stalin's henchmen. The Markishes, Bergelsons, Kulbaks, and Kvitkos are no more, and unless the general Soviet attitude toward the Jewish problem is radically altered, there is little hope that others will come to take their place.

Yet with all the reservations, *Sovyetish Heymland* must still, in the opinion of this author, be judged as a positive phenomenon. And though its literary merits are negligible, occasionally one is struck by a poem or short story that rings with passion and verisimilitude. Its politics are depressing, yet it enables the Yiddish writer in the Soviet Union to be (at least at times) apolitical. It fulfills its function as a weapon of Soviet propaganda, yet it also provides the Soviet Jew with a modicum of cultural self-esteem, and the outside world with a glimpse of Jewish life in the U.S.S.R. It is ideologically dedicated to the assimilation of the Soviet Jews, yet its internal dynamics propel it in the opposite direction. Above all, after years of cultural attrition, after a period that witnessed the annihilation of the most talented representatives of Yiddish letters in the Soviet Union, it offers proof, however pitifully meager, of the enduring vitality of the Jewish spirit.

II

1965: New Winds?

The paper by my late father, which spans the first three years of *Sovyetish Heymland,* ends on a rather despairing note. Although in the final analysis he viewed the only Yiddish journal in the Soviet Union as a "positive phenomenon," it is clear that in his mind the "reservations" concerning the journal's politics, its ideological rationale, and its literary merits far outweighed its significance either as an accurate mirror of Jewish life in Russia, or even as a testimonial to "the enduring vitality of the Jewish spirit"—or put differently, as a literary and social document.

When, in a talk delivered at the Conference on the State of Ethnic Minorities in the Soviet Union, held at Brandeis University in late 1965, I presented what amounted to the quintessence of my father's findings, I was met with considerable criticism by some who felt that I had exaggerated the faults of the magazine and underrated its more laudable features. In doing so, my critics were influenced more by some of the recent issues of *Sovyetish Heymland* than by its previous volumes—more specifically, by *certain* items that have appeared in recent months, than by the magazine as a whole. For it cannot be emphasized too strongly that the first issues of *Sovyetish Heymland* were steeped, by and large, in the kind of "socialist realist" cant that even the most reactionary Soviet Russian journals would be reluctant to display; that its affirmations of the "Jewish spirit" were, unfortunately, few and far between; and that the over-all reaction, therefore, of a critical reader could be only one of sorrow and dismay.

Yet since January, 1965, when *Sovyetish Heymland* began to appear as a monthly—or perhaps more accurately since about April of that year—the journal has begun to move in what might be termed a qualitatively new direction. For reasons that will be explored later, there has been a marked improvement in its literary quality, a more daring political tone, a growing and frequently quite astonishing attempt at broadening the limits of Jewish national identification, and a tendency, however hesitant, to catch up with the achievements of Russia's "liberal" writers and intellectuals. This is not to say that some of these features had not existed before. Their increasing frequency, however, would seem to indicate that a new trend in Soviet Yiddish literature, and perhaps an improvement in the status of Soviet Jews in general, is in the offing. Whatever the final assessment of this trend—and given the realities of Soviet politics and the absence of institutional guarantees for the free cultural expression of the Jewish minority, this assessment is bound to be guarded as well as tentative—it is sufficiently interesting to merit our most careful scrutiny.

It should be emphasized, however, that whatever the improvements made during the past year, the over-all quality of *Sovyetish Heymland* is still abysmally low. What is so striking about the bulk of the contributions is not only the rhetoric, the tendentiousness, the fraudulence and all the other traits that we have come to expect from the practitioners of socialist realism. It is, rather, something more profound and at the same time less definable: a lacklusterness, an insipidness, an absence of vitality, of characterization, of genuine dramatic conflict. Typical in this respect is the novella *"Khavele Gefen,"* by Joseph Rabin (1),* which deals, in a remarkably plotless and colorless way, with the revolutionary events in the city of Vilna during 1917–18. And only in *Sovyetish Heymland* can we find a poem such as this by Abraham Gontar (1):

Vemen geystu alts dertseyln
az geven bist sheyn?
dakht zikh, darfst kartofl sheyln,
zits un sheyl.

(Whom will you tell/that you had been pretty?/It seems you're to peel potatoes/then sit and peel); or, for example, the following poem, written by Chaim Gurevich, and published under the rubric "New Voices" (1). With all the allowances for someone presumably still young and lacking in literary experience, it is so incredibly jejune a performance that one wonders how the editors of *Sovyetish Heymland* had the audacity to publish it. The translation below preserves the unique flavor of the poem, as well as its metric and other prosodic qualities:

In my village near the Pripet, in my dear, sweet home
The air is heavy with aromas of fresh hay and tar.
Mother carries fresh and frothy milk from near-by barn,
And the flowers in the garden are so soft and tender.
Full is our heady orchard—full of plums and pears,
And the stork, like some big planner, sits upon a wheel.
Apple-wine from barrels flows and quenches our thirst,
And *kolkhozniks* wish each other happiness and joy.

Typical of the more pernicious items that still find their way into the pages of *Sovyetish Heymland* is the novella "Today a New World Is Born," by Nathan Zabare (2). Skillfully told, its primitive intellectual content reminds one of the noxious "anti-Western" products of the Stalin-Zhdanov era rather than of even the most mediocre works of contemporary Soviet fiction. The locale is postwar Berlin, the protagonists are American officers working in cahoots with ex-Nazis, and the heroes are the Soviet military who eventually succeed in exposing a German-American black-market ring. As an example of the author's familiarity with American customs, the following description of "the coctail" (*sic*) mixed by an American will

* Numerals in parentheses refer to monthly issues of 1965.

suffice: "He had his own recipe. Only he knew the secret of how much whisky, how much gin and vermouth, and how much clean alcohol to mix into the drink."[23] In addition, there is also the inevitable gum-chewing American colonel who addresses his lieutenant as "Mr. Mike," refers to General Marshall as "Mister Marshall," and who delivers himself of the following oration on American aims in the postwar world:

> We Americans respect and value thrifty people, people who understand that life here, in Europe, is a battleground, a war, a war that is greater than one between two armies. Business is the weapon now. The best soldier is the golden [!] dollar, and it is these soldiers who will win the mightiest victory. All the struggles which we are engaged in all over the globe will be determined by money, by the dollar, and we shall benefit from it. We shall be victorious.

In yet another vein, though still in the same category, is "A Simple Story," by Tevye Geyn (6)—incidentally one of the stanchest among the Yiddish "conservatives"—which describes the joys of a group of young people off to work in the distant regions of the Soviet Far East. To see the profound differences between a person of Geyn's persuasion and those of some of Russia's new leading writers, one need only compare Geyn's description of Soviet youths—dedicated, enthusiastic, disarmingly naïve and forthright—with the characters of the novels by Vasily Aksionov (e.g., in *A Ticket to the Stars*) or Yuri Kazakov. It is also instructive to compare the *programmatic* statements by the editors of and some contributors to *Sovyetish Heymland* with editorial statements in *Novyi mir*.[24] Again, this is not a matter of *Weltanschauungen* diametrically opposed to each other. Among the Russian writers there are many hacks à la Geyn, and among Yiddish writers the "liberals," no doubt, predominate. But whereas there are dozens of Russian literary magazines, there is only *one* Yiddish journal, edited, moreover, by a man whose natural inclinations are more akin to those of a Gribachov or Sofronov[25] (even though these luminaries of crypto-Stalinism are notorious anti-Semites) than to those of Tvardovski (editor of *Novyi mir*) or, for that matter, Ehrenburg. It may be maintained with considerable justification that, currently, the Party has no consistent policy, that the struggle between the "conservative" and the "liberal" intellectuals is a reflection of a similar struggle at the top echelons of the Party, or that, for one reason or another, the Party has decided to leave the conflicting issues unresolved. Statements by Vergelis *et al.*, however, about "the tasks of Soviet Yiddish literature" carry the uncomfortable ring of official approval.[26]

Nevertheless, whether or not the Yiddish "liberal" writers have had the blessings of Vergelis, they have made considerable gains within the past year. Let us, then, turn to the areas in which the most salient changes have taken place.

This area embraces, first and foremost, what might be termed bona fide literary criticism: discussion and controversy over matters of style and substance where the hallowed principles of "party-mindedness" or other aesthetic dogmas are not invoked, and perhaps deliberately disregarded. For instance, issue No. 10 carried a rather remarkable exchange between a reader of *Sovyetish Heymland* who objected to certain linguistic aberrations in the memoirs of Itsik Kipnis (which appeared in the first issue) and one M. Shapiro, identified as a Candidate of Philological Sciences. The reader raised a number of grammatical and lexical problems, all of which were analyzed by the respondent with commendable objectivity and an impressive grasp of the subject matter. In the same issue we also find an interesting note about a work by Moyshe Beygun in Russia's first Yiddish-language publication, *Kol Mevaser* (1862–72), written by Beygun's grandson, Alexander Drobinski. Yet another example is an article reprinted from the Warsaw Yiddish monthly *Yidishe Shriftn,* which deals with "the oldest verse in Yiddish," a recently discovered manuscript dating from the thirteenth century (8). These examples may not strike the reader as particularly exceptional, yet when one remembers that it was not very long ago that any deviation from the "class-conscious" approach to literary matters was virtually equated with treason, it becomes clear that a respectable literary discussion in the pages of *Sovyetish Heymland* is no mean accomplishment.

In dealing with questions of literary scholarship or history, the authors frequently—albeit indirectly—refer to names, works, or concepts that had at one time been officially proscribed, thus in effect contributing to the resurrection and rehabilitation of the Yiddish literary tradition *in toto*. This tendency has already been described in the first part of this study, but in view of its more pronounced character a few illustrations seem to be called for.

Item: An otherwise routine bibliographical review, which demands greater accuracy and comprehensiveness from Soviet Yiddish literary historians, refers, in passing, to the late historian Y. Shatski, the American historian M. Kossover, and the Yiddish philologist Yudl Mark (now living in the United States).

Item: The above-mentioned reprint from *Yidishe Shriftn* contains a laudatory reference to Max Weinreich.

Item: "Literary Notes," by Oizer Holdes (5), refers, *inter alia,* to the American Yiddish writers and poets H. Leivick, Moyshe Leyb Halperin, Joseph Opatoshu, and Moyshe Nadir, all of whom had at one time flirted and subsequently broken with Communism, the last one after the Nazi-Soviet Pact—surely, the writer adds, with perhaps more than unconscious grimness, because he did not understand its "true significance." The same essay also contains a reinterpretation of the second part of Stalin's famous dictum "socialist in content, national in form," defining it so broadly as to include not only language (lexicography, syntax, folklore, etc.), but also "traditions that reveal the psychology of the masses." Since at least a considerable segment of the Jewish masses had been traditionally considered to be infested with "petty-bourgeois mentality" and "clericalism," Holdes' reinterpretation may not be without significance.[27]

Item: Issues 2 and 3 include a re-evaluation of the literary historian I. Tsinberg, by Hillel Aleksandrov, plus a selection of Tsinberg's correspondence with, among others, A. G. Leyeles (the American Yiddish poet and essayist, who died in 1967) and Joseph Opatoshu. In a commentary on this series (10), M. Notorovich paid warm tribute to the great scholar "whom the cult of personality did not spare," noting that the series cannot be read "without emotion."

The tendency—*pace* Mr. Vergelis—to increase the latitude of tolerance toward Yiddish literature in all its aspects would not be so noteworthy did it not coincide with an even more unusual demand for a fuller grant of recognition to Hebrew and Hebrew literature. Characteristically, this demand is usually voiced under the guise of respectable ideological formulas. Thus in a review of the second volume of *The Short Literary Encyclopedia* (in Russian), the critic L. Podriadchik chastises the authors of the article on Jewish literature for paying insufficient attention to Hebrew literature in which, after all, the "socialist ideas" of the nineteenth century were first expressed.[28]

However, the ideological rationale is not always present: Even in the above-mentioned review there are several excellent pages devoted to Hebrew literature of the Middle Ages, and in issues 6 and 7 we find translations from the works of Hebrew poets of the Spanish epoch, among them Yehuda Halevi and Moshe Ibn Ezra.[29] More than that: Issue No. 10 carries a slightly abbreviated translation of the introduction to and a chapter from *Biblical Legends* by a Polish Biblical scholar, Zenon Kosidowski, in which parts of the Old Testament (especially Genesis) are subjected to a refreshingly sensible historical interpretation, free of the usual Marxist-Leninist jargon.[30] Of more contemporary significance are occasional notes in the "Chronicles," dealing with anniversaries of modern and/or contemporary Hebrew writers, e.g., a note on the eightieth birthday of I. D. Berkovich, Sholom Aleichem's son-in-law, who has been living in Israel since 1928.

The growing recognition of the place of Hebrew in Jewish letters has also been accompanied by an attempt to liberate Soviet Yiddish literature from its ideological hostility to Hebraisms. This hostility had at one time led to ridiculous excesses,[31] but its residue lingers on. This is borne out by Oizer Holdes in his aforementioned "Literary Notes," where he explicitly pleads for an end to old prejudices and for a more judicious approach to the place of Hebraisms in modern Yiddish. Similarly—and indeed more explicitly—the authors of a warm tribute to the Soviet Yiddish linguist Elie Spivak ("a victim, in 1949, of the cult of personality"), single out Spivak's criticism of those who regarded Hebraisms exclusively as expressions of "religious-spiritual" concepts. "It is thus absolutely incorrect," the authors state, "to be against Hebraisms in general," a position "fully in accord with the current practice in our literary language."

There is no doubt that the "current practice" in Soviet Yiddish literature conforms to this principle, so much so, in fact, that some writers have taken to employing Hebrew words in a demonstrative manner. Thus an eighteen-line poem by Moyshe Teyf, published in issue No. 10, is replete with startling rhymes, pairing both standard and more unusual Hebraisms with words either of Slavic or Germanic origin or with other Hebraisms (e.g., *boydemer—hisboydedes, oytsres —melyoytsen, meshuge-shures*). Perhaps the most impressive use of traditional Yiddish folk idiom is made by the elderly Yiddish writer Yekhiel Shraybman.

The growing appreciation of Hebrew, as well as the new flowering of a traditional Yiddish idiom, which is used to evoke the once-despised milieu of a *shtetl,* are all reflections of an intense desire to forge a bond with the Jewish community at large, both in space and in time. This is more than a matter of nostalgia. Rather, it is a deliberate, though understandably cautious, attempt to broaden the area of national self-expression, to remove those doctrinal fiats that at one time tended to tear Yiddish literature from its historic roots and reduce it to a feeble component of "homogenized" Soviet culture. How far this process will be allowed to go is an open question. A few examples, however, will suffice to demonstrate its current viability.

Item: Officially, religion is as much an "opiate" now as it was in the past. Yet in Samuel Gordon's novella "Spring" (6) we find a moving description of a Jewish soldier who, in the midst of the war, on the night of Yom Kippur, is irresistibly drawn to a synagogue. "To avoid going to a synagogue altogether was unpleasant. Father used to go, so did grandfather. . . . Why shouldn't he go? Should he be the one to give it up altogether?" In the synagogue, the Red Army soldier is transfixed by the sight of a man lost in prayer: "He couldn't make out the words of the prayer, each of which was followed by a wail that seemed to split the heavens. There was no submissiveness in that prayer. A mighty oak, buffeted by a storm, stood before him. Proud and mighty, with the lingering light of the candles upon him, he took his God to task."

Item: The official line is that Jews are not a distinctive "international" people. It is a dogma that, however inconsistently applied at various periods of Soviet history, remains in force today no less than it had been under Lenin and Stalin. In light of this formula, a (generally unfavorable) review of Hannah Arendt's *Eichmann in Jerusalem* (6), in which the verdict on the "revolting criminal . . . who had caused the Jewish people [*not* "masses"] so much unspeakable suffering" is passionately approved, is probably not devoid of significance. Even more revealing was a brief review of the *Atlas of the Peoples of the World,* published by the Ethnological Institute of the U.S.S.R. Academy of Sciences, which gave the author an opportunity to inform his readers that there is a total of 15 million Jews throughout the world (9).

Item: The official Soviet attitude on Yiddish schools remains decidedly negative. So is the official attitude of *Sovyetish Heymland.*[32] In issue No. 7, however, we find a poignant memoir by Samuel Ortenberg, in which he describes the visit of the dean of early "proletarian" Yiddish poets, Morris Vinchevski, to a Yiddish school in the Ukraine in 1925. The elderly poet, the writer recalls, was moved to tears by the sight of Jewish children reciting his poems.

Item: Officially, *Sovyetish Heymland* was established only and exclusively in order to satisfy the needs of a small segment of the Soviet Jewish population that still regards Yiddish as its mother tongue. This position, it would seem, implies that there is no room for promotional campaigns, as it is in the nature of such campaigns to create or at least to *stimulate* interest and curiosity, rather than merely to satisfy it. One wonders how this principle is congruent with a letter by one David Peskin, published in issue No. 11, and the editorial reply to it. Mr. Peskin, who described himself as a dedicated friend and disseminator of "the Soviet book in general and the Yiddish in particular," admonished the editors for not doing enough to raise the circulation of the magazine. Somewhat sheepishly, the editors assured their correspondent that a series of "broad measures" were now being undertaken with a view not only to "reach those who wish to read the magazine," but also to win "new readers and new public disseminators."

Perhaps no issue has rocked the Soviet literary world in recent years as much as the question of how to assess and how much to reveal about the Stalin era in Soviet history. The most famous novel on the Stalinist terror is, of course, Solzhenitsyn's *One Day in the Life of Ivan Denisovich*. Yet this has not been the only work that has tried to portray the horrors of the past. Despite attempts of the guardians of official orthodoxy either to limit the publication of such works, or at least to portray the victims of Stalinism as stalwart Bolsheviks who remained loyal to their Party in the face of all adversities,[33] there has been an increasing outpouring of novels, memoirs, and short stories on the Stalinist era, most of them sympathetic to the "little man," the hapless victim of circumstances, the "anti-hero," rather than to the spurious "positive hero" demanded by the die-hard "conservatives."

Given the special circumstances of Jewish life in Russia, it is not surprising that this subject would long remain taboo for Yiddish writers. Yet the ferment in the Soviet literary arena at large, combined with the need to "tell the truth"—a need felt most acutely by Jews, who more than other ethnic groups in the Soviet Union had felt the full brunt of Stalinist brutality—has now brought about a breakthrough in this area, too. The process has been slow, halting, and not without contradictions. Thus in "Pages from My Life," by Itsik Kipnis (1) (who suffered both under the onslaught of the Yevsektsia and under Stalin for his incurable sin of "bourgeois nationalism"),[34] one finds a pathetic mixture of standard rhetoric, poignant recollections of and tributes to Yiddish writers who perished under Hitler—but not a word about the author's own years in Soviet prisons and concentration camps. Similarly, in the welter of memoirs about Yiddish writers exterminated by Stalin one looks in vain for descriptions of their arrests and subsequent fates. At best there will be one barren sentence: So-and-so "fell victim to the cult of personality"—or more boldly: "to the cult of Stalin."[35]

Nevertheless, the subject of purges, arrests, and terror during the Stalin era is no longer avoided by Yiddish writers. These matters are referred to, for instance, in Note Lurye's novel *The Sky and the Earth.* In "After the Golden Peacock," by Rive Baliasne (6), there is a harrowing description of the persecution, arrest, and confinement of a woman because her father was a member of the bourgeoisie (even though he had left for America when she was a mere child). The main character of this novella is a simple woman, incapable of feats of heroism. At the same time, the novella contains passages that probably sanitize it against possible attacks by the official critics: e.g., a portrait of an old Bolshevik, a woman who, though paralyzed and subjected to indignities, remains true to her faith. The author also suggests that the terror was not really characteristic of those years: "Everywhere the people built, the people worked; *that* was the luminous sign of the times" (italics added).

Quite a different note is struck in the short story *"Di Untershte Shure* (loosely, "The Summing Up"), by Noyekh Lurye (not to be confused with Note Lurye). Indeed, this is a work that deserves the highest praise both for its literary merits and its uncompromising honesty about the crimes of the Stalin era. There is nothing specifically Jewish about this story, nothing, in fact, that would prevent it from being published in one of the Russian "liberal" journals. Yet the fact that it did appear in *Sovyetish Heymland,* and that the editors saw fit to indicate that the manuscript had been gathering dust for nearly a decade (it was written in November–December, 1956), may possibly augur well for future works in the same genre.

The story is simple: Alexander Yosifovich Braslavski, a man in his late fifties, lives with his son in a large Russian city. Though not a member of the Party, it transpires that he had nevertheless been an active informer under Stalin, and had even denounced—and thus caused the death of—a childhood friend of his, Borya Maryasin. Not that Braslavski had really understood what was happening during that "typhus of 1937," yet the less he understood, "the stronger were his professions of faith, the more pious were his words, and the more frequently did his ecstasy shine through them." In 1955, his brain reels under the impact of even more inexplicable events—the rehabilitation of former "enemies of the people," the return of thousands upon thousands of concentration camp inmates, each with a more agonizing story of his personal experiences to be told to relatives and friends who had long given him up as dead.

It is clear that Braslavski is *not* overcome with pangs of conscience and that the feeling of guilt is alien to him. He is simply confused, disturbed, dismayed, and, above all, lonely. His son, apparently having gotten wind of his father's erstwhile "profession," avoids him; their relations are at a breaking point. He is ostracized by his friends. In desperation, he seeks out the widow of his one-time friend and victim Borya Maryasin, who seems to be unaware of the role he had played in her husband's death. During one of these visits, he meets another returnee, also a former friend of Maryasin, who had been with the latter in the same camp. Apparently (though this is never made quite clear) he *does* know of Braslavski's denunciation. Braslavski's dismay turns to panic. His loneliness increases and becomes almost unbearable.

Shortly thereafter, he hears that Maryasin's widow has died, and he attends a commemorative ceremony in her honor. Upon hearing the words of a speaker ("She embodied the gentlest qualities of the new Soviet man"), he is overcome with joy: "Platitudinous words of eulogy!" Upon returning home that night, he tells his son of the widow's death, and in an attempt to dispel his son's suspicions (which had never been voiced openly), he informs him that Maryasin, curiously enough, had several friends with rhyming names—Braslavski, Zaslavski, Varshavski. . . . The son grasps at this stratagem, and their relations improve. But the father's fear and discomfiture are not easily assuaged, and a few nights later he rises from his bed, takes a sheet of paper, and pens a letter to the late widow—a desperate *cri de coeur:* "Anya, Anya! Anya, light of my heart, my good Anya, do not reject me, do not punish me! I am all alone, I have no one. No one, no one except you. Do not turn away! Help me!" He rises again, numbly searches for a place to "put away the unusual letter for which there was no address," and finally inserts it among the yellowed pages of a book that, twenty years ago, had concealed his reports on conversations and copies of denunciations to the police. "It was there that he inserted the written pages, and then, after wrapping the volume in a newspaper and putting a string around it, he hid it in some corner, out of the way, so no one would see it." And thus the story ends.

I have already spoken of the devices employed by Yiddish writers to communicate their views, feelings, the use of Aesopian language, the introduction of novel concepts under the guise of ideological respectability, etc. A few more words on this subject seem to be called for, primarily with regard to poetry, which by its very nature lends itself better than any other medium to the use of the symbol, the innuendo, and the allusion.

Parenthetically, it should be noted that the general quality of the poetry appearing in *Sovyetish Heymland* (a selection of which was published in 1965 in *Horizontn fun der Hayntsaytiker Yidisher Dikhtung*) is depressingly mediocre. It suffices to compare the poetry in the anthology *A Shpigl Oyf a Shteyn* (*A Mirror on a Stone*) with the poems in *Sovyetish Heymland* to realize the enormous chasm that separates the giants of Soviet Yiddish literature, e.g., Leyb Kvitko, Moyshe Kulbak, Izi Kharik, and David Hofshteyn, from the present representatives of Yiddish poetry in Russia. The differences go far beyond the choice of subjects or themes.

Contemporary Yiddish poetry in Russia, whatever its shortcomings, does offer important clues to the emotional and intellectual climate of Soviet Jewry in general. It would not seem to be fortuitous that side by side with the usual hosannas to "socialist construction," the primitive affirmations of Soviet patriotism, we find a significant number of poems in which the themes of old age, grief, sadness, melancholy, anxiety—in short, the private world of the poet—predominate. This emphasis on highly individualistic themes, so strikingly at odds with the traditional specious note of collective optimism, is by itself testimony to the greater self-assertiveness and passion for verisimilitude on the part of Soviet Yiddish writers. At times, however, the themes, though expressed in an indirect fashion, become considerably bolder. Could one, for instance, mistake the meaning of the following poem by Mendl Lifshitz (3):

Ikh far zikh darf gornit hobn,
far di fraynd darf ikh a velt.
Oyfgrobn, vos iz fargrobn,
Oyfdekn, vos iz farshtelt.

(For myself I yearn for nothing/for my friends—the world at large./ Excavate what has been buried/rip the veil from what's been veiled.)

With every new issue of *Sovyetish Heymland,* there are more and more implicit references to past sufferings, often coupled with expressions of hope that they have gone forever. At times the tone is one of passivity, as in this poem by David Bromberg (6):

Bay mir shoyn demolt iz/dos lebn sheyn un zis/
un alts arum iz lib mir/un iz tayer/
ven s'shpalt zikh nit di erd/unter di fis
un s'shit zikh funem himl nit/keyn fayer.

(Life for me is sweet and beautiful, and all that surrounds me is dear to me if the earth no longer splits under my feet and no fire rains from the skies.)

Or by the same author, referring to his five-year-old grandson:

Ver mit zayn heym geven iz lang tsesheydt
der vet farshteyn mayn tsiterdike freyd.

(He who had long been separated from his home will understand my trembling joy.)

Yet occasionally—very occasionally—a note of anger in protest is sounded, as in this poem by M. Grubyan, called "My Bonfire":

Nit bam himl/kh'vel betn/oysbrenen fun haldz/di lid fun mayn langn tsorndikn veg/vos farfolgt mikh un plogt/ikh vel aleyn/vi a hogl/zi tsetretn/baynakht vel ih a shtern/a rayb ton in shukh/un a shayter tsetsindn—/far di, vos hobn a veg/durkh groyl un fintsternish gezukht/ zol zey likhtik zayn/vi bay tog!

(I shall not implore the skies/to burn out/the song of my long and furious road/from my throat/the song which follows and haunts me/ I myself shall stamp it out, like hail/At night I shall/rub a star in my shoe/and light a bonfire/for those who sought a path/through horror and darkness/let the light, as by day, shine upon them!)

The most impressive poem of all, though not necessarily artistically the best, is "Moloch," by Hirsh Osherovich (3). It is the only poem of an allegorical nature that has appeared thus far, and one that may surely be read as a parable on the stark horror of the Stalin era. In choosing as his subject the Phoenician god who demanded the periodic sacrifice of children, the poet succeeds in evoking the bestiality and insanity of that chapter in Soviet history, fulminating against those who had brought it into being:

Vey tsu di, velkhe bashafn
zayendik bahersht fun shrek!

(Woe to those who create/when possessed by fear.)

After the inhabitants of the land turn in anger against Moloch and the orgy of destruction is over, the poet exclaims:

Neyn, nit dikh—dem glomp fun ayzn
undzer blindkayt shlogn mir!

(No, not you, you lump of iron/our blindness we now scourge!)

For a final example, let us turn to a review of two anthologies of Yiddish literature published in Israel, one specifically devoted to Soviet Yiddish prose, and the other partly to Soviet Yiddish poetry (10). What is unique about this review is not only its mild, and indeed even generous, attitude toward the editors of the two anthologies, who can hardly be suspected of pro-Soviet bias, but its almost transparent use of irony and sarcasm with regard to "official" truth. "Unfortunately," says the critic, with singular restraint, "the assessment of the most important developments in Soviet Yiddish poetry, and of individual poets [in the anthology of poetry] is not devoid of tendentiousness and false conceptions." After indignation, high comedy: "The compiler tries to prove that, ostensibly, Soviet Yiddish poets came into conflict with the policy of the Soviet Government, which, ostensibly, impeded the free development of their creativity. He does not understand that it was precisely their loyalty to the policy of the Soviet Government and of the Communist Party that constituted the strength of Yiddish poetry." "Ostensibly!" "Precisely!" Or the following passage from an otherwise highly laudatory review of the anthology of Soviet Yiddish prose: "In keeping with anti-Soviet propaganda, D. Knani [the editor of the anthology] goes out of his way to discover a special 'Jewish question' in the U.S.S.R." As if to underline the absurdity of this accusation, the reviewer follows it immediately with the following comment: "The anthology contains a brief yet conscientiously compiled bio- and bibliographical section on the life and work of the writers represented in it (compiled by Khone Shmeruk)."

Khone Shmeruk, Professor of Literature at the Hebrew University of Jerusalem, is a distinguished literary historian and the author of numerous works on Soviet Yiddish literature, among them (in collaboration with others) the afore-mentioned *A Mirror on a Stone*. This writer is not familiar with the work reviewed in *Sovyetish Heymland,* but if its bibliographical section is anything like the one in *A Mirror on a Stone,* then it most decidedly reveals the existence of "a special Jewish question in the U.S.S.R.," and the reviewer's criticism thus constitutes a remarkable tribute to the objectivity of an anti-Communist scholar.

Having dealt with the new trends in *Sovyetish Heymland* over the past year or so, I am left with the uncomfortable feeling of having given an impression of vast and radical changes, of a fundamental departure from the principal features that had characterized the journal in the first three years of its existence. At the risk of repeating myself, let me therefore stress once more that these new tendencies are reflected in only a very minor portion of the works that have appeared in *Sovyetish Heymland* since January, 1965, and that the majority of the short stories, novels, poems, and critical reviews (though this is less true of the last category) are still of a blatantly inferior quality, aesthetically or otherwise. For evidence the reader need only turn to issue No. 12. Its contents would almost lead one to suspect that the editors had become somewhat alarmed by the tenor of the earlier issues (especially No. 10), and, in an attempt to imbue the journal with the proper "balance," filled its literary sections with predictably safe items: monotonously enthusiastic reportage from various areas of the Soviet Union, as well as fiction and poetry in the same genre. Thus Moyshe Altman in his short story "A Day of Rest": "Humanity had had Athens and Jerusalem, Rome and Paris; philosophy and art which had risen to the heights of philosophy; morality which became transmuted into great passionate poetry; revolutionary pathos of the folkmasses, which had erupted and was subsequently stifled. . . . Now humanity has the essence of humanism—Moscow. And Moscow is the harmony of all spiritual forces and the powerful march towards the future. Moscow. . . . Who among us is able to praise thee, to praise thee?" The only exception to this tedium are several poems by Shloyme Roytman, one of the most genuinely talented poets writing in Yiddish today.

Yet despite the inconsistencies, the zigzags, and the relative paucity of what others, in referring to Russian literature of the post-Stalin era, have described as its "dissonant voices," these voices *have* made themselves heard increasingly over the past year. We are therefore justified in posing the questions "Why?" and "What do they augur for the future?"

The answers are unavoidably speculative. Nevertheless, they deserve to be considered. First, the decision to publish *Sovyetish Heymland* on a monthly rather than bimonthly basis and the partial "liberalization" of its contents are, it would seem, the result of a basic decision of Soviet authorities to liberalize their policy toward Soviet Jews in general. Thus we have recently seen a conspicuous diminution in the volume and virulence of "anti-Judaistic"—that is, antireligious—works published in the Soviet Union; a marked disappearance of pejorative references to Jewish "economic criminals"; the partial lifting of the ban on matzoth-baking; and on the positive side, specific condemnations of anti-Semitism, one in *Pravda* of September 5, 1965, and one in a speech delivered by Premier Kosygin in Riga on July 18, 1965. In the cultural sphere, the innovations in *Sovyetish Heymland* have been accompanied by the publication of three Yiddish books: the aforementioned anthology of poetry; *Azoy Lebn Mir,* a rather depressing collection of essays, mostly reprinted from *Sovyetish Heymland,* about Jewish life in the Soviet Union;[36] *Erev* (*On the Eve*), by Elie Shekhtman, an exceptionally well-written novel set in Russia circa 1905, which had previously been serialized in *Sovyetish Heymland.* In addition, in 1965, the amateur Yiddish artistic ensemble in Vilna was formally recognized as a "People's Theater" (along with groups performing in other languages) by official decree.

This shift in Soviet policy toward the "nonexistent" Jewish problem was motivated by and large by the same considerations that were responsible for the decision to publish *Sovyetish Heymland* in the first place, namely by an effort to counter the adverse effects that years of quasi-official repression and discrimination have had on liberal, "progressive," and even Communist public opinion in the West. In recent years, largely as a result of the publication of Kichko's *Judaism Without Embellishment* in 1963, and the odious attacks on Jews in connection with the "anti-economic crimes" campaign in 1961–64, public criticism of Soviet injustices toward the Jews has, if anything, increased. The continuing demands for an end to all forms of persecution, direct as well as indirect, the condemnation of the treatment of the Jewish minority, especially in the context of rights granted to other, less numerous nationalities, have all contributed to the improvement of the status of Soviet Jews in the legal sphere and in matters of religious and cultural rights. It may be assumed, in fact, that Vergelis has argued for at least a few token concessions, if only to improve his own position vis-à-vis his critics abroad. There is a note of quiet triumph, for instance, in his report on a conversation with someone he met during a recent visit to France: "In response to the criticism that no Yiddish books have been published in the Soviet Union, I answered briefly: We are embarking upon just such a publication program. Soon our readers will receive their first presents from the talented vanguard of Yiddish Soviet writers." (8)

There is another factor, too, and that is the inexorable dynamics of a process once set in motion. Just as in Soviet arts and literature in general the "thaw" began rather hesitantly, gaining momentum when it became clear that the authorities were not decidedly opposed to it, so in the sphere of Yiddish culture one small victory leads to another, each encouraging further attempts, each contributing to a lessening of fear and to a more permissive political atmosphere.[37]

The very existence of a magazine in Yiddish is in itself a spur for writers who had either given up in despair or had written "for the drawer" (and the dates in the *Horizontn* anthology offer clear testimony that even during the most repressive years of Stalinist terror some Yiddish authors continued to write). "I don't think I am exaggerating," noted the novelist Note Lurye at a four-day conference on Soviet Yiddish prose, "when I say that numerous works that have recently enriched our literature had come to life as a result of the appearance of *Sovyetish Heymland.* For example, I began writing my novel *The Sky and the Earth* when, as good fortune had it, our magazine was born. This applies to almost all of our prose writers, who with their works have demonstrated that they have something to say." Only four years earlier on a visit to a branch of the public library in Odessa, I found that Lurye's novels, as well as all other Yiddish books, had been untouched since 1948 and were sequestered in a "spetsotdiel," a special section inaccessible to the reading public because of "lack of space." *Sovyetish Heymland* has thus given Lurye and all those who have "demonstrated that they have something to say" a new lease on life. There is no doubt that the decision to widen the latitude of freedom of expression still further has had an encouraging effect on the many Yiddish writers who had so long been denied access to their public.

What, then, of the future? Regrettably, there is still no cause for too much optimism. This is not simply because the improvements are meager, and the volume of creditable works slender. Nor is optimism precluded simply because the most talented Yiddish writers in the Soviet Union have been ruthlessly destroyed. The immense social calamities of the past did not succeed in stopping the spiritual and cultural progress of the Jewish people. It is rather that all these factors, *combined* with the fundamental insecurity of Jews in the Soviet Union, with the lack of institutional safeguards for free cultural self-expression, and with the lack of sympathy (if not outright hostility) of the Soviet authorities to any *meaningful* expansion of cultural activities (e.g., Yiddish schools) and to the very concept of national self-preservation, produce a situation in which the unhampered flourishing of any manifestation of the Jewish tradition is well-nigh impossible. One example of the difficulties faced by Yiddish writers in the Soviet Union, all recent concessions notwithstanding, will serve to illustrate this point: The January, 1965, issue of *Sovyetish Heymland* had announced that six Yiddish books would be published in 1965. Only three have been published thus far, and in pitifully small editions at that. Furthermore, it seems clear that these volumes have been published primarily for external consumption;

some of them were practically unobtainable in the Soviet Union months after they had officially seen the light of day.[38]

The slowly awakening self-confidence of the Jewish intelligentsia and the literary and political achievements they have scored, however meager, deserve both sympathy and approval. Yet it would be foolish to overestimate their importance. Gogol's publication, in 1842, of *Dead Souls* was not a reflection of Czar Nicholas I's intention to depart from his repressive policies. Russian literature in the nineteenth century was subjected to far less rigorous censorship (especially in *aesthetic* terms) under the Czars than under the Soviets. Was the former, then, to be necessarily preferred to the latter?

Turning again to the Soviet experience, the post-Stalin "protest literature" of 1954–56 was followed by a severe tightening of the reins in 1957, and the renewed permissiveness of 1960–62 was superseded by a violent onslaught of the combined forces of the Party and cultural reactionary forces from which the liberals have not yet fully recovered.[39] The 1966 trial of two distinguished Soviet literary critics and translators, Andrei Sinyavsky and Yuli Daniel, on charges of having published (under the pen names, respectively, of Abram Tertz and Nikolai Arzhak) "vicious anti-Soviet works" abroad, demonstrates how far the Soviet regime is from any meaningful conception of artistic and literary freedom.[40] All of which is not merely to underscore the problems faced by all decent and creative forces in the Soviet Union, but keeping in mind the special situation of Soviet Jews, to emphasize the *special* difficulties faced by Russia's Yiddish-speaking intelligentsia. In the last analysis, their fate is intimately bound up with the fate of the Soviet intelligentsia in general. Every step forward by the latter is followed, however belatedly, by half a step forward by their Yiddish-speaking colleagues. Conversely, however, each step backwards for the Russian intellectuals inevitably results in a two-step-backward reversal for the Jews. At best, then, *Sovyetish Heymland* is a distorted mirror of Soviet reality. But it is there that one must look for clues to the future of Yiddish culture in the U.S.S.R.

NOTES

1. R. A. Abramovich, in *Algemeyne Entsiklopedye in Yidish* (*General Encyclopedia in Yiddish*), Vol. Yidn–D (New York, 1950), pp. 388–89.
2. C. S. Kazhdan, in *The Jewish People, Past and Present* (New York, 1945), II, 133.
3. Solomon Schwarz, *The Jews in the Soviet Union* (Syracuse, N.Y., 1951), pp. 205–7.
4. See Sh. Katcherginsky, *Tsvishn Hamer un Serp* (*Between Hammer and Sickle*) (Buenos Aires, 1950), pp. 55–114. See also, Schwarz, *op. cit.*, pp. 205–7.
5. Jacques Fernier, "Judaism with Embellishment," *Problems of Communism,* XIII, No. 6 (November–December, 1964), 46.
6. V. I. Lenin, "The Bund's Position Within the Party," *Iskra,* October 22, 1903.
7. V. I. Lenin, as quoted in Schwarz, *op. cit.*, p. 53; see also, pp. 241–56.
8. As quoted in a press release on the "Report of an International Socialist Study Group on the Situation of Jews in the Soviet Union," April 15, 1964, p. 4.
9. Nikolai Gribachov, in *Krokodil* (Moscow), February 20, 1953.
10. See Vergelis' introduction to Sholom Aleichem, *Geklibene Shriftn* (*Selected Works*) (Moscow, 1959).
11. See *Leksikon fun der Nayer Yidisher Literatur* (*Biographical Dictionary of Modern Yiddish Literature*) (New York, 1964), III, 497–98.
12. According to *Pechat v SSSR v 1962 godu* (*The Press in the USSR in 1962*), the Udmurt nationality group, with a population of 625,000, had nine newspapers; Mari (504,000), seven newspapers; Komi and Komi-Permiaks (431,000), two newspapers; Chechen (419,000), four newspapers; and Yakut (237,000), ten newspapers and magazines. The print-run of *Sovyetish Heymland* is 25,000 copies.
13. *Ogoniok* (Moscow), No. 38 (1961).
14. [Anonymous] "Diary of a Soviet Jew," *Di Zukunft* (New York), May–June, 1963, p. 235.
15. These included such distinguished figures as Peretz Markish, recipient of the Order of Lenin and member of the Jewish Anti-Fascist Committee, who was arrested in 1948 and shot, with a large group of other writers, on August 12, 1952; poet Itsik Fefer, a Soviet lieutenant-colonel, holder of many official awards, articulate apologist for Stalin, and a member of the Jewish Anti-Fascist Committee, who visited the United States with actor Solomon Mikhoels—arrested in 1948 and shot on August 12, 1952; and Mikhoels, director of the Yiddish State Theater and chairman of the Jewish Anti-Fascist Committee—murdered under mysterious circumstances (still unexplained, despite promises of investigation). See Miriam Broderzon, "An Eyewitness to History," in *A Decade of Destruction* (New York, 1958), p. 28. The author is a Yiddish actress, widow of the poet Moshe Broderzon, who was purged by Stalin.
16. Hayim Sloves, French Jewish leftist, had this to say on his return from a visit to the Soviet Union: "The Soviet Yiddish writers are perhaps more creative today than ever before. 'Not a day passes without my writing,' everyone tells you. And everyone has work ready for the press—volumes of poetry, novels, dramas."—*Yidishe Kultur* (New York), February, 1959. Allowing for some exaggeration, Sloves' statement is accurate.

17. Alexander Pomerantz, *Die Sovyetishe Harugey Malkhus* (*The Tragic Fate of Jewish Writers and Literature in the Soviet Union*) (Buenos Aires, 1962), pp. 102–3.
18. Madame Furtseva made a statement to this effect to André Blumel, vice-chairman of the Franco-Soviet Friendship Society; General Dragunski said the same thing during his 1960 visit to France.
19. Only nine of all the Yiddish writers whose works appeared in *Sovyetish Heymland* are from the Jewish Autonomous Province.
20. Alexander Pomerantz asserts that this "explanation" has no basis in fact and is "absolutely false and nonsensical" (*op. cit.*, p. 106).
21. Article 123 reads: "The equality of the rights of citizens of the Soviet Union, irrespective of nationality or race, is an irrevocable law in all spheres of economic, public, cultural, social, and political life. Any direct or indirect restriction of rights . . . because of race or nationality, as well as any advocacy of racial exclusiveness, hatred, or contempt, is punishable by law."
22. For the full text of the exchange, see *Commentary,* January, 1965, pp. 35–37.
23. This reminds me of a scene, which my father related to me, from a novel that appeared in a prewar Yiddish newspaper in Warsaw. The novel dealt with the dissolute life of "high society" circles in Poland. The author was apparently casting about for a suitable symbol of the moral degeneration of the Polish plutocracy. He finally found it: it was *cocoa.* And so, in an appropriately vivid description of an orgy, the author exclaimed: "And cocoa was flowing like water!" Twenty-five years later, in the Soviet imagination, cocoa had been replaced by "the cocktail."
24. See the note by the editors of *Novyi mir*—the vanguard of Soviet liberal intellectuals—No. 9 (1965), reaffirming their adherence to the principle that "there is no truth, no genuine truth, which our literature is not in need of, or which may be harmful or insignificant, nor is there any lie which could be in any way useful to it." This is a bold rejection of the official Soviet aesthetic theory, which is based on the negation of perceivable reality and the glorification of the desired, or "future," truth—in other words, of *lies.*
25. Respectively, a novelist and the editor of the popular weekly *Ogoniok.*
26. Here, for instance, is the answer to the question "How should the artist reflect life?," offered by H. Remenik, who might be described as the "official" literary critic of *Sovyetish Heymland:* "Literature must educate and mobilize the Soviet man for stupendous achievements, and that can only be accomplished by the truthful description of every-day achievements and by unmasking the negative phenomena of life, the prejudices and survivals of alien ideology in the consciousness of man, bureaucratism, individualism, nationalism, theft, bribery, etc." (4). Or the following remark made by the writer Tevye Gen at a conference on Soviet Yiddish prose (8): "How do I conceive of the positive hero? Above all, he is a man made of blood and flesh, all that is human is not alien to him, but in addition he must have a strong character, be brave and active. He is deeply rooted in our Soviet reality. He must represent a lofty and generalized embodiment of our contemporary Soviet Jew." Needless to say, the very concept of a "positive hero" is anathema to liberal Soviet writers.
27. See the more traditional formulation of this problem in a review by Chaim Loytsker of a book on Sholom Aleichem written in Russian by H. Remenik

(3). Loytsker's objection to a certain passage in the book stemmed from the fact that while Remenik considered Tevye der Milkhiker and Menakhem Mendl, the two heroes of Sholom Aleichem's most famous works, as "almost antipodes inasmuch as the former represents the folk-masses which are close to the working class" while the other "personifies the psychology of those circles [i.e., strata] of the Jewish population which were filled with the aspiration . . . to join the camp of the bourgeoisie," Loytsker felt that they were *complete* antipodes. Of such is the stuff of traditional literary criticism in the Soviet Union.

28. Significantly, this volume had been published two years earlier. Apparently the reviewer had not considered it safe to make these comments until 1965.
29. Here is one poem by Yehuda Halevi that was, significantly, included in this collection: "When the source of song became besmirched/I turned from it with a shudder, and my soul revolted against it/for how should a young lion come out to his shores/when small foxes are snorting on his path?"
30. The Bible, says the author, is "one of the greatest chef-d'oeuvres of world literature, a work of great realism, one which pulsates and seethes with true life."
31. For some fascinating examples, see the annotations in *A Shpigl Oyf a Shteyn* (*A Mirror on a Stone*), ed. B. Hrushovsky, A. Sutskever, and Kh. Shmeruk (Tel Aviv, 1964), a superb anthology of the works of twelve masters of Yiddish prose and poetry in Russia.
32. This view was expressed to me personally in no uncertain terms by Mr. Vergelis and his editorial colleagues during a two-hour interview in Moscow in September, 1961.
33. The most common "conservative" criticism of Solzhenitsyn was that the author had portrayed Ivan Denisovich as a meek, ordinary man rather than as a courageous fighter for Communism. Since the appearance of Solzhenitsyn's novel, two other novels have appeared that were deliberate attempts to present the "other side" of the coin. See Leopold Labedz and Priscilla Johnson (eds.), *Khrushchev and the Arts* (Cambridge, Mass., 1965).
34. See S. Niger, *Yidishe Shrayber in Soviet Rusland* (*Jewish Writers in Soviet Russia*) (New York, 1958), p. 463.
35. One salient exception is the case of Peretz Markish. Although there is still no mention in Soviet sources of how he met his death, he has been fully rehabilitated; there was complete coverage of a meeting held in his honor in October, 1965.
36. For an incisive review of this anthology, see *Jews in Eastern Europe* (London), May, 1965, p. 60.
37. Another example of this trend is the aforementioned discussion about how better to disseminate *Sovyetish Heymland.* Issue No. 12 features a photograph of "the public press-disseminator R. Mistislavskaia" accepting subscriptions to *Sovyetish Heymland* in Chernovitz for the year 1966.
38. See *Jews in Eastern Europe* (London), May, 1965, pp. 58–59.
39. See Labedz and Johnson (eds.), *op. cit.*
40. See Abraham Brumberg, "Traitors in the Dock," *Problems of Communism,* XV, No. 2 (March–April, 1966).

11

The Legal Position of the Jewish Community of the Soviet Union

WILLIAM KOREY

In the Soviet multinational society, nationality is a fundamental component of citizenship carrying vital psychological, cultural, and even political ramifications. From the very inception of the Soviet state, the Jewish community has been accorded the legal status of a nationality. Even if Bolshevik ideologists, prior to the October Revolution, denied that the Jewish community had the specific characteristics that they considered essential for nationhood, most notably a continuous territory and an agricultural base,[1] they nonetheless recognized that Jews had a "common 'national character.' "

As early as March, 1914, Lenin drafted a bill on nationality that clearly defined the future legal status of the Jewish community in the state as a distinct nationality entity. The bill was to provide for "the repeal of all restrictions upon the rights of Jews, and, in general, of all restrictions based on a person's descent or nationality." After noting that the "citizens of all nationalities of Russia" were to be equal before the law, Lenin's draft went on to specify the removal of barriers against Jews.[2] Five years later, after the Bolsheviks had seized power, Lenin once again juxtaposed Jews and the nationality question when he called for

> Particular carefulness in regard to the national feelings of nations that were oppressed (for example, on the part of the Great Russians, Ukrainians, and Poles toward Jews, on the part of Tatars toward Bashkirs, etc.); support not only for real equality in rights, but also for the development of the language, the literature of the toiling masses of the formerly oppressed nations.[3]

Significantly, a Communist Party resolution, adopted at its Tenth Congress in 1921, after referring to the "equality of nationalities" and "the right of national minorities to free national development," specifically mentioned Jews among a very small list of examples.[4]

Formal political expression to the acknowledged legal status of a Jewish nationality was given in January, 1918, when a Commissariat for Jewish National Affairs was established as a special section of the Peoples' Commissariat for National Affairs. The Peoples' Commissariat, or Narkomnats, had been established with Stalin at its head only one day after the Bolshevik seizure of power. Its function, the official text stated, was that of being "the initiator of the entire Soviet legislation on the national question . . . measures regarding the economic and cultural uplifting of the nationalities, etc."[5] But the establishment of "the dictatorship of the proletariat in the Jewish street"—the spreading of the ideas of the Bolshevik Revolution among the Jewish masses, became the principal task of the Commissariat for Jewish National Affairs. (In this capacity, it sought the abolition of the existing autonomous institutions of the Jewish community and the transfer of their funds and property to itself.[6] A formal decree of August 5 accomplished this task.)

Alongside the Jewish Commissariat (and its provincial sub-bodies), the Communist Party in 1918 created "Jewish Sections" (*Yevsektsii*) to carry out Communist Party policy and propaganda among Jewish workers in the Yiddish language and "to see to it that the Jewish masses have a chance to satisfy all their intellectual needs in that language."[7] While the Commissariat passed out of existence in early 1924 (as did the Peoples' Commissariat itself), the Jewish Sections continued to exist until January, 1930, when they, too, were liquidated. But the category of a Jewish nationality remained.

The reference to language in the functions of the Jewish Sections reflected the fact that Yiddish was formally recognized as integral to the legal identity of the Jewish nationality.[8] Indeed, the Belorussian Republic—which contained the greatest number of compact Jewish communities and where 90.7 per cent of the Jews, in the 1926 census, called Yiddish their mother tongue—decreed that Yiddish was one of the four official languages of the government.[9]

If the Jewish community qua community has a fixed legal status as a nationality so, too, does the individual born of Jewish parents. A Jew is not someone who chooses to identify himself as such; he is a juridically defined person who inescapably is a part of the Jewish nationality by being born of Jewish parents.

The legal decree fixing the identity of a person of Jewish parentage as being a Jew by nationality was not introduced until late 1932.

Ironically, it appeared under circumstances that bore no direct relationship to the nationality question. On December 27, 1932, the Central Executive Committee and the Council of Peoples' Commissars adopted a decree[10] creating the "single passport system" for the U.S.S.R.—a system still in force. The decree stipulated that the passports, to be issued in 1933 to urban residents sixteen years of age and over, were to state the "nationality" of the bearer.

The principal reason for the introduction of the passport was the severe housing shortage in the major urban areas. The passport was to be the basis for regulating the distribution of apartments. As the decree noted, the objective was "an improved registration of the population of the cities, of workers from villages and new factories, and the combing out from living quarters those persons not connected with production or labor in institutions and schools, and not engaged in socially useful labor . . . and also with the purpose of removing from these living quarters concealed kulaks, criminals, and antisocial elements."

The passport system was first introduced in the major cities, but the decree specified that the system was to be extended to all localities in the U.S.S.R. Nationality ranked high among the specifications in the passport. It was listed immediately after name, date, and place of birth, and before social position, permanent residence, and place of work. The decree noted further that the passport would include a list of documents providing proof of nationality. Among the documents required was a birth certificate, which, among other types of "proof," stated the nationality of the person involved.

The listing of the nationality of the registering sixteen-year-old is a virtually automatic process.[11] He is required to produce papers stating the nationality of each of his parents. If both are of the same nationality—the usual case—then that nationality is put in the passport. Only persons with parents of different nationality have the option of choosing between two nationalities.

Since the passport is the principal means of identification in the U.S.S.R., not merely in obtaining housing, but in application for jobs and, indeed, in dealing with all governmental institutions, it is a potentially powerful means for either discrimination or favoritism on nationality grounds.

The fixed personal legal category has particular significance for the Jews since, unlike most other nationalities, they lack a distinct geographical national base. There is, of course, the Jewish Autonomous Region of Birobidzhan, established in 1934. But despite government pronouncements in the mid-1930's recommending Birobidzhan as a "homeland" for Soviet Jews, the area attracted relatively few Jews as permanent residents, so that today only 8.8 per cent of the Region's population—14,270 persons—are of Jewish nationality.[12] Of the Region's five representatives in the Soviet of Nationalities of the Supreme Soviet, one is identified as a Jew.[13] The name of the Region is thus an anomaly, and the applicability to it of Article 110 of the U.S.S.R. Constitution, stipulating that "judicial proceedings" are to be "conducted in the language" of the Region, becomes meaningless.

Numbering, according to the census of 1959,[14] 2.268 million, the Jews are dispersed throughout all of the fifteen Union Republics: 38 per cent in the Russian Republic; 37 per cent in the Ukraine; 7 per cent in Belorussia; another 15 per cent in Uzbekistan, Georgia, Lithuania, Moldavia, Latvia, and Estonia; and the remaining 95,000 in the other six republics. Everywhere they constitute a small minority, their highest percentage of the Republic population being in Moldavia (3.3 per cent) and in the Ukraine (2 per cent). On a national level, Jews form but 1.09 per cent of the total population. But this small percentage does not reflect their relative weight in the nationality pattern. Actually, they rank eleventh among the 108 nationalities. Nonetheless, they are a minority everywhere and, therefore, more vulnerable to the abuses of the passport system.

The dispersal of Jews, together with the fact that they are one of the most highly urbanized nationalities in the U.S.S.R. (95 per cent live in urban areas), has no doubt accelerated the normal trend to linguistic assimilation. This is reflected in the 1959 census figures on the use by Jews of their native "mother tongue." In contrast to the census figures of 1926, when more than 70 per cent of the Jews indicated Yiddish as their native language, in the 1959 census, approximately 18 per cent, or a little more than 400,000, did so.[15] Jews ranked far and away the lowest among the nationalities to claim the language of the nationality to which they belonged as their native tongue. Other dispersed nationalities came next: the Poles with 45 per cent; the Gypsies with 59 per cent; the Germans with 75 per cent.

But, as one Soviet Yiddish specialist, Yakov Kantor, has indicated, the structuring of the census questionnaire made for a distorted and exaggerated picture of the extent of linguistic assimilation. In an analysis published by the Warsaw Jewish Historical Institute,[16] Kantor notes that since the census instructions did not define "native language," many Jews thought it meant "language spoken." In consequence, "many people who speak and read Yiddish, enjoy Yiddish books, and appreciate Yiddish plays nevertheless gave Russian as their language because they speak Russian at work, in the street, and even at times at home."

Besides, the over-all percentage obscures the fact that, in the territories incorporated into the Soviet state in 1939–41, the percentage of Jews specifying Yiddish as their native tongue is fairly high—69 per cent in Lithuania, 48 per cent in Latvia, and 50 per cent in Moldavia. A Soviet linguistic scholar at the University of Leningrad, M. Friedberg, has criticized as "wholly incorrect" the assertion in the *Large Soviet Encyclopedia* that the Soviet Jewish community is on the road to "complete linguistic assimilation."[17] He noted the extensive use of Yiddish in areas in the Ukraine and Belorussia that have compact Jewish populations.

The distinctiveness of the Jewish community as a nationality having a dispersed character is further complicated by the legal status accorded to the Jewish religious community. A government decree of June, 1944,[18] which formally established the Council for the Affairs of Religious Cults, specifically mentioned the Jewish religious community among the approximately dozen non-Russian Orthodox faiths granted formal status. The Council, according to the decree, is directly responsible to the U.S.S.R. Council of Ministers and is assigned the task of maintaining liaison between the government and the recognized religious communities.

Participation in the Jewish religious community, as distinct from the category of the Jewish nationality, is, from a legal viewpoint, a voluntary act of a Jew (or any citizen). According to an official report to the United Nations, "the laws in force in the Soviet Union on religious matters bar any State registration of citizens of the Soviet Union according to religion."[19] In consequence, "no indication of religious affiliation is given in State documents such as passports or in State censuses," and, indeed, "no statistics or numerical records concerning religious affiliation are kept."

Figures on the number of persons affiliated wth the Jewish religious community are unavailable, although, in 1960, a member of the Council for the Affairs of Religious Cults offered an estimate—undoubtedly inflated—of 500,000 "practicing" Jews.[20] The Chief Rabbi of Moscow stated in 1963 that there were ninety-six synagogues in the country (the Novosti Press Agency reported it as ninety-seven).[21] In addition, there are an unknown number of *minyanim,* private prayer groups of ten or more having no legal status. (To acquire status a group of "not less than twenty citizens" who combine "to form a religious association" must register and be approved by the local authorities.)[22]

Notwithstanding the voluntary character of membership in the Jewish religious community, the same root term for both the nationality and the religion—"Jew" or "Jewish"—makes the complete separation of the two in the public mind difficult. The intertwining of nationality and religion become particularly apparent in the atheist campaign directed by the Party. The Jewish religion is frequently attacked either on grounds that it stimulates *nationalist* feelings or that it expresses "national exclusiveness." Thus, the "voluntary" character of adherence to the Jewish religion may be less voluntary than the law requires. In the minds of readers of atheist propaganda, "Jew" might take on the character of an objective category in which nationality and religion are conjoined.

Nonetheless, the laws on the status of the Jew are clear. He is entitled to a set of constitutionally prescribed rights embracing the areas of nationality, religion, and civil law. What follows is an inquiry into both the laws governing the rights of Jews in the Soviet Union and the reality of their implementation.

As a distinctive nationality in the U.S.S.R., the Jewish community was and is entitled to enjoy a host of national rights, inscribed in law, that stretch back to the early days of the Soviet regime. Only a week after the seizure of power, on November 15, 1917, the government issued a formal Declaration of Rights of Peoples, which proclaimed the "free development of national minorities and ethnic groups inhabiting Russian territory."[23]

In keeping with the principle, Article 22 of the first Soviet Constitution of 1918[24] stipulated that "to oppress national minorities or impose any limitations whatsoever on their rights" is "contrary to the fundamental laws" of the regime. Following the formation of the U.S.S.R. in 1922 and the enactment of the new federal constitution in 1924,[25] the principle of equality of rights for nationalities was restated in the constitutions of individual republics.

Article 13 of the Constitution of the R.S.F.S.R. stipulated that citizens "have the right to use their native language freely in meetings, in the courts, in administrative bodies and in public affairs." It further specified that the national minorities "have the right to receive education in their native tongue."

In both the Ukraine and Belorussia, where sizable compact Jewish communities existed, statutes were enacted to guarantee linguistic rights. The Ukrainian Code of Criminal Procedure of 1922 permitted court proceedings "in the language of the majority of the population concerned."[26] A Ukrainian decree of August 1, 1923, "concerning measures to ensure the legal equality of languages"[27] provides that in localities where one of the minority nationalities was spoken by a majority, the authorities were to use the language of the nationality. A subsequent decree in July, 1927, restated this right and specified the teaching of the native language together with both Russian and Ukrainian in minority schools.[28]

Belorussia's Declaration of Independence of August 1, 1920, recognized Yiddish as one of the four "legal" languages enjoying "equality" with Belorussian, Russian, and Polish.[29] A decree of July 15, 1924, "concerning practical measures to implement the policy on nationalities," guaranteed both native schools and the use of the "mother tongue in dealing with any kind of organ and institution of the Republic."[30]

In the Ukraine and Belorussia the decrees, in the 1920's, led to the establishment of a complex of Jewish administrative and judicial institutions in areas where Jews constituted a sizable and compact group. However, with the stepped-up industrialization campaign of the 1930's, the compactness of old Jewish communities broke up, a dispersion of their population to new industrial areas followed, and the complex of institutions disintegrated. Administrative pressures and voluntary acts by assimilationists contributed to this disintegration. Nevertheless, the school apparatus remained. By the end of 1940, according to Jacob Lestchinsky, some 85,000–90,000 Jewish children—about 20 per cent of the Jewish student population—attended schools in which Yiddish was the language of instruction.[31]

The 1936 Constitution of the U.S.S.R.[32] no longer made reference to the right of use of the native language in meetings, courts, and administrative bodies. Article 121, however, reaffirms the right of "instruction in schools . . . in the native language." Similar provisions exist in the constitutions of all the Union and autonomous republics.

In August, 1962, the U.S.S.R. ratified the UNESCO Convention Against Discrimination in Education, which obligated it, according to Article 5 (1c) "to recognize the right of members of national minorities to carry on their own educational activities, including the maintenance of schools and . . . the use or the teaching of their own language."[33]

Ratification of the UNESCO Convention was reflected, earlier, in a law adopted on April 16, 1959, in the Russian Republic "Concerning the Strengthening of the Connection of the Schools with Life and the Furthest Development of the System of Peoples' Education in the R.S.F.S.R." The law, in Article 15, declared: "The education in schools will be conducted in the native language of the students. The right is given to parents to decide with what language to register their children in schools."[34] A 1956 letter from the Deputy Minister of Education of the Russian Republic, A. Arsenyev, stated that Soviet law requires that in the event that ten parents request that their children be educated in their mother tongue, "the organization of such a class [in the "mother tongue"] in any school" will be arranged.[35]

The Party Program adopted by the Twenty-second Congress in 1961 underscored the Soviet commitment to the teaching of the native language. The Party guarantees "the complete freedom of each citizen of the U.S.S.R. to speak and to rear and educate his children in any language, ruling out all privileges, restrictions, and compulsion in the use of this or that language."[36]

Notwithstanding the numerous laws and decrees governing education in the native tongue, there is today not a single Yiddish school or Yiddish class in all of the U.S.S.R. The Jewish schools in the Ukraine and Belorussia destroyed by the Nazis have not been reopened. Efforts to re-establish a Yiddish school system in Lithuania after the liberation from the Nazis came to naught.[37] And, by 1946, the few Jewish schools that had existed in Birobidzhan were closed.

Two arguments have been advanced by Soviet authorities to explain the absence of Jewish schools. One is based on the costliness of establishing schools for a widely dispersed nationality. The validity of this argument becomes suspect in view of recent school developments involving another dispersed Soviet nationality—the Germans.

Numbering more than 1.6 million persons (according to the 1959 census) and dispersed, since an August 28, 1941, decree, over a wide area embracing eastern parts of the R.S.F.S.R. and almost a dozen other Union republics, the former Volga Germans received full restitution of their national rights by a 1964 decree of the Presidium of the U.S.S.R. Supreme Soviet.[38] The decree reveals that "in districts of a number of provinces, territories and republics that have a German population, there are secondary and elementary schools where teaching is conducted in German or German is taught children of school age."

In March, 1964, the Soviet teachers' journal[39] offered some details concerning the extent of the rehabilitation of the linguistic school rights of the Germans in the R.S.F.S.R. Under the headline "Two Native Languages," the article observed that "at present there exist hundreds of schools in the R.S.F.S.R. where, beginning with the second grade, the German language as the mother tongue is used in teaching." Thirteen textbooks on the teaching of German as a mother tongue have been published and republished in 431 editions. Teachers were being trained in four pedagogical institutes for higher grades and in three seminars for lower grades.

The Soviet German weekly *Neues Leben* on January 20, 1965, carried an article complaining that in one village where the Germans number one-third of the local population, the teaching of German as a "native language" had been introduced only in the lower grades. A week later, the newspaper published an article by a Kirghiz school official who disclosed that 5,000 German pupils in 33 schools of various regions in Kirghizia were learning their "native language," and that, in 1960, the Council of Ministers of that republic had promulgated a decree that all schools with classes of ten or more German pupils had to introduce the teaching of German as a "native language if their parents so requested."[40]

The second argument that is offered for the absence of a Jewish school system is the extent of assimilation of Jews. A parliamentary delegation of French Socialists was told by Khrushchev in 1956 that assimilation is so advanced that "Even if Jewish schools were established, very few would attend them voluntarily."[41] He added that "If the Jews were compelled to attend Jewish schools, there would certainly be a revolt. It would be considered some kind of ghetto."

This type of argument raises more questions than it answers. Assuming there are insufficient prospective students for Jewish schools, why are there no special Jewish classes? If all that is required is that ten parents request such classes, is it conceivable that in areas of large Yiddish-speaking populations (as in Vilna, Kovno, Riga, and elsewhere in the western Ukraine, western Belorussia, and Moldavia), no such request should be forthcoming?

Simply to put these questions is to suggest the determination of school administrators to discourage such requests or to fail to inform parents of their rights to make such requests. A recent article in the Soviet German weekly had criticized a high-school principal in one village with a considerable German minority for his failure to inform German parents of their legal rights to request teaching in the "native language."[42] Might this failure be a deliberately created widespread phenomenon in dealing with Jewish parents? The external stimulation from "on high" of a popular desire or request is a frequently used device of Soviet policy makers to arouse support for one or another position. In contrast to the press stimulation of German parents, there has not appeared a single article in the press to stimulate such interest on the part of Jewish parents.

But, perhaps, a more fundamental question would be the following: Is not the assimilation of Jews a product, at least in part, of the absence of specific Jewish institutions to perpetuate its language and culture, rather than the converse? A leading Soviet Jewish researcher, the author of an authoritative work on Jewish institutions, observed recently that

> Such things as schools of all kinds, museums, theaters, libraries, even sections of academies and so on, all work toward the consolidation, the support, and the strengthening of minority cultures.
>
> Unhappily, the Jews belong to that group of national minorities where such supporting and strengthening factors for their culture do not exist. They have not existed for a number of years, since the time of the reinforced cult of the personality.[43]

The value judgment implied in the word "unhappily" reflects the author's conviction that the absence of schools and other cultural institutions is the decisive factor in causing assimilation, and not a reflection of it. It is significant that this penetrating analysis was published in Warsaw and not in the Soviet Union, where the author lived until his death in September, 1964.

The elimination of the last Jewish schools in the U.S.S.R. was followed by the destruction of the complex of Jewish cultural institutions. Already during 1946–47, much of the remaining extensive prewar publishing structure was dismantled. And then, in November, 1948, the Yiddish publishing house, Der Emes of Moscow, which brought out the triweekly *Aynikayt* and which had issued a total of 110 publications during the three-year postwar period, was closed down.[44] Early in 1949, the famed Jewish State Theater in Moscow was closed, its leading actor, Solomon Mikhoels, having been murdered by the secret police a year earlier.[45] (The organization of which he was a leading official, the Jewish Anti-Fascist Committee, was dissolved in November, 1948. Most of its other officials were also liquidated.)

For eleven years the Jewish national scene in the U.S.S.R. was a cultural desert—no theater, no books, no publications (except for the *Birobidzhaner Shtern,* a small triweekly with a circulation of 1,000 produced locally in Birobidzhan). Only the popular Yiddish concerts by traveling singers provided some linguistic sustenance. Beginning in 1959, a small trickle of publications began to seep through to the parched Yiddish-reading population. A book by Sholem Aleichem appeared that year, followed during the next three years by four other Yiddish books by deceased Jewish authors. Then, between 1962 and 1964, nothing was published. In 1965, in response to a growing outcry in the Western world, the Soviets published some books—a volume of poetry by living Yiddish poets and a series of essays by contemporary Jewish writers about how they live.

The most important development was the establishment in August, 1961, of a bimonthly Yiddish literary review, *Sovyetish Heymland,* with a press run of 25,000. This journal, like the few Yiddish books, would probably never have appeared except for foreign reaction to the discriminatory policy on Yiddish culture. In 1961, the then Soviet Minister of Culture, Yekaterina Furtseva, told André Blumel, Vice-Chairman of the Franco-Soviet Friendship Society, that, if the Soviet Union "did anything at all" for Yiddish culture, "it would not be for domestic reasons but to please our friends abroad."[46]

Sovyetish Heymland, which, in January, 1965, was turned into an enlarged monthly, has become a focal point of the very limited Jewish activity. Besides publishing the writings of over 100 Jewish authors, it has organized a number of well-attended literary conferences. The Yiddish theater, however, has not been restored. Instead, in 1962, a touring Yiddish repertory company was launched under Veniamin Schwartser, a former member of the Moscow Jewish State Theater.[47]

The brisk sale of Yiddish books and of *Sovyetish Heymland,* the sizable audiences at the literary conferences, at performances of Schwartser's company, and particularly at Yiddish concerts—a semi-official estimate puts them at a half million per year[48]—testify to the continuing vitality of the *"Yiddish Vort."*

There exist no laws or statutes in the U.S.S.R. guaranteeing the cultural rights of minorities, but these rights have been implicit in the Party policy on the nationality problem enunciated in the 1920's. As early as March, 1921, the Tenth Party Congress resolved that it must assist the nationalities "to set up a press, schools, theaters, community centers, and cultural and educational institutions generally, using the native language."[49] The early postwar period was marked by a decisive reversal of this policy so far as the Jewish national culture was concerned. This new policy has been continued by Stalin's successors, with the exception of the minor changes introduced in 1959 and afterward.

The ultimate objective of a "single common culture," as expressed by Stalin, has been given a greater degree of urgency and immediacy by the Party, which, in its new Program, called for "the effacement of national distinctions . . . including language distinctions."[50] Khrushchev, while heaping ridicule on those "who complain about the effacement of national distinctions," told the Party that "Communists are not going to freeze and perpetuate national distinctions."[51] In a report to the U.N. in late 1963, the Soviet Government gave expression to the new Program by emphasizing that its nationalities are "drawing closer in a spirit of mutual fraternal aid and friendship."[52]

A leading Soviet analyst of the national question, M. S. Dzhunusov, has stressed the "drawing closer" process by citing statistics on the changing ethnic composition of the Union republics (particularly the greater number of Russians and Ukrainians in the various non-Slavic republics), the wider use of the Russian language by non-Russian nationalities (over 10 million according to the census), and the frequency of intermarriage.[53] (According to the Soviet report to the U.N., there are in urban areas 151 mixed families per 1,000 families in the U.S.S.R. as a whole, 108 in the R.S.F.S.R., 263 in the Ukraine, and 237 in Belorussia. To what extent intermarriage involves the highly urbanized Jewish community is not known.[54]

The blocking of channels for the perpetuation of a distinctly Jewish national culture is accompanied by other devices to restrict an awareness about the past of that culture. Thus, whereas the first edition of the *Large Soviet Encyclopedia* carried 116 pages about Jews, the current, second, edition has but two. More significantly, history textbooks published during 1958–60 for use in Soviet high schools scarcely mention Jews, let alone Jewish culture.[55]

Though the martyrdom of Jews by the Nazis is a fundamental part of the immediate past consciousness of Soviet Jewry, it has been minimized by the authorities. The events surrounding the publication of Yevgenii Yevtushenko's poem "Babi Yar" is illuminating. The poem recalled Jewish martyrdom throughout history and noted that there were no monuments commemorating the massacre of the Jews of Kiev by the Nazis in September, 1941.[56] The literary establishment immediately labeled the poem an insult and "provocation" to Russian patriotism. Khrushchev joined the chorus of attack, observing that the poem was oriented toward a *"national"* martyrdom, whereas Communists must approach situations from a "class" viewpoint.[57]

An analysis of the press and radio treatment in the Communist countries of the trial of Adolf Eichmann in Israel similarly illustrates official Soviet indifference to Jewish martyrdom. In contrast to the extensive and sympathetic coverage given the trial in Poland, Hungary, and Czechoslovakia, Soviet coverage was limited and critical.[58] In the same way, the twentieth anniversary of the Warsaw Ghetto uprising was handled by a single article in *Izvestiia,* which, in large part, was given over to an attack on the government of West Germany.[59]

A recent debate at a U.N. seminar in Yugoslavia throws some light on the resistance of Soviet authorities to formal ties between Soviet Jews and Jews abroad.[60] One of the topics on the agenda of the seminar, which dealt with multinational societies, was "measures to be taken to ensure the preservation by ethnic, religious, linguistic, or national groups of their traditions, characteristics, or national consciousness." Included was a discussion of the right of members of ethnic and religious groups to associate across national boundaries. When the issue was posed in terms of the special responsibility of one-party states to permit association across national borders, the Soviet response was violently negative. The Soviet spokesman vehemently argued that individuals had no standing in international law, and therefore could not be granted rights of association. The right of association existed only for organizations.

The fierce opposition of the Soviet officials to the right of individuals to associate with their ethnic brethren elsewhere found no support. Isolated, they finally agreed to endorse the view of the conference participants that the "right of association" included "the right of individuals to associate both with national organizations in other countries and with international organizations, and the right of individuals in one country to associate with individuals in other countries."

Whether and in what way, if any, the Soviets will adhere to the U.N. seminar proposal is uncertain. Decisions reached at the seminar are merely recommendations to the U.N. Commission on Human Rights and are not binding on the participants. Implementation of the proposal in a meaningful manner would involve a radical reversal of recent attitudes and practices on the part of the Soviet Union. In view of the character of the implementation of prescribed nationality rights so far as the Jewish nationality is concerned, an excessive degree of optimism would seem unwarranted.

Dedicated to "scientific materialism" and to the idea that religion is the "opiate of the masses," the Soviet Communist Party conducts an unceasing, vigorous campaign against all religions. At the same time, the Soviet state distinguishes between the Party's conduct toward religion and its own. "There are fundamental differences between the two [state and Party]. In its legislation on religion, the Soviet state . . . accords unrestricted freedom of worship to citizens of the Soviet Union who are believers."[61]

The Soviet Government goes on to state that while the state guarantees freedom of worship, the Communist Party, "on the other hand, on the basis of the law on freedom of conscience, carries on scientific atheist propaganda among the population."[62]

The reference to the legal basis for Party propaganda work against religion is of interest. The earlier R.S.F.S.R. Constitutions of 1918 (Article 13) and of 1925, as part of their "Bill of Rights," provided for both "freedom of religious and antireligious propaganda." However, a law of April, 1929,[63] that regulated the activities of religious organizations of the Soviet Union deprived religious bodies of the right of religious propaganda. The 1936 Constitution took account of this change by deleting reference to "religious propaganda." Only "antireligious" propaganda is permitted, although "freedom of religious worship" is legally assured.[64] Article 124 reads: "In order to ensure freedom of conscience, the Church in the U.S.S.R. is separated from the state, and the school from the Church. Freedom of religious worship and freedom of antireligious propaganda are recognized for citizens."

There were some who had proposed that Article 124 prohibit "religious rites" along with religious propaganda. But this proposal was rejected after Stalin described it as "running counter to the spirit of our Constitution."[65]

The rights guaranteed to the recognized religions are spelled out (in addition to the Constitution) in the still valid decree of the Council of Peoples' Commissars of January 23, 1918, in the Order of the All-Union Central Executive Committee and the Council of Peoples' Commissars of the R.S.F.S.R. of April 8, 1929, and in various criminal codes. The Soviet Government has provided the United Nations with a detailed listing of and commentary on these rights in two major documents that are available in *Study of Discrimination in the Matter of Religious Rights and Practises,* Conference Room Paper, No. 35, and *Manifestations of Racial Prejudice and Religious Intolerance,* Doc. A/5473/Add.1.

Equality of all religions lies at the very heart of the decree of July, 1918, abolishing the dominant position enjoyed by Russian Orthodoxy under the Czars and prohibiting governmental actions that would "establish any kind of privileges or advantages on the grounds of religious affiliation of citizens."[66] In a number of vital respects, the principle of equality of religious rights is observed in the breach insofar as Judaism is concerned. This became apparent in the immediate postwar period when, according to one authority, "favorable treatment" by the state was given to Russian Orthodoxy, Islam, and other religions, while Judaism was held in "disfavor."[67]

One crucial area is the right to organize a central or federative body. The Order of April 8, 1929, enables

> religious communities of the same denomination . . . [to] form religious associations which may or may not coincide geographically with the administrative subdivisions of the Union of Soviet Socialist Republics . . . and may set up *religious centers*. . . . These *religious centers,* which are governed by their own rules and regulations, may hold republic or All-Union congresses, church councils, and other conferences on matters related to the administration of church affairs. [Italics added.][68]

The Order further notes that the "religious centers" may publish "periodicals and the necessary devotional literature."

Unlike the other recognized religious bodies, Judaism has not had any semblance of a central or coordinating structure since 1926. In June, 1919, the Soviet Government banned the then existing central Jewish body, the Central Board of Jewish Communities.[69] The last time a conference of rabbis met in the Soviet Union was in 1926. The absence of a central or federative structure for Judaism has brought about a fragmentation of religious life, limits effective resistance to the antireligious campaign, and makes the enjoyment of specified as well as unspecified rights difficult if not impossible. Thus, while the "religious centers" of the other faiths are able to publish periodicals and devotional literature, Judaism cannot. It has not published a Hebrew Bible since the late 1920's,[70] whereas the Russian Orthodox, in 1957, printed 50,000 copies of their Bible, the Baptists, in 1958, printed 10,000, and the Moslems, in 1958, printed 9,000 copies of the Koran.

Jewish prayer books are scarce.[71] The state has assured those faiths without "religious centers" a supply of the "necessary paper and the use of printing plants,"[72] but apparently this privilege has been extended to Judaism in a most restrained manner. In 1957, for the first time since the 1920's, permission was granted for an edition of the *Siddur* (prayer book)—all of 3,000 copies.[73] Lacking a religious center, Judaism has also been denied the opportunity of producing such essential devotional articles as the *tallith* (prayer shawl) and the *tefillin* (phylacteries). The Soviet Government has stated that it extends to "religious organizations" the right "to set up undertakings, such as candle factories and ikon painting studios, for the manufacture of the requisite articles for religious worship,"[74] a right that is meaningless without a religious center.

Of even greater significance is the fact that religious centers enable the religions of the U.S.S.R. to have formal, official contacts with their coreligionists abroad. This was spelled out in an official Soviet memorandum to the U.N. in 1963, which listed about a dozen Soviet religions that are connected with international bodies.

Jews are conspicuous by their absence from among the enumerated religions. The U.N. seminar in Yugoslavia throws added light on this question. The Soviet representative insisted that only organizations, not individuals, have status in international law and that, consequently, members of an ethnic or religious group cannot be accorded the right of association with international bodies of the same ethnic or religious affiliation.[75] The fact that Judaism had no religious center in the U.S.S.R. precluded its right to "association" with coreligionists abroad. Only at the very end of the seminar did the Soviet representative agree to accept the principle of the right of association of individuals. Whether it will be implemented so far as Judaism is concerned is uncertain.

Besides permitting formal contacts between religious organizations, the Soviet Government allows students of many of its faiths to study at foreign seminaries or theological institutions. Judaism is an exception, as this report from the Soviet Government to the U.N. indicates:

> The Soviet Government does not impede the training of ministers at theological institutions abroad. In the last five years students from religious groups in the U.S.S.R. have studied at the following educational establishments abroad: The Moslem Theological Academy in Cairo, Baptist colleges in the United Kingdom, the Theological Faculty of Oxford University, the Lateran University of the Vatican, Göttingen University (Federal Republic of Germany), Bethel Theological Seminary, McMaster University (Canada), and the Moslem University in Syria.[76]

With regard to the training of theological students, Judaism operates under a heavy burden. One Yeshiva was finally permitted in Moscow in 1957, while the Orthodox, for example, were allowed to open a number of seminaries immediately after the war.[77] Since the opening of the Yeshiva, two students have been ordained. Of the thirteen students at the Yeshiva in April, 1962—eleven of whom were over forty years of age—nine who came from communities in Georgia and Daghestan were prevented by Soviet authorities from returning to Moscow on grounds of a housing shortage. Rabbi Levin of Moscow told an American delegation of rabbis in 1965 that the Soviet Government would permit twenty students to register in the Yeshiva in the fall of that year.[78]

The shortage of Yeshivas seriously affects the future course of Judaism. Without replacements for an aging rabbinate (the average age is close to seventy years) numbering approximately sixty persons, Judaism may soon find itself without spiritual leadership. The special pressures on Judaism are exemplified by the manner in which the authorities have handled the baking and sale of matzoth (unleavened bread), an indispensable dietary article for the observance of the Passover. In its report to the U.N., the Soviet Government reported that "on days preceding particularly important holidays," such as "Passover in the case of the Jews," the stores of "the State trading organizations sell . . . matzoth . . . for Orthodox Jews . . . to enable worshippers to perform the appropriate ritual."[79]

But, as early as 1957, restrictions on the baking and sale of matzoth began to be imposed, first in Kharkov. In succeeding years, the ban spread to other cities and, by 1962, virtually the entire country was affected. On March 16, 1963, the Chief Rabbi of Moscow formally announced that the authorities had banned all public baking and selling of matzoth. He advised his congregation to bake the unleavened bread at home.[80] In 1964, although the public baking and sale of matzoth was still forbidden, the Moscow Jewish community was granted permission, just prior to the Passover, to rent a small bakery for production of the dietary article. The outcry from abroad, in 1965, was accompanied by a loosening of previous restrictions. Synagogues in a few major communities were allowed to bake matzoth, and the Chief Rabbi told an American delegation that he has been assured an adequate supply of flour for the baking of matzoth in the future.[81] But that assurance does not extend to the rest of the country.

Certain features of the Party-supervised antireligious campaign against Judaism carry distinctive overtones that have ramifications beyond the antireligious intent itself. A 1954 policy resolution of the Central Committee of the Party[82] warns against "offensive attacks of any sort against believers and the clergy" and calls for a "tactful" and "considerate" approach toward those who "still remain under the influence of various religious beliefs." The resolution specifically objects to placing "Soviet citizens under political suspicion because of their religious convictions."

Notwithstanding the caveat against "offensive" language, the anti-Judaism propaganda has frequently been characterized by the kind of vulgarity that encourages and reinforces anti-Semitic stereotypes. Synagogue leaders have been depicted as money worshipers who use the religious service, kosher slaughtering, religious burial, matzoth baking, and other ritual practices to exploit a duped congregation.[83] A typical example is an article in a Minsk newspaper in 1961, stating that "money is the God of the Minsk Jewish religious community and its aides."[84] And the notorious *Judaism Without Embellishment* has this to say: "Who is the secular god [of the Jews]? Money. Money is the jealous God of Israel."[85]

Even though the Party's Ideological Commission accepted the fact that the latter book had anti-Semitic overtones, it recommended as a "useful publication" a book by A. Osipov, which carried such crudities as: "Where Jews are concerned, the principal blood sucker turns out to be God himself;" "The first thing we come across is the preaching of intolerance, the bloody extermination of people of other faiths. . . . God recommends real racial discrimination to the Jews."[86]

An American Communist theoretician has observed that crude antireligious propaganda, "when it is directed against the Jewish religion in particular, leads to anti-Semitism."[87] He then states:

> For even while we reject the idea that any criticism of Judaism is of necessity anti-Semitic, the fact is that historically the maligning of the Jewish faith has been an intrinsic part of anti-Semitism—for example, the notorious blood libels which falsely ascribe to Jews the practice of using human blood in religious rituals and even of ritual murders. It is necessary to be extremely sensitive to such things, otherwise anti-religious propaganda can all too easily degenerate into anti-Semitism and encourage such expressions of it as the Kichko book.

The point is effectively made.

Another distinctive characteristic of the anti-Judaism campaign has been the attribution of potential or actual disloyalty to religious practitioners. Judaism is depicted as an instrument of Israel, which, in turn, is linked to American imperialism. Thus, as one typical article put it: "Judaism kills love for the Soviet motherland."[88] A more recent article charges Judaism with conducting "ideological subversion . . . of the working Jews in our country."[89]

Current Soviet law against incitement to hatred is limited to national and racial incitement. The earlier criminal code had provided for prison sentences for those who engaged in "propaganda and agitation" aimed at arousing "religious enmities" as well as "national" enmity.[90] The new code deleted the reference to religion because, so Soviet commentators have argued, there had been no prosecutions on religious grounds for a number of years.[91] But other Soviet specialists have observed that religious intolerance may be a veiled form of hostility on nationality grounds and, therefore, punishable under the current criminal code.[92] It remains to be seen whether this interpretation will receive support. But it is of interest that the crudities directed at Judaism have declined and warnings have been issued to use "extreme caution" in dealing with religious believers and to refrain from "offenses against religious feelings."[93]

In response to charges of discrimination against the Jewish community *qua* community on either national or religious grounds, Soviet authorities and spokesmen usually shift the discussion to a different plane by pointing to statistics about the broad participation of Jews in numerous professions and in public life.[94] Stress is therewith placed upon the rights of Jews as *individuals;* the argument is arbitrarily shifted from *communal* to *civil* rights. What, then is the state of civil rights for Jews?

Under the Czars, the civil rights of Jews were severely limited as to residence, military service, participation in government or in elections, schooling, etc.[95] The Provisional Government that came to power in March, 1917, abolished all ethnic, religious, and social discrimination.[96] When the Bolsheviks seized power in November, 1917, they immediately gave assurances about the hard-won civil rights. On November 15, 1917, the new regime issued a Declaration of Rights, signed jointly by Lenin as head of government and by Stalin as Commissar of Nationalities, which formally abolished "all national and national-religious privileges and restrictions."

The first Soviet Constitution reaffirmed the Declaration, at least as far as nondiscrimination on ethnic grounds was concerned. The new Republic constitutions adopted after the formation of the U.S.S.R. contained similar affirmations of civil rights. Thus, the Constitution of the R.S.F.S.R., adopted in 1925, stated that "the principle of the equality of rights of all citizens without distinction of race or nationality" was fundamental and "any restriction" of these rights and, "still more, the granting or toleration of any national privilege whatsoever, whether direct or indirect, are wholly incompatible with the fundamental laws."

The 1936 Constitution of the U.S.S.R. stresses the civil rights of all Soviet citizens and spells out the areas covered:

> Equality of rights of citizens of the U.S.S.R., irrespective of their nationality or race, in all spheres of economic, government, cultural, political, and other public activity is an indefeasible law.
>
> Any direct or indirect restriction of the rights of, or conversely, the establishment of any direct or indirect privileges for citizens on account of their race or nationality . . . is punishable by law.

All Soviet citizens, "irrespective of race or nationality," are eligible to vote and to be elected.[97] The constitutions of each of the fifteen Soviet republics contain similar formulations.

Constitutional provisions on civil rights are undergirded by the provisions of the new Criminal Codes. The law on the Fundamentals of Criminal Jurisprudence emphasizes that all citizens are equal in the eyes of the law and the courts. The recently adopted Criminal Code of the R.S.F.S.R. (January 1, 1961) is especially pointed in its treatment. Its Article 74, which is entitled "Infringement of National and Racial Equal Rights," specifies that "any direct or indirect limitation of rights or the establishment of direct or indirect privileges" on ground of race or nationality will be punished by a deprivation of freedom for a period of from six months to three years or by exile from two to five years.[98]

In a number of areas, Jews enjoy the civil rights spelled out in the legal statutes. Residential restrictions are nonexistent, and there are no barriers to participation in various aspects of social life—the Party, trade unions, army, the social services, clubs. Employment opportunities in a number of fields—particularly in science, medicine, law, and the arts—are widespread. As of December 1, 1960, there were 427,100 Jewish technical specialists working in the economy—290,700 with a higher education, the balance with a secondary-technical school education,[99] a greater number than any of the nationalities except Russians and Ukrainians. Further, Jews constitute 14.7 per cent of all doctors; 10.4 per cent of all lawyers; 8.5 per cent of writers and journalists; and 7 per cent of all actors, sculptors, musicians, and other artists.[100] Jews rank especially high in the sciences, numbering over 36,000, or 8.8 per cent of all scientists.

Approximately 10 per cent of the prestigious Academy of Science is made up of Jews, and the same percentage have won the Lenin Prize in science.[101]

Notwithstanding the numerous constitutional provisions and criminal statutes, however, discrimination against Jews in vital and decision-making fields does exist. Indeed, there is indirect evidence suggesting that, in some instances, unpublished governmental regulations have been issued, either written or oral, setting quotas for the number of Jews in specific areas. And there is no evidence that criminal proceedings have been started against anyone for discriminating against Jews on racial or national grounds.

In December, 1927, S. Ordzhonikidze, Commissar for Workers' and Peasants' Inspection, reported at the Fifteenth Congress of the Communist Party that Jews (who then constituted 1.8 per cent of the population) held 10.3 per cent of the administrative posts in Moscow, 22.6 per cent of the civil service posts in the Ukraine (where Jews constituted 5.4 per cent of the population), and 30.6 per cent of the posts in Belorussia (Jews here were 8.2 per cent of the population).[102]

The 1930's and 1940's saw a sharp drop in these percentages. Three interviews in 1956 with top Soviet officials bore out the contention that the central and republic governments had established quota systems restricting Jewish employment.

Khrushchev told a visiting parliamentary delegation of the French Socialist Party on May 12, 1956:

> Our heterogeneous populations have their republics. . . . Each of them has an autonomous government. Formerly backward and illiterate, these peoples now have their engineers and professionals. . . .
>
> Anti-Semitic sentiments still exist there. They are remnants of a reactionary past. This is a complicated problem because of the position of the Jews and their relations with the other peoples. At the outset of the Revolution, we had many Jews in the leadership of the Party and State. They were more educated, perhaps more revolutionary than the average Russian. In due course we created new cadres.[103]

At this point, Khrushchev was interrupted by Pervukhin, who attempted to clarify Khrushchev's "new cadres." Pervukhin explained: "Our own intelligentsia." The "we" and "they" type of bigotry was obvious. Khrushchev continued, driving home the rationalization for a quota in a particularly vulgar fashion:

> Should the Jews want to occupy the foremost positions in our republics now, it would naturally be taken amiss by the indigenous inhabitants,

who would react unfavorably to such pretensions, especially as they do not consider themselves either less intelligent or less capable than the Jews. For instance, when a Jew in the Ukraine is appointed to an important post and surrounds himself with Jewish collaborators, it is understandable that this should create jealousy and hostility toward Jews.

In a second interview a month later, Yekaterina Furtseva told a correspondent of the *National Guardian:* "The government has found in some of its departments a heavy concentration of Jewish people, upwards of 50 per cent of the staff. Steps were taken to transfer them to other enterprises, giving them equally good positions and without jeopardizing their rights."[104]

The third interview was conducted in August by J. B. Salsberg, a former Canadian Communist leader, with a number of key Soviet officials. One of them corroborated Furtseva's statement: "He tried terribly hard to prove to me with examples that the transfer or dismissal of Jewish employees in once-backwards republics, that now have 'their own' intelligentsia and professional people capable of occupying posts previously held by Jews or Russians, has nothing to do with anti-Semitism."[105]

Six years later, Khrushchev was to return to the same theme in an unpublished speech to a meeting of artists held on December 17, 1962.[106] He told the audience that were Jews to occupy too many top positions it would tend to create anti-Semitism.

That discriminatory employment practices may adversely affect current efforts to stimulate production was suggested in an editorial in *Pravda* on September 5, 1965.[107] After stating that Lenin "violently denounced all manifestations of nationalism, and in particular demanded an increasing 'struggle against anti-Semitism, that malicious exaggeration of racial separateness and national enmity,' " the editorial went on to say: "It is necessary to keep in mind that the growing scale of Communist construction requires that the cadres of various peoples be exchanged. Therefore any manifestations of national separateness in the *training and employment* of personnel of various nationalities in the Soviet Republics are intolerable." [Italics added.]

This was the first time in twenty years that *Pravda* editorially inveighed against anti-Semitism and emphasized its condemnation by quoting Lenin. The editorial's importance was further underscored when numerous newspapers throughout the country reprinted it.[108] Whether the editorial means that new policy directives will be issued reversing earlier national and local instructions is as yet not known.

A discriminatory pattern, whether deliberate or not, has also been evident in political life since the 1940's. The Supreme Soviet has seen a drastic decline in the number and percentage of Jews since 1937.[109] In that year, 32 of the 569 deputies of the Soviet of the Union (or 5.6 per cent) and 15 of the 574 deputies of the Soviet of Nationalities (or 2.6 per cent) were Jews. By January, 1946, the percentage of Jews in the Soviet of the Union had dropped to 0.8 per cent—5 of 801 deputies.[110] In March, 1950, there were only 2 Jews among the 678 deputies (0.3 per cent) of the Soviet of the Union and 3 among the 638 members (0.5 per cent) of the Soviet of Nationalities. In April, 1958, only 3 of the 1,364 deputies of both houses, or 0.25 per cent of the total, could be identified as Jews. Of the 1,443 members of the current Supreme Soviet, only 8 (0.5 per cent) are Jews.[111]

Although the Soviet Union has claimed that "one of the clearest indications of the absence of discrimination against citizens of the U.S.S.R. on grounds of nationality is the multinational membership of the Supreme Soviet of the U.S.S.R., the highest organ of state power,"[112] evidently Jews are an exception. Constituting over 1 per cent of the population, they have, since the 1940's, numbered 0.5 per cent at the most in the highest legislative organ. Since the selection of candidates for deputy is Party-controlled, it is difficult to avoid the conclusion that some understanding exists to prevent placing more than a token number of Jews on the ballot. The situation in the Supreme Soviets of the fifteen Union republics is even more egregious.[113] Of 5,312 deputies in these bodies in 1959, only 14 (0.26 per cent) were Jewish. There was only 1 Jewish deputy among the 835 deputies in the Russian republic; 1 Jew (0.22 per cent) among the 457 deputies in the Ukraine (where the Jewish population constitutes 2 per cent of the total); and 2 Jews (0.45 per cent) among the 407 deputies in Belorussia (with a Jewish population of 1.9 per cent of the total).

Percentages in the non-Slavic republics, with the exception of Lithuania, presented a similarly disparate picture. Not a single one of the 281 deputies in Moldavia (where Jews constitute 3.3 per cent of the population) was a Jew. Latvia, too, had no Jews among its 200 deputies, even though Jews comprise 1.7 per cent of the population. No Jewish deputies were elected in Estonia, Georgia, Armenia, and Kirghizia; 1 Jewish deputy was elected in Azerbaidzhan, Tadzhikstan, and Turkmenia; and 2 Jewish deputies were elected in Uzbekistan and Kazakhstan. Only in Lithuania did Jewish representation parallel its percentage in the population—3 of 209 deputies, or 1.44 per cent.

Paralleling the sharp decline in Jewish representation in the

Supreme Soviet is a drastic drop in representation in the elitist Central Committee of the Communist Party.[114] In 1939, the percentage of Jews in this body was 10.8, higher than the combined percentage of Ukrainians and Belorussians. By 1952, the percentage of Jews dropped to 3; in 1956, to 2; and, in 1961, to 0.3. Currently, only one of the 330-man body, Veniamin Dymshits, is a Jew.

Restrictions in the Party leadership do not, however, apply to Party membership. Recently reported data[115] on Party membership suggest that there are tens of thousands of Jewish members. Of the 11,758,200 members and candidates, 1,035,300 are listed as belonging to "other nationalities and peoples." (Detailed figures are given for the principal nationality of each of the fifteen republics.) The sizable figure in the residual category points to the likelihood of a considerable number of Jews.

In addition to the political area, discriminatory patterns appear to be evident in fields involving foreign contacts.[116] While data on this subject are sketchy and fragmentary, at least partial validation can be obtained by examining a 1962 list of names of top Soviet officials in the Ministry of Foreign Affairs and the Ministry of Foreign Trade.[117] Of 475 persons serving in key positions in the Foreign Office and in embassies abroad, only 5 or 6 appear to have Jewish names, in marked contrast to the 1920's or 1930's, when numerous Jews played prominent roles in the ministry. Similarly, of 94 top officials in the Ministry of Foreign Trade, only 1 or 2 appear to have Jewish names.

The quota system in admissions to universities, which is the key to advancement in Soviet society, is perhaps the most disturbing aspect of the discriminatory pattern. In 1963, *Kommunist,* by implication, and the *Bulletin of Higher Education,* explicitly, acknowledged the existence of "annually planned preferential admission quotas."[118] Nicholas DeWitt, an American specialist on Soviet education, has stated that the quota system operates "to the particularly severe disadvantage of the Jewish population."[119] He offers data that between 1935 and 1958, "the index of representation rose for most nationalities, but fell for Georgians and all national minorities, with a drastic decline for the Jews."

Soviet data released in 1961[120] show that at the end of 1960 there were 77,177 Jewish students in higher education—3.2 per cent of the total number of university enrollments. (Yeliutin had contended that it was 10 per cent.) Although on a percentage population basis, Jewish enrollment ranks highest among all nationality groups, it marks a sharp drop from 1935, when Jewish enrollment was 13 per cent.[121] Furthermore, in view of the fact that 95 per cent of all Jews live in urban areas, the statistics suggest "that in those republics where Jews constitute an above-average proportion of the urban population, their representation among university students is well below the rate of the general population's access to higher education."[122] The quota device in education may be one of the factors (among others, including the widening character of education generally) in the sharp percentage decline of Jews in the science field. While the figures show an absolute increase from 24,400 in 1947 to 36,200 in 1961, the percentage of Jews among total scientific personnel dropped from 16.8 in 1947 to 8.8 in 1961.[123]

Besides banning discrimination on national and racial grounds, Soviet statutes make the overt expressions of anti-Semitism a state crime. As early as July, 1918, the Council of Peoples' Commissars issued an order aimed at destroying "the anti-Semitic movement at its roots" by outlawing "pogromists and persons inciting to pogroms."[124] The R.S.F.S.R. Criminal Code of 1922 provided a minimum of one year solitary confinement (and death in time of war) for "agitation and propaganda arousing enmities and dissensions."[125] The R.S.F.S.R. Criminal Code of 1927 provided for loss of freedom of "no less than two years" for "propaganda or agitation aimed at arousing national or religious enmities and dissension," as well as the dissemination, manufacture, or possession of literature of such nature.[126] Article 74 of the present R.S.F.S.R. Criminal Code, which went into effect in 1961, reads: "Propaganda or agitation aimed at inciting racial or national enmity or discord . . . is punishable by loss of personal freedom for a period of six months to three years, or exile from two to five years."[127] This section of the Code is based on Article 11 of the Fundamentals of Criminal Jurisprudence of the U.S.S.R., adopted by the Supreme Soviet in December, 1958.[128]

In the 1920's, the Soviet press from time to time reported instances of anti-Semitic activity as well as the judicial proceedings against offenders.[129] Party organs condemned anti-Semitism and called for vigilant and energetic action against its manifestations. In the 1930's, the number of anti-Semitic incidents declined sharply and press reports of such incidents became infrequent. That anti-Semitism would not, however, be countenanced by the Party was made clear in a speech by V. M. Molotov, Chairman of the Council of Peoples' Commissars, at the Eighth Soviet Congress in November, 1936, and carried in *Pravda*.[130]

In contrast, not only was anti-Semitism not condemned in the immediate postwar period, but beginning in 1948–49 with the campaign against "cosmopolitanism," there was open incitement against Jews, resulting in the ominous anti-Jewish atmosphere of early 1953 stirred up by the "Doctors' Plot." The death of Stalin and the subsequent exposure of the plot as a fraud brought an end to the anti-Semitic provocation. But neither *Pravda* nor any other major organ, nor, indeed, any top Soviet official then or later, called the plot a specifically anti-Semitic manifestation.

Until recently, no specific editorial condemnation of anti-Semitism has appeared in any major publication in the U.S.S.R. And, with one exception, there has been no public airing of charges of anti-Semitism that have appeared in the Western press. The exception is the book *Judaism Without Embellishment,* by T. Kichko, published in October, 1963, by the Ukrainian Academy of Sciences. The 192-page book accuses Judaism of fostering hypocrisy, bribery, greed, and usury, and links it with Zionism, Israel, Jewish bankers, and Western capitalists in a world-wide conspiracy. The vulgarities of the text are accompanied by a series of viciously anti-Semitic caricatures. Only after world-wide protests, including outspoken condemnation by leading Western Communist parties, did the Soviet authorities react with some vigor. The Central Committee's Ideological Commission, in April, 1964, criticized the book for "erroneous statements and illustrations likely to offend believers and which might be interpreted in a spirit of anti-Semitism."[131] The wording was somewhat vague: No specific charge of anti-Semitism was leveled at the book itself, and the author was not accused of violating any provisions of the Criminal Code of the Ukraine.[132]

Though some action may have been taken on the Kichko book,[133] nothing was done about a similar book by F. S. Mayatsky,[134] published in 1964, which uses material prepared during the "Doctors' Plot" to prove the existence of a conspiracy between Zionism, Jewish bankers, and Western intelligence agencies. Numerous other tracts containing the same crude provocations have appeared in the late 1950's and early 1960's, apparently with either official blessing or indifference.

Nor was any *public* action taken in connection with an anti-Semitic episode in 1959. Just prior to the High Holy Days in October of that year, the synagogue in Malakhovka, a small community near Moscow, was set on fire and vicious anti-Semitic leaflets appeared, signed by an anonymous "committee," calling upon Russians to "beat Jews and save Russia."[135] At first, Soviet officials called Western reports of the episode a "monstrous lie," but in January, 1960, one official acknowledged that it had taken place, saying that when anti-Semitic feelings are "too strongly manifested, the persons involved are prosecuted and punished according to the law for the protection of nationalities." In the fall of the following year, André Blumel was told by a high official that the culprits had been apprehended, tried, and sentenced to ten and twelve years' imprisonment, respectively.[136] But Soviet publications carried no notices of the alleged trial.

During the intensive campaign against economic crimes (1961–64), the press occasionally stressed the Jewish national origin of some of those charged with and executed for such crimes.[137] But Khrushchev publicly denied that anti-Semitism was involved, terming it "a crude concoction, a vicious slander on the Soviet people, on our country."[138]

Only very recently have any statements appeared in the press condemning anti-Semitism. In July, 1965, *Pravda* published a speech of Premier A. N. Kosygin delivered before a large rally in Riga, Latvia, in which he denounced "the manifestation of nationalism, great-power chauvinism, racism, anti-Semitism" as "absolutely alien to and in contradiction to our world view."[139] Whether these statements will inaugurate efforts to wipe out anti-Semitic manifestations, using the full force of Soviet law to do so, is uncertain. As previously indicated, such efforts might be considered necessary to cope with problems that impede national production problems. For the time being, however, the observance of laws on anti-Semitism, like the observance of some civil-rights laws affecting Jews, leaves much to be desired.

The discrepancy between law and reality, the constitutional "fiction"—to use Lenin's term—has set in motion the kind of contradiction that violates a principal Communist objective. If, on the one hand, the "fiction" of nationality rights for Jews serves the higher Party aim of assimilation, the "fiction" of civil rights in specific areas, on the other hand, psychologically stirs a national consciousness, an awareness that the nationality identification in the passport does define the Jew. Those who have spent some time in the Soviet Union have testified that discriminatory practices have caused many Jews, particularly young ones who no longer speak Yiddish and know nothing about Jewish history or Jewish culture, to become keenly aware of their Jewishness.[140]

Since the ordinary channels for expressing such consciousness are severely restricted, particularly in view of the limited knowledge of

Yiddish, it is hardly surprising that substitute forms of expression have become manifest. They may take the form of electrifying responses to Yevtushenko reading his "Babi Yar," of cheering a visiting Italian company's production of *The Diary of Anne Frank,* of enthusiasm over Shostakovich's Thirteenth Symphony (based on "Babi Yar"), of assembling by the thousands outside the synagogue on Simohath Torah (the traditional joyous holiday celebrating the end of a year's reading of the Torah), or of asking Jewish visitors from abroad questions about Israel.[141] Clearly, Jewish self-identification remains vibrant despite growing state pressures—indeed, precisely because of the contradictory character of these pressures.

NOTES

1. See particularly I. Stalin, *Marksizm i natsional'no-kolonial'nyi vopros* (Moscow, 1937), pp. 6, 8. This section is Stalin's well-known essay of 1913 on the nationality question.
2. V. I. Lenin, *Sochineniia* (3d ed.; Moscow, 1937), XVII, 292. If Lenin at times denied that the Jews could be considered even a genuine nationality (see S. Schwarz, *Jews in the Soviet Union* [New York, 1951], pp. 50–56), he nonetheless accepted the legal category that identified the Jews as a nationality.
3. Lenin, *op. cit.*, XXIV, 96.
4. Stalin, *op. cit.*, p. 209.
5. A. Vyshinsky, *Sovetskoe gosudarstvennoe pravo* (Moscow, 1938), p. 247.
6. *Izvestiia,* June 19, 1919.
7. From S. Dimanshtein's speech to a caucus of Party delegates at a conference of Jewish Sections and Jewish Commissariats in October, 1918, as cited in Schwarz, *op. cit.*, p. 97.
8. In contrast, the Hebrew language was considered "reactionary" and an instrument of Zionism. After being permitted a shadowy existence for a few years, Hebrew schools were suppressed or taken over by local officials. See Schwarz, *op. cit.*, p. 131; and B. Z. Goldberg, *The Jewish Problem in the Soviet Union* (New York, 1961), p. 360. Interestingly, a new Hebrew-Russian dictionary was published in July, 1963.
9. *Prakticheskoe reshenie natsional'nogo voprosa v Belorusskoi SSR,* Part I (Minsk, 1927), p. 120.
10. *Pravda,* December 28, 1932. Oddly, this vital decree has not been referred to in the various standard works on the U.S.S.R. For a discussion of the important current statistical uses of the passport system, see *Vestnik statistiki* (July, 1965), pp. 16–21. The article indicates that in various rural areas the passport system has not yet been introduced.
11. See *The New York Times,* February 18, 1963, and the findings of André Blumel, as reported in a Paris press conference and published in the *Jerusalem Post,* October 23, 1960.
12. Tsentral'noe statisticheskoe upravlenie, *Itogi vsesoiuznoi perepisi naseleniia 1959 goda: SSSR* (Moscow, 1962), p. 204. For a description of the region's non-Jewish character, see Max Frankel's report in *The New York Times,* May 1, 1959.
13. Information obtained from the biographical sketches in *Deputaty Verkhovnogo Soveta SSSR* (Moscow, 1962).
14. The data are in *Pravda,* February 4, 1960. Since respondents were not required to produce proof of nationality, it is quite possible that a considerable number of Jews, especially those involved in mixed marriages, may have declared a nationality other than that indicated on their passport. In this connection, it is to be noted that parents were given the right of specifying the nationality of their children. See United Nations General Assembly, *Manifestations of Racial Prejudice and National and Religious Intolerance,* Doc. A/5473/Add.1, September 25, 1963, p. 42. Parents in a mixed marriage relationship could have chosen the non-Jewish designation for their children.

   According to a Soviet Jewish source, the Jewish population has increased commensurate, percentage-wise, with the general population increase of 20 million between 1959 and 1964. S. Rabinovich, *Jews in the USSR* (n.p. [1965]), p. 18.

15. Tsentral'noe statisticheskoe upravlenie, *Chislennost', sostav, razmeshchenie naseleniia SSSR* (Moscow, 1961), p. 25; and *Itogi vsesoiuznoi perepisi naseleniia 1959 goda: SSSR,* pp. 184–202. Georgian was indicated by 35,700 Jews, while 20,800 indicated Tadzhik and 25,400 indicated Tatar. The adjusted figure for the total number of Jews who declared their native language to be that of their nationality is 487,800.
16. Y. Kantor, "Aynike Bamerkungen un Oisfiren tsu di Fareffentlichte Sachhakalen fun der folks-tselung in Ratenverband dem 15 Yanuar, 1959," *Bleter far Geshichte* (Warsaw), XV (1962–63), 146–47. This work did not appear until early 1964.
17. The author has examined a section of the article by M. Friedberg, "Slozhnopodchinennoe predlozhenie v idish-taich, XVI–XVIII vv.," in *Voprosy sintaksisa romano-germanskikh iazikov* (Leningrad, 1961).
18. The decree is dated June 30, 1944, and is noted in *Pravda,* July 1, 1944. The decree establishing the Council for Affairs of the Russian Orthodox Church is in *Pravda,* October 8, 1943.
19. Commission on Human Rights, *Study of Discrimination in the Matter of Religious Rights and Practises,* Conference Room Paper, No. 35, January 30, 1959, pp. 3, 8. Hereafter referred to as *Conference Room Paper, No. 35.*
20. *Jewish Telegraphic Agency,* January 13, 1960.
21. *USSR,* April, 1963; "Jews in the Soviet Union," *Novosti Press Agency* (n.p. [1963]).
22. *Conference Room Paper, No. 35,* p. 17.
23. *Istoriia sovetskoi konstitutsii v dokumentakh 1917–56* (Moscow, 1956), pp. 57–58.
24. *Sobranie uzakonenii i rasporiazhenii,* No. 51 (1918), pp. 599–609.
25. *Sistematicheskoe sobranie deistvuiushchikh zakonov Soiuza Sovetskikh Sotsialisticheskikh Respublik* (Moscow, 1927). The Constitution called for "freedom of national development of peoples" and "equal rights of peoples."
26. *Sobranie uzakonenii i rasporiazhenii rabochego i krest'ianskogo pravitel'stva Ukrainskoi SSR* (Kiev), No. 41 (1922), Item 598.
27. *Ibid.,* No. 42 (1923), Item 435.
28. *Sobranie uzakonenii i rasporiazhenii rabochego i krest'ianskogo pravitel'stva Ukrainskoi SSR* (Kiev, 1927), No. 34, Item 157.
29. *Prakticheskoe reshenie natsional'nogo voprosa Belorusskoi SSR,* Part I (Minsk, 1927), p. 120.
30. *Ibid.,* pp. 133–39.
31. Cited in Schwarz, *op. cit.,* p. 137.
32. *Konstitutsiia SSSR. Konstitutsii soiuznikh i avtonomnykh sovetskikh sotsialisticheskikh respublik* (Moscow, 1960).
33. Commission on Human Rights, *Study of Discrimination in Education,* Doc. E/CN.4/Sub.2/210, January 5, 1961, p. 6. See also the statement made by the Soviet Government to UNESCO: "The Union of Soviet Socialist Republics reports that every Soviet citizen may have his children taught in any language he wishes." See Commission on Human Rights, *Periodic Reports on Human Rights Covering the Period 1960–1962,* Doc./E/CN.4/861/Add.2 (December 20, 1963), p. 42.
34. *Novaia sistema narodnogo obrazovaniia v SSSR* (Moscow, 1960), p. 79.

35. A photostat of the Russian letter is in J. B. Shechtman, *Star in Eclipse: Russian Jewry Revisited* (New York, 1961), p. 151. The author has been unable to locate the decree upon which the letter is based.
36. *Pravda,* November 2, 1961.
37. Concerning these efforts and their failure, as well as the school closures in Birobidzhan, see E. Schulman, "The Jewish School System in the Soviet Union, 1918–48" (Ph.D. dissertation, Dropsie College, 1965).
38. *Vedomosti Verkhovnogo Soveta SSSR,* No. 52 (1293), p. 931. The decree was published on December 28, 1964, but it was signed earlier on August 29, 1964. Figures on the dispersal of Germans in a dozen Soviet republics are in A. Bohmann, "Die Deutsche Bevoelkerung in der Sowjetunion," *Aussenpolitik* (January, 1961), p. 267.
39. *Uchitel'skaia gazeta,* March 12, 1964.
40. *Neues Leben,* January 27, 1965.
41. *Réalités,* May, 1957. Furtseva told Blumel in 1961 that "the Jews may feel hurt if we push them towards Yiddish." (*Jerusalem Post,* January 29, 1961.) On the other hand, a recent U.N. Seminar on Multinational Societies, at which the U.S.S.R. was present, urged that society provide educational facilities in the language of a minority "even if the minority itself was disinterested in the provision of educational facilities for its children." And the Seminar further recommended that "special attention" be paid "to the question [of] providing facilities for scattered minorities."
42. *Neues Leben,* January 20, 1965.
43. Kantor, *op. cit.,* p. 148. His standard work was Y. Kantor, *Natsional'noe stroitel'stvo sredi Yevreiev SSSR* (Moscow, 1934).
44. See C. Szmeruk, "Soviet Jewish Literature: The Last Phase," *Survey* (April–June, 1961), pp. 71–77. In the prewar period, the Yiddish publishing house had turned out, during 1933–37, 852 books in over 6 million copies. In 1939 alone, 339 books were published. In addition, there were three daily newspapers and five literary journals, as well as about a score of permanent Yiddish theatrical companies.
45. The revelation about the murder is in *Sovetskaia Litva,* January 13, 1963.
46. *Jerusalem Post,* February 3, 1961.
47. *Jewish Chronicle* (London), March 29, 1963.
48. "Jews in the Soviet Union," *Novosti Press Agency.*
49. Stalin, *op. cit.,* p. 207.
50. *Pravda,* November 2, 1961.
51. *Materialy XXII s"ezda KPSS* (Moscow, 1961), p. 192.
52. *Manifestations,* Add.1, p. 38.
53. The article from *Istoriia SSSR,* No. 3 (1962) is translated in *Soviet Sociology,* I, No. 2, 10–28.
54. *Manifestations,* Add.1, p. 48.
55. The textbooks examined are S. P. Alexeev and V. G. Kartsov, *Istoriia SSSR* (Moscow, 1960); F. P. Korovkin, *Istoriia drevnogo mira* (Moscow, 1959); L. P. Bushchik, *Istoriia SSSR* (Moscow, 1958); K. V. Bazilevich, S. V. Bakhrushin, A. M. Pankratova, and A. V. Fokht, *Istoriia SSSR,* Part II (Moscow, 1958); and K. V. Bazilevich, S. V. Bakhrushin, A. M. Pankratova, and A. V. Fokht, *Istoriia SSSR,* Part III (Moscow, 1959). The first book is used in the fourth class; the second in the fifth and sixth classes; the third in the eighth class; the fourth in the ninth class; and the last in the tenth class.

56. For a background analysis of this episode, see W. Korey, "A Soviet Poet as Rebel," *The New Republic,* January 8, 1962.
57. *Pravda,* March 10, 1963.
58. W. Korey, "Reporting the Eichmann Case," *Survey,* December, 1961.
59. *Izvestiia,* April 19, 1963.
60. The author has examined the preliminary U.N. report, *Seminar on the Multinational Society,* Doc. ST/TAO/HR/23. For an intimate description and survey of the debate, see D. P. Moynihan, "Breakthrough at Ljubljana," *National Jewish Monthly,* September, 1965, pp. 15–17. Moynihan, then Assistant Secretary of Labor, was head of the American delegation.
61. See *Conference Room Paper, No. 35,* p. 6.
62. *Ibid.,* p. 7.
63. The text of the law is in *Izvestiia,* April 26–28, 1929.
64. The 1936 Constitution (Article 135), in contrast to previous constitutions, permitted clergy to vote and run for elective office. Election of deputies is declared to be "universal."
65. J. Meisel and E. Kozera (eds.), *Materials for the Study of the Soviet System* (Ann Arbor, Mich., 1953), p. 241.
66. *Conference Room Paper, No. 35,* p. 5.
67. J. Curtiss, "Religion as a Soviet Social Problem," *Social Problems,* VII, No. 4 (Spring, 1960), 328–39.
68. Articles 20–21 of the Order specify this right. See *Conference Room Paper, No. 35,* p. 19.
69. See Schwarz, *op. cit.,* p. 112.
70. C. Szmeruk, *Pirsumim Yehudiim Bivrit Hamoatzot* (Jerusalem, 1961), p. 23.
71. A *New York Times* correspondent reported, for example, that among the "overflow crowd of several thousand worshipers" on Yom Kippur, there were only a "few lucky owners of prayer books." *The New York Times,* September 29, 1963.
72. *Conference Room Paper, No. 35,* p. 14.
73. M. Decter, "The Status of the Jews in the Soviet Union," *Foreign Affairs* (January, 1963), pp. 420–30.
74. *Conference Room Paper, No. 35,* p. 17.
75. D. P. Moynihan, *op. cit.,* pp. 15–17.
76. *Manifestations,* Add.1, p. 52.
77. Curtiss, *op. cit.,* p. 329. For other information on the Yeshiva, see Decter, *op. cit.*
78. *The New York Times,* July 27, 1965. He was similarly quoted in a press interview in *Jewish Chronicle* (London), June 25, 1965.
79. *Conference Room Paper, No. 35,* p. 11.
80. *Jews in Eastern Europe* (London), September, 1963, p. 27.
81. *The New York Times,* July 26, 1965.
82. *Pravda,* November 11, 1954.
83. See numerous examples in the publication of the Anti-Defamation League of B'nai B'rith, *Facts,* October, 1960; and in *Jews in Eastern Europe* (London), May, 1960.
84. *Minskaia pravda,* April 4, 1961.
85. M. Kichko, *Iudaizm bez prikras* (Kiev, 1963). This book is discussed on page 341, below.
86. The recommendation of the Ideological Commission is in *Pravda,* April

4, 1964. The Osipov book is *Katikhiz's bez prikras* (Moscow, 1963), pp. 276, 281.

87. H. Lumer, *Soviet Anti-Semitism—A Cold War Myth* (New York, 1964), p. 9. The reference to the blood libel in the pamphlet suggests the Daghestan incident of 1960. A local newspaper carried an antireligious article alleging that Jews mixed Moslem blood with water for ritual drinking purposes. The article appeared in the Buinaksk *Kommunist* of August 9, 1960. Two days later the article was labeled "a political error."
88. *Sovetskaia Moldavia,* July 23, 1959.
89. *Zviazda* (Minsk), February 2, 1965.
90. *Ugolovnyi kodeks RSFSR* (Moscow, 1953), Sec. 59, Art. 7, p. 23.
91. V. D. Men'shagin and B. A. Kurinov, *Nauchno-prakticheskii kommentarii k zakonu ob ugolovnoi otvetstvennosti za gosudarstvennye prestupleniia* (Moscow, 1960), p. 34.
92. M. I. Iakubovich and V. A. Vladimirov (eds.), *Gosudarstvennye prestupleniia: uchebnoe posobie sovetskomu ugolovnomu pravu* (Moscow, 1960), p. 99. Propaganda or agitation directed toward stimulating racial or national hostility "can also be expressed in arousing hostility or dissension."
93. See G. Anashkin, "O svobode i sobliudenii zakonodatel'stva a religioznikh kul'takh," *Sovetskoe gosudarstvo i pravo,* No. 1, January, 1965. A leading atheist propagandist has been rebuked in the official atheist publication, *Nauka i religiia,* for the crudeness of her attacks on religion. See *The New York Times,* April 26, 1965.
94. See, for example, the joint letter, signed by five distinguished Soviet Jewish citizens, distributed by Novosti Press Agency in April–May, 1962, and Aron Vergelis' articles in *Moscow News,* June 12 and June 26, 1965. Also see Khrushchev's comments at the National Press Club in Washington, D.C. in September, 1959.
95. For a listing of some of these legal restrictions, see I. P. Tsamerian and S. L. Ronin, *Equality of Rights Between Races and Nationalities in the USSR* (Nijmegen, 1962), pp. 17–21.
96. *Sbornik ukazov i postanovlenii Vremennogo Pravitel'stva,* March 12–May 18, 1917 (Petrograd, 1917), pp. 8, 46.
97. One must be eighteen years old to vote and twenty-three to run for office. Article 135 also permits religious citizens to vote and be elected. Whether a religious person has ever run for office in the U.S.S.R. is doubtful.
98. *Ugolovnyi kodeks RSFSR* (Moscow, 1964), p. 39. The Ukrainian criminal code provides for imprisonment from six months to three years. The codes of other republics specify similar penalties.
99. Tsentral'noe statisticheskoe upravlenie, *Vysshee obrazovanie v SSSR* (Moscow, 1961), p. 49.
100. "Jews in the Soviet Union," *Novosti Press Agency.*
101. See *ibid.; The New York Times,* June 16, 1964; and the lists of Lenin Prize winners in *Pravda,* April 22, 1964, and April 22, 1965.
102. *XV s"ezd vsesoiuznoi kommunisticheskoi partii* (*b*) (Moscow, 1928), pp. 400–401.
103. The transcript of the interview is in *Réalités,* No. 136 (May, 1957).
104. *National Guardian,* June 25, 1956.
105. Salsberg's visit is reported in *Vochenblatt* and in *Morgen Freiheit.* The series of articles appeared on an irregular basis from October 25 to December 20, 1956. The quoted section is translated in J. B. Salsberg, "Anti-Semitism in the USSR?," *Jewish Life,* February, 1957, p. 38.

106. Its contents were revealed by the London *Observer,* January 13, 1963.
107. "Leninskaia druzhba narodov," *Pravda,* September 5, 1965. No doubt the desire to blunt foreign criticism also played a role. The editorial stated that "we must keep . . . in mind" the imperialists who "slander" the U.S.S.R. "in conducting our ideological work."
108. *The New York Times,* September 11, 1965.
109. *Vybory v Verkhovnyi Sovet SSSR i v verkhovnye sovety soiuznykh i avtonomnykh respublik, 1937–38 gg.* (Moscow, 1939), p. 12.
110. Schwarz, *op. cit.,* pp. 355, 364.
111. Information extracted from *Deputaty Verkhovnogo Soveta SSSR* (Moscow, 1962).
112. Commission on Human Rights *Periodic Reports on Human Rights,* Doc. E/CN.4/860, December 20, 1963, p. 175.
113. *Sostav deputatov verkhovnykh sovetov soiuznykh, avtonomnykh respublik i mestnykh sovetov trudiashchikhsia, 1959* (Moscow, 1959). Data on the composition of later republic Supreme Soviets have not been published.
114. S. Bialer, "How Russians Rule Russia," *Problems of Communism,* XIII, No. 5 (September–October, 1964), 46, 48.
115. See *Partiinaia zhizn',* No. 10 (May, 1965), pp. 8–17.
116. See M. Hindus, *House Without a Roof* (New York, 1961), p. 315.
117. The lists were drawn from a variety of sources and made available to the author.
118. See V. Komarov and V. Artamoshkina, "Takova ikh nauchnaia ob'ektivnost'!," *Vestnik vysshei shkoly* (December, 1963), p. 78.
119. See N. DeWitt, *Education and Professional Employment in the USSR* (Washington, D.C., 1961), pp. 358–60. However, Hindus observes that the quotas against Jews are less rigid in Leningrad than in Moscow and almost nonexistent in Siberian universities. See Hindus, *op. cit.,* p. 315.
120. *Vysshee obrazovanie v SSSR,* p. 85.
121. F. Lorimer, *The Population of the Soviet Union* (Geneva, 1946), pp. 55–61.
122. N. DeWitt, *The Status of Jews in Soviet Education* (Mimeo., 1964), p. 11. It is interesting to note that a top education official recently criticized university admission policies, noting that in "past years, the universities and institutes enrolled many young people with poor knowledge of the fundamentals of learning." See *Pravda,* August 31, 1965. The criticism was principally directed against the preference extended to workers.
123. DeWitt, *The Status of Jews in Soviet Education,* p. 25.
124. *Izvestiia,* July 27, 1918.
125. *Ugolovnyi kodeks RSFSR* (Moscow, 1922), Sec. 83, p. 18.
126. *Ugolovnyi kodeks RSFSR* (Moscow, 1953), Sec. 59, Art. 7, p. 23.
127. *Ugolovnyi kodeks RSFSR* (Moscow, 1964), Art. 74, p. 39.
128. For a commentary upon Article 11, see Iakubovich and Vladimirov, *op. cit.,* pp. 98–100.
129. The subject is treated at length in Schwarz, *op. cit.,* pp. 241–99.
130. *Pravda,* November 30, 1936.
131. *Pravda,* April 4, 1964. Initially, the Soviets avoided response to the criticism by observing that Kichko was merely engaged in antireligious propaganda, protected by the Constitution. See the statement of Novosti Press Agency, March 24, 1964.
132. Article 66 of the Criminal Code of the Ukraine provides for imprisonment of six months to three years or exile from two to five years for

"propaganda or agitation calculated to stir up racial or national hatred or discord." The contents of the Article are reported by the Ukrainian S.S.R. in U.N. document *Manifestations,* August 9, 1963, p. 59. The Ukraine further makes the flat statement that "there are no instances of racial prejudice or of national and religious intolerance either *de jure* or *de facto.*"

133. Alexei Adzhubei reported that the remaining copies of the book had been seized and destroyed. See *Jewish Chronicle* (London), April 10, 1964.
134. F. S. Mayatsky, *Sovremennyi Iudaizm i Sionizm* (Kishinev, 1964).
135. The episode is detailed in Goldberg, *op. cit.,* pp. 284–86.
136. See the *Jerusalem Post,* October 23, 1960, for a report of André Blumel's findings.
137. For a detailed and carefully evaluated examination of the anti-Semitic facets of the economic crimes campaign, see "Economic Crimes in the Soviet Union," *Journal of the International Commission of Jurists,* Summer, 1964, pp. 3–47. The past year has been marked by a very sharp reduction of press reports of executions and of Jews involved.
138. In his letter to Bertrand Russell in *Pravda,* February 28, 1963. One of *Izvestiia*'s editors, in describing the crimes charged to two Jews, went out of his way to observe that he was deliberately mentioning the "Jewish family names" of the accused—Roifman and Shakerman—"because we pay no attention to the malicious slander . . . in the Western press." See *Izvestiia,* October 20, 1963. The provocative character of the statement is self-evident.
139. *Pravda,* July 19, 1965.
140. See, for example, Hindus, *op. cit.,* pp. 322–24; and H. Salisbury, *A New Russia?* (New York, 1962), pp. 70–71. Also note the observation made by *The New York Times* correspondent in Moscow: "The legal insistence that a Jew retain his ethnic nationality although he is denied cultural rights accorded to other nationalities has produced a psychological depression among many young Soviet Jews. They speak of a feeling of separateness in Soviet society that conflicts with their yearning to belong." (*The New York Times,* February 8, 1963.)
141. Each of these incidents has been reported at length in the Western press.

THE CONTRIBUTORS

EDWARD ALLWORTH, Associate Professor of Turco-Soviet Studies in the Department of Middle East Languages and Cultures of Columbia University, is the author of *Central Asia—A Century of Russian Rule,* among other works.

JOHN A. ARMSTRONG is Professor of Political Science at the University of Wisconsin, where he is Director of the Russian Area Studies Program. He is the author of, among other works, *Ukrainian Nationalism, 1939–45* and *The Soviet Bureaucratic Elite.*

YAROSLAV BILINSKY is Associate Professor of Political Science at the University of Delaware, and the author of *The Second Soviet Republic.*

ABRAHAM BRUMBERG is the editor of *Problems of Communism.* A frequent contributor to *The New Leader, The New Republic,* and other journals, he also edited *Soviet Russia Under Khrushchev.*

JOSEPH BRUMBERG was a leader of the Jewish Bund of Poland between the two world wars, and the Director of the Medem Sanatorium. In the United States, he served as an executive officer of the American Jewish Labor Committee.

ERICH GOLDHAGEN is Director of the Institute of East European Jewish Studies and Assistant Professor of Politics, Brandeis University.

VSEVOLOD HOLUBNYCHY is currently Lecturer in the Graduate Department of Economics at Hunter College of the City University of New York. He is the author of many articles on the Soviet economy.

WILLIAM KOREY is Director of the International Council of B'nai B'rith. He has written a biography of Zinoviev and numerous articles on the state of minorities in the Soviet Union.

MARY KILBOURNE MATOSSIAN, Associate Professor of History at the University of Maryland, is the author of *The Impact of Soviet Policies in Armenia.*

JACOB ORNSTEIN is a member of the Institute of Languages and Linguistics, Georgetown University, and the author of many articles on Soviet linguistic policy.

JAAN PENNAR is American Counsellor to the Institute for the Study of the USSR. He is co-editor of *The Politics of Soviet Education.*

GARIP SULTAN, a specialist on the Turkic peoples in the Soviet Union, is a member of the Institute for the Study of the USSR.

NICHOLAS P. VAKAR, Professor of History at the University of Ohio, is the author of *Belorussia: The Making of a Nation.*